DEATH, ECSTASY, AND OTHER WORLDLY JOURNEYS

DEATH, ECSTASY, AND OTHER WORLDLY JOURNEYS

edited by

John J. Collins
Michael Fishbane

State University
of New York
Press

Published by
State University of New York Press, Albany

© 1995 State University of New York

All rights reserved

Production by Susan Geraghty
Marketing by Bernadette LaManna

Printed in the United States of America

For information, address State University of New York Press, State University
Plaza, Albany, N.Y., 12246

10 9 8 7 6 5 4 3 2 1

Library of Congress Cataloging-in-Publication Data

Death, ecstasy, and other worldly journeys / edited by John J.
  Collins, Michael Fishbane.
        p.   cm.
    Includes bibliographical references and index.
    ISBN 0-7914-2345-X (alk. paper). — ISBN 0-7914-2346-8 (pbk. :
  alk. paper)
        1. Death—Religious aspects. 2. Ecstasy. 3. Near-death experiences—
Religious aspects. I. Collins, John Joseph, 1946– . II. Fishbane,
Michael A.
    BL504.D37 1995
    291.2'3—dc20
                                                                    94-13469
                                                                         CIP

CONTENTS

Introduction   ix

ANTIQUITY   1

Chapter 1   Wisdom's Place   3
            Jonathan Z. Smith

Chapter 2   Ascent to the Stars in a Mesopotamian Ritual:
Social Metaphor and Religious Experience   15
            Tzvi Abusch

LATE ANTIQUITY   39

Chapter 3   A Throne in the Heavens: Apotheosis in Pre-
Christian Judaism   41
            John J. Collins

Chapter 4   The Seven Heavens in Jewish and Christian
Apocalypses   57
            Adela Y. Collins

Chapter 5   Paul and the Beginning of Jewish Mysticism   93
            Alan F. Segal

Chapter 6   The Practice of Ascent in the Ancient
Mediterranean World   121
            Martha Himmelfarb

Chapter 7   Mystical Descents   137
              Guy G. Stroumsa

The Crown of Immortality: Toward a Redescription
of Christian Martyrdom   153
              Arthur J. Droge

Chapter 9   Abathur, A New Etymology   169
              Nathaniel Deutsch

MEDIEVAL   179

Chapter 10   The Imagination of Death in Jewish
Spirituality   181
              Michael Fishbane

Chapter 11   Weeping, Death, and Spiritual Ascent
in Sixteenth Century Jewish Mysticism   207
              Elliot R. Wolfson

Chapter 12   Between Authority and Indeterminacy:
Some Reflections on Kabbalistic Hermeneutics   245
              Moshe Idel

Chapter 13   Hekhalot and Mi'rāj: Observations on the
Heavenly Journey in Judaism and Islam   265
              David J. Halperin

Chapter 14   The Role of the "Anima Mundi" as Mediator
Between the Divine and Created Realms in the Twelfth
Century   285
              Bernard McGinn

EARLY MODERN   317

Chapter 15   Death and the Distribution of Sacral Power
in Early Japanese Mythistory   319
            Gary L. Ebersole

Chapter 16   To Hell and Back: Death, Near-Death
and Other Worldly Journeys in Early Medieval China   339
            Robert Ford Campany

Chapter 17   Sir Henry Vane: Mystical Piety
in the Puritan Revolution   357
            W. Clark Gilpin

CONTEMPORARY   377

Chapter 18   Death, and Near-Death Today   379
            Carol Zaleski

Contributors   405

Biblical References Index   411

Nonbiblical Authors and Works Index   415

Modern Authors Index   421

INTRODUCTION

As to paradise in heaven, we heard about it from the priests. But
we wanted to see for ourselves what it is like, so we sent our scout
there, Yuri Gagarin. He circled the globe and found nothing in
outer space—just complete darkness, he said, and no garden at all,
nothing that looked like paradise. We thought the matter over and
decided to send up another scout. We sent Herman Titov and told
him to fly around a bit longer this time and take a good look—
Gagarin was only up there for an hour and a half, and he might
have missed it. He took off, came back and confirmed Gagarin's
conclusion. There's nothing up there, he reported.

Nikita Khrushchev, 1961

The quest for another world beyond this one, a world of spirits
immune to death, is as old as recorded civilization, and attested in
cultures East and West, North and South. In the paleolithic cave of
Lascaux a bird-faced man is depicted falling backward or lying dead
in the path of a wounded bison. Some paleoanthropologists and
historians of religion have suggested that the man is a shaman of
sorts, and that the bird face symbolizes flight to the spirit world.[1]
Whether this particular interpretation is justified or not, there is no
doubt that belief and interest in life beyond death is attested from
the dawn of civilization. Many of the great monuments of early
societies, such as the pyramids of Egypt or the mound of New-
grange, testify to the fascination with the world beyond. Shamans,
the prototypical otherworldly travelers, are found among Eskimos
at the Arctic Circle and among the aborigines of Australia, at the
other end of the world, as well as in Central Asia and Siberia. The
worldwide distribution of beliefs and practices relating to a spirit
world cannot be explained by diffusion from a single source in
historical time. If these notions can be traced to a common source it
is lost in pre-history, before humanity dispersed to the remotest
corners of the globe.

The ultimate way to experience the world of spirits is by death
and transformation into a spiritual existence. Unfortunately, most

people who make this transition do not come back to tell about it. From antiquity to modern times, however, people have been fascinated by stories of near-death experiences. In the tenth book of his *Republic,* Plato tells the story of Er the Pamphylian, who was slain in battle but revived on the funeral pyre and told what he had seen in the other world. His account was mainly concerned with the judgment of the dead, and the rewards and punishments that awaited them. He also told how all souls eventually choose the lives in which they will be reincarnated and how only those imbued with wisdom will be able to choose wisely. Plato tells the story as a myth, which he bends to his purpose, to underline the importance of the philosophical life. We have no way of verifying whether Er even existed.

In the modern world, however, there have been numerous cases of near-death experiences, ones in which the subjects have been available for examination and interrogation. Raymond Moody claimed to provide evidence of such experiences, "not in darkened rooms in circumstances contrived by witch doctors, but in the bright light of emergency and operating rooms, presided over by physicians."[2] These modern accounts typically involve an experience of being separated from one's own body, an encounter with a being of light, a review of one's life, a strong attraction to the afterlife, and a reluctant return to the body.[3] The significance of these experiences has been very controversial.[4] Despite some extravagant claims, they cannot be taken to prove the reality of life after death; at most they reveal a penultimate stage in the process of death. Neither do they corroborate the elaborate visions of heaven and hell that we find in traditional religions. They do, however, attest to a dimension of experience that is only rarely available for public discussion and that bears a strong resemblance to traditional accounts of the separation of soul from body. As such they suggest that religious beliefs about the flight of the soul have some foothold in human experience, however enigmatic that experience may be.

Excursions into the spirit world are not confined to the moment of death. They are also the stuff of dreams, visions, and ecstatic practices. Otherworldly journeys can take place spontaneously in a dream. So, for example, an Akkadian text from the seventh century B.C.E. tells of a terrifying vision in a night dream in which a visionary named Kummaya goes down to the netherworld and is hauled before Nergal, god of the netherworld.[5] When he wakes in terror, he pledges his devotion to the Nergal and the other gods. It is virtually impossible to tell whether a text such as this reports an actual dream or is a literary fiction. There certainly were literary compositions of this sort. The death dream of Enkidu in the Epic of Gilgamesh is an early example. But the literary convention was presumably modeled on the experience of dreaming.

In some cases we read of dreams and visions that were induced by the visionaries. The shaman has been described as "above all the specialist in ecstasy,"[6] able, at will, to pass out of his body and undertake mystical journeys through all the cosmic regions. As part of his training, the shaman learned the techniques of ecstasy, by which he could contact the spirits of the other world and get their support. One of the most famous otherworldly journeys is that of the Zoroastrian Arda Viraf, who was supposedly elected by the assembly to test the truth of Zoroastrianism. He was reluctant to go, because of the objections of his seven wives. Before his departure he made a will and performed the rites of the dead for himself. Then he drank three cups of a special liquid (wine and henbane) and went to sleep on a couch, watched over by the priests. After seven days he awoke cheerful and joyous, bringing greetings to the assembly from Ahura Mazda, Zarathustra, and the gods of the dead.[7] Moshe Idel has described the techniques by which Jewish mystics attained the ascent of the soul. In the formulation of R. Hai Gaon:

> When one seeks to behold the *Merkavah* and the palaces of the angels on high, he must follow a certain procedure. He must fast a number of days and place his head between his knees and whisper many hymns and songs whose texts are known from tradition. Then he perceives within himself and in the chambers [of his heart] as if he saw the seven palaces with his own eyes, and it is as though he entered one palace after another and saw what is there. . . . For God . . . shows to the righteous, in their interior, the visions of his palaces and the position of his angels.[8]

The fact that a procedure is followed does not lessen the authenticity of the experience. It does, however, underline the cultural specificity of all experience. The Jewish mystic does not encounter Zoroaster, nor does the Persian see the Merkavah. Not only the techniques of ecstasy, but also the content of the ecstatic vision is learned from a specific tradition. Visionaries see what is believed in their culture to be possible.

Consequently, we find considerable variation on the geography of the other world. Khrushchev's assumption that it would suffice to go up in a spaceship and look around was far too simplistic for even the most literalistic believer. The netherworld appears as the destination in otherworldly journeys more often than the heavens. Gilgamesh entered the "other world" through the base of a mountain. For much of antiquity, all the dead were consigned to the netherworld. Only in the Hellenistic period were the blessed dead relocated to the heavens. The elaborate cosmology of late antiquity and the Middle Ages typically had seven heavens, although various other numbers are also attested. This was a more complex world than any imagined by Soviet astronauts. Visionaries have never lacked for spaceships. Jewish and Christian visionaries are typically propelled upward by spirit, wind or clouds. Chinese Taoist immortals are also "carried by the wind in a chariot of clouds." We also hear of more exotic means of heavenly travel. Among the Taoists

> first in order of importance was the crane, white or black, but wild ducks and even tigers would do on occasion, and even special shoes like the cloud-raising shoes made by Sin Pin from fish skin were thought to be efficacious. The famous emperor Chi reached the heavenly immortals by ascending to them on a winged horse, or according to another version on the back of a long-bearded dragon capable of carrying seventy people at once.[9]

Not all otherworldly travel was so picturesque. We have noted already the view of Hai Gaon that the mystic sees within the chambers of his own heart *as if* he were seeing the palaces of heaven. Already in antiquity philosophers such as Plato and Philo saw the ascent of the soul as an allegory for a spiritual journey toward the truth or God. Awareness of the mental character of the otherworldly journey is most acute in Buddhism. The Tibetan Book of the Dead consists of manuals for the intermediate states (*bardos*) through which people pass in their illusory journey through existence. The manuals are recited to the deceased to help them recognize that the lights and the deities they encounter are only projections of the mind. To realize this is to escape from the cycle of becoming and dying.[10]

Modern accounts of near-death experiences are often taken as evidence for the reality of life after death. In traditional societies this is seldom an explicit issue; the reality is assumed. Several other reasons for recounting these experiences come to the fore. Wilhelm Bousset, in the heyday of the *religionsgeschichtliche Schule,* argued that the ascent of the soul was an anticipation of its ascent after death.[11] This correspondence is quite clear in several Christian and some Jewish apocalypses, which culminate in the transformation of the visionary into an angelic state, such as he hoped to attain after death.[12] Other accounts serve rather to establish the authority of the figure who makes the ascent. The *mir'aj* of Muḥammad is an important example. This motif of divine authorization is already evident in the call narratives of the Hebrew prophets, who received their commissions when they stood in the council of the Lord.[13] In other cases the emphasis lies on the message which the visionary brings back to earth. The Myth of Er provides a notable example. Any code of conduct on earth is reinforced if it shown to be the basis of the judgment after death, or if it is received from a deity or an angel in the course of an otherworldly journey.

Nonetheless, ecstasy and otherworldly journeys are most profoundly connected to the ultimate human problem of death. Peter Berger has written that "the power of religion depends, in the last resort, upon the credibility of the banners it puts in the hands of men as they stand before death, or more accurately, as they walk, inevitably, toward it."[14] The most imposing banner by far is one that proclaims that death is not the end, that there is another, spiritual, world where souls can dispense with their bodily garb. The existence of such a world need not be dismissed as a calculated fiction. It is adumbrated, however elusively, by dreams, visions, and near-death experiences. Small wonder, then, that human beings have always tried to glimpse what lies behind the veil, or to extrapolate what lies beyond from the resources and values of religious traditions. The result is the elaborate construction of multilayered heavens or of a netherworld peopled with divinities and monsters. These "other worlds" are not such that they could be verified by an astronaut. They do not tell us about the world "out there" so much as about the fantastic ability of the human mind to construct a world where it can feel secure and where ethical actions remain worthwhile despite the apparent finality of death.

The issues discussed in this volume were at the center of the scholarly agenda of Ioan Culianu. He published two monographs on the ascent of the soul in western traditions: *Psychanodia I: A Survey of the Evidence Concerning the Ascension of the Soul and Its Relevance* (Leiden, 1983) and *Expériences de l'extase: Extase, ascension et récit visionnaire, de l'Hellénisme au Moyen-Age* (Paris, 1984). His last book, *Out of This World: Otherworldly Journeys from Gilgamesh to Albert Einstein* (Boston, 1991), was an attempt to provide a comprehensive survey of otherworldly journeys in the religions of the world. Inevitably, a survey of this breadth could be little more than an inventory, but it assembled the resources for a far-reaching study.

In May 16–17, 1991, Culianu hosted a conference at the University of Chicago entitled "Other Realms: Death, Ecstasy and Otherworldly Journeys in Recent Scholarship," to mark the publication of *Out of This World*. Most of the articles in this volume originated as papers for that conference. It was expected that they would appear under Culianu's editorship. Unfortunately that was not to be. On May 19, two days after the end of the conference, he was shot to death in Swift Hall where the meetings had taken place. The murder has not been solved, but is widely believed to be related to political turmoil in his native Romania. His sudden and violent death gave added poignancy to the topic of the conference and of much of his life's work. This book is dedicated to his memory.

In keeping with the scope of the original conference, the topics treated below cover a broad historical, cultural and methodological range, from the Epic of Gilgamesh to modern accounts of near-death experiences. Topics are drawn from ancient and medieval Judaism and Christianity, Islam, and Chinese and Japanese religion. Nevertheless, there is a notable thematic coherence to the whole. One will particularly observe the recurrent treatment of the mystical ascent, the cosmological context in which the descent is imagined, the conjunction of mystical experience and death, and the relationship between martyrdom and the spiritual transfiguration of death (through interpretation and its ritual). Overall, diverse types of death-defying behavior emerge; and these often bear on the centrality of salvation in the minds of those involved. Moreover, in line with the dominant metaphor of the journey, one may perceive diverse typologies of place as they relate to death. In some cases, the places of this world are central; in others, places out of this world or in the spiritual spaces of the soul are the goal. The paradox, however, is that journeys or quests in earthly space are quite often inner pilgrimages as well; correspondingly, the ascent or descent of the adept to other realms is ritually grounded in this-worldly acts. Ritual or ritualized space thus serves as a permeable zone for transcendent experiences.

The reader will find in this book, then, an integrated collection of data dealing with death and ecstasy. Their value to the study of religion is enhanced by elegant uses of the comparative method. Some of the studies focus quite intently on comparative evidence within a given culture; others are sharpened by cross-cultural perspectives. The results deepen our understanding of death, ecstasies, and otherworldly journeys. Taken all together, the essays gathered here reveal the power of the religious imagination to transfigure mortal existence and provide materials for imitation and interpretation. Ioan Culianu's fascination with these connections between cultural hermeneutics and the history of religions was an animating aspect of his personality. We hope that these essays will serve as an appropriate memorial.

John J. Collins
Michael Fishbane

NOTES

1. H. Kirschner, "Ein archäologischer Beitrag zur Urgeschichte des Schamanismus," *Anthropos* 47(1952) 244–86; M. Eliade, *Shamanism: Archaic Techniques of Ecstasy* (New York, 1964), 147; C. Zaleski, *Otherworld Journeys: Accounts of Near-Death Experience in Medieval and Modern Times* (New York, 1987), 12–13.

2. R. A. Moody, "Commentary on 'The Reality of Death Experiences: A Personal Perspective' by Ernst Rodin," *The Journal of Nervous and Mental Disease* 168(May 1980) 265.

3. R. A. Moody, *Life after Life The Investigation of a Phenomenon—Survival of Bodily Death* (Atlanta, 1975) 21–22.

4. See Zaleski, *Otherworld Journeys*, 161–83.

5. The text is called "The Vision of the Nether World." See H. Kvanvig, *Roots of Apocalyptic The Mesopotamian Background of the Enoch Figure and of the Son of Man* (WMANT Neukirchen-Vluyn; 1988) 390–91.

6. M. Eliade, "Nostalgia for Paradise," in *Myths, Dreams, and Mysteries* tr. Philip Mairet (New York, 1960) 61.

7. I. P. Culianu, *Out of This World* (Boston, 1991) 107–13.

8. M. Idel, *Kabbalah: New Perspectives* (New Haven, 1988) 90.

9. Culianu, *Out of This World,* 73.

10. Zaleski, *Otherworld Journeys,* 24–25; Culianu, *Out of This World,* 92–98.

11. W. Bousset, "Die Himmelsreise der Seele," *Archiv für Religionswissenschaft* 4(1901) 136.

12. M. Himmelfarb, "Revelation and Rapture: The Transformation of the Visionary in the Ascent Apocalypses," in J. J. Collins and J. H. Charlesworth, eds., *Mysteries and Revelations: Apocalyptic Studies after the Uppsala Colloquium* (Sheffield, 1991), 89–102; *Ascent to Heaven in Jewish and Christian Apocalypses* (New York/Oxford, 1993), 47–71.

13. See G. Widengren, *The Ascension of the Apostle and the Heavenly Book* (Uppsala, 1950).

14. P. Berger, *The Sacred Canopy: Elements of a Sociological Theory of Religion* (New York, 1967) 51.

Antiquity

CHAPTER 1

Wisdom's Place

Jonathan Z. Smith

The so-called Gilgamesh Epic formally entered the world of western scholarship in December 1872.[1] Although it first drew interest because of the possible relationship between the Flood narrative in Tablet 11 and the biblical Flood stories, this concern has yielded to a universalizing interpretation that relates to one of the foci of this volume: Gilgamesh, we are told, learns that he cannot escape death. Death is the common lot of humankind. This theme is addressed at least three times in the separate, second-millennium Sumerian texts that form part of the background for the later Akkadian compositions.[2]

In *Gilgamesh, Enkidu and the Netherworld* (the second half of which is translated as Tablet 12 of the late Akkadian recension) there is a catalogue of the various modes of human death: one dies of "fever" or a "sudden death," or one is "killed in battle" (147–49; cf. the repeated formulae 51–53, 58–60, 66–68, 72–74).

In *Gilgamesh and the Land of the Living*, it is Gilgamesh seeing the ordinary human mortality surrounding him in Uruk that leads him to undertake a heroic adventure in the hope of achieving an everlasting name:

> In my city, man dies, oppressed is the heart,
> Man perishes, heavy is the heart,
> I peered over the wall,
> Saw the dead bodies . . . floating on the river.
> As for me, I will come to the same end—truly this is so. . . .
> I would set up my name. . . . I would raise up my name.
>
> (A: 23–31)

And so Gilgamesh sets off, guarded by the deity Utu, accompanied by his servant Enkidu, and fifty unmarried men of Uruk, having neither "house" nor "mother" (A: 46–53), to do battle—actually a holy war—against the monstrous Huwawa in the "Land of the Cedar."

The most explicit Sumerian text, *The Death of Gilgamesh,* is in fragmentary condition. It contains an unrestorable dream narration and follows with an interpretation:

> O Lord Gilgamesh, the meaning of the dream is—
> [Enlil] has determined you for kingship, O Gilgamesh,
> For eternal life he has not determined it.
> . . . Be not sad of heart,
> Be not aggrieved, be not depressed.
>
> (34–37)

Later, there appears to be a vision of the underworld, and Gilgamesh seems to respond by crying (68–83). In the badly damaged second section of the text (B: 1–42), there may be a funeral ritual for Gilgamesh.

It is interesting to note both what is and is not said in these three passages from the Sumerian tradition. Death is the common lot of humankind; it cannot be escaped. There is no hint that Gilgamesh asks for, or seeks, immortality. At best, he seeks to offset death's anonymity. He hopes for a memorial, an act of inscription, which will ensure that his name and his heroic deeds are remembered.

A somewhat different set of concerns animate the later Akkadian versions which, beginning with the Old Babylonian versions (2000–1600 B.C.E.), welded some of the separate incidents in the Sumerian tradition into the complex epic we know today as *Gilgamesh.* This work was completed in something like its present form c. 1300 B.C.E. and is represented by diverse tablets dated between 800 and 200 B.C.E.

One of the literary achievements of the later recensions was to provide the epic with a prologue, the oldest element of which (see Old Babylonian, Nippur fragment) appears to be an account of Gilgamesh's status and conception as a divine king:

> The offspring of Lugalbanda, Gilgamesh is perfect in strength,
> The son of the august cow, Rimat-Ninsun . . . Gilgamesh is
>   perfect in awesomeness . . .
> Who can be compared to him in kingship?

Who like Gilgamesh can say, "I am king indeed"?
Gilgamesh was summoned [to kingship] by name from the
  very day of his birth.
Two-thirds of him is god; one-third of him is human.
The image of his body (the mother goddess) designed . . .
                                              (I.i.33–ii.1–5)

This description is repeated at an early stage of Gilgamesh's journey to the Land of the Remote: his "body is the flesh of gods . . . two-thirds of him is god, one-third of him is human" (9.2.14, 16), and reenforced by the parallel Hittite version:

The great gods made Gilgamesh's form,
The heavenly sun god to him . . . gave,
The storm god gave him courage.
Gilgamesh, created by the great gods,
His height was 16½ feet; the width of his chest, 6½ feet.
                              (Hittite Gilgamesh 1.1, 3–8)

To take these passages seriously is to decisively alter our usual understanding of *Gilgamesh* and to end the universalizing interpretation. Gilgamesh is *not* everyman; he is a divine/human mixture, a god/man. One of the major trajectories of the later versions of the epic is to explore the limits and implications of this claim. Seen in this light, *Gilgamesh* is, among other things, a taxonomic inquiry. Death, in *Gilgamesh,* when applied to god/men, is a taxic indicator. Death is characteristic of human beings. This is the presupposition of the epic, not its conclusion. Not dying is characteristic of gods. What, then, is the case when one is a mixture, a divine king, "two-thirds god, one-third human," possessing a bodily frame which, in size, is more typical of divinities? (Compare the portrait of the birth and body of the king-god, Marduk, in *Enuma elish* 1.83–100.)

The narrative of the later recension begins with a second trajectory that is, likewise, taxonomic: the proper placement of the king. It also serves to present the reason for the figure of Enkidu whom the Akkadian recensions raise from the status of a servant (as in the Sumerian compositions) to that of Gilgamesh's "friend" and double. For all is not well in Uruk. Rather than serving as a maintainer of order—the chief role of the king—Gilgamesh is disordering the city. Although the exact nature of the disorder is not clear,[3] what is clear in all the later versions is that the gods either directly observe

the disorder, or that the people's complaints reach them. What is to
be done? Again, we must take seriously the viewpoint of the prologue. The rectification of a divine king, one "summoned" to kingship by the gods, is not an affair of humans. The gods have created
the problem; they must solve it.[4]

The solution is the divine creation of Enkidu in a process analogous to that of Gilgamesh. Enkidu will be Gilgamesh's double:
"He looks like Gilgamesh," only slightly "shorter in stature, but
stronger in bone" (Old Babylonian 2.5.15–17); "they will rival
each other in battle that Uruk may have peace" (1.2.32). A problem that haunts royal narratives—the simultaneous presence of
rival claimants—is here subjugated to the taxonomic interest: a
god/man can only be checked by another god/man; human beings
are mere spectators of the struggle.

Before Enkidu can enter Uruk and challenge Gilgamesh, there
is a further taxonomic issue. Being not human (not like us) can
signal divinity; it can also signal animality or incivility (savagery).
The first person to speak to Enkidu after his formation in his
uncivil state expresses this ambivalence: "Wise are you, O Enkidu,
you are like a god; / Why then do you run around with the wild
animals on the steppe?" (1.4.34–35). Enkidu must be reclassified
(reduced) to at least a partially human state.

In the various versions, Enkidu's nonhumanity is described
in terms of four taxic indicators: physical appearance, diet,
dress, and habitat. He has long hair; his body is covered with
hair. He eats grass and drinks the milk of wild creatures or
slurps water from ponds. He is ignorant of grain and beer. He is
either naked or wears a garment of skins (like the god of wild
game). "He does not know people or civilized land"; he lives in
the steppes; he mingles freely with wild beasts (Old Babylonian
Penn. 2.12–3.23; Akkadian Uruk frag. obverse, 4–26; Hittite
Gilgamesh 1.2.7–12; "standard version" 1.2.36–41). This picture shares many features with the mythic portrait of the First
Human, "Man-as-he-was-in-the-beginning" (lullû amēlû), as Enkidu is called (1.4.6, 13, 19). Enkidu must "become human"
(Old Babylonian Penn. 3.25); his divinity/animality must become a mixture. This is accomplished by introducing Enkidu,
through the mediation of the prostitute Shamhat, to sex, human
discourse, clothes, beer and wine, and the use of oils. The immediate effect is to make him smell like a human rather than an

animal. The ultimate effect is to move him from the marginal realm of the steppes to the central world of the city.[5]

Enkidu enters Uruk and confronts Gilgamesh in the center of the city. They wrestle. Gilgamesh is the victor in a close match, and Enkidu acknowledges his kingship. They then set off on a series of heroic adventures. This has the desirable effect of removing Gilgamesh from the populace he has disordered, but it introduces another problem of placement: the king who is absent from the center, exploring the periphery.

The pair's first adventure is the encounter with Huwawa, the legitimate, though monstrous, guardian of the Cedar Forest. The pair defeat Huwawa and cut off its head. Unlike the predecessor Sumerian version of this incident, *Gilgamesh and the Land of the Living,* there is no suggestion here that the adventure is undertaken because of Gilgamesh's awareness of death and the desire to do deeds that will result in a memorable name. From the surviving Akkadian texts, the adventure appears unmotivated, although there is an expressed delight in the excitement of combat, which eliminates all fear of death (4.6.36). Gilgamesh's mother exclaims that Shamash has given Gilgamesh a "restless heart" (3.3.10), and, in a secondary rationalization, Gilgamesh explains that he wished to rid the land of evil (4.5.2; cf. the heavily restored 3.3.7).

Flushed with their victory, the pair return to Uruk, where Gilgamesh attracts the attention of Ishtar, who proposes, "you shall be my husband and I shall be your wife" (6.9). What is being offered is no mere erotic dalliance but rather the sacred marriage of king and goddess, one of the chief ritual duties of the divine king that ensures the perpetuation of civic life.[6] Gilgamesh's rude refusal reintroduces the theme of royal disorder. And there is more. In an insulting speech to the goddess, Gilgamesh catalogues the fate of her former consorts. This introduces, for the first time in the Akkadian epic, the possibility of a divine king dying. Gilgamesh charges the goddess with engineering the death of her prototypical consort, Dumuzi/Tammuz (6.60–63) as well as that of another consort, Ishullanu (6.76). Gilgamesh's refusal expresses his determination to avoid a similar fate (7.78).

In retribution for her rejection, Ishtar sends the Bull of Heaven against Uruk, but Gilgamesh and Enkidu defeat it. Enkidu hurls its severed thigh at Ishtar. This crowning insult to the goddess provides the motivation for a meeting of the divine council which decrees Enkidu's death. A god/man, it would appear, can only be killed by divine action.

At first, the pair are unaware of these fatal consequences and bask in the glory and the immortality of the name of heroes:

> Riding through the main streets of Uruk
> The people of Uruk gathered and gazed at them.
> Gilgamesh addressed his retainers:
> "Who is finest among the young men?
> Who is proudest among the males?"
> [They answer] "Gilgamesh is finest among the young men!
> Gilgamesh is proudest among the males!"
>
> (6.178–85)

The fatal decision of the council is conveyed to Enkidu in a prophetic dream. The complex structure of Tablet 7, cols. 3–4 is one of the intellectual centers of gravity of the late version of the epic. First, Enkidu learns he is to die. He reviews his career and regrets it, concluding with a curse against the prostitute who civilized him. Second, the god Shamash intervenes in direct speech and rejects the curses. After all, he argues, the prostitute gave Enkidu the gifts of civilization. Gilgamesh has treated Enkidu as a friend and a brother, bestowing on him great honor. After Enkidu's death, Gilgamesh will provide him with a splendid funeral and will mourn him in extreme fashion. Third, upon hearing this, Enkidu's "angry heart grew quiet" (7.3.50). Fourth, this calming vision is immediately superseded by a profoundly distressing vision of the Land of the Dead. The old heroic ideal is relativized. Not even Etana, the king of Kish who was translated to heaven, escaped death. He, along with divine kings, prophets, and priests, is seen in the Land of the Dead in Enkidu's portentious dream:

> In the House of Dust which I entered,
> I looked at [rulers], their crowns put away;
> I [saw princes], those born to the crown,
> Who had ruled the land from days of yore.
> [These doubles] of Anu and Enlil were serving meat roasts.
> . . . .
> In the House of Dust which I entered,
> Reside high priest and acolyte,
> Reside incantory and ecstatic,
> Reside the laver-anointers of the great gods,
> Resides Etana . . .
>
> (7.4.40–49)

The initial taxonomic question can now be answered. Neither divine kingship nor participation in the cult provides an escape from death. The "one-third human" is sufficient, in the case of god/man figures like Gilgamesh and Enkidu, to offset the "two-thirds divine." Any admixture with divinity produces a classification as wholly human with respect to mortality. There is no *triton genos,* no *tertium quid,* such as the later Pythagoreans would proclaim with respect to divine kings.

Following Enkidu's death, Gilgamesh draws the appropriate conclusion:

> Shall I not die too? Am I not like Enkidu?
> Grief has entered my heart.
> I am afraid of death.
>
> (9.1.3–5)

But, one line later, he immediately recalls one last mythic precedent (9.1.6), the case of Utnapishtim and his wife, sole survivors of the Flood, who were reclassified as *wholly* divine by the command of Enlil (11.193–94; cf.9.3.4). Could not the same be done for Gilgamesh? It is to answer this taxonomic question that Gilgamesh undertakes the arduous journey from Uruk to the realm of Utnapishtim-the-Far-Away (10.5.24; 10.6.40; 11.1, 195–96, 205, 219, 229, 258)—the latter's reclassification being expressed in both classificatory and spatial distance. In a journey that reverses the course of the sun, Gilgamesh travels through a succession of essentially uninhabited lands (unlike the monstrous lands in royal Indo-European quest narratives), forewarned, in one version, by Shamash that his quest will be a failure (Old Babylonian 10.1.8).

The Old Babylonian tradition, but not the later Akkadian recensions, introduces, at this point, the *carpe diem* theme. Siduri, the "wise old bawd," one of the few typical individuals Gilgamesh encounters, after hearing his story delivers a wisdom speech:

> Gilgamesh, where are you running?
> The life which you seek you will not find.
> For when the gods created humankind,
> They allotted death to humankind,
> But life they kept within their keeping.
> As for you, Gilgamesh, let your belly be full,
> Make merry each day and night.
> Of each day make a feast of rejoicing,
> Day and night, dance and play.
>
> (Old Babylonian, Megiddo, 3.1–9)

This Babylonian conclusion appears to be rejected by the late Akkadian versions which, by contrast, focus relentlessly on the taxonomic issue and the question of whether Utnapishtim and his wife constitute a viable precedent.

When Gilgamesh finally encounters Utnapishtim and his wife, the precedent, at least momentarily, seems plausible. For there is nothing "special" about them as compared to Gilgamesh:

> I look at you, Utnapishtim,
> And your limbs are no different, you are just like me.
> Indeed, you are not at all different, you are just like me.
> . . . .
> Tell me how you came to stand in the assembly of the gods
> and received eternal life.
>
> (11.2–7)

But Utnapishtim instantly disabuses him. The Flood was a unique, unrepeatable event. It is not a precedent, and it will never recur. (So much for the ancient Near East's notion of cyclical, mythic time!) Enlil, Utnapishtim narrates:

> Seized my hand and led me up.
> He led up my wife and made her kneel down by my side.
> He touched our foreheads, stood between us, blessed us:
> "Until now Utnapishtim was mortal, but, henceforth,
> Utnapishtim and his wife shall be as we gods are.
> Utnapishtim shall dwell far off at the mouth of the rivers."
> [The gods] took me and made me dwell far off, at the mouth
>   of the rivers,
> So now, who can gather the gods on your behalf,
> That you may find the eternal life which you seek?
>
> (11.190–98, emphasis added)

What occurs next is complex and difficult to interpret. What seems to be a contest turns into one, if not two, apparent rituals of rebirth. Gilgamesh is challenged by Utnapishtim to stay awake for six days and seven nights. He sleeps the entire period, but after he awakes, he is washed:

> He washed in water his filthy hair . . .
> He threw away his skins, and the sea carried them away.
> His body was soaked until it was fresh.
> He put a new headband in his hair.
> He wore a robe as a proud garment,
> Until he came to his city,

Until he came to his journey's end.
[Until then] the garment would not discolor,
and stayed absolutely new.

(11.248–55; cf. 239–45)

His corpselike appearance is changed into that of a newborn, his old robes of skin into a new garment. From a literary point of view, Gilgamesh is becoming recivilized, thus paralleling the transformation of Enkidu as, in Gilgamesh's journey up to this point, he increasingly took on Enkidu's animalistic/savage attributes (see above, note 5). Furthermore, Gilgamesh is granted a boon, a "secret knowledge of the gods." If he will plunge to the bottom of the sea, he will find a hidden plant called "An-old-man-grows-into-a-young-man." It will be difficult to locate and painful to hold, but if Gilgamesh persists and takes the plant back to Uruk, he will have the capability of regeneration:

With it [the plant] a man may win the breath of life.
I shall take it back to Uruk; I shall give it to an old
man to eat, and thus try it out . . .
I too shall eat it and turn into the young man I once was.

(II. 279–82)

Although the ordeal of the plunge to the bottom of the sea as well as the plant which tears his hands reads like some initiatory scenario, there are no known ritual parallels in Akkadian tradition.

Immediately after gaining the plant—and here we must read most carefully, for, as in the Israelitic so-called Fall Story, crucial events are narrated with extreme economy—Gilgamesh sets off on his return to Uruk with plant in hand. He stops to bathe in a pool, and a snake steals the plant, thereby gaining the gift of shedding its skin and rejuvenation. The universalistic interpretation takes this to be the final denouement, but it is not: the snake drops the plant, and the sea tides carry it away to a distance the equivalent of which Gilgamesh has walked that morning (11.297; cf. 283). That is to say, Gilgamesh *could* recover the plant, but he chooses not to: "I shall give it up (11.297). Rather, he continues to Uruk, where he becomes a proper, in-place ruler. (As in the nonepic Sumerian tradition, he becomes, after death, re-placed as a judge in the Underworld.)

In the present conclusion of the epic, the late Akkadian redactor announced the moral of the tale. Gilgamesh speaks to the boatman who has accompanied him on the latter part of his journey:

> Go up onto the wall of Uruk and walk around,
> Inspect its base, examine its brickwork.
> Is not its brickwork of kiln-fired brick?
> . . . .
> One square mile is city, one square mile is orchards,
> One square mile is claypits, as well as the open grounds of Ish-
> tar's temple.
> Three square miles and the open ground comprise Uruk.
>
> (11.303–7)

The Sumerian Gilgamesh's desire for heroic memorialization has been here transmuted into civic achievement. Gilgamesh's memorial is his wall and the careful organization of the divisions of his city. It is this taxonomic bounding and ordering of Uruk that makes it truly a city, one established and maintained by an in-place king. In the late version of the epic, Gilgamesh is no longer a figure of heroic *furor;* his *ek-stasis* is his wall.

A late Akkadian editor, effectively employing the device of ring-composition, retrojected the invitation to view the walls of Uruk to the prologue as well (1.16–21), thus framing the entire narrative. Also, at a late stage, wisdom materials were added to the formerly heroic prologue:

> He who saw everything . . .
> The hidden he saw, the undisclosed he discovered . . .
> [He] achieved a long journey, exhausted but at peace.
>
> (1.1.1,5,7)

Gilgamesh's "peace" is the sort of salvation expressed in the biblical passage "he sets up salvation as walls and bulwarks" (Isaiah 26:1). Rather than presenting salvation exclusively as escape from death, as transcendence or ascension to other realms, *Gilgamesh* reminds us of another sort of salvation, one that is achieved, often arduously, through efforts of placement.

NOTES

1.   G. Smith, "The Chaldean Account of the Deluge," *Transactions of the Society of Biblical Archaeology* 2 (1873) 213–34.

2.   I have drawn on the following translations: A. Heidel, *The Gilgamesh Epic and Old Testament Parallels,* 2nd ed. (Chicago, 1949); S. N.

Kramer and E. A. Speiser in J. B. Pritchard, ed., *Ancient Near Eastern Texts Relating to the Old Testament,* 2nd ed. (Princeton, 1955) 44–52, 72–99; S. Dalley, *Myths from Mesopotamia* (Oxford, 1989) 50–153; M. G. Kovacs, *The Epic of Gilgamesh* (Stanford, 1989). Above all, I have utilized the magisterial work of J. H. Tigay, *The Evolution of the Gilgamesh Epic* (Philadelphia, 1982).

3. On the basis of the damaged late Akkadian version (1.2.6–30), some scholars have claimed that Gilgamesh introduced forced labor on civic projects. The Old Babylonian seems to suggest that Gilgamesh exercised *droit de seigneur* (Old Babylonian, Penn. 4.32–34). The Hittite versions suggests that there are athletic contests in which Gilgamesh bests the young men of Uruk, perhaps claiming their women as prizes or, less likely, that Gilgamesh is an instance of the "stranger-king" pattern, the king from the outside who, after contest, gains the throne and the women (Hittite 1.1.10–13).

4. Note the parallel to the Priestly version of the Israelitic Flood story where the admixture of the divine and the human (Gen. 6:1–4) likewise requires a divine solution.

5. Note that later in the epic, after Enkidu's death, when Gilgamesh begins his journey to the Land of the Remote, leaving the city of Uruk, he reverses the transformation of Enkidu. As Shamash predicts, after Enkidu's death, Gilgamesh "will make himself wear unkempt hair, he will don a lion's skin and roam over the steppe" (7.3.47–48). Compare Gilgamesh's self-description in 10.5.29–32, which contains a rudimentary zoological taxonomy.

6. Note the possible foreshadowing of this theme at the beginning of the epic. In the Old Babylonian, when Enkidu first enters Uruk, he blocks Gilgamesh from performing what appears to be a sacred marriage ritual (Old Babylonian 2.5.24–26).

CHAPTER 2

Ascent to the Stars in a Mesopotamian Ritual: Social Metaphor and Religious Experience

Tzvi Abusch

Visions of the heavens or the netherworld and journeys thereto are well represented in Mesopotamian mythology. Aspects of these themes are found in such works as the Descent of Inanna/Ishtar, the Epic of Gilgamesh, Etana, Adapa, and An Assyrian Prince's Vision of the Netherworld, and they are preserved in traditions about antedeluvian sages and kings from which the Enoch literature derives.[1] This body of mythological works is not of a piece. For Mesopotamian mythology seems to have undergone a major change sometime during the early historical period.

Early Mesopotamian religious thought focused upon issues of vegetation and fertility and emphasized the cyclical quality of nature. Gods of life and death, of the earth and netherworld, might once have even been aspects of the same power and possessed a unitary identity, for the earth/netherworld was both the source of life and the receiver of the dead. Initially, Mesopotamian mythology grew out of and gave expression to this religion of fertility and thus recognized the fluidity as well as the cyclical nature of movement between earth and netherworld. These two realms formed a continuum, and thus movement back and forth between the world of the living and that of the dead was possible and was even part of the natural order. Life and death themselves were parts of the same continuum. Even the separation of the human and the divine was not yet definitive, for divinity and deathlessness did not coincide, and thus gods, like humans, could die and sojourn in the nether-world.

Later a sharp distinction was drawn. No longer were the afore-mentioned realms seen as parts of a single continuum that are set off from each other by means of porous boundaries. Rather, they were now regarded as separate; consequently, one could no longer belong to two realms at the same time, and movement from one realm to another tended to become permanent and irreversible. Even the organic unity underlying the identity of some of the gods was divided into sharply differentiated forms. There was an increasing stratification and firming-up of boundaries and a loss of the fluid movement reminiscent of natural flux. At least in the standard works of mythology, a sharp dichotomy between life and death was introduced; the earth and the netherworld, the world of the living and that of the dead, were no longer perceived as forming a continuum. Fluid movement now constituted a threat to the more rigid cosmic structure and could easily lead to the break-down of that structure. Thus, for example, forced entry into the netherworld would lead paradoxically but logically to the over-whelming of the realm of the living by the dead (e.g., Descent of Ishtar).

But with the drawing of a sharp distinction between earth and netherworld, a tripartite structure of reality (netherworld/earth/heavens) developed in order to accommodate a new reality that increasingly drew sharper distinctions than had existed before. For example, no longer was a god who disappeared for a season consid-ered to be dead for that period of time and to be a proper resident of the netherworld; rather, he would now have to reside in what had become the proper residence for immortal beings, the heavens. Accordingly, some of the roles of the netherworld were transferred to the heavens, so we find some gods who have disappeared residing in the heavens rather than the netherworld. But now, there is also greater movement between the earth and the heavens, a movement facilitated perhaps by a concomitant growing emphasis in Mesopo-tamia upon heavenly bodies and gods of the sky.

Transmitted accounts of travel to the heavens and the nether-world reflect and give expression to concepts and attitudes that belong to the two stages of thought that we have described: even in late mythological texts that actually treat our theme, the very abili-ty to move between the realms and perhaps even to change one's identity reflects the earlier stage and/or mode, while many narrative details, descriptions of the divides between the realms, and the consequences of crossing over often reflect the later stage (e.g., Descent of Ishtar and Adapa). Many of these mythological texts should perhaps be reexamined in light of the distinctions that I have just drawn.[2]

However, even in some later materials, the new stratified hierarchical structure and sharp distinction between the earth and netherworld were not carried through consistently. For these new developments seem to have had little effect upon the familial and personal experiences surrounding funerals and upon rituals on behalf of, or involving, the dead. Even after death, a human being could move back and forth along the continuum, for people retained their integrity so long as their form—their skeletal remains—was not destroyed. In the interaction of the living and the dead, personal contact as well as movement and interchange between the realms remained normal. Thus, for example, at the end of the month of Abu, there occurs an all-souls day when the dead rise up, appear in this world, and interact with the living.

Here, then, I wish to draw not upon a myth but upon the realm of magic and ritual to document an ascent to the heavens and a descent to the netherworld. In a ceremony whose context is the all-souls day mentioned above, we have an instance of human ascension to the stars, and it is to this ascension and its context that I wish now to turn. More specifically, this chapter will draw upon several incantations in the Babylonian magical series *Maqlû;*[3] the incantations are found in the introductory section of the work (Tablet 1. lines 37–60) and in other structurally significant sections that belong to the same recension as the introduction. By examining the mythic framework and personal experience described in this magical text, I shall try to shed a bit of light on the religious experiences and images associated with the cosmic journey. I trust that similarities with later texts that describe attempts to ascend to heaven and join the world of divinity will be obvious.

INTRODUCTION: BACKGROUND

Before turning to the passages in which the relevant personal experience of the participant—his transformation, ascent to heaven, and mission to the netherworld—comes to special expression, we need to recall a few general characteristics of the text.[4]

The *Maqlû* series contains about one hundred incantations and accompanying rites. It preserves the text of a single complex ritual and is composed of three major subdivisions: Tablets 1–5, Tablets 6–7. line 57, and Tablets 7. line 58–8. The first two divisions were performed during the night, the third during the early morning hours of the following day. The primary participants were the exorcist or incantation-priest (*āšipu*), who served as the ritual expert and director, and his client or patient, a bewitched man (sometimes the king), who was the speaker or ritual actor. The latter acted not only on his own behalf but also on behalf of the community. On occasion, he may even have taken on the identity of a priest and messenger of the gods. The ceremony took place at the end of the month of Abu,[5] the time of year when spirits move back and forth between the netherworld and this world, the living and the dead interact, and judgments can be made in this world by both heavenly and netherworld deities. The purpose of the *Maqlû* ceremony was symbolically to judge, punish, and expel all witches, whether dead or alive. Dead witches were unearthed and held captive; live witches were killed. All witches were then utterly destroyed and were thus deprived of the possibility of burial. They were thereby prevented from finding a permanent place in the netherworld and were expelled from the cosmos.

In keeping with the setting and purpose of *Maqlû*, the introduction to the work (1.1–72) is directed to the nighttime sky and its gods and to the netherworld and its gods and thus establishes a cosmic framework.[6] This introductory section constitutes the indictment of the witches and their imprisonment; only in the following sections of the work are the witches then judged and executed.

It seems that the witches have disregarded a compact to which they were bound. The *māmītu* ("oath") of our text (1.38) designates, I believe, a code of behavior to which members of society, including the witches, have been bound by oath under the threat of punishment. This social compact prohibits hostile behavior of an antisocial, seditious nature, behavior that either refers to or is construed as the performance of witchcraft.

The aforementioned *māmītu* is authorized and guaranteed by the powers of the heavens and the netherworld. For their crimes, the witches are to be punished and excluded from the organized community of humanity, which encompasses the living and the dead. Accordingly, the speaker in these incantations attempts to gain the assistance of the heavens in support of his accusation and to persuade the netherworld that the shades of witches should not be allowed into that realm.

SOCIO-COSMIC LEVEL: THE SPEAKER AS MESSENGER

We turn now to 1.37–60, the unit comprising the second, third, and fourth incantations (lines 37–41, 42–49, and 50–60, respectively) in the introduction to the work.[7] The speaker's mission at this point in *Maqlû* is to invoke and enforce the compact. The first incantation was directed to the heavens against live witches. Now in the second (1.37–41), the *māmītu* of the netherworld is invoked against dead witches:

> Netherworld, netherworld, yea netherworld,
> Gilgamesh is the enforcer of your oath.
> Whatever you have done, I know,
> Whatever I do, you do not know,
> Whatever my witches do, there will be no one to overlook,
>   undo, release.

In this incantation, the speaker invokes the netherworld and then declares that the witches are under an oath administered and enforced by Gilgamesh; hence, it is an oath sanctioned by the netherworld.

Having invoked the oath, the speaker seeks to ensure its preservation and enforcement; he must prevent any divine being from aiding the witches and revoking the *māmītu*. To this end, he undertakes the activities described in the third and fourth incantations. In the third, he calls upon the gods of the sky for their assistance; then, in the fourth, he calls upon the netherworld goddess, Bēlet-ṣēri, here in the role of scribe of the netherworld and guardian of its borders.

The celebrant must approach Bēlet-ṣēri at the border between the heavens and the netherworld, where a passageway or crossing (*nēbiru*) serves as an entry point from the netherworld into the heavens. Here, where the two worlds meet, there is a place to imprison[8] and hold back those who wish to follow a cosmic circuit but who must now not be allowed to go either forward into the inhabited world (and then on into the netherworld) or backward,

like the planets, into the netherworld.[9] The speaker must ensure
that the dead witches who had ascended during the festival of the
dead be confined for trial at a point between heaven and the
netherworld and not permitted to return to the netherworld,
whence they could reascend in subsequent years.

The speaker imagines himself able to address and interact with
the gods of both cosmic regions and to journey to both. He wishes
to go to Bēlet-ṣēri to ask for her support. But to do so, he must be a
messenger of the gods, an emissary of the heavenly court (see lines
42–72). However, he is a member of the laity, not a priest, and is
thus not automatically a messenger of the gods.[10] To understand
how a member of the laity may become their messenger, we must
turn to the third incantation (1.42–49), where the speaker faces
the gods of the night sky and addresses them as follows:

> My city is Zabban, my city is Zabban,
> Of my city Zabban, two are its gates:
> One for the rising of the sun, the second for the setting of the
>   sun,
> One for the rising of the sun, the second for the setting of the
>   sun.
> Raising up a broken palm frond and *maštakal* plant,
> I offer water to the gods of the sky (and say):
> "As I purify you yourselves,
> May you purify me myself."

The setting and description of Zabban are central to our text.
Historical sources contain references to a city Zabban; it is, therefore, possible that our lines refer to the terrestrial city Zabban. But
while it is possible to interpret our text as if it were set in that
terrestrial city, the text contains a number of indications that suggest that the city may also have a cosmic setting. For example, the
statement that the city contains two gates, one for the rising of the
sun and the other for its setting (1.43–45), is intended to emphasize less the direction of the earthly city's gates and more the fact
that the city faces, perhaps even contains, the very gates through
which the sun rises and sets. These gates are on the horizon, and
through them pass the sun and other heavenly bodies when they
enter and leave the sky and return to the netherworld. Thus, the
gates of Zabban lead into the heavens and the netherworld, and
the city, together with its "inhabitant," our speaker, guards the
entrances into and out of those regions. Moreover, the city is situ-

ated on a cosmic shore. Located on the horizon, its quay and pass serve as entry points through which cosmic travellers and ghosts normally pass, without hindrance, from the netherworld into the heavens, but where they may also be temporarily imprisoned.

Thus even if "Zabban" is a normal terrestrial city, here in *Maqlû* it is also a cosmic locale identical perhaps with West Semitic Ṣāphôn,[11] an *Axis Mundi* that connects the earth, heavens, and netherworld and draws together the human, divine, and infernal communities. Here the speaker is not only at the point of contact between the earth and the night sky but also at the point where heaven, earth, and the netherworld meet.

Thus, while the speaker is on earth, he is also in the heavens. In this sense, his vision is like Isaiah's vision of God, a vision that is both terrestrial and heavenly: "I beheld my Lord seated on a high and lofty throne; and the skirts of His robe filled the Temple" (Isa. 6:1).[12]

Our Mesopotamian speaker imagines himself able to journey shaman-like to both the heavens and the netherworld in the guise of a star. Let us now examine his specific actions. In the opening incantation, the speaker, standing on a rooftop, invoked the gods of the night sky and perhaps received an oracular response from them. Still standing on a roof, the speaker in the third incantation again faces the gods of the night sky, the stars. In lines 46–47, he says:

> Raising up a broken palm frond and mashtakal plant,
> I offer water to the gods of the sky.

The offer perhaps takes the form of sprinkling water towards the heavens. But why does the speaker offer water to the gods of the sky? The answer lies in the following two lines (1.48–49), where he says to the gods:

> As I purify you yourselves,
> May you purify me myself.

It is to the previously mentioned act of giving water that he alludes when he tells the gods that he has purified them; now he asks them to purify him in turn.

Why does he ask them to purify him? The purpose of this purification may be construed in several ways: as preparation for an eventual dream incubation;[13] as protection against demonic forces, generally, and witchcraft, specifically; as reaffirmation of the judgment of innocence given previously in the first incantation (1.21–26) and there symbolized by a purification in the presence of the gods of the night sky; and as preparation for entering the world of the gods. Of these, the last seems to be the most significant, for here, I think, purification is requested by the speaker primarily so that he may be incorporated into the court of the gods of the night sky.

I need hardly emphasize that the underlying concept or experience here of ascent to the world of the gods is also found in early Jewish apocalyptic and hekhalot literatures, where the participant ascends to heaven to join the divine world,[14] and in early Pythagoreanism and in Hellenistic literature, where the soul at death returns to the heavens and is to be found among or as one of the stars.[15] These traditions, it should be noted, are linked, in one way or another, to ancient Mesopotamia and are rooted in an ecstatic, trance, or dream experience.

To return to the speaker: he is stationed in a cosmic locale or area that connects heaven and the netherworld; it is a place from which he can ascend into heaven and then descend to the netherworld. But to enter the netherworld he must assume the identity of an astral body that routinely travels through the heavens and the netherworld. On a mythological level, that is, he must become a member of the company of the stars, the heavenly host or retinue of the gods of heaven Anu and Antu, for only then can he serve as their emissary and present himself to Bēlet-ṣēri in the manner of lines 52–53: "Anu and Antu have sent me saying, 'Whom shall I send to Bēlet-ṣēri?'"[16] Hence, he asks the gods to purify him, thus preparing him for incorporation into their company. At his request, the gods of the sky prepare him, induct him, and introduce him into the presence of Anu and Antu. The latter, in turn, commission him as their messenger, thus providing him with the authorization and support that he requires in order to travel to Bēlet-ṣēri.

The situation is not unlike the induction of Isaiah; the prophet is purified so that he may participate in the divine court and serve as the Lord's emissary:

> Then one of the seraphim flew to me carrying in his hand a glowing coal. . . . He touched my mouth with it and said, "See, this has touched your lips; your iniquity is removed, and your sin is wiped away." Then I heard the Lord saying, "Whom shall I send? Who will go for me?" And I answered, "Here am I; send me." He said, "Go and tell this people. . . ." (Isa. 6:6–9)[17]

Having joined the gods of the night sky, taken on the identity of a heavenly body, and ascended into the sky, our speaker in the fourth incantation (1.50–60) now descends to address Bēlet-ṣēri in the netherworld.

> I have enclosed the ford, I have enclosed the quay,
> I have enclosed (therein) the witchcraft of all the lands.
> Anu and Antu have sent me, (saying):
> "Whom shall we (lit., I) send to Bēlet-ṣēri?"
> Place locks on the mouth of my warlock and witch,
> Place the sealing of the sage of the gods, Marduk,
> When they call to you, do not answer them,
> When they speak to you, do not listen to them,
> When I call to you, answer me,
> When I speak to you, listen to me.
> By the command of Anu, Antu, and Bēlet-ṣēri.

The speaker's purpose is to keep the witches confined prior to trial here in the pass and quay, at the entrance to the netherworld, and to prevent the witches from persuading netherworld officers to abrogate the oath. In lines 52–53, he presents himself to Bēlet-ṣēri as a fully accredited messenger of the sky gods and presents his credentials. He turns to her because her approval is necessary for entrance into the infernal realm, and she herself has the authority to abrogate the oath. Like the necromancer who calls to the dead for information, so too both the messenger and the witches call to Bēlet-ṣēri in the netherworld for a response. The messenger asks that Bēlet-ṣēri not heed the witches' call for assistance but instead respond to his call. He calls upon the goddess to keep them imprisoned, to sustain the ban invoked against them, and not to heed their request to abrogate it and allow them into the netherworld. In this manner, the witches are to be kept confined for the trial and prevented either from entering the heaven and attacking the earth and/or from returning to the netherworld and finding a haven there.

PHENOMENOLOGICAL LEVEL: THE SPEAKER AS RITUAL PARTICIPANT

The speaker identifies with the stars in order to become a messenger of the heavenly court. But there are other reasons, as well, for his identification with the gods of the night sky, the stars; and it is noteworthy that his transformation into a heavenly body belongs not only to the social sphere but at the same time also to the individual sphere. The actor is not only a messenger who takes on a social role and functions on a socio-cosmic level but also an individual who participates in a ritual and is thereby psychologically transformed.

The ritual actor's assumption of a new identity, his astral identification or transformation, is no less desirable on a ritual level than it was on a social level, for, as we shall see, the new identity and experience will serve to protect and preserve him during the ritual and will allow him to experience and exercise power.

The participant has joined the company of the stars. In this connection, we note that in the course of a discussion of the Mesopotamian attitude toward the phenomena of nature,[18] the late Thorkild Jacobsen cited *Maqlû* 6.1–8 (alongside 3.151–52, where the speaker takes over the identity of the heavens and the netherworld) and suggested that through such identifications with gods and sacred emblems, the Mesopotamian attained immunity from witchcraft by taking over the quality of sacred inviolability. In Jacobsen's words:

> One such self might infuse itself into other different selves and, in a relation of partial identity, lend them of its character. We may illustrate by quoting a Mesopotamian incantation by which a man sought to become identical with Heaven and Earth:
>
> > I am Heaven, you cannot touch me,
> > I am Earth, you cannot bewitch me!
>
> The man is trying to ward off sorcery from his body, and his attention is centered on a single quality of Heaven and Earth, their sacred inviolability. When he has made himself identical with them, this quality will flow into him and merge with his being, so that he will be secure from attacks by witchcraft.
>
> Very similar is another incantation in which a man endeavors to drench every part of his body in immunity by such identification with gods and sacred emblems. It reads:
>
> > Enlil is my head, my face is the day;
> > Urash, the peerless god, is the protecting spirit leading my way.
> > My neck is the necklace of the goddess Ninlil,
> > My two arms are the sickle of the western moon,
> > My fingers tamarisk, bone of the gods of heaven;
> > They ward off the embrace of sorcery from my body;
> > The gods Lugal-edinna and Latarak are my breast and knees;
> > Muhra my ever-wandering feet.

Here again the identity sought is only partial. Qualities of these
gods and sacred emblems are to infuse the man's members and
make him inviolable.[19]

Jacobsen was surely on the right track, but behind the identification there seems to be more than just a desire to attain sacred
inviolability. The actor's astral identifications serve several purposes. We have already seen that his identification with the stars
allows him to become their messenger and liaison; now let us try
to explore additional dimensions of the experience.

When *Maqlû* was turned into a nocturnal ceremony, the experiences and images of night and sleep came to dominate the ceremony and the work. *Maqlû* now began not with the original opening address to the sun but with an address to the bodies of the
night sky and to the watches of the night.[20] The work was expanded and now encompassed three ceremonial divisions, each
corresponding to and overseen by one of the three watches (the last
extending into the early morning). Simply put, the stars were now
called upon in large part because they were the powers then present or visible in the sky.

The speaker stands on the rooftop of an earthly house and
recites the incantations. Before him is the expanse of the heavens.
He beholds the visible stars and heavenly bodies. In the first place,
they are asked to assist in the judgment and render decisions. But it
is not enough for the ritual actor just to see and call upon the sky.
More important, perhaps, he must also become part of the sky.
The speaker invoked the stars and other heavenly bodies in order
to identify himself with these inhabitants of the night sky, an identification that comes to particular expression precisely in sections
of *Maqlû,* such as the introduction of the first division and the
framework of the second division, that were added to the work to
give it structure as it developed into a lengthy nighttime ceremony.
On a topographical level, this transformation is possible because
he is in a locale that is not only terrestrial but also heavenly and
that draws together the human and heavenly communities.

As we saw, the identification allows him to become a messenger of the gods. He imagines himself to be one of the stars and
ascends into the sky and journeys through it to the netherworld.
The identification has other purposes as well. Most of all, it serves
to allow the ritual actor to take on the quality of wakefulness or
sleeplessness associated with the stars. But before developing this

theme, we must first understand why this particular quality is so very important and even necessary.

The actor must protect himself and combat a diabolic enemy. At least one of the witches that he must counteract has a spectral or even demonic quality.[21] For she is assuredly a creature of the night and increasingly assumes forms associated with the night. Basic to the normal experience of nighttime are the activities of sleeping and dreaming.[22] Not surprisingly, a powerful experience underlying the imagery and fear of the witch is the nighttime dream. The witch becomes the one who sends the dream or such associated forms as clouds, and she is now more readily thought of as a wind (see, e.g., 5.82–88; cf. 7.1–7). This set of associations further reinforces the notion of the witch as a shade, for in Mesopotamia winds, ghosts, and demons are closely associated, even identified.

Notions of witchcraft and images associated with the night, particularly the dream, are brought together.[23] On occasion, then, to dream an evil dream is to be bewitched. Standard conceptions of bewitchment are overlaid or replaced by images drawn from or associated with the experience of dreaming. The terrifying dream carries with it a double set of metaphors: images associated with dreams generally (clouds, smoke) and images associated with terrifying dreams specifically (evil gods). These images are then equated with witchcraft. Perhaps the witch appears in the dream; perhaps another dead human that the witch has enlisted appears in it. The evil dreams, themselves demonic powers or beings, became primary concerns.[24] But not only dreams, also sleep—which allows one to dream—becomes a matter of concern. For sleep may lead to or turn into death.[25] Moreover, death itself is often described as a form of sleep, and the verb ṣalālu, "to be asleep," is used to designate a peaceful death.[26] And the danger, the possibility of dying while asleep, is especially present and immediate when sleep is associated with dreams of a deathly nature.

But it is not only nighttime but also the very calendrical or festival setting itself that make it so very appropriate and necessary for the participant himself to identify with stars. We need again recall that the Maqlû ceremony was performed, principally at night, during a festival of the dead at the end of the month of Abu. All nights are dangerous, but this one is particularly so, for the aforementioned dangers are especially present during the festival of the dead.

The *Maqlû* ceremony was performed at a time of year when ghosts return to this world. On this night, normal ghosts are "awake" before going back to sleep, their permanent rest in the earth. Although not necessarily malevolent as such, they are dangerous while they are awake. But at the end of the night they resume their sleep; they return, that is, to the netherworld for another year.

Not all the dead are worthy, well intentioned, and benign. The manes of dead witches also reappear in this world together with the other dead. These "infernal" witches are also now awake, and like all ghosts they are dangerous. In addition, however, they are essentially evil. Moreover, since one of the purposes of *Maqlû* is to keep them from returning to the netherworld, they are particularly dangerous because they themselves are trying to stave off the threat of permanent extinction.

On this night, one is perhaps susceptible to harm from all ghosts, but one is particularly vulnerable to witches. Especially the main participant in the ceremony must be protected against these witches and their powers, for he becomes their target, perhaps precisely because he sets out to destroy them.

It follows, therefore, that going to sleep during this night—when the dead, particularly the dead witches, are present among the living—constitutes a very real danger, an even greater danger than normal, for asleep, one is at the mercy of malevolent forces that roam around in the external world and, especially, at the mercy of those that can take control through internal means and do harm through the medium of sleep. The occasion requires a vigil.

Astral Identification

The *Maqlû* ritual must protect the ritual participant from the dangerous dead and from the fearful (dream) experiences of the night brought on by the witches, and it must provide assurance that they will not again reappear. Hence, in order to protect himself against attack, the actor identifies himself with the denizens of the night sky. He does so in order to acquire the quality of inviolability that the heavens and heavenly bodies possess (cf. Maql 5.11–20 and 7.55–57). But the form of the necessary inviolability that he seeks is not so much sacredness as wakefulness. It seems to me that his identification with the heavenly bodies is governed primarily by his desire to take over their quality of wakefulness, for the stars are present in the sky throughout the night.

This is evident, for example, from 6.1–18 and 7.50–57, the parallel incantations that open and close the second, that is the middle, division of *Maqlû*. While these incantations serve as the present frame of the second division, they are actually secondary and were added to the text of *Maqlû* only at a relatively late stage of development after most, if not all, of the other materials in the division were already present; their inclusion in the text is part of a late revision that represents the introduction of an Ekur related tendency that centers upon dreams.[27] These two incantations are all the more important, therefore, because they were introduced into the ceremony in order to provide a new structuring principle and to define the new interest of the text as a concern with the night sky, the night, and dreams. In these incantations, the participant reaffirms the aforementioned identification; for example, "Enlil is my head, Sirius is my visage."[28] The quality to be assumed by means of the identification is stated expressly in the latter incantation, 7.50–57, where subsequent to the identification, the speaker asserts in line 54 that the heavenly powers with which he identifies—the stars—are *attunu ilī rabûti ša ina šamê napḫātunu*, "the great gods who are visible in the heavens." They are thus powers that themselves partake in, and imbue him with, the quality of wakefulness.

He wishes to remain awake in order not to succumb to sleep, for awake he remains impervious to attacks of witchcraft that may come in the form of terrifying dreams which augur death or of a deathly sleep which may carry the sleeper into death. Accordingly, in the opening incantation of Tablet 6, we find the speaker addressing an "evil god" immediately following the identification:

> Whoever you are, o evil god whom the warlock and witch
> Have sent against me to kill me:
> If you are awake, do not come here (to me),
> If you are asleep, do not rise up (to me).
>
> (6.10–13)

The evil god seems here to be a power that can do harm by appearing and travelling at night. Perhaps this "evil god" is a ghost or a dream, more properly, a power that appears like a *zaqīqu* in a dream. The fact that these lines occur in the opening incantation of the ceremonial division that centers upon a rite of fumigation is consistent with our interpretation, for in *Maqlû* a major purpose of fumigation—the burning in a censer of a prepared mixture of ingredients in order to produce incense or smoke—is to counteract attacks of witchcraft imagined as dreams that themselves come in the form of smoke, clouds, or the like.

But just as the *Maqlû* ritual as a whole serves both apotropaic and destructive purposes, so too the rite of fumigation in *Maqlû* not only is a protective act but also serves aggressive purposes, for it disperses and destroys witchcraft. It is thus also a rite that scatters evil dreams and drives away the spiritual remains of both the live witches who in the preceding portion of the ceremony have just been killed and their bodies destroyed and the dead witches who have just been exhumed.

This witch, then, is a shade who must not be allowed to make the rounds of heaven and the netherworld together with the stars.[29] Perhaps she is even a star.[30] In any case, she can be identified and outwitted by a star.

As for the ritual actor, he is able to assume an aggressive identity in addition to his defensive posture. This comes as no surprise in view of his role as an astral messenger of the gods. Thus, for example, in 5.82–88, he identifies himself with such meteorological forces as a wind and attacks the witch.[31] A comparable textual segment occurs also in 7.1–7, where the speaker assumes a meteorological (=rainbow, see line 3), perhaps even an astral, identity (line 1, if *manzâd* refers to the speaker and not the witch) in his confrontation with the witch. As a star, the ritual actor discerns which heavenly forces are evil and are actually either the demonic witch or her emissaries. He has the power to confront her, withstand her power,[32] and cast her into the wilderness or transform her into a formless wind that sweeps along the steppe.[33]

CONCLUSION AND FURTHER SPECULATION: THE SOCIO-PSYCHOLOGICAL EXPERIENCE

It is surely not a coincidence that this discussion has centered upon the introduction to *Maqlû*, in which the speaker addresses the host of the night sky and is inducted by them into their company, and upon 6.1–7.57, the very division that begins and ends with incantations that center upon the speaker's identification with stars and wherein such other incantations as the opening one in Tablet 7 also show the speaker assuming a heavenly visage. For in *Maqlû* the ritual actor takes on an astral identity and seems to remain awake throughout the first two ceremonial divisions. Now, in preparation for the morning, he can perhaps rest or even sleep. Hence, the next three incantations of the second division (7.23–57 // 9.141ff.[34]) center upon the act of salving the ritual actor, for salve both relaxes and protects. And in the morning, the actor will be purified, his evil dreams nullified by the sun, Shamash, and the powers of water, Ea and Asalluhi, and the witches will be finally destroyed both as humans (by being thrown to jackals) and as demons (by being sent off into Apsu, the abyss).

But here let us return for a moment to the themes of sleep and wakefulness. It is in the calendrical context of Abu that the issues of sleep and death of the celebrant and of the witch come together. It is not unimportant for the understanding of *Maqlû* that the concepts 'awake' and 'asleep' appear in the first incantation of the second division in a significant context alongside the speaker's identification with stars, for these are among the central themes of the ceremony.

Here in *Maqlû*, wakefulness serves both offensive and defensive purposes. Like the stars, the celebrant must remain awake during the night and not sleep. If he were to sleep, his diabolic enemies would seize him; asleep he is vulnerable. But by remaining awake, he may fend off the witches and destroy them. And destroy them he must; they must be punished for their crimes; moreover, not unlike vampires, if after having been awake during the night they succeed in going back to sleep at the end of the festival, they will have returned to a secure place in the netherworld and will be able to rise up again in the following year. Therefore, he wishes to prevent them from returning to the netherworld and enjoying the rest of the dead.[35] They are to be destroyed; they may, for example, be sent off to roam in the steppe, the land of formlessness and meaningless movement that is outside of the settled community and organized cosmos. There the witch as shade becomes a formless wind.

The text of *Maqlû* has a cosmic framework, and this setting serves as the stage for the enactment of the celebrant's wakefulness and of his ascent to heaven and descent to the netherworld. Hence in the introduction to *Maqlû*, we encounter not simply the usual and expected witchcraft incantations that are rooted in rituals involving such gods as Shamash and Ea, but rather incantations revolving around the gods of the heavens and the netherworld and around "Zabban." Zabban is a terrestrial and a cosmic intersection that is a point of connection between this world and the netherworld, a place where the living and the dead meet, where in the festival of the dead the two human communities come together. But, in addition, it draws together earth, heaven, and the netherworld.[36] The cosmic "Zabban" allows the human to ascend into the heavens, to become an astral divinity, and to descend to the netherworld in order to enlist its help.

The psycho-ritual experience behind his astral identification may be that of the dream. Here I would speculate that the witch threatens to bewitch her victim by means of a dream, and perhaps he now counteracts her by undertaking an incubation rite.[37] Perhaps it is in the course of a dream that he becomes a star and attacks the witch. (He is able to remain awake, then, because of this identification with the stars that he attains, paradoxically, by means, perhaps, of a dream.) But it is a wakeful dream or night vision wherein like Balaam he is in a trance but in a wakeful state:

> The word of Balaam son of Beor,
> the word of the man whose sight is clear,
> the word of him who hears the words of God,
> who shares the knowledge of the Most High,
> who with opened eyes sees in a trance
> the vision from the Almighty.[38]

It is even possible that the celebrant experiences an ecstatic trance and that this experience underlies his earlier role as a messenger. Certainly, such an experience would explain his ability to assume the identity of a star. And we may now even wonder whether the speaker's soul has not left his body and travelled to the supernatural world.

It would be remiss of me to end this discussion without noting that the picture that is slowly emerging bears some resemblance to the activities in Europe of shamanistic individuals and groups that fought witches and other evils. Here we have in mind primarily Carlo Ginzburg's description of the *benandanti* and related phenomena.[39] When the *benandanti* reached manhood, they received a summons, and then for about twenty years, they were thought to go forth in spirit while asleep, four times a year, to do battle with the witches. The *benandanti* fought with fennel stalks, the witches with sorghum reeds. The success or failure of the community's crops was dependant upon the outcome of this battle. The *benandanti* were also believed to have the ability to recognize witches and their crimes and the power to detect and cure the victims of withcraft. Moreover, they witnessed processions of the dead and discovered the fate of the dead in the other world.[40] There was a "profound bond which joined the two currents, the 'agrarian' and 'funereal' benandanti. . . . [B]oth the conventicles of witches and the processions of the dead could be reached by the benandanti only 'in spirit'. . . . And that state of lethargy . . . was sought after as the ideal way to reach the mysterious and otherwise unobtainable world of the dead, of those spirits that wandered over the face of the earth without hope of peace. In the 'agrarian' version of the cult these spirits retained the fearful traits of the ancient 'Wild Hunt', whereas in the 'funereal' form they assumed an aspect which was more orderly and conformed more closely to the Christian tradition. . . . Thus we discern the fundamental similarity between the wandering dead and the witches against whom the benandanti fought at night."[41] In sum, such folk as the *benandanti* and the livonian werewolves were "particular men and women who—in a state of trance, and often in an animal form or riding upon animals —travelled to the realm of the dead in order to bring prosperity to the community."[42]

In this context, it is of interest to note that the work of the last thirty years has revealed for Europe that "Behind the diabolical withcraft of the witch-hunters has been discovered a more traditional, neighbourly witchcraft. Behind this in turn we are seeing glimpses of a still more archaic, shamanistic witchcraft."[43] Here we may end by asking whether it is not possible that a similar developmental scheme is discernible also in ancient Mesopotamia.[44] More to the point here, we notice the similarities between our Mesopotamian ritual actor and the later *benandanti*.[45] And, in any case, we should at least raise the possibility that an archaic structure similar to that mentioned above might for Mesopotamia provide the background for and explain the ritual actor's ability to travel to the heavens and the netherworld.

NOTES

Drafts of this essay were read by D. F. Baum, K. Kravitz, L. Pearce and H. Pitmann. I am grateful to them for their helpful criticism and support. This essay was composed while I was a Fellow of the Center for Judaic Studies of the University of Pennsylvania.

1. For a comprehensive treatment of the Enoch materials and their Mesopotamian background, see Helge S. Kvanvig, *Roots of Apocalyptic: The Mesopotamian Background of the Enoch Figure and of the Son of Man* (Neukirchen-Vluyn, 1988).

2. I intend to provide such a reexamination in the near future. The preceding statements are intended simply to convey my general orientation. Although happily and not suprisingly coinciding in many respects with Thorkild Jacobsen's reconstruction (see, e.g., *The Treasures of Darkness: A History of Mesopotamian Religion* [New Haven, 1976]), the present orientation emerged independently from my own restudy of Mesopotamian mythology. An essay is in preparation in which I will provide the detailed reasoning underlying my conclusions.

3. For the text of *Maqlû,* see provisionally, G. Meier, *Die assyrische Beschwörungssammlung* Maqlû (Archiv für Orientforschung supp. 2; Berlin, 1937), and idem, "Studien zur Beschwörungssammlung *Maqlû,*" *Archiv für Orientforschung* 21 (1966) 71–81.

4. See T. Abusch, "Mesopotamian Anti-Witchcraft Literature: Texts and Studies. Part I: The Nature of *Maqlû:* Its Character, Divisions and Calendrical Setting," *Journal of Near Eastern Studies* 33(1974) 251–262, and "The Socio-religious Framework of the Babylonian Witchcraft Ceremony *Maqlû.* Some Observations on the Introductory Section of the Text, Part I."

5. See "Mesopotamian Anti-Witchcraft Literature," 259–61 and "The Socio-religious Framework, Part I."

6. In my estimation, the introduction was created in the first millennium, was added to one of the latest versions of the text, and encapsulates its conceptual world. For the history of *Maqlû,* see especially my "The Demonic Image of the Witch in Standard Babylonian Literature: The Reworking of Popular Conceptions by Learned Exorcists," in J. Neusner et al., eds., *Religion, Science, and Magic in Concert and in Conflict* (New York, 1989) 38–50, 56–58; "An Early Form of the Witchcraft Ritual *Maqlû* and the Origin of a Babylonian Magical Ceremony," in T. Abusch et al., eds., *Lingering Over Words: Studies in Ancient Near Eastern Literature in Honor of William L. Moran* (Atlanta, 1990) 1–57; "The Ritual Tablet and Rubrics of *Maqlû:* Towards the History of the Series," in M. Cogan and I. Eph'al, eds., *Ah Assyria . . . Studies in Assyrian History and Ancient Near Eastern Historiography Presented to Hayim Tadmor* (Scripta Hierosolymitana 33; Jerusalem, 1991) 233–53; and "Ritual and Incantation: Interpretation and Textual History: A Consideration of *Maqlû* VII:58–105, IX:152–59," in M. Fishbane and E. Tov, eds., *"Sha'arei Talmon": Studies in the Bible, Qumran, and the Ancient Near East Presented to Shemaryahu Talmon* (Winona Lake IN, 1991), 367–80.

7. The following section is an abridgement of parts of my "The Socio-religious Framework of the Babylonian Witchcraft Ceremony *Maqlû:* Some Observations on the Introductory Section of the Text, Part II," in S. Gitin et al., eds., *Festschrift Greenfield* (Winona Lake IN, 1995). For detailed argumentation and additional aspects, see there.

8. In my opinion, the *kāru*, "quay," in our text also serves as a jail in which prisoners—here, the witches—are held prior to trial. It seems likely that the ford and quay in our text are connected to the waters, or river, that lead to and from the netherworld.

9. Should we also compare the prison house for the stars at the end of the heaven and earth in 1 Enoch 18:12–16?

10. In acting as if he were a priest, the speaker, a victim or patient, behaves like the speaker in the following Sumerian incantation against evil demons: "If a man, a lonely man, is one who walks at night in the street, then let him say 'I am Enki's messenger, I am Damgalnunna's messenger, I am the messenger Asalluhi.' Let him say 'I am the man of Eridu.'" (M. J. Geller, *Forerunners to UDUG-HUL: Sumerian Exorcistic Incantations* [Stuttgart, 1985] 30–33: 198–202.) The evil demons will think him a priest and not attack him.

11. The name of the city here in *Maqlû* may be read Ṣappān (ṣap/ṣa-ap-pan) rather than *Zabban.* While influenced by Canaanite models, our composer would have viewed the cosmos through Mesopotamian eyes and transformed a cosmic mountain into a cosmic city. Hence, Mount Ṣāphôn has become the city Ṣappān. Compare, for example, the casting of the biblical city Jerusalem in terms drawn from the mythological characteristics and designations of Mount Ṣāphôn. Of course, if the incantation was composed in the first millennium, as I imagine it to have been, a form with *ā,* rather than the Canaanite *ō,* would suppose an Aramaic context—a context compatible with the mode of contact of Assyria with the West.

12. Translation: *NJPS.*

13. Cf., e.g., *STT,* vol. 1, 73:83, where the sprinkling of water to specific stars is contextually linked to the request for a dream incubation (see E. Reiner, "Fortune-Telling in Mesopotamia," *Journal of Near Eastern Studies* 19 [1960] 27).

14. Cf., e.g., I. Gruenwald, *Apocalyptic and Merkavah Mysticism* (Leiden, 1980), esp. 32–51, 98–109, 119–121.

15. Cf., e.g., W. Burkert, *Lore and Science in Ancient Pythagoreanism* (Cambridge, Mass., 1972) 350–64.

16. This formula is unusual. These lines are a neologism created for our text by means of a conflation of two discrete formulae: (1) *anu u antu išpurū'inni,* "Anu and Antu have sent me," and (2) *mannu lušpur,*

"whom shall I send." The formula supports my interpretation of the induction scene, for this formulation is meant to explain to the addressee, here Bēlet-ṣēri, why she does not recognize the messenger and, therefore, represents the induction scene of an irregular or ad hoc messenger and makes clear that the speaker was originally not a regular divine- or priestly-messenger but rather one who has only now become a member of the heavenly court and a messenger of the gods.

17. Translation: *NEB*.

18. Th. Jacobsen, "Mesopotamia," in H. Frankfort et al., *The Intellectual Adventure of Ancient Man: An Essay on Speculative Thought in the Ancient Near East* (Chicago, 1946) 130–35.

19. Jacobsen, "Mesopotamia," 132–33.

20. See Abusch, "Early Form," 25 ff.

21. See Abusch, "Demonic Image," for a discussion of the demonic witch.

22. See Abusch, "Demonic Image," 45–50, for a somewhat fuller discussion of the dream and its relationship to witchcraft.

23. For a clear example of this association, see the morning incantation, 7.170–77.

24. Dreaming, moreover, may be perceived as a unitary experience and force in which the witch is both a demonic power who sends the dream and the demonic dream itself. And even when the unitary experience of dreaming is split into the power that brings the dream and the dream itself, the demonic nature of both holds the two together.

25. Such death would surely have overcome Gilgamesh, for example, when he fell into a deep sleep in Tablet 11 of the Epic had he not been awakened; uninterrupted his sleep would have turned into death.

26. For this use of *ṣalālu*, cf., e.g., J. Bottéro, "Les inscriptions cunéiformes funéraires," in G. Gnoli and J.-P. Vernant, eds., *La mort, les morts dans les sociétés anciennes* (Cambridge, 1982) 377, 382–83.

27. See Abusch, "Mesopotamian Anti-Witchcraft Literature," 256; "Demonic Image," 47–49; "Early Form," 55–56; and "Ritual Tablet and Rubrics," 252–53.

28. The several gods and objects mentioned in these two incantations refer to heavenly bodies and configurations; a detailed discussion of these incantations will be presented elsewhere.

29. Ghosts and demons travel back and forth between the netherworld and the upper world. In this regard, they resemble the sun, the moon, and the stars; the latter travel a circuit between the heavens and the netherworld, spending part of their time below the horizon, together with the denizens of the netherworld, and the rest of their time above the horizon, together with the inhabitants of this world. Also, the dead witch

returns to this world: she is a human being and, as such, her ghost may ascend, especially during the festival at the end of Abu.

30.   The meteorological or astral forms of confrontation and attack seem to be directed particularly against forms of witchcraft (such as evil dreams, omens, and specters) that are associated with (i.e., either assumed by or controlled by) the dead or cosmic witch. But especially given the identification of the ritual actor with astral beings, perhaps these forms of confrontation should be seen as directed also against other astral beings as well. And it is therefore relevant that the witch, too, is associated with such beings: The aforementioned evil god, for example, can be either a dream, a ghost, or perhaps even a star. The description is evocative, and it occurs in an incantation that opens with the speaker's own express identification with astral powers. And if the evil god is a star, the witches surely control that star, for they are said to have the power to send it. Perhaps also the witch herself is occasionally a star. Thus, for example, in 7.8–9, the witches are associated with "sailors," that is, stars, who are now asleep. Actually, the witches are the sailors, as demonstrated by the fact that the witches' (astral) captivity was earlier described in 1.50ff in forms drawn from these very lines. Still, the identification of the witch with astral bodies remains highly speculative; note, therefore, that my contention that the ritual actor assumes an astral identity depends in no way on that identification.

31.   Whoever you are, o witch, who like the Southwind . . .
. . . .
Has formed clouds against me and stood over me.
I rise up against you like the shearer of the heavens, the Northwind.
I scatter your clouds, I destroy your storm.
I scatter your witchcraft that you have piled up over me night and day
And the emissaries of *zikurrudâ* that you have repeatedly sent against me.

32.   As a star, he is a power that remains active throughout the night. Perhaps the enigmatic statement in 1.39–40 reflects this astral transformation, for there he says to the witches "Whatever you have done, I know; whatever I do, you do not know."[a] How can a mortal say such words to his witches, especially when they are not human witches but rather supernatural demonic witches who can themselves even assume forms such as the wind, the clouds, and the dream?[b] The meaning or explanation of this statement may lie in what the speaker imagines himself to be: he has identified himself with the gods of the night sky, the stars, and imagines himself to be a member of the nocturnal heavenly court. His knowledge and capacity would then derive from his power to

function as one of the gods of the night sky and to watch over the witch. In turn, he cannot be recognized (and attacked) because of his astral identification.[c]

a. The significance of this utterance is highlighted by the contrast provided by the bewitched man's more standard utterance in prayers that he does not know who the witch is.

b. The demonic quality of the witch in 1.37–41 as well as the speaker's cognitive powers there may be inferred from such other incantations as 6.120–27, 128–35, 136–44, 145–51, where the nighttime witch is said to partake of the qualities of wind or fire that sends witchcraft in the form of clouds, smoke, dreams, and the speaker, for his part, asserts *anāku īdema attakal takālu* (6.123 // 131 // 139 // 148), thus claiming knowledge, as in our 1.39: *anāku īde,* and setting up a protection. He thus claims to recognize such phenomena as wind, smoke, and dreams as forms of the witch and witchcraft and asserts that the witches cannot disguise themselves or their witchcraft. Their identity and demonic character are recognizable even when they are disguised.

c. He is stronger for having become a star, while the witches, for their part, are now cut off and perhaps imprisoned on or in the earth, at or below the horizon. He functions as a spy of the stars and also as a jailer of the demonic witches who are imprisoned at the entrance from the netherworld to the heavens (1.50–51). They are unable to see (recognize?) his activities but he is able to see theirs. Hence, he is able to say that he knows what the witches do but they do not know what he does.

   The witches are now unable to disguise themselves or their deeds in the form of sleep or dreams. They can no longer escape or attack him, for as a star he remains awake and is both invulnerable to sleep and able to see them. He will recognize them even if they take on the further disguises or forms of winds, clouds, etc. By contrast, however, he is able to do what he wishes without their knowledge. For he is no longer earth bound; he has assumed a new identity as a star or among the stars and cannot be recognized. In his new form, he is protected against them, and having taken on a new form, he can do what he wishes. Thus, he asserts that he knows everything that the witches do. They can neither harm nor escape, for they are presently constrained—perhaps even incarcerated. Their every act is known and they will be unable to find a way out of their present predicament.

   33. Are Bēlet-ṣēri's connections to the steppe of particular relevance here?

34.   For the text of these lines, see Abusch, "Ritual Tablet and Rubrics," 238–39.

35.   But perhaps on this night, he first wishes to render them asleep temporarily, for in order to destroy them, he must keep them confined for the night in jail or paralyzed in sleep until their trial and, preferably, their execution.

36.   Note further that the connection of the earth with the heavens and the netherworld can be understood to exist on either a horizontal or a vertical plane; thus, e.g., one may travel from earth to netherworld on an east-west plane (horizontal), but, alternatively, the grave itself or a mountain may connect earth, heaven, and netherworld (vertical).

37.   Above I noted that purification may also have served to prepare the speaker for a dream or, preferably, a vision. This experience is also suggested by Geštinanna/Bēlet-ṣēri's association with dreams and the necromantic character of his address to Bēlet-ṣēri.

38.   Num. 24:15–16; cf. 24:3–4. Translation: Revised English Bible with the Apocrypha (Oxford, 1989).

39.   See C. Ginzburg, *The Night Battles: Witchcraft and Agrarian Cults in the Sixteenth and Seventeenth Centuries* (Baltimore, 1983), *Ecstasies: Deciphering the Witches' Sabbath* (London, 1990), and "Deciphering the Sabbath," in B. Ankarloo and G. Henningsen, eds., *Early Modern European Witchcraft: Centres and Peripheries* (Oxford, 1990) 121–37.

40.   See Ginzburg, *The Night Battles*, esp. chaps. 1–2, *Ecstasies*, esp. part two, chap. 3, and "Deciphering the Sabbath," 124–25. Note also the discussion of Ginzburg's work in such essays as G. Henningsen and B. Ankarloo, introduction, in Ankarloo and Henningsen, *Early Modern European Witchcraft*, 6–7, and esp. R. Rowland, " 'Fantasticall and Devilishe Persons,' " in Ankarloo and Henningsen, *Early Modern European Witchcraft*, 181–88.

41.   Ginzburg, *The Night Battles*, 58–59. The similarity between the wandering or unrelenting dead and the witches is one that should be constantly kept in mind when studying *Maqlû* and its ceremonial setting.

42.   Ginzburg, "Deciphering the Sabbath," 132.

43.   Burke, "The Comparative Approach to European Witchcraft," in Ankarloo and Henningsen, *Early Modern European Witchcraft*, 441. Elsewhere (see e.g., Abusch, "Demonic Image," 32–34 [the paper cited there, p. 54, n.17, has since appeared as "Ritual and Incantation," 367–380]), I have reconstructed for Mesopotamia an early stage of "popular" witchcraft comparable to this archaic stage. In the popular form, the "witch" is not of necessity an evil being and doer of illegal acts but may in fact perform various magical acts (both normative and non-normative forms of witchcraft) on behalf of others and even against "evil" witches.

In this popular form, the "witch" seems to exhibit associations with ecstatic types of practitioners (see, especially, my analysis of *Maqlû* VII 84–105). Such associations may well be significant, for they recall the occasional coalescance of peripheral possession and witchcraft. In certain social circumstances, the same individual may both utilize spirit posssession and be employed as an exorcist but then also be labelled as a witch (I. M. Lewis, *Ecstatic Religion; An Anthropological Study of Spirit Possession and Shamanism* [Harmondsworth and Baltimore: 1971] 121–122).

44.   See my "Demonic Image," where I identified several stages in Mesopotamian witchcraft and already suggested a similar scheme for ancient Mesopotamia.

45.   To forstall confusion, I note again here that like the *benandanti*, our ritual actor acted not only on his own behalf but also on behalf of the community and, also like them, fought against witches; but unlike the *benandanti*, the performer of magic here in *Maqlû* has not been identified or equated with the witch but is seen as one who serves "good."

Late Antiquity

CHAPTER 3

A Throne in the Heavens: Apotheosis in pre-Christian Judaism

John J. Collins

In 1982 Maurice Baillet published the fragments of the War Scroll from Qumran Cave 4.[1] There were originally seventy of these fragments. The number was reduced by joining fragments like pieces of a jigsaw puzzle to produce the thirty-seven printed by Baillet. These fragments include a number of passages without parallel in the well-known copy of the War Scroll from Cave One, including a particularly intriguing passage that Baillet dubbed "a canticle of Michael."[2]

This fragment begins by stating that the righteous will exult because of the power of God, but then it goes on to boast of the glory of the speaker.[3] First it refers to "a mighty throne in the congregation of the gods. None of the kings of the East shall sit in it and their nobles shall not . . . No Edomite shall be like me in glory. And none shall be exalted save me, nor shall come against me. For I have taken my seat . . . in the heavens . . . I shall be reckoned with gods and established in the holy congregation." Reading the remainder of the fragment is rendered difficult by lacunae. I cite only phrases that seem reasonably clear: "my desire is not like flesh . . . all that is precious to me is in glory [or: in the glory of] . . . who has been deemed as plunder because of me,[4] and who is like to me in glory? who will return like those who go to sea and narrate . . . " The passage appears to boast of the speaker's ability to endure evil ("who . . . griefs like me and who . . . evil like me") and speaks more clearly of his incomparable prowess as a teacher and legal expert ("who will restrain the utterance of my lips and who will arraign me and equal my judgment?"). The end of the passage affirms, "I shall be reckoned with gods, and my glory, with [that of] the king's sons."

Baillet placed the fragment immediately before the account of battle in cols. 16–17 of 1QM but admitted that the joining is "only probable." He identified the speaker as the archangel Michael, who is given dominion among the *elim* in 1QM 17.7. This proposal was rejected with characteristic vehemence by Morton Smith, who has published the only other study of the passage to date. We need not accept all Smith's objections, for example, that an archangel would not compare himself to such small fry as the Edomite Herod. Assumptions about what an archangel may or may not do in this kind of literature are risky. It is true, however, that Michael never speaks in the War Scroll, and nothing in the text requires the identification. The hymn gives the impression that the speaker has come to be reckoned among the gods but was not of heavenly origin. The reference to prowess as a teacher also suggests a human speaker. Indeed, if Baillet's positioning of the fragment is correct, then it is most probably a hymn recited by the high priest before the battle. According to 1QM 15.4 the priest is to read aloud the prayer in time of war, and also all their hymns, and this passage is reflected in the fragments of 4QM 10.2, which immediately precede the "canticle of Michael" in Baillet's edition. The "canticle," then, was not necessarily composed as part of the War Scroll, but may have been an independent hymn, comparable to the Hodayot.[5] Indeed, Smith "thinks immediately of the author of the Hodayot" and lists the similarities, noting especially the fellowship with the angels in the hymns.[6]

There is an important difference, however: "This speaker's claim to have been taken up and seated in heaven and counted as one of the gods (*elim*) is more direct and explicit than anything I recall in the Hodayot or in any other of the Dead Sea documents hitherto published." Smith took it as an illustration of "speculation on deification by ascent towards or into the heavens, speculation which may have gone along with some practices that produced extraordinary experiences understood as encounters with gods or angels."[7] Already in his controversial book *Clement of Alexandria and a Secret Gospel of Mark*, Smith had claimed that "the notion of ascent to the heavens was an important element in Jesus' Palestinian background and had led to the development of a technique for ascent which Jesus might have practised." He had also claimed that "those who ascended were thought to become like the gods in form . . . and to be enthroned in the heavens," which he declared to be the goal of the hekalot mystics.[8] He then claimed to have found in 4QM a "clear and complete" example of this phenomenon in a pre-Christian text.

I do not propose here to discuss all aspects of Smith's theses, especially those regarding a technique for ascent, which are closely bound up with the controversial Secret Gospel of Mark. What I propose is to put the 4QM text, and specifically the motif of heavenly enthronement, in the context of Judaism in the Hellenistic period.

ASCENT IN PRE-CHRISTIAN JUDAISM

Evidence of ascents in pre-Christian Judaism is scarce. Part of the reason may be ideological, since the editors of the Hebrew Bible were not sympathetic to accounts of ascent to heaven. The deuteronomist insisted that the divine commandment was neither too difficult nor too far away: "It is not in heaven that you should say, 'who will go up to heaven for us, and get it for us so that we may hear it and observe it?" (Deut. 30.12). The sages tended to be skeptical. "Who has ascended to heaven and come down?" asked Agur, son of Jakeh (Prov. 30:4). There is, of course, a long tradition of prophetic visions of the divine throne, dating back to the preexilic period with Micaiah ben Imlah and Isaiah.[9] We might assume that the prophet who stands in the council of the Lord has been transported to heaven, but the ascent of the prophet is never the subject of description in the Hebrew Bible. The location of the vision is not an issue. Isaiah apparently had his vision in the temple; Ezekiel "in the land of the Chaldeans by the river Chebar." In no case does a prophetic vision of the divine throne imply that the visionary himself will be enthroned or divinized in any way. These visions typically serve two functions: they establish the credentials of the visionary and legitimate him as an intermediary between heaven and earth, and they provide revealed information, typically about the future course of events.

The closest we come to a description of a heavenly ascent in the Hebrew Bible (as distinct from an allusion to one) is in the Sinai narrative in Exodus 24. There Moses, Aaron, Nadab, Abihu, and the seventy elders "went up and they saw the God of Israel. Under his feet there was something like a pavement of sapphire stone, like the very heaven for clearness" (Exod. 24:9–10). Even this is not quite an ascent to heaven. God has come down on Mount Sinai, and so they are meeting him halfway. It is also possible that the statement in Genesis that Enoch "walked with *elohim*" refers to an ascent prior to his final translation. The figure of Enoch was modeled to a great degree on the Mesopotamian Enmeduranki, king of Sippar, founder of the *baru* guild of diviners.[10] Enmeduranki, seventh king in the Sumerian king list, was taken up to heaven and shown the tablets of the gods. Enoch is seventh from Adam in Genesis, and in the pseudepigraphical literature he is said to have read the heavenly tablets. The analogy with Enmeduranki would suggest that Enoch ascended to heaven and returned to earth before his final translation. A "round-trip" ascent of Enoch may well be presupposed in Genesis, but if so, it has been downplayed by the priestly writer.

The earliest Jewish description of a "round-trip" ascent to heaven is found in the Book of the Watchers in 1 Enoch. Although such ascents eventually became the dominant medium of revelation in apocalypses, they are quite rare in the pre-Christian period. Apart from Enoch, the only account of an ascent in a Semitic language is that of Levi in the Aramaic Levi apocryphon from Qumran, of which a later form is found in the Greek Testaments of the Twelve Patriarchs.[11] The familiar pattern of ascent through a numbered series of heavens, usually seven, is not attested in Judaism before the Christian era.[12] Both the pre-Christian Aramaic ascents are pseudonymous, a factor which complicates their relevance to Jewish religious practice of the period. For a Jewish writer who claims to have ascended to heaven (apart from 4QM), we must wait until St. Paul.

Nonetheless, there are some indications that Enoch's ascent reflects practices that were not involved in the prophetic visions in the Hebrew Bible. To begin, the location is of interest. Enoch is said to have been by the waters of Dan, in Dan which is southwest of Hermon (1 Enoch 13:7). The proximity to waters is often mentioned in visionary accounts (Ezekiel, Daniel) but the location in Dan is surprising. Dan was the site of one of the Israelite sanctuaries in the preexilic period. In Hellenistic times there was a shrine of the Greek god Pan at the foot of Mount Hermon. The choice of this site, then, is hardly indifferent, although we can only guess at its significance.[13]

Enoch is identified not as a prophet but as a scribe. This identification is not grounded in the biblical text. He presents a petition in the heavenly courtroom on behalf of the Watchers. This has no precedent in the prophetic texts and would seem to be conceived by analogy with a scribe at an earthly court.

Enoch read out the record of the Watchers' petition until he fell asleep. There is no biblical precedent for such a practice, but some form of incantation is often used in visionary experience.[14] The account of the ascent not only describes what Enoch saw but narrates a series of actions ("I went into the tongue of fire," 14:10) and records the experience of feeling ("hot as fire and cold as snow," 14:13). In this respect it has more in common with the later mystics than with the earlier prophets.

The features of the scene that have no clear literary precedent invite the suggestion that the author was recording his own visionary experience in the name of Enoch. At the least, he knew the kinds of things visionaries do, and was apparently familiar with some techniques, such as incantation, which were not derived from the Hebrew scriptures.[15] Even if 1 Enoch 14 is not a record of the author's experience, it can still be taken as indirect evidence for the practice of ascent. The Levi apocryphon is less suggestive in this regard. Neither the Aramaic nor the Greek account of Levi's ascent mentions preparatory practices such as we found in the case of Enoch, and so the account is more easily taken as a purely literary composition, although the fragmentary character of the Aramaic must be borne in mind. It is, however, significant that the second-century B.C.E. author of the Aramaic Levi apocryphon introduces an ascent of Levi, which has no basis in the biblical text, and this again supports the currency of such ideas in the Judaism of the period.

The notion of the ascent of the visionary appears in Judaism in close proximity to the notion of heavenly afterlife. There were a few exceptional instances of translation in the Hebrew Bible: Enoch, Elijah, and possibly Moses. The notion that lesser righteous people might hope for a heavenly afterlife first emerges clearly in the apocalyptic literature, in the second century B.C.E. Perhaps the clearest formulation is in 1 Enoch 104:2, 4: "you will shine like the lights of heaven and will be seen, and the gate of heaven will be opened to you . . . for you will have great joy like the angels of heaven." The earliest attestation of this idea in Jewish tradition is probably in Daniel 12:3: "Those who are wise shall shine like the brightness of the sky, and those who lead the many to righteousness, like the stars forever and ever."

In view of the importance of Enoch in early apocalypticism it is reasonable to assume that his translation was paradigmatic for righteous humanity. Explicit documentation of this linkage is surprisingly rare. The Similitudes of Enoch, probably composed around the mid first century C.E., concludes with the assumption of Enoch and adds that "all . . . will walk according to your way, inasmuch as righteousness will never leave you; with you will be their dwelling, and with you their lot, and they will not be separated from you for ever and for ever and ever" (1 Enoch 71:16). The righteous share in the immortality of Enoch. There is possibly an earlier appeal to the paradigm of Enoch in Psalm 73:24, where the psalmist affirms that "afterward there is glory, you will take me,"[16] but the allusion is doubtful, since there is no explicit reference to Enoch in the psalm. The earliest account of the abodes of the dead in the Enoch literature (in the Book of the Watchers, 1 Enoch 22) locates them, not in heaven with the angels, but in a hollow or cave inside a mountain, with a spring of water and light.[17] This abode is only a holding area until the judgment, but the final dwelling place of the chosen appears to be on a transformed earth, with fruit from the tree of life, when God "comes down to visit the earth for good" (1 Enoch 25). Bousset's theory that the ascent of the visionary is an anticipation of the ascent of the soul after death can be supported from many apocalypses of the Christian era, but this motif is not apparent in the earliest ascents of Enoch and Levi.[18]

Instead these early ascent accounts seem to function in much the same way as the call visions of the Hebrew prophets. The ascent of Enoch establishes his role as mediator between heaven and earth. When Enoch presents his petition to the Most High, he is told to "go say to the Watchers of heaven who sent you to petition on their behalf: 'you ought to petition on behalf of men, not men on behalf of you'" (1 Enoch 15:2). The official intercessors of the people were the priests, and so the account of the Watchers has been read as antipriestly polemic.[19] Martha Himmelfarb has underlined the temple imagery in Enoch's ascent vision. The outer and inner houses correspond to the structure of the earthy temple, with its main hall and holy of holies.[20] In the earthly temple, only the High Priest was allowed to enter the Holy of Holies. Yet Enoch, who is not a priest but a righteous scribe, here penetrates to the inner "house" and the very presence of God. May we infer that the author, too, was not a priest, but a scribe? Whether all this constitutes a polemic against the Jerusalem priesthood is debatable, since the priesthood is never explicitly mentioned. It is undeniable, however, that the passage elevates a scribe to an unprecedented height, and must surely have served to lend legitimation and authority to scribes as mediators of divine revelation.

The ascent also has a revelatory aspect because it provides the point of departure for further revelations, which Enoch receives in his subsequent tour of the ends of the earth.[21] It does not, however, involve the enthronement of Enoch, nor is it, at least explicitly, an anticipation of his final assumption in glory.

Similar comments might be made about the ascent of Levi, although in that case the specific purpose of the ascent is rather different. When Levi enters the heavenly temple and sees the throne of glory, he is told by the Most High: "Levi, I have given to you the blessings of the priesthood." The angel who brings him down to the earth gives him a sword and tells him to execute vengeance on Shechem (Test Levi 5:1–3). The function of the ascent then is quite transparent: to confirm the priesthood of Levi and to authorize the destruction of Shechem, quite probably in the service of Hasmonean propaganda. There is also a revelatory aspect of the vision, which may be the result of secondary expansion. There is no suggestion, however, of enthronement for Levi or that his ascent is an anticipation of the afterlife.

HEAVENLY ENTHRONEMENT

The paradigmatic case for the view that visionary ascent had its goal in heavenly enthronement is provided by Enoch in the Hebrew Book of Enoch or 3 Enoch. There Rabbi Ishmael narrates that when he ascended on high to behold the vision of the chariot he was greeted by Metatron, who has several names, including Enoch son of Jared. Metatron tells him how he was taken up from the generation of the Flood, and how "the Holy One, blessed be he, made for me a throne like the throne of glory" (10:1).[22]

There are problems with any attempt to regard Enoch/Metatron as paradigmatic for visionary ascent in the Hellenistic period. First, and most obvious, is the late date. Although the Hebrew Book of Enoch may contain old traditions, it is unlikely to be older than the sixth century C.E. Even in 3 Enoch it is not suggested that Rabbi Ishmael was given a throne. Indeed, the book contains evidence that the enthronement of Metatron was controversial. In a passage that is probably a secondary addition, we read that when Aher came to behold the chariot and saw Metatron sitting on the throne he exclaimed, "There are indeed two powers in heaven."[23] Then Metatron was given sixty lashes of fire and made to stand on his feet.

Nonetheless, in several instances beings other than God are said to be enthroned in heaven. Perhaps the first candidate to come to mind is the Messiah. Akiba is said to have expounded the plural "thrones" of Daniel 7 as "one for God, one for David."[24] The antiquity of the idea that the Davidic king had a throne in heaven is a matter of debate. Psalm 110, "The Lord said to my Lord, sit at my right hand," could be interpreted in that way, but it could be metaphorical or could refer to a ritual enthronement in the temple.[25] In Psalm 89:36–37, "His line will continue forever, and his throne endure before me like the sun; It shall be established forever like the moon, an enduring witness in the skies," the analogy between the throne and the heavenly bodies lies in its permanence, not in its location.[26] The idea that the King/Messiah is enthroned in heaven is attested from the first century, in the New Testament (Col. 3:1; Heb. 1:3) and in the Similitudes of Enoch. Jesus is a special case insofar as his enthronement presupposes his resurrection and ascension. In the Similitudes it is the "Son of Man" figure of Daniel's vision who sits on the throne of glory (compare Matt. 19:28; 25:31). This figure is also called "Messiah" in the Similitudes (1 Enoch 48:10), but he is a heavenly preexistent figure, rather than an exalted human.[27]

The original meaning of the one like a Son of Man in Daniel's vision is, of course, perennially disputed. I have argued elsewhere that the most likely referent is the archangel Michael.[28] Daniel, Chapter 7, doesn't actually describe the enthronement, but it is reasonable to infer that one of the thrones was set for the one like a Son of Man, and this is in accordance with the fact that dominion, glory, and kingship are given to him. In adaptations of this scene in the Similitudes of Enoch and in Matthew the corresponding figure is enthroned as judge.[29] A further adaptation of this tradition is found in the Testament of Abraham where Abel (son of Adam) sits on a throne to perform judgment.[30]

The idea that righteous human beings will have thrones in heaven as an eschatological reward becomes current from the first century C.E. In the Gospels, the apostles are promised that they will sit on thrones judging the twelve tribes of Israel.[31] In 1 Enoch 108:12, an appendix to 1 Enoch of uncertain provenance,[32] God "will bring out into shining light those who love my holy name, and I will set each one on the throne of his honor." Rev. 3:21 promises the one who conquers "to sit on my throne with me," and in Rev. 20:4 the visionary sees "thrones, and those seated on them were given authority to judge." According to the *Ascension of Isaiah* 9:24–26, those who believe will receive "robes and thrones and crowns." Enthronement bespeaks heavenly glory. The function of judgment is often associated with enthronement, but is not necessarily implied.

All the instances of heavenly enthronement we have considered thus far are eschatological and relate either to the final judgment or to the final destiny of the just. To my knowledge, there is only one scene of heavenly enthronement in pre-Christian Judaism that is not, or is not necessarily, eschatological. This is found in the Hellenistic

Jewish tragedy, the *Exagoge,* of Ezekiel, whose work was excerpted by Alexander Polyhistor in the early first century B.C.E. One excerpt concerns a dream of Moses:

> I dreamt there was on the summit of mount Sinai
> A certain great throne extending up to heaven's cleft,
> On which there sat a certain noble man
> Wearing a crown and holding a great scepter
> In his left hand. With his right hand
> He beckoned to me, and I stood before the throne.
> He gave me the scepter and told me to sit
> On the great throne. He gave me the royal crown
> And he himself left the throne.
> I beheld the entire circled earth
> Both beneath the earth and above the heaven,
> And a host of stars fell on its knees before me;
> I numbered them all,
> They passed before me like a squadron of soldiers.
> Then seized with fear, I rose from my sleep.[33]

Jethro then interprets the dream:

> you will raise up a great throne
> And it is you who will judge and lead humankind;
> As you beheld the whole inhabited earth,
> The things beneath and the things above God's heaven,
> So will you see things present, past, and future.[34]

This dream occurs in a self-conscious literary work. There is no question of a reflection of an actual experience of ascent. In fact, what is described is not really an ascent in any case. Moses sees the throne on top of Mount Sinai, not in the heavens. What is intriguing, however, is that the figure on the throne vacates it for Moses. Jethro's interpretation does not comment on this figure, but the one enthroned on top of Mount Sinai can hardly be other than God. Moses then gets to sit on the divine throne. What is implied in the vision, then, is the virtual apotheosis of Moses.

More than twenty years ago, Wayne Meeks traced the relevant traditions in his article "Moses as God and King."[35] Meeks took his starting point from a passage in Philo's Life of Moses: "For he was named god and king of the whole nation. And he was said to have entered into the darkness where God was, that is, into the formless and invisible and incorporeal archetypal essence of existing things, perceiving things invisible to mortal nature."[36] The notion that Moses was named god has a clear basis in Exod. 7:1: "I have made you a god to Pharaoh." Since king is one of the attributes of God, this is also taken to mean that Moses was made king. The kingship of Moses is affirmed again in the midrashim (citing Deut. 33:5, "he became king in Jeshurun")[37] and in Samaritan tradition.[38] The passage in Ezekiel shows that the tradition is much older than Philo. In Philo the apotheosis is further linked with Moses' ascent of Mount Sinai, into the cloud (Exod. 20:21). In Ezekiel, the dream occurs early in the drama (before the burning bush), but the fact that the throne is on Mount Sinai may reflect a similar tradition. Although our earliest sources for this tradition are in Greek, from the Egyptian Diaspora, its later emergence in the midrashim suggests that it had its origin in the exposition of the Book of Exodus in the land of Israel.

Here then we have at least one example of the enthronement of a visionary. The visionary in question is Moses, and his case is exceptional. It is warranted, to a degree, by the biblical text, which made him a god to Pharaoh. Nonetheless, it involves a considerable extrapolation beyond the biblical text. Although the enthronement of Moses can be grounded exegetically, it is not demanded by exegesis and would hardly have occurred to an exegete who was not already familiar with some traditions of heavenly exaltation, though not necessarily the particular ones that are attested in the Christian era.[39]

The function of Moses' enthronement bears some similarity to the ascents of Enoch and Levi. The vision establishes the authority of Moses. In Psalm 110 the king is given authority by being seated on God's right hand. Moses is seated on God's own throne and promised dominion over men. In addition, he is given knowledge of "things past, present and future," a formula describing prophecy.[40] The manner in which his dominion is to be exercised is not described; one supposes that it was through the medium of the law. The drama, however, seems to have stopped short of the giving of the law on Mount Sinai, and it concluded with the arrival at the palm trees of Elim, an area of a shaded meadow and well-watered trees. Near this place they see a strange bird, usually identified as the phoenix.[41] The introduction of the phoenix here is suggested by the Greek word for palm tree, φοινιξ,. The phoenix, however, had ancient symbolic significance in Egypt, where it was associated with the creator god and the renewal of life, but also with Osiris and the renewal of life through death.[42] The apotheosis of Moses can hardly be temporary. The symbolism of the scene at Elim suggests that the drama concluded with the intimation of immortality.

The enthronement of Moses, then, has some of the functions commonly associated with the call visions of prophets and with the ascents of Enoch and Levi, but may also include the kind of eschatological anticipation that Bousset considered intrinsic to ecstatic experience.

THE TEXT FROM QUMRAN

We return now to the text from Qumran Cave 4. Despite its fragmentary nature, it seems clear that the author claims to have sat on the mighty throne in the congregation of the gods and to have been reckoned with the gods, to have undergone a virtual apotheosis. As we have seen, such a claim was not typical in the texts describing ascents. The author refers to his heavenly enthronement. He does not describe how it took place or give any account of the heavenly geography. He does not describe an ascent. We may assume that someone who has sat on a throne in the heavens has somehow been transported upwards, but the cosmology receives no attention here.

In fact, there are a number of accounts of mystical experience in the distinctively sectarian scrolls, and none of them describes an ascent such as we find in the apocalypses. At the end of the Community Rule we find a hymn whose author boasts that

> my eyes have gazed on that which is eternal
> on wisdom concealed from men,
> on knowledge and wise design [hidden] from the sons of men,
> on a fountain of righteousness and on a storehouse of power,
> on a spring of glory [hidden] from the assembly of flesh.
> God has given them to His chosen ones as an everlasting
>   possession
> and has caused them to inherit the lot of the Holy Ones.
> He has joined their assembly to the sons of Heaven
> to be a Council of the Community,
> a foundation of the building of Holiness,
> an eternal Plantation throughout all ages to come.[43]

Here again there is no account of the manner in which the revelation was received. It is as if the space between the community and heaven has disappeared and the experience is unmediated. Similarly in the Hodayot (1QH 4:23): "Thou hast revealed Thyself to me in Thy power as perfect Light . . . " The kind of experience implied here seems to be akin to that of the biblical psalmist rather than to that of Enoch. There is nothing to indicate that any technique other than contemplative concentration was involved.

The claim to be reckoned with the gods is akin to the frequent claim to fellowship with the angels in the scrolls, especially in the Hodayot: "I walk on limitless level ground, and I know there is hope for him whom Thou hast shaped from dust for the everlasting Council. Thou hast cleansed a perverse spirit of great sin that it may stand with the host of the Holy Ones and that it may enter into community with the congregation of the Sons of Heaven" (1QH 3:21–22). This conception is rightly recognized as a kind of realized eschatology.[44] The members of the community enjoy in the present what is promised to the righteous after death in Daniel and Enoch. The "I" of this hymn is the typical sectarian, not a unique individual. The passage from 4QM, however, claims more than this. The mighty throne implies a claim to sovereignty of some sort. This is apparent by the insistence that no Edomite can sit upon it. If Smith is correct that this is a reference to Herod, the author is comparing himself with the most powerful contemporary ruler in the land. It is likely, then, that he is a leader of the sect rather than an ordinary sectarian.

One possibility that occurs at this point is that the author is a messianic figure, or messianic pretender. We have seen that the enthronement of the Messiah is a matter of eschatological expectation but also that realized eschatology is typical of Qumran. Nonetheless, the scrolls always refer to messiahs as figures who are to come in the future.[45] There is no sound evidence that the Teacher, or any other figure at Qumran, actually claimed to be a messiah,[46] although the leaders of the community seem to have exercised the functions that the messiahs would fill in the future (e.g., the chief priest's role would correspond to that of the messiah of Aaron, and there was also expectation of one who would teach righteousness at the end of days).[47]

The closest parallel we have found for the enthronement of a human being before the eschaton is not the Messiah, but Moses, and the parallel is of considerable interest here. The author of the hymn in 4QM is evidently a teacher and legal expert: "who will contain the flow of my speech and who will arraign me and be my equal?" Inevitably one thinks here of the Teacher of Righteousness. The author of the so-called Teacher Hymns in the Hodayot is "the man whose mouth Thou has confirmed" (2: 17) and whose mouth is a fount of living waters which shall not fail (8: 16).[48] In the Damascus Document, the Teacher must be identified with the mehoqeq, the interpreter of the law (CD 6:7). If he is not a new Moses, at least he is the complement of Moses. If Moses had a throne in heaven, we can understand how the teacher might claim one too, and also lay claim to the royal prerogatives of Moses. The claim to the heavenly throne is obviously a claim to authority, but as in the case of Moses there is also a claim of deification, of being reckoned among the *ēlîm*, with the implication of immortality.

There is an obvious difficulty, however, with identifying the author of this hymn as the Teacher who was active in the origin of the sect. If the Edomite referred to is indeed Herod, the hymn must have been composed considerably later than any plausible date for the activity of the Teacher. Besides, there is a striking difference in tone between this hymn and the alleged Teacher Hymns of the Hodayot. Although the author of this hymn boasts of his ability to bear griefs, he does not complain about persecution, as does the author of the Hodayot. Neither does this hymn show the sense of human sinfulness typical of 1QH, the sense of being snatched from the Pit and of being a creature of clay. The tone of this hymn is more confident and probably reflects a different phase in the history of the sect. It is probable, however, that Teacher/Interpreter of the Law was not just the title of the founding father but an office in the sect, held by various teachers in succession and destined to be fulfilled by an eschatological figure at the end of days.[49] The author of this hymn may have been, not the Teacher, but a teacher in the late first century B.C.E. who saw himself, like Moses, enthroned in the heavens and issuing teachings and rulings of irresistible power.

CONCLUSION

Morton Smith rendered a service to scholarship by directing our attention to this enigmatic fragment embedded in the War Scroll. He was surely right that it records the claims of a human figure and should not be attributed to an angel. His conclusions require some qualification. This is not precisely an example of ascent, at least as ascents are described in the apocalypses, although it is a related phenomenon. Also, not all ascents had deification as their goal. There were, however, traditions associated with Moses that envisaged deification by enthronement, and this text may be understood as an adaptation of those traditions. In what sense the author experienced this deification we cannot say. We do not even have a description of the experience, only a claim that it occurred. Such claims are quite rare in the Judaism of the period, and they are made by exceptional individuals. That such a claim should be made by a sectarian teacher in the late first century B.C.E. is obviously of great interest for the milieu in which Christianity developed.

NOTES

1. M. Baillet, *Qumrân Grotte 4.3 (4Q482–4Q520)*. (Discoveries in the Judean Desert 7; Oxford, 1982) 12–72.

2. Ibid., 26–30.

3. The following translation is adapted from that of M. Smith, "Ascent to the Heavens and Deification in 4QM^a," in L. H. Schiffman, ed., *Archaeology and History in the Dead Sea Scrolls: The New York University Conference in Memory of Yigael Yadin;* Sheffield, 1990) 181–88.

4. Or: deemed worthy of contempt (so Baillet; Heb. לבוז נחשב). Smith translates in "Ascent to the Heavens": "I do not desire [gold] as would a man of flesh: everything precious to me is in the glory of [my God]. [The status of a holy temple,] not to be violated, has been attributed to me" (restoring איא לבוז rather than מיא לבוז). He comments: "he was given the status of a *hieron asylon* . . . a legal status much sought after in the late Roman Republic" ("Ascent to the Heavens," 186). There is no parallel for such an idea at Qumran.

5. According to Baillet, elements of the same canticle are found in another manuscript from Cave 4, provisionally designated 4QS1 86. See Baillet, "Le volume VII de 'Discoveries in the Judaean Desert' Présentation," in M. Delcor, ed., *Qumrân: Sa piété, sa théologie et son milieu* (Paris/Leuven, 1978) 79, n. 19.

6. Smith, "Ascent to the Heavens," 187.

7. Ibid.

8. Morton Smith, *Clement of Alexandria and a Secret Gospel of Mark* (Cambridge, Mass., 1973) 238.

9. I. Gruenwald, *Apocalyptic and Merkavah Mysticism* (Leiden, 1980). 31.

10. See J. C. VanderKam, *Enoch and the Growth of an Apocalyptic Tradition* (Washington, D.C., 1984) 33–45.

11. On the relationship between the Aramaic apocryphon and the Greek Testament see M. de Jonge, "Testament of Levi and Aramaic Levi," in *Jewish Eschatology, Early Christian Christology and the Testaments of the Twelve Patriarchs* (Leiden, 1991) 244–62.

12. The account of the seven heavens in Test Levi 3 is clearly a redactional addition and is not reflected in the Aramaic fragments.

13. G. W. E. Nickelsburg, "Enoch, Levi, and Peter: Recipients of Revelation in Upper Galilee." *Journal of Biblical Literature* 100(1981) 586 suggests that 1 Enoch 12–15 emanated from circles in upper Galilee and, further, that "in point of historical fact, this was a place where one went for revelation" (590).

14. M. Idel, *Kabbalah: New Perspectives* (New Haven, 1988) 88–96.

15. See S. Niditch, "The Visionary," in J. J. Collins and W. G. E. Nickelsburg, eds., *Ideal Figures in Ancient Judaism;* Missoula, Mont., 1980) 163.

16. M. Dahood, *Psalms II* (Anchor Bible 17: Garden City, N.Y., 1968) 195.

17. The location inside a mountain is reminiscent of Babylonian traditions. See M. T. Wacker, *Weltordnung und Gericht: Studien zu 1 Henoch 22* (Würzburg, 1982) 173–75. The spring of water, however, is a motif from Orphic eschatology. See H. Diels, in W. Kranz, ed., *Die Fragmente der Vorsokratiker,* 10th ed. (Berlin, 1960–61) 1:15–18; T. F. Glasson, *Greek Influence in Jewish Eschatology* (London, 1961) 34.

18. For Bousset's theory, "Die Himmelsreise der Seele," *Archiv für Religionsgeschichte* 4(1901) 136. For illustrations from the Christian era, M. Himmelfarb, "Revelation and Rapture: The Transformation of the Visionary in the Ascent Apocalypses," in J. J. Collins and J. H. Charlesworth, eds., *Mysteries and Revelations: Apocalyptic Studies after the Uppsala Colloquium* (Sheffield, 1991) 89–102.

19. D. Suter, "Fallen Angel, Fallen Priest: The Problem of Family Purity in 1 Enoch 6–16," *Hebrew Union College Annual* 50(1979) 115–35. Nickelsburg, "Enoch, Levi, and Peter," 586, sees 1 Enoch 12–15 as polemic against the Jerusalem priesthood.

20. Martha Himmelfarb, "From Prophecy to Apocalypse: The Book of the Watchers and Tours of Heaven," in A. Green, ed., *Jewish Spirituality,* vol. I, *From the Bible through the Middle Ages* (New York, 1986) 151.

21. J. D. Tabor, *Things Unutterable: Paul's Ascent to Paradise in its Greco-Roman, Judaic, and Early Christian Contexts* (Lanham, Md., 1986) 75, classifies Enoch's ascent as "ascent to receive revelation."

22. Trans. P. Alexander, "3 (Hebrew Apocalypse of) Enoch," in J. H. Charlesworth, ed., *The Old Testament Pseudepigrapha* (Garden City, N.Y., 1983) 1.263. See nos. 13, 894 in P. Schäfer, with M. Schlüter and H. G. von Mutius, *Synopse zur Hekhalot-Literatur* (Texte und Studien zum Antiken Judentum 2; Tübingen, 1981).

23. For the controversy on this topic see A. Segal, *Two Powers in Heaven* (Leiden, 1977).

24. Hag. 14a, Sanh. 38b.

25. See H. J. Kraus, *Psalms 60–150* (Minneapolis, 1989) 348. Smith, *Clement of Alexandria, 238,* implausibly reads this text as a claim of ascent on behalf of Simon Maccabee.

26. Pace P. Mosca, "Once Again the Heavenly Witness of Ps 89:38," *Journal of Biblical Literature* 105 (1986) 33–36.

27. See my essay "The Son of Man in First Century Judaism," *New Testament Studies* 38(1992) 448–66.

28. *The Apocalyptic Vision of the Book of Daniel* (Missoula, Mont., 1977) 123–47.

29. In Daniel, Chapter 7, the "Son of Man" figure arrives after the judgment.

30. Testament of Abraham 13:1–4. In the Ascension of Isaiah, the

visionary sees angelic figures enthroned in several of the heavens, though not in all.

31.   Matt. 19:28, Luke 22:30.

32.   G. W. E. Nickelsburg, *Jewish Literature between the Bible and the Mishnah* (Philadelphia, 1981) 151; M. Black, *The Book of Enoch or 1 Enoch* (Leiden, 1985) 323.

33.   Eusebius, *Praeparatio Evangelica*, 9.29.4–5. Trans. C. R. Holladay, *Fragments from Hellenistic Jewish Authors II: Poets* (Atlanta, 1989) 363–65. See also H. Jacobson, *The Exagoge of Ezekiel* (Cambridge, 1983).

34.   *Praep. Ev.* 9.24.6; Holladay, *Fragments,* 367.

35.   "Moses as God and King," in J. Neusner, ed., *Religions in Antiquity: Essays in Memory of Erwin Ramsdell Goodenough* (Leiden, 1968) 354–71.

36.   *Vit. Mos.* 1.155–58.

37.   Bamidbar R. 15.13, Tanḥuma, ed. S. Buber, 4.53–54; cited by Meeks, "Moses as God and King," 356.

38.   Memar Marqah 4.6; Meeks, "Moses as God and King," 358.

39.   See P. W. van der Horst, "Moses' Throne Vision in Ezekiel the Dramatist," *Journal of Jewish Studies* 34(1983) 21–29.

40.   Ibid., 28.

41.   On the identification, see H. Jacobson, "Phoenix Resurrected," *Harvard Theological Review* 80(1987) 229–33.

42.   M. Walla, *De Vogel Phoenix in der antiken Literatur und in der Dichtung des Laktanz* (Vienna, 1969) 1–50; R. van den Broek, *The Myth of the Phoenix According to Classical and Early Christian Traditions* (Leiden, 1972).

43.   1QS 11:5–9; trans. G. Vermes, *The Dead Sea Scrolls in English* (Harmondsworth, 1975) 92–93.

44.   H.-W. Kuhn, *Enderwartung und gegenwärtiges Heil* (Göttingen, 1966); G. W. Nickelsburg, *Resurrection, Immortality and Eternal Life in Intertestamental Judaism* (Cambridge, Mass., 1972) 146–56.

45.   1QS 9:11; 1QSa 2:12, 20; CD 12:23–13:1; 14:19; 19:10–11; 20:1.

46.   M. A. Knibb, "The Teacher of Righteousness—A Messianic Title?" in P. R. Davies and R. T. White, eds., *A Tribute to Geza Vermes* (Sheffield, 1990) 51–65.

47.   See further J. J. Collins, *The Apocalyptic Imagination* (New York, 1984) 122–26.

48.   On the identification of the Teacher Hymns see G. Jeremias, *Der Lehrer der Gerechtigkeit* (Göttingen, 1963) 168–267.

49.   CD 6:11; see Collins, *The Apocalyptic Imagination,* 125–26.

CHAPTER 4

The Seven Heavens in Jewish and Christian Apocalypses

Adela Yarbro Collins

The *religionsgeschichtliche Schule* of the late nineteenth and early twentieth centuries attempted to explain the origin and development of the Israelite, Jewish, and early Christian religions in terms of their interaction with other cultural traditions. The traditions of Sumer, Babylon, and Persia and the phenomena of "Hellenistic Oriental syncretism" were brought to bear on Israelite, Jewish, and Christian texts because the explanation of origins was thought to go a long way toward illuminating meaning and function. The complex of ideas related to the motif of the ascent to heaven was a major topic addressed by members of the history of religions school. Although some scholars argued for the origin of the tradition in Babylon, and others in Persia, they shared the assumption that the number of heavens involved was an indication of the cultural origin of the notion of ascent.

The first influential study of ascents to heaven in antiquity was Anz's *Ursprung des Gnostizismus,* published in the series Texte und Untersuchungen in 1897.[1] Study of the Mithras mysteries and Gnostic systems suggests that the later teaching is connected with belief in seven planetary star gods.[2] Anz argued that the teaching of seven heavens was connected with the seven planetary gods and that the whole complex originated in Babylonian tradition.

Even more influential than Anz's study was that of Wilhelm Bousset, "Die Himmelsreise der Seele," published in 1901.[3] Bousset argued that Persian religion is the home of the notion of the ascent of the soul. This notion involved both the ecstatic ascent during a human being's lifetime and a final ascent after death. He agreed with Anz that the teaching of seven heavens originated in late Babylonian religion but argued that many texts contain evidence for an older view, namely, that there were three heavens and over these, Paradise. This older view, according to Bousset, was Persian in origin. Therefore, one can speak only of a secondary influence of Babylonian religion.

The views of these two scholars have been challenged by Ioan Culianu. He has argued that the motif of the seven planetary heavens could not be derived from Babylonian religion because, for the Babylonians, the seven planets moved on the same plane, that is, at the same distance from the earth. It was the Greek astronomers during the time of Plato who first conceived the idea that the planets moved at different distances from the earth. This idea arose as an explanation for the differing lengths of time it took each planet, supposedly, to circle the earth.[4] He argued further that the Babylonian cosmology made use of a variable number of heavens, from one to ten, with the exception of six. The notion of three heavens was no less conventional than seven. But since the Babylonians never arrived at the idea that the planets circled at different distances from the earth, there was never a link between the vaults of heaven and the planets. Thus Culianu rejected the argument of the history of religions school that a cosmological scheme involving seven planetary spheres was borrowed from the Babylonians.[5]

In discussing the Jewish and Jewish-Christian apocalypses, Culianu has remarked that an important feature of all these works is the absence of any relation between the seven heavens and the seven planets.[6] His own proposal for a classification of ascents involves two types: (1) the "Greek" type, in which beliefs concerning ascent are conformed to scientific hypotheses, and (2) the "Jewish" type, involving a journey through three or seven heavens, which are never identified with planetary heavens. He indicated that the myth of Er in Book 10 of Plato's *Republic* and the eschatological myths of Plutarch either belong to the "Jewish" type or to a third, "mixed" type. With regard to the second, "Jewish" type, he suggested that it may have developed under Babylonian influence, but he did not pursue this point.[7]

Culianu's criticism of the theories of Anz and Bousset has reopened the question of the origin of the motifs of the three and the seven heavens in the Jewish and early Christian apocalypses. His brief suggestion that these motifs may have been borrowed from

Babylon without any link to the seven planets requires exploration. If the seven heavens were not linked to the seven planets, what did they signify? It is this question that I would like to address in this chapter.

I shall begin with a short discussion of the usage of the Hebrew Bible and its Greek translation, raising the question whether they presuppose multiple heavens. After a brief look at the Book of the Watchers, I shall examine the oldest Jewish and Christian texts that speak of a plurality of heavens and give them a definite number. These texts date from the end of the second century B.C.E. to the second century C.E. Some are apocalypses, and the others manifest an apocalyptic perspective. Among the texts that I will discuss, three are Jewish works: *The Life of Adam and Eve*, the Apocalypse of Abraham, and 2 Enoch. Two are Christian in their present form, but were probably Jewish compositions originally, namely, the Testament of Levi and 3 Baruch. The Martyrdom and Ascension of Isaiah as a whole is a Christian work in two parts. The first part, the story of Isaiah's martyrdom, is probably based on a Jewish work. The account of Isaiah's ascent, however, which is the part relevant to this study, is a Christian composition. Paul's account of his ascent in 2 Corinthians, chapter 12, is of course a Christian text, but it may provide evidence also for the practice of ascent in the type of Judaism to which Paul had belonged. I shall also mention the Similitudes of Enoch, another Jewish work, since it seems to reflect the motif of three heavens.

THE HEBREW BIBLE AND ITS OLD GREEK TRANSLATION

The word for heaven in the Hebrew Bible is *shāmayim*. According to von Rad, this abnormal plural can only be regarded as a secondary shortening. Its etymology is obscure.[8] He concludes that Israel was not acquainted with the idea of many intersecting heavenly spheres, although there may be an echo of this Babylonian view in the phrase *shəmē hashāmayim*. This phrase could be translated "heaven of heavens," as von Rad does, or "heaven of heaven," as Bietenhard takes it.[9] If the translation "heaven of heavens" is correct, the phrase implies the existence of at least three heavens. If "heaven of heaven" is the meaning, the phrase distinguishes two heavens: the heaven above the earth that human beings see and a heaven that is above the visible heaven.[10] The phrase occurs in the climax of the historical review of Deuteronomy (10:14), in the prayer of Solomon at the dedication of the temple (1 Kings 8:27), in Ezra's confession in Neh. 9:6, and in other prayerful contexts.[11] Though the phrase may reflect Babylonian ideas, it may have been used simply as rhetorical hyperbole.[12]

In the Old Greek translation of the Hebrew Bible, the singular of the Greek word for heaven, *ouranos,* is the almost exclusive translation of the Hebrew *shāmayim* and its Aramaic equivalent.[13] In the Old Greek, *ouranos* occurs fifty-one times in the plural. This usage is rare in classical Greek and probably came into Greek usage through the Septuagint, the Greek translation of the Hebrew Bible. In the earlier writings of the Septuagint, the plural *ouranoi* should probably be taken as a "translation-plural," reflecting the hyperbole or fullness of expression typical of hymnic and liturgical style.[14] In later writings, the plural is more common and should be taken, in many cases, as a true plural.[15] In the phrase "who created the heavens and the earth," which occurs in Judith, Psalms, and Proverbs, *ouranoi* is probably a true plural, reflecting the idea of a plurality of heavens. This idea most likely became more common among Jews from the time of the Babylonian exile and indicates the influence of Babylonian cosmology on Jewish writers.

THE BOOK OF THE WATCHERS

The oldest part of the composite work known as Ethiopic Enoch or 1 Enoch consists of the first thirty-six chapters, usually called the Book of the Watchers. It is characterized by the story of the fallen angels or Watchers, found in chapters 6–11, and by Enoch's journeys to heaven and to the ends of the earth. In chapter 1, verse 4, Enoch utters a "parable" regarding an eschatological epiphany of God. In the Greek version, it is said that God will appear in the power of his strength from the heaven of the heavens.[16] It is likely that this phrase is hyperbolic, since, when Enoch travels to the heavenly throne of God in chapter 14, there is no indication of a plurality of heavens.

THE TESTAMENT OF LEVI

The work entitled the Testaments of the Twelve Patriarchs has been preserved in Greek, Armenian, and Slavonic versions. All three versions are Christian in their present form. A number of scholars have argued that this work was originally a Jewish composition and that it has been revised by one or more Christian editors. If the probably Christian passages are left aside, internal evidence suggests a date toward the end of the second century B.C.E.[17] Since 1955 several fragments of one or more Aramaic Levi documents have been discovered at Qumran.[18] One of these fragments shows clearly that at least one such document contained an account of a vision of Levi that involved more than one heaven.[19] Some of the Aramaic fragments overlap with the Greek version. Thus the conclusion is warranted that the Christian Greek version was based on a Jewish work written in Aramaic.

The Testament of Levi contains an account of Levi's ascent into heaven (chaps. 2–3). There are two recensions of the Greek version. The earlier of these involves three heavens; the later speaks of seven.[20] Both recensions may have existed in Aramaic. Another possibility is that the Aramaic Levi documents involved only three heavens and the motif of seven heavens was first added at some stage in the Greek transmission of the work. Thus the possibility must also be kept in mind that it was a Christian redactor who added the motif of the seven heavens.

The first Greek recension describes Levi's ascent as follows:

> And behold, the heavens were opened, and an angel of the Lord said to me, "Levi, Levi, come in." And I entered the first heaven and I saw there much water hanging. And I saw yet a second heaven that was much brighter and more radiant. For there was unlimited height[21] in it. And I said to the angel, "Why are these things so?" And the angel said to me, "Do not marvel concerning this [heaven], for you will see another heaven more radiant and beyond comparison [with it]. And when you go up there, you will stand near the Lord, and you will be a minister to him, and you will announce his mysteries to human beings, and you will make a proclamation concerning the coming redemption of Israel.[22] (T. Levi 2:6–10)

In the following chapter (T. Levi 3), the angel instructs Levi about the heavens. The lower heaven is sad or gloomy because it sees all the unrighteous deeds of humanity. It contains fire, snow, and ice, prepared for the day of judgment. In it also are the winds or the spirits associated with the punishment of humanity. In the second heaven are the heavenly powers that are to punish the spirits of error and of Beliar. And in the highest dwelling of all is the Great Glory above all holiness.

It is possible that the notion of the three heavens in this work results from an inner Jewish development, based perhaps on a reading of *shəmē hashāmayim* in the Hebrew Bible as "heaven of heavens," that is, implying three heavens. It is more likely that its use implies a picture of the world based on Babylonian cosmology.

According to W. G. Lambert, the basic picture of the universe current in Mesopotamia in the first millennium B.C.E. involved "superimposed levels, the earth being roughly in the middle, the stars and heaven above, and cosmic water and the underworld below."[23] He also notes that the Babylonians had a doctrine of several superimposed heavens.[24] He implies that the most conventional number of heavens, at least in the second and early first millennia B.C.E., was three.[25] He notes that the fullest exposition of the levels of the Babylonian universe occurs in a nonliterary text that has been preserved in a short and a long form. Both forms speak of three heavenly levels: the upper heavens, the middle heavens, and the lower heavens.[26] In the shorter, older form, the upper heavens are the abode of Anu, the nominal ruler of the universe. Each level is made of a different precious stone. The lower heavens are made of jasper, from which the sky derives its blue color. The stars are visible to those on earth from this level.[27]

An indication that the cosmology of the Testament of Levi may be based on Babylonian tradition is that what is called "the first heaven" in T. Levi 2:7 is called "the lower [heaven]" in 3:1.[28] In chapter 3, the third heaven is called "the upper dwelling" (3:4).[29] The terms *lower* and *upper* with respect to heavenly levels are reminiscent of typical Babylonian expressions.

The "much water hanging" that Levi sees in the first heaven reflects the idea that there are waters above the firmament expressed in Gen. 1:7.[30] This motif probably derives from Babylon also, since it appears in the Enuma elish 4.139–40. The notion that the first heaven contains fire, snow, ice, and winds prepared for the day of judgment is probably based on older Jewish tradition.[31]

Unfortunately, there does not seem to be sufficient evidence to determine when the recension of the Testament of Levi that refers to seven heavens originated. All that we can say is that it was created sometime after the end of the second century B.C.E.[32] It is striking that this recension does not add any new information about the content of the heavens. It simply divides the information given in the first recension among a greater number of heavens. This state of affairs supports Charles's conclusion that the notion of seven heavens is secondary.

It is not likely that the motif of seven heavens is the result of an inner-Jewish development. Like the notion of three heavens, it was probably inspired by Babylonian tradition. According to F. Rochberg-Halton, the two most common numbers of the heavens in Babylonian and Assyrian tradition are three and seven.[33] In a forthcoming article on Babylonian cosmology, she argues that the plurality of heavens and earths is not an innovation of first-millennium Babylonia. Sumerian incantations of the late second millennium already refer to seven heavens and seven earths.[34] As an example, she cites a short incantation which has the frequently used incipit "heavens are seven, earths are seven," expressing a common mythological theme.[35] Since their nature and extent are not discussed in this early literature, she suggests that the seven heavens may be another derivation from the magical properties of the number seven, like the seven demons or the seven thrones, rather than evidence of an early stage in the development of a consistent cosmography.[36]

According to R. Campbell Thompson, the Babylonians cultivated one of the most elaborate and intricate systems of ancient magic that we know.[37] Much of Babylonian magic is concerned with "the Seven," seven malefic spirits who were thought to cause much evil and destruction.[38] The number seven appears frequently in magical ritual. One of the Assyrian incantation texts in the series *Maqlû* involves two sets of seven figures representing two sets of seven female magicians.[39] In an incantation for healing, "the seven wise ones of Eridu" are called upon for help.[40]

According to a certain spell, a person suffering from chills and fever was to be anointed seven times with water from a bowl to which various preparations had been added.[41] An Assyrian tablet dealing with the laying of ghosts calls for seven small loaves.[42] A prayer to use when a dead man appears to a living man for evil, to turn him back, involves a ceremony in which seven knots are tied in a thread.[43] An incantation to break a spell is to be recited seven times.[44] A text on the seventh tablet of the *Šurpu* series specifies that seven loaves of pure dough should be prepared to cure a person who has fallen sick.[45] Another incantation in the same collection seeks absolution for one in danger of death. Among others, the seven winds are adjured to release his oath.[46]

The hypothesis that the seven heavens in Sumerian and Babylonian tradition derives from magical thought and practice fits the usage of the motif in the second recension of the Testament of Levi. In that recension there is no mention of seven planets. A simple distinction seems to have been introduced into the second recension between the lower three heavens, which are concerned with the punishment of evil, and the upper four heavens, which are holy.[47] But for the most part, there is little interest in the contents and layout of each of the heavens. What seems to be of primary importance is the number of the heavens itself.

If the motif of seven heavens was added by a Christian redactor at some time in the first or second century C.E., other influences may have been at work. Such influences will be discussed below.

THE SIMILITUDES OF ENOCH

Another part of the composite work known as Ethiopic Enoch or 1 Enoch consists of chapters 37 to 71 and is usually called the Similitudes of Enoch. The latest historical allusion in it is to the activity of Herod the Great. Thus it probably dates to around the turn of the era. The similitudes or parables involved contain divine revelation focusing on a heavenly savior, based on Daniel 7, who is called the Son of Man, Messiah, and the Elect One. Another important motif in this work is the translation of the living Enoch to a heavenly existence (chaps. 70–71). None of the similitudes has been preserved in Aramaic or Greek, and only the Ethiopic version attests them, so we are rather far removed from the wording of the original. Nevertheless, it should be noted that a plurality of heavens seems to be presupposed in two passages of chapter 71. Verse 1 reads, "And it came to pass . . . that my spirit . . . went up into the heavens."[48] Verse 5 speaks about Enoch being carried off into "the highest heaven"[49] or "the heaven of heavens."[50] Bietenhard interprets verse 5 as a reference to three heavens.[51] This chapter of the Similitudes may reflect the Babylonian notion of three heavens, but if so, the motif is undeveloped.

PAUL THE APOSTLE

Second Corinthians, chapters 10–13, come from a "painful letter" or "letter of tears" (cf. 2:3–9) that Paul wrote to defend his apostleship against some "superapostles" who were threatening Paul's leadership role among the Christians at Corinth. One of the legitimating characteristics of these "superapostles" was apparently their extensive experiences involving "visions and revelations of the Lord" (2 Cor. 12:1). Although he acknowledges that it is foolish to boast of such things, Paul proceeds to recount his own experience in that regard (12:2–10). He begins in the third person, either out of modesty or as a token preservation of the esoteric character of the experience, but soon lapses into the first person (compare v.2 with vv.6–7).

Thus this passage provides a first-person account of an ascent to heaven, dating from the fifties of the first century of the common era:

> I know a person in Christ who fourteen years ago was caught up to the third heaven—whether in the body or out of the body I do not know; God knows. And I know that such a person—whether in the body or out of the body I do not know; God knows—was caught up into Paradise and heard things that are not to be told, that no mortal is permitted to repeat. (2 Cor. 12:2–4)

Bousset argued that "the third heaven" (v. 2) and "Paradise" (v. 4) represent two different stations on the heavenly journey. Otherwise, the repetition would be senseless.[52] The repetition, however, could be for rhetorical effect, so it is not so clear that Paul envisioned paradise as a place above the third heaven, a fourth heavenly region. If Paul envisioned three heavens, this passage may be taken as evidence that the original Babylonian tradition of three heavens had become conventional, probably already in the Judaism to which Paul belonged before becoming an apostle of Christ.

The Greek word παράδεισος and its Hebrew equivalent come from on Old Persian word meaning "park" or "garden" without any particular religious significance. The Hebrew form of the word does not occur in the story of Adam and Eve in Genesis, chapters 2–3. The Greek form, however, was used in the Septuagint version of these chapters. When the idea of an abode of the righteous after death had developed, this dwelling was identified with the Garden of Eden, that is, Paradise. This identification may be presupposed already in 1 Enoch 20:7 (third century B.C.E.) and probably in Pss. Sol. 14:3 (first century B.C.E.).[53] The location of Paradise is not specified in these early texts. For Paul, it is apparently in the third heaven.

There does not seem to have been a consistent world-picture among Christians in the first two centuries C.E. As we have just seen, Paul speaks of three heavens. The letter to the Colossians, probably written in the sixties, speaks of a plurality of heavens without indicating their number (Col. 1:5). The situation is the same with the letter to the Ephesians, written somewhat later (4:10, 6:9). The book of Revelation, probably written around 95 C.E., seems to know only one heaven. The letter to the Hebrews, written sometime between 60 and 115,[54] clearly envisages more than one heaven, but this motif is not developed (4:14, 7:26).

THE LIFE OF ADAM AND EVE

Rabbinic literature contains many legends regarding Adam and Eve and their children. But no pre-Christian collection of such legends in Hebrew or Aramaic has survived. Many Christian Adam books have been preserved in various languages. The following discussion relates to the Latin "Life of Adam and Eve" and to a closely related Greek work published by Tischendorf in 1866 under the title "The Apocalypse of Moses."[55] M.D. Johnson has dated the original composition upon which both the Greek and the Latin depend to the period from 100 B.C.E. to 200 C.E., more probably to the end of the first century C.E.[56]

In the Latin version, chapters 25–29 contain Adam's account of his ascent to heaven, accompanied by the archangel Michael. He begins as follows:

> Listen, Seth my son, and I will tell you what I heard and saw after your mother and I had been driven out of Paradise. When we were at prayer, Michael the archangel, a messenger of God, came to me. And I saw a chariot like the wind, and its wheels were fiery; and I was caught up into the Paradise of righteousness. And I saw the Lord sitting; and his face was a flaming fire that no man could endure. And many thousands of angels were on the right and on the left of that chariot. (25:1–3)[57]

God reveals to Adam that he must die because of his sin. Adam asks for mercy and God promises that at least some of his descendants will always serve God. After Adam worships God, the text continues as follows:

Michael the archangel of God immediately took hold of my hand and ejected me from the Paradise of visitation and of God's command. And Michael held in his hand a rod and touched the waters which were around Paradise and they froze. I crossed over and Michael with me, and he took me to the place from where he had seized me. (29:1–3)[58]

It is apparent that in this work there is both a heavenly and an earthly Paradise. When Adam speaks about being driven out of Paradise (25:2), he refers to the earthly Garden of Eden. The Paradise of righteousness to which he ascends is clearly a heavenly place, the dwelling of God (25:3). This heavenly region is also called the Paradise of visitation (29:1).[59] This correspondence between an earthly and a heavenly entity is ultimately rooted in Babylonian thinking.[60] The notion may have already become part of Jewish tradition by this time, since it appeared in the discussion of the sanctuary built in the wilderness (Exod. 25:9).

Although the Latin version gives no indication of a plurality of heavens, the Greek version speaks of seven heavens. As Adam lies dying, Eve goes out to pray. The angel of humankind, that is, Michael, comes to her, lifts her up, and says, "Rise, Eve, from your repentance, for behold, Adam your husband has gone out of his body. Rise and see his spirit borne up to meet its maker" (32:3–4).[61] As Eve watches, the divine chariot comes to fetch Adam. Eve calls Seth to come and see things that no eye has seen. When Seth arrives, Eve says: "Look up with your eyes and see the seven heavens opened, and see with your eyes how the body of your father lies on its face, and all the holy angels are with him, praying for him" (35:2). Eventually, the Lord of all takes Adam, hands him over to Michael, and instructs him to take him up into Paradise, to the third heaven (37:4–5).[62] The next scene is a description of the return of the divine chariot to heaven and the taking of Adam's body into the heavenly Paradise (chap. 38). In the following scene, Seth is mourning over the body of Adam in the earthly Paradise (chap. 39). In the next scene Adam and Abel are buried in the earthly Paradise with cloths of linen and silk and fragrances brought from the heavenly Paradise (chap. 40).

It is unlikely that the motif of the seven heavens in the Greek version of this work derived from the tradition of seven planetary spheres known to Plato and Eudoxos. Virtually the only astronomical interest appears in the narration that two Ethiopians accompany the divine chariot when it comes to fetch Adam. These two dark-skinned persons are identified as the sun and the moon, who are not able to shine in the presence of the Light of all (35–36). Support for the conclusion that the motif of seven heavens derives from Babylonian tradition, is its combination with the notion of the correspondence between the earthly and the heavenly Paradise. There is little interest in the planets as such. It seems that the tradition known to Paul, in which Paradise is in the third, which is the highest, heaven, has been combined with the tradition of seven heavens. This hypothesis is supported by the fact that nothing is said about the dwelling of God being in the seventh heaven. In fact, no information is given about any of the heavens except the third.

THE APOCALYPSE OF ABRAHAM

The Apocalypse of Abraham is a Jewish work dating to the latter part of the first century, shortly after the fall of Jerusalem in 70 C.E.[63] It is preserved only in Slavonic. Chapters 1–8 consist of the story about Abraham's conversion from idolatry. Chapters 9–32 describe Abraham's ascent to heaven, which is connected with the sacrifice offered by the patriarch in Genesis 15.

In 10:9, the angel who accompanies Abraham on his ascent says, "I am Iaoel and I was called so by him who causes those with me on the seventh expanse, on the firmament, to shake." H. G. Lunt suggests that "on the firmament" may be a gloss explaining "on the seventh expanse."[64] He points out that three Slavic roots, all synonyms of the ordinary word for "heaven," appear in this work. One of these (*tvĭrdĭ*) surely translates the Greek *stereōma*, translated here as "firmament." The other two (*protjaženie* [a pulling out tightly] and *prostĭrtie* [a spreading out broadly]) probably reflect forms of the Greek τείνω and are usually translated "expanse."[65]

In 15:4–5, Abraham says, "And we ascended as if (carried) by many winds to the heaven that is fixed on the expanses. And I saw on the air to whose height we had ascended a strong light which cannot be described." This is apparently the highest point of the heavenly world, for it is here that Abraham sees God as fire on a throne of fire, surrounded by many-eyed ones. This "heaven," the highest point of the heavenly world, is also called "the seventh firmament" in 19:4. One of the concerns of the description of the heavens seems to be to assure Abraham, and the reader as well, that there is no other power in any of them other than the one God (19:2–4).

Abraham is allowed to see what is in the "expanses" below the firmament in which he is standing. Their contents are described, beginning with the seventh, which is identical with the firmament on which he stands. In that place he saw a spreading fire, and light, and dew, angels, a power of invisible glory from above, the living creatures, and no one else. In the sixth expanse, he saw a multitude of spiritual angels, without bodies, who do the bidding of the fiery angels on the seventh firmament; there was no power on that expanse either, only the spiritual angels. In the fifth expanse, he saw the starry powers, the commands they are bidden to fulfill, and the elements of earth that obey them (19:2–9). The description breaks off here, and the contents of the first four expanses are not discussed.

The image of something "pulled out tightly" or "spread out broadly" fits the Babylonian world-picture better than the Greek. Lambert has pointed out the lack of evidence for the theory that the Babylonians imagined the shape of the sky or heaven to be vault- or domelike.[66] The Hebrew term in Genesis, chapter 1, traditionally translated as "firmament" actually means "a strip of beaten metal." This term was used to describe the expanse stretched out to separate the upper and the lower waters.[67] As noted earlier, this idea appears also in the Enuma elish.[68] The later Greeks, including Plato, considered the seven heavens to be spherical. Since the Apocalypse of Abraham includes no indication of a curved shape for the seven heavens or "expanses," it is clear that the motif was not adapted from Greek tradition, at least not from Greek tradition informed by astronomy.

Like the Christian situation, there was no consistent world-picture among Jews in the first two centuries of the common era. As just noted, the Apocalypse of Abraham speaks of seven heavens or "expanses." Two other Jewish apocalypses also written in reaction to the destruction of Jerusalem, 4 Ezra and 2 Baruch, speak of only one heaven. Yet a fourth apocalypse, apparently responding to the same crisis, speaks of multiple heavens, 3 Baruch. But before discussing that work, an earlier one should be mentioned.

2 ENOCH

Like the Apocalypse of Abraham, 2 Enoch has been preserved only in Slavonic. There are two recensions, one long and the other short. The consensus is that the shorter recension is more original. It is clearly a Jewish composition. It was probably written in the first century C.E., prior to the destruction of the temple, since sacrifices play a major role in the work.[69]

According to this text, Enoch experiences an ascent to heaven when he is 365 years of age. He is conducted by two angels through seven heavens. In the first heaven he sees elders, who are rulers of the stellar orders. He also sees a vast sea, which is greater than the earthly sea, and the treasuries of snow, clouds, and dew (chaps. 3–6).[70] In the second heaven he sees the imprisoned rebellious angels, who ask him to intercede for them, a motif also found in the Book of the Watchers (chap. 7). Next the angels take him to the third heaven and set him in the midst of paradise, which is described as the eternal inheritance of the righteous (chaps. 8–9). North of the third heaven, or in the northern heaven or region, is a terrible place. Characterized as the eternal inheritance of the wicked, it involves torture as punishment for their sins (chap. 10). In the fourth heaven, Enoch is shown all the movements of the sun and moon, their doors or gates, and armed troops worshiping (chaps. 11–17). In the fifth heaven, Enoch sees the nonfallen Watchers, who mourn for the fallen; Enoch exhorts them to worship God again and they do (chap. 18). In the sixth heaven there are seven equal angels who rule all, seven phoenixes, seven cherubim, and seven six-winged creatures who sing songs that cannot be reported. These are God's footstool (chap. 19). In the seventh heaven he sees archangels, angels, ophannim, and the Lord sitting on his throne; also present are heavenly armies, glorious ones, hosts of cherubim, and six-winged angels who cover the throne, singing. At this point the two angels depart from Enoch. Gabriel presents him before the Lord, and the Lord speaks to him. Then Michael takes off his earthly garments, anoints him with oil, and clothes him with glorious garments (chaps. 20–22).

2 Enoch seems to share certain traditions with the Testament of Levi 2–3. Both speak of "much water" or a "sea" in the first heaven.[71] Both teach that there is snow and ice in the first heav-

en.[72] Both associate the second heaven with the wicked angels.[73] A striking difference between the two is the far greater interest in 2 Enoch in astronomical phenomena. When Enoch is in the first heaven, the angels show him the movements and aberrations of the stars from year to year (4:1).[74] In the fourth heaven, they show him the movements (and in some manuscripts the displacements) of the sun and the moon (11:1–2). There is interest in the shortening and lengthening of the days and the nights (13:1). The discussion of the various gates in the east and west through which the sun rises and sets is related to the annual movement of the point across the horizon where the sun appears to rise and set (13:1–15:3).[75] At the end of this discussion it is stated that "these gates the Lord created to be an annual horologe" (15:3). The idea seems to be that these gates keep track of the days of the year in the same way as a sundial keeps track of the hours of the day.[76] In the account of the fourth heaven, there is also a discussion of the movements and the gates of the moon (16:1–8). The moon goes in and out by each of these gates for a period ranging from twenty-two to thirty-five days.

The astronomical notions of 2 Enoch do not conform to the most advanced scientific ideas of its time. For example, the fixed stars are placed in the first heaven, rather than above the seven planetary spheres.[77] The picture of the movement of the the sun and the moon is either mythical or literary personification. They do not seem to move as part of an intrinsically orderly cosmic system; rather, they are moved, or at least directed, by the angels who accompany them.[78]

Some of these astronomical traditions are either derived from or shared with the Book of the Heavenly Luminaries, an originally independent work dating from the third century B.C.E., which is preserved in 1 Enoch 72–82. The discussion of the gates of the sun in the east and in the west is closely related to 1 Enoch 72.[79] The discussion of the gates of the moon has some points of contact with 1 Enoch 73 and 75.[80] The Book of the Heavenly Luminaries could not be the source of 2 Enoch's idea of seven heavens, since the older work knows only one heaven. The motif of seven heavens could have been borrowed directly from Babylonian tradition, or more likely, it had already become one of several Jewish traditions about the number of heavens. The relation of the astronomical ideas of 2 Enoch to Babylonian and Egyptian thought is a matter that requires further study. They do not seem to have much connection with Greek astronomical thought.

THE MARTYRDOM AND ASCENSION OF ISAIAH

The Martyrdom and Ascension of Isaiah is probably a composite Christian work, made up on an originally independent Martyrdom of Isaiah and a Christian ascent text. The account of Isaiah's ascent is given in chapters 6–11 of the Ethiopic version of the composite work. The ascent text was written toward the end of the first or in the second century C.E.[81]

The world-picture implied by the ascension involves a "firmament" that separates the earth from the seven heavens. When an angel takes Isaiah up to the firmament, he sees Sammael, apparently equivalent to Satan, and his hosts. There is strife among the angels of Satan because of jealousy. Isaiah comments that what happens in the firmament happens similarly on earth (7:9–12). Then Isaiah is taken above the firmament to the first heaven. In it he sees a throne,[82] with angels on the right and left. Those on the right have greater glory; all sing praises to God and the Beloved (7:13–17).

The angel then takes him to the second heaven, whose height is the same as (the distance) from the firmament to the earth. There he sees a throne, with angels on the right and left. The one seated on this throne has greater glory than the rest. Isaiah begins to worship the one seated on the throne. The angel instructs him not to worship any angel or throne in the (lower) six heavens, because his throne, garments, and crown are set above these heavens. Isaiah rejoices that those who love the Most High and his beloved will be taken up to the seventh heaven by the angel of the Holy Spirit (7:18–23).

The arrangement of the third heaven is like that of the second. Each heaven has greater glory than the one beneath it. Here Isaiah comments that his face is being transformed, presumably into angelic glory (7:24–27). When Isaiah reaches the fourth heaven, he comments that the height from the third to the fourth is greater than the (distance) from the earth to the firmament. The contents are like those of the third, only more glorious (7:28–31). The same pattern continues in the fifth heaven (7:32–37).

Next the angel takes Isaiah up first into the *air* of the sixth heaven, then into the sixth heaven itself. The glory is greater there than in the five lower heavens. Here and upwards there is no one seated in the middle on a throne and no angels on the left because they are directed by the power of the seventh heaven. When Isaiah addresses the angel with the phrase "my lord," the angel tells him that he is his companion, not his lord. Isaiah and the angel praise with the angels of the sixth heaven. The angel also tells Isaiah that he must return to earth, because his time for entering the seventh heaven permanently had not arrived yet (8:1–28).

Then they enter the *air* of the seventh heaven. Isaiah's entry is challenged by the one in charge of the praises of the sixth heaven, but he is allowed passage by the Lord Christ. Then they enter the seventh heaven itself. There is marvelous light and innumerable angels. All the righteous from the time of Adam are there: Abel, Enoch, and later Seth, are mentioned. They have been stripped of their garments of the flesh and are wearing garments of the world above, like angels, standing in great glory. They have not yet received their thrones or crowns because the Beloved has not yet descended. Then a summary of the descent and ascent of the Beloved is given. Isaiah sees many garments, thrones, and crowns stored up for those who believe in the Beloved. Isaiah sees One (Beloved), another glorious One (angel of Holy Spirit), and the Great Glory. Isaiah and the angels cannot look upon the Great Glory, but the righteous can. Then all worship the Great Glory (9:1–42).

There follows a description of the descent and transformation of the Beloved. He is not transformed in the sixth heaven; the angels there recognize and worship him. But he is transformed to look like the angels of fifth and lower heavens, so they do not perceive his descent. The keepers of the gate of the third heaven demand a password, and the Lord gives it. The same thing happens in the second and first heavens and in the firmament where the prince of this world dwells. Then he descends to the air and made himself like the angels there. It was not necessary to give them a password, because they are too busy doing violence to one another (10:1–31).

Chapter 11 contains stories about the birth, infancy, life, and crucifixion of the Lord. Then his ascent through the seven heavens is described. He ascends first to the firmament. Since he has not transformed himself, the angels of the firmament and Satan worship him. They lament and ask how his descent was hidden from them. The same thing happens in (the first) through fifth heavens, except the angels there do not lament. Intead they worship and praise him. In each heaven the praise increases. All praise in the seventh, and he sits down at the right hand of the Great Glory. The angel of the Holy Spirit is seated on the left; this angel sends Isaiah back to earth. Near the end there is an exhortation in the second person (apparently to the readers) to keep watch in the Holy Spirit so that they may receive their garments, thrones, and crowns of glory that are stored up in the seventh heaven (11:1–43).

There is virtually no astronomical interest in this work. The primary distinction within the heavenly world is between the air above the earth and the firmament, on the one hand, and the seven heavens above the firmament, on the other. The air above the earth and the firmament are the abode of Satan, the prince of this world, and the wicked angels. The seven heavens appear to be holy, yet there are distinctions among them as well. The sixth and seventh heavens are considerably more holy and glorious than the lower five; each of the lower five has a ruler or throne in its midst and angels on the left who are inferior to those on the right. When the Beloved descends, he is not transformed in the sixth heaven, because it is in full harmony with the seventh. There is a further distinction between the third and lower heavens and the fourth and higher ones: in the third and lower heavens, and at least in theory in the firmament, a password is required for passage. Such a requirement does not seem to apply to the fourth and upper heavens.[83] This distinction between the lower three and the upper four heavens recalls an analogous distinction in the later recension of the Testament of Levi.[84]

The transformation of the Beloved in the fifth and lower heavens during his descent and the need for the use of a password in the lower three heavens suggest some degree of opposition between these lower heavens and the upper two. The relation of this mild opposition to the theories of the Valentinians and the Ophites requires further investigation.[85]

As noted above, each heaven, according to the ascension of Isaiah, is more glorious than the one below it. The sixth heaven, in particular, has much greater light than those beneath it. This motif calls to mind the pattern in the Testament of Levi, in which the second heaven is brighter than the first and the third is incomparably brighter than the second (T. Levi 2:6–10). Another similarity between these two works is the name "Great Glory" used of God.[86]

Both the Ascension of Isaiah and the Apocalypse of Abraham associate the seventh heaven with a marvelous or indescribable light.[87] They differ, however, in a striking way: the description of enthroned angels or powers in the lower five heavens of the Ascension of Isaiah contrasts vividly with the remarks in the Apocalypse of Abraham that there is no power besides God in all the expanses. Thus the Ascension of Isaiah may represent or be related to the kind of tradition against which the relevant part of the Apocalypse of Abraham was written.[88] The Ascension of Isaiah lacks the motif of Paradise as such, but it emphasizes the salvation of the faithful and their exalted destiny in the seventh heaven.[89] Unlike 2 Enoch, the Ascension of Isaiah has little interest in the punishment of the wicked.

The Ascension of Isaiah is the oldest certainly Christian composition to make use of the motif of seven heavens. This motif was most likely borrowed from Jewish tradition.

THIRD BARUCH

Third Baruch is probably a Jewish composition that has undergone some Christian reworking. The Jewish form of the work was produced during the second century C.E.[90] It was composed in Greek and is preserved both in Greek and Slavonic. The following discussion is based on the Greek version. It begins with the lament of Baruch, the scribe of Jeremiah, over the destruction of Jerusalem and its temple. Presumably, the earlier destruction is chosen as the fictive setting because of the parallel with the destruction of 70 C.E. The Lord sends an angel to comfort Baruch and to guide him through the heavens and reveal their mysteries to him. After his ascent, Baruch is returned to earth to communicate what he has seen to others.

At the beginning of the journey, the angel takes Baruch to the place where the heaven was set fast and where there is a river which no one is able to cross (2:1). The statement that "the heaven was set fast" may imply a domelike or semispherical shape for heaven.[91] Then the angel leads Baruch to a large door which is the door of heaven (2:2). They enter as on wings about the distance of a thirty day's journey. The angel says later that the door is as (thick) as the distance from earth to heaven. Inside is the first heaven that contains a plain whose width is the same distance. On the plain are men with faces of cattle and horns of deer and feet of goats and loins of sheep. These are those who built the tower of the war against God, that is, the Tower of Babel (2:2–7).

The the angel takes Baruch to a second door. They enter, flying about the distance of a sixty days' journey. Inside is the second heaven that contains a plain with men on it who look like dogs; their feet are like those of deer. These are those who plotted to make the tower, forcing people to make bricks (chap. 3).

Next the angel and Baruch pass through doors, making a journey of about 185 days. Inside is the third heaven, which contains a plain and a serpent whose belly is Hades. This serpent feeds on the wicked. In the third heaven is the place where the sun goes forth; the chariot of the sun is drawn by forty angels and accompanied by the phoenix. Apparently in the third heaven also are 365 gates of heaven by means of which light separates itself from darkness (i.e., dawn; cf. 6:13–14). The sun passes through the third heaven (cf. 7:2). Baruch views the setting of the sun whose crown has to be removed and renewed because it has been defiled by the earth. The moon and the stars are also apparently in the third heaven. The moon is in the form of a woman and rides in a chariot (chaps. 4–9).

The angel then takes Baruch to the fourth[92] heaven and in it he sees an unbroken plain with a lake in the middle. Around it are birds that are unlike those on earth and that continuously praise the Lord. The plain is the abode of the righteous; the water is the life-giving water that is rained onto earth, the dew that produces fruit (chap. 10).

Next the angel leads Baruch to the fifth heaven, at the entrance of which is a closed gate; this the angel explains, only Michael can open. Michael appears to receive the prayers of humanity. Angels bring baskets of flowers, which represent the virtues of the righteous. Michael eventually departs and the doors close. The angel and Baruch wait while Michael carries the virtues to God; he then returns and gives oil to those who had brought flowers. When the door closes a second time, the angel returns Baruch to earth (chaps. 11–17).

Third Baruch shows more interest in cosmological matters than the Ascension of Isaiah, but this interest is limited. The firmament (heaven) is pictured as resting on the ends of the earth. A river surrounds the earth, but it is not named. The thickness of the doors of the various heavens is emphasized, probably to dramatize the vastness and greatness of the heavenly world compared with the earthly.

The placement of Hades in the third heaven (4:3) reflects a development beyond the eschatological functions of the heavens in the Testament of Levi. In the latter work, fire, snow, ice, and winds are held in the first heaven for the day of judgment. These materials are apparently to be used in a way similar to the plagues in the book of Revelation. In the second heaven, according to the Testament of Levi, heavenly powers await the time when they will punish the spirits of Beliar and of error. In Third Baruch, in contrast, punishment of wicked humans at least is not postponed to the final day of judgment but presumably occurs immediately after death. Second Enoch also goes beyond the Testament of Levi in that the rebellious angels are already imprisoned in the second heaven (2 Enoch 7). But Paradise, the "eternal inheritance of the righteous," and the "terrible place" that is the eternal reward of the wicked are not yet occupied in the narrative time of 2 Enoch. They are "prepared," that is, held ready in waiting, for use after the general resurrection and the final judgment. Thus, of the three works, the eschatology of 3 Baruch seems to be the most fully realized.

In both Second Enoch and Third Baruch, Hades or its equivalent is placed in the heavenly world rather than under the earth. This placement may reflect a new cosmography. The old view is expressed, for example, by Plato in the *Phaedrus* 249A–B: the wicked are punished under the earth and the good are rewarded in a heavenly place. The new view is typical of Plutarch (c. 46- 122 C.E.). According to his dialogue *On the Face of the Moon*, when the soul leaves the body, it must spend some time in the sphere of the moon. The unjust are punished there; the just also need purification on the meadow of "Hades."[93] In another dialogue, the widespread motif of the tortures of the wicked in the underworld is taken up, but placed in the heavenly regions. Likewise, the islands of the blest are shifted to the heavenly world.[94] It is not clear whether the new cosmography was due to a more scientific view of the world, involving the shift from the picture of a more or less flat earth to one of a spherical earth, or simply to another form of popular religion.[95] In any case, language about "the underworld" continued to be used alongside descriptions reflecting the new world-picture.[96]

Besides the discussion of Hades, the account of the third heaven also includes matters of astronomical interest: the nature and movement of the sun; the 365 gates of heaven; the nature, movement, and waxing and waning of the moon; and the stars. This material is clearly more mythical or literary than scientific. The fact that the sun, moon, and stars appear in the same heaven make clear that the notion of the planetary spheres as distinguished from the sphere of the fixed stars plays no role in this work.

Some of the more intriguing questions about Third Baruch are how many heavens the work presupposes and whether it originally described more than the four with a glimpse of the fifth that appear in the work in its present form. The angel tells Baruch several times that he will see the glory of God (e.g., 7:2, 11:2). Yet Baruch never does see the glory of God in the present form of the work. The reader's expectation of a description of the divine throne may be deliberately aroused and frustrated. The descriptions of Michael going *upward* to God from the fifth gate may imply that there are higher heavens.[97] If the work presupposes more than five heavens, seven is the most likely number. It may never have contained descriptions of the upper (three) heavens. It appears to be roughly a mirror image of the Apocalypse of Abraham, which describes only the upper heavens, the seventh, sixth, and fifth.

PRELIMINARY CONCLUSION

Most of the Jewish and Christian works discussed so far presuppose that there are three or seven heavens. The main options for the origin of the notion of three heavens are: (1) it is an inner Jewish development, based on the phrase "heaven of heavens" in the Hebrew Bible, or (2) it was borrowed from one of the typical Babylonian pictures of the universe. Given the basically rhetorical use of the Hebrew phrase and the extensive contact of Jews with Babylonian culture, the second option is more likely. The use of the terms *lower heaven* and *upper heaven* and the presence of a heavenly sea in the Testament of Levi support this conclusion. The major options for the origin of the motif of seven heavens are: (1) it was borrowed from the Greek world-picture involving seven planetary spheres, or (2) it was borrowed from Babylonian magical tradition. Since the later recension of the Testament of Levi and the other relevant works discussed do not connect the seven heavens with planetary spheres, the second option is more likely. I would now like to turn to texts that explicitly link the seven heavens and the seven planets.

THE SEVEN PLANETS: EXPLICIT LINKS

Although there is no explicit connection between the seven heavens and the seven planets in the early Jewish and Christian apocalypses, certain other texts explicitly associate the two. The oldest of these seems to be *Poimandres,* which dates to the second century C.E.[98] According to chapter 9 of this work, divine intellect engendered rationally a second intellect as craftsman. The latter created seven "controllors," that is, the planets, called "governors" in astrology,[99] which encompass the visible world in orbits. Their control is called "destiny." In chapters 24–26 there is a discussion about the ascent of the soul. As the human soul speeds upward through the framework of the orbits, it gives up to each of the seven zones (planetary spheres) the quality that it had wrought in it as it had descended earlier to enter a body. Stripped of those undesirable qualities, the soul comes to the nature of the eighth heaven. Eventually it comes to be within god; that is, it becomes god.[100]

In his recent study, David Ulansey has shown that the Mithraic mysteries were closely related to astronomy and astology.[101] From this point of view, it is not surprising that the seven planets appear frequently in Mithraic iconography. Some of the examples are undated.[102] Two of the relevant monuments have been dated to the second half of the second century C.E. In the Mithraeum of the Seven Spheres in Ostia,[103] the floor of the central aisle is covered with mosaic showing representations.[104] In the white-black mosaic floor near the entrance there is a dagger, and behind it follow seven half circles, which represent the seven spheres of the planets. The Mithraeum of the Seven Gates, also in Ostia, is dated to about 160–70 C.E.[105] On the threshold of the mosaic paved floor of this mithraeum,[106] there is a large central arch formed by two pilasters; this main arch is flanked by three minor arches on either side. The seven arches are thought to represent the seven spheres of the planets. Other evidence, to be discussed below, suggests that the initiate expected to ascend through the planetary spheres after death.

The work entitled the *Chaldaean Oracles* was probably written by Julian the Theurgist in the second half of the second century C.E. An extant fragment speaks figuratively about the seven planets in connection with the ascent of the soul.[107] The initiate is instructed not to look downward, because there is an abyss that threatens to tear him from the ladder with seven gates, under which is the throne of Necessity.[108]

In Book 1, chapter 30 of *Against Heresies,* Irenaeus describes the teaching of "others," presumably a group of Gnostics. They say that Wisdom's offspring, Ialdabaōth, emitted an offspring; this third one did the same, until there were seven. "Thus, according to them, the septet was completed, with the mother [Wisdom] occupying the eighth position" (1.30.4).[109] The names of the seven are Ialdabaōth, Iaō, Sabaōth, Adōnaios, Elōaios, Oraios, and Astaphaios.[110] The snake who persuaded Eve was the agent of Wisdom.[111] Ialdabaōth cast the snake, along with Adam and Eve, from heaven into this lower world. "And it . . . engendered six offspring, with itself serving as the seventh in imitation of that septet which surrounds its parent [Ialdabaōth]. And—they say— these are the seven worldly demons, which always oppose and resist the race of human beings, because it was on account of these that their parent [the snake] was cast down."[112] Later it is said that this lower septet introduced humanity to all kinds of evil, beginning with apostasy from the upper, holy septet, presumably the septet associated with Ialdabaōth. The holy septet is then identified with the seven heavenly bodies called "planets."[113]

Later in the same account, Irenaeus says that they teach that the anointed [preexistent] Christ descended and entered into the human Jesus. Christ descended "through the seven heavens, having assumed the likeness of their offspring, and it gradually emptied them of any power; for—they say—the whole secretion of light rushed to it."[114] The "seven heavens" here are presumably equivalent to "the holy septet," who were identified with the seven planets earlier. The allusion to their "power" may reflect astrological ideas of destiny.

According to Origen, Celsus, following Plato, asserted that souls could make their way to and from the earth through the planets. Origen then discusses Jacob's vision of the ladder, saying that it may point to the same things Plato had in view or to something greater than these.[115] Origen goes on to say that Celsus speaks about a representation (*symbolon*) used in the Mithraic mysteries. This representation concerned a ladder with seven gates (and on the top of it, an eighth gate) that represented the soul's passage through the seven planetary spheres. Celsus apparently argued that the Mithraic teaching was similar to that of the Christians, implying some derogatory conclusion about the latter.[116] Perhaps anticipating this argument, Origen claims in the prior passage that the Christian scriptures do not teach any specific number of heavens.[117]

Symbols for the seven initiatory stages in Mithraism are found associated with symbols of the seven planets in mosaics found in the Mithraeum of Felicissimus at Ostia, dated to the second half of the third century C.E.[118] The central aisle has a mosaic pavement with the symbolic representations of the different mithraic grades; each of these grades is associated with one of the planetary deities.

THE SEVEN PLANETS: PROBABLE LINKS

Certain other texts can be taken as probably presupposing an association of the seven heavens with the seven planets, because of their similarity to texts that make the association explicitly. One of these texts is Irenaeus's account of the Gnostic myth according to Ptolemy; Irenaeus attributes it generally to "the Valentinians."[119] According to this account, the Demiurge created seven heavens, above which they say that he exists. And on this account they term him the seventh and his mother the eighth, "preserving the count of the primal and first octet of the fullness. They say that the seven heavens are intellectual and postulate that they are angels; . . . Likewise, they say that paradise is above the third heaven and is virtually the fourth archangel; and that Adam got something from it [or him] when he passed time within it [or conversed with him].[120] These seven heavens associated with seven angels are analogous to the holy septet that Irenaeus says "others" identified with the seven planets.[121]

Another such text is an account of the teachings of the Gnostic sect of the Ophites in Origen's *Contra Celsum* 6.24–38.[122] An important part of their teaching was the ascent of the soul after death (6.27). To reach its goal in the realm of the Father and the

Son, the soul had to pass through a "Barrier of Evil" (or "fence of wickedness"—φραγμὸν κακίας), which is defined as "the gates of the archons which are shut for ever" (6.31). There are seven archons controlling the gates; in ascending order they are: Horaeus, Aiolaeus, Astaphaeus, Adonaeus, Sabaoth, Iao, and Ialdabaoth. To persuade the archons to let him pass, the soul must address them by name, recite the correct formula, and show to each of them a "symbol" (symbolon). These symbols are perhaps to be connected with the "seal" (sphragis) which, according to 6.27, was bestowed by the Father on the "Youth and Son."[123] Having passed through the realms of the seven archons, the soul reaches the eighth (sphere)—the Ogdoad, ruled over by "the first power" (6.31). The Ogdoad seems to be equivalent to an eighth heaven. The names of the seven archons in this text are almost the same as those given by Irenaeus in his account of "others."[124] Irenaeus says that these are the "holy septet," who are identified with the seven planets. A contrast between the two texts is that in Irenaeus the planets seem to be ambivalent, whereas in Origen they are somewhat more malefic.

Sometime before 350 C.E., a Gnostic work entitled *The Reality of the Rulers* or *The Hypostasis of the Archons* was written. According to this work, there is a "veil" (katapetasma) that divides the world above and the realms that are below.[125] This veil separates the seventh heaven from the eighth.[126] When Sabaōth repented and condemned his father Sakla (= Ialtabaōth or Ialdabaōth), he was caught up and appointed in charge of the seventh heaven, below the veil between above and below.[127] Wisdom had her daughter Life sit at Sabaōth's right hand to teach him about the things in the eighth heaven.[128] This text seems to presuppose the same basic myth and cosmography as Irenaeus's account of the "others."

Around 375 C.E., Epiphanius wrote *Against Heresies*, which contains a discussion of the teachings of "the Phibionites," apparently a Gnostic group. He says that they speak of many rulers, but gives the names of the ones they consider to be the greater ones. There follows a list of names associated with seven heavens: five of the seven names agree with the list given by Irenaeus in discussing "the others." It is likely, then, that this text also is evidence for a link between seven rulers and the seven planets.[129]

Finally, at the end of the fourth or beginning of the fifth century C.E., a work entitled the *Life of Joseph* (the husband of Mary) was written.[130] In chapter 21, Death, Hades, the Devil, and evil demons approach Joseph on his deathbed. Jesus drives these powers away and calls Michael and Gabriel to accompany Joseph and to show him the way until he has passed through the "seven aeons of darkness."[131] The identity of these seven aeons is not clear, but, if "aeons" maybe taken as a synonym for "rulers," they may be associated with the planets. If so, they are pictured in malefic terms.

EXPLICIT REFERENCES TO THE PLANETS, BUT NOT TO SEVEN

In the Gnostic work *The First Thought in Three Forms,* one of the events of the final struggle is the undoing of planetary determinism:

> And the lots of destiny and those which traverse the houses [the planets which traverse the sectors of the celestial sphere] were greatly disturbed by a sharp thunderclap. And the powers' thrones were disturbed and overturned, and their ruler became afraid. And those which follow destiny [the planets] gave up their numerous circuits along the way.

The planets then complain to the powers that the way on which they travel is no longer established.[132] The lack of interest in the number of planets and spheres is noteworthy.

Chapter 136 of *Pistis Sophia* is usually classified as part of Book 4 of that work, which is dated to the first half of the third century C.E.[133] In that passage it is said that Jeu bound 1800 archons and placed 360 archons over them, and he placed five other great archons as rulers over the 360 and over all the bound archons. In the human world these five are named Kronos, Ares, Hermes, Aphrodite, and Zeus. The order given here is neither the so-called Chaldaean nor the Egyptian.[134] It may be that seven planets are presupposed but that for some reason the sun and moon are omitted.

NUMBER OF HEAVENS NOT CONNECTED WITH PLANETS

In Irenaeus's account of the Gnostic myth of Basilides, he remarks:

> And out of the power together with wisdom (there were engendered) authorities, rulers, angels. These he calls "first" ones. And

by them the first heaven was crafted. By an act of emission on their part, other angels came into being, and they made another heaven closely resembling the first one . . . [and so forth] (up to a total of) 365 heavens. And it is because of them that the year has that quantity of days, corresponding to the number of heavens . . .

They locate the positions of the 365 heavens just as astrologers do; for they accept the astrologers' principles, adapting them to their own kind of system. And the ruler of them (the heavens) is named Abrasaks, and that is why this (ruler) has the number 365 within it $(1 + 2 + 100 + 1 + 200 + 1 + 60 = 365)$. (1.24.3, 7)[135]

Thus Basilides, who was active in Alexandria at about 132–35 C.E., seems to have had a more complex cosmography than many other Gnostics.

A passage from Epiphanius was cited above as evidence that the Phibionites presupposed seven heavens. In another passage, the implication may be that they knew 365 heavens, each ruled by an archon.[136]

The Apocalypse of Paul from Nag Hammadi speaks of ten heavens (22–23). The First Apocalypse of James, also from Nag Hammadi, says that there are 72 heavens that are under the authority of the twelve rulers (26).

Thus, is it impossible to speak of a standard Gnostic cosmography.

CONCLUSION

There is no clear indication in the early Jewish and Christian apocalyptic writings that there is any connection between the seven heavens and the seven planets. Such a connection first becomes visible in Hermetic texts, Mithraic monuments, and Celsus's discussion of Mithraic mysteries. The connection is clearly made under the influence of Greek astrology. The motif of seven heavens was probably borrowed from Babylonian tradition by Jewish apocalyptic writers. The reasons for adapting this motif probably included the magical properties of the number. The tradition of the sabbath and the motif of the seven archangels may also have reinforced the choice of this motif.

If the motif of the seven heavens was added to the Testament of Levi by a Christian redactor, that recension and the ascension of Isaiah would be the earliest Christian apocalyptic writings to make use of the motif. There is virtually no indication of any astronomical or astrological interest in these two works.

The only explicit evidence in the first three centuries that Christians connected the seven heavens with the seven planets is Irenaeus' account of the teaching of "the others," presumably a Gnostic group.[137] The connection was probably made by Ptolemy, the follower of Valentinus, and the Ophites (as described by Origen).[138] Some Gnostic groups probably combined the magical idea of seven malefic spirits or seven demons with the astrological idea of the planets as controllers of destiny.

Thus Culianu was right in rejecting the hypothesis of the history of religions school that the seven heavens in Jewish and Christian apocalyptic writings derived from a Babylonian tradition concerning seven *planetary* heavens or spheres. As he conceded in an aside, however, the picture of seven heavens probably does derive from Babylon. The context of this borrowing probably involved magical rather than cosmographical ideas. The main concern of the history of religions school was to interpret Jewish and Christian *origins*. One may say that, with regard to this tradition at least, they were right in looking to Babylon.

NOTES

This essay is dedicated to the memory of the primary organizer and host of the conference at which it was presented, Professor Ioan P. Culianu. I would like to thank F. Rochberg-Halton for her help with the relevant Sumerian and Babylonian material. She, of course, is not responsible for any errors that this essay may contain.

1. Wilhelm Anz, *Zur Frage nach dem Ursprung des Gnostizismus: Ein religionsgeschichtlicher Versuch* (TU 15.4; Leipzig, 1897).

2. Wilhelm Bousset, "Die Himmelsreise der Seele," *Archiv für Religionswissenschaft* 4(1901) 236–37, with reference to Anz.

3. Bousset, "Die Himmelsreise der Seele," 136–69, 229–73.

4. Ioan P. Culianu, *Psychanodia 1: A Survey of the Evidence of the Ascension of the Soul and its Relevance* (Leiden, 1983) 27–28.

5. Ioan P. Couliano, *Expériences de l'extase: Extase, ascension et récit visionnaire de l'Hellénisme au Moyen Âge* (Paris, 1984) 10.

6. Culianu, *Psychanodia,* 56.

7. Couliano, *Expériences de l'extase,* 20.

8. Gerhard von Rad, "οὐρανός, B. Old Testament." *Theological Dictionary of the New Testament* 5(1967) 502.

9. Ibid., 503; Hans Bietenhard, *Die himmlische Welt im Urchristentum und Spätjudentum* (WUNT 2; Tübingen, 1951) 11.

10. Bietenhard, *Die himmlische Welt*, 11.

11. Ps. 148:4; 2 Chr. 2:5, 6:18.

12. Von Rad, "Old Testament," 503.

13. Helmut Traub, "οὐρανός. C. Septuagint and Judaism," *Theological Dictionary of the New Testament* 5(1967) 509.

14. Ibid., 510.

15. 2 Chr. 28:9; 2 Macc. 15:23; 3 Macc. 2:2; Wis. 9:10, 16; 18:15; Tob. 8:5; see Traub, "Septuagint and Judaism," 511.

16. ἀπὸ τοῦ οὐρανοῦ τῶν οὐρανῶν; see Matthew Black, *Apocalypsis Henochi Graece* (Leiden, 1970) 19.

17. Robert Henry Charles, *The Greek Versions of the Testaments of the Twelve Patriarchs* (Oxford, 1908; reprint, Hildesheim, 1960) ix.

18. 4Q213 TestLevi[a]; originally published by J. T. Milik in *Revue Biblique* 62 (1955) 398–406; see the discussion in H. W. Hollander and M. de Jonge, *The Testaments of the Twelve Patriarchs: A Commentary* (Leiden, 1985) 17–18. Another fragment is 4Q Test Levi[a] 8 III, published and discussed by J. T. Milik, *The Books of Enoch: Aramaic Fragments of Qumran Cave 4* (Oxford, 1976). Milik has announced the discovery of fragments of a second document, 4Q Test Levi[b] (*Revue Biblique* 73 [1966] 95, n. 2 and *The Books of Enoch*, 214). Fragments of an Aramaic Levi-document were also found in the first cave at Qumran (Hollander and de Jonge, *Testaments of the Twelve Patriarchs*, 18).

19. 4Q TestLevi[a] col. II, lines 11–18.

20. Charles argued that the two Greek recensions were translations of two Hebrew recensions; since the Aramaic fragments have been discovered, the hypothesis of a Hebrew original has been discarded (Charles, *Greek Versions of the Testaments*, xxxviii).

21. Charles emends to "light" (ibid., 30, n. 38).

22. Charles considered the words "the coming redemption of" to be a Christian modification of the text (ibid., 31, n. 55).

23. W. G. Lambert, "The Cosmology of Sumer and Babylon," in Carmen Blacker and Michael Loewe, eds., *Ancient Cosmologies* (London, 1975) 44–45.

24. Ibid., 58.

25. See also Alasdair Livingstone, *Mystical and Mythological Explanatory Works of Assyrian and Babylonian Scholars* (Oxford, 1986) 82–86.

26. Livingstone's translation of the same or a similar text speaks of "the upper heaven," "the middle heaven," and "the lower heaven" (ibid., 82–83).

27. Lambert, "Cosmology of Sumer and Babylon," 58–59.

28. ὁ κατώτερος; see Charles, *Greek Versions*, 32.

29. τῷ ἀνωτέρῳ . . . καταλύματι; ibid., 33.

30. For further references in the Bible, the Apocrypha, and the Pseudepigrapha, see Hollander and de Jonge, *Testaments of the Twelve Patriarchs*, 134.

31. Compare Job 38:22–24, Sir. 39:28–29; for further references see Hollander and de Jonge, *Testaments of the Twelve Patriarchs*, 137.

32. See the discussion of date in Charles, *Greek Versions of the Testaments*, xlii–xliv.

33. Personal communication.

34. Rochberg-Halton, "Babylonian Cosmology," in N. Hetherington, ed., *Encyclopedia of Cosmology* (forthcoming).

35. J. van Dyjk, A. Goetze, and M. I. Hussey, *Early Mesopotamian Incantations and Rituals* (Yale Oriental Series, Babylonian Texts 11; New Haven, 1985) 44; cf. 13 and plate 66.

36. Rochberg-Halton, "Babylonian Cosmology;" cf. Livingstone, *Mystical and Mythological Explanatory Works*, 159. On the seven thrones, see a Sumerian blessing of the royal throne in van Dyjk, Goetze, and Hussey, *Early Mesopotamian Incantations and Rituals*, 39; cf. 12 and plate 59. On the seven demons or evil spirits, see below.

37. R. Campbell Thompson, *Semitic Magic: Its Origins and Development* (New York, 1971; originally published in 1908) 1.

38. R. Campbell Thompson, *The Devils and Evil Spirits of Babylonia* (London, 1903) 1.50–53, 62–65, 68–69, 72–79, 154–55, 190–99. Cp. Erica Reiner, *Šurpu: A Collection of Sumerian and Akkadian Incantations* (Archiv für Orientforschung 11; Graz, 1958) 24, line 172. See also the enumeration of seven prayers, the seventh of which involves "the Seven" (Reiner, 27, lines 60–66).

39. Gerhard Meier, ed., *Die assyrische Beschwörungssammlung Maqlû* (Archiv für Orientforschung 2; Berlin, 1937) 33; cf. 43, line 79. The majority of the tablets of this series comes from the libraries of Assurbanipal and Assur.

40. Ibid., 48. line 49; cf. 17, line 24.

41. Thompson, *Semitic Magic*, lii–liii.

42. Ibid., 32.

43. Ibid., 33; cf. 166–67, 170; cf. Meier, *Maqlû* 60, line 73.

44. Ibid., 188.

45. Ibid., 206–7; cf. 208. See the edition and translation of this text by Reiner, *Šurpu*, 37, lines 54–59. The majority of the tablets of the series *Šurpu* also come from the libraries of Assurbanipal and Assur.

46. Reiner, *Šurpu*, 17, lines 166–67. Cf. the reference to seven generations (ibid., 19, line 6).

47.   Compare the last sentence of T. Levi 3:3 in the two versions (Charles, *Greek Versions of the Testaments*, 33).

48.   Translation by M. A. Knibb, in H. F. D. Sparks, ed., *The Apocryphal Old Testament* (Oxford, 1984) 255; E. Isaac also translates with the plural "heavens" (in *The Old Testament Pseudepigrapha* 1.49).

49.   Knibb, *The Apocryphal Old Testament*, 255.

50.   Isaac, *The Old Testament Pseudepigraphia*, 49.

51.   Bietenhard, *Die himmlische Welt*, 11.

52.   Bousset, "Die Himmelsreise der Seele," 143.

53.   H. K. McArthur, "Paradise," *Interpreter's Dictionary of the Bible* 3.655.

54.   Harold Attridge, *The Epistle to the Hebrews* (Hermeneia; Philadelphia, 1989) 6–8.

55.   See the discussion by M. Whittaker in *The Apocryphal Old Testament*, 141–42.

56.   M. D. Johnson in *The Old Testament Pseudepigrapha* 2.252.

57.   Translation by L. S. A. Wells, revised by M. Whittaker, in *The Apocryphal Old Testament*, 153.

58.   Translation by Johnson, *The Old Testament Pseudepigrapha* 2.268.

59.   Wells and Whittaker translate "Paradise of God's Reckoning," *The Apocryphal Old Testament*, 154.

60.   Bietenhard, *Die himmlische Welt*, 14.

61.   Translation by Johnson, *The Old Testament Pseudepigrapha* 2.287.

62.   Some manuscripts lack the reference to the third heaven (ibid., 291, n. f).

63.   G. H. Box, *The Apocalypse of Abraham* (London, 1919) xv.

64.   The notes to R. Rubinkiewicz's translation were written by H. G. Lunt (*The Old Testament Pseudepigrapha* 1.694, n. c).

65.   Ibid., 698, n. 19a.

66.   Lambert, "Cosmology of Sumer and Babylon," 61.

67.   T. H. Gaster, "Firmament," *Interpreter's Dictionary of the Bible* 2.270.

68.   Enuma elish 4: 139–40.

69.   John J. Collins, "The Jewish Apocalypses," *Semeia* 14 (1979) 40.

70.   The chapter numbers correspond to those of the translation by F. I. Andersen, in *The Old Testament Pseudepigrapha* 1.105–213; A. Pennington uses a different scheme in the translation in *The Apocryphal Old Testament*, 329–62.

71.   Cf. the older recension of T. Levi 2:7 (Charles, *Greek Versions of the Testaments*, 30) with 2 Enoch 4:2.

72.   Cf. the older recension of T. Levi 3:2 (Charles, *Greek Versions*

of the Testaments, 32) with 2 Enoch 5:1 (some manuscripts read "cold" instead of "ice"; see Pennington, in Sparks, *The Apocryphal Old Testament,* 330, n. 3.)

73. Cf. the older recension of T. Levi 3:3 (Charles, *Greek Versions of the Testaments,* 33) with 2 Enoch 7.

74. "Movements" refers to regular movements, like the rising and setting of the sun. "Aberrations" refers to perturbations in those regular movements, such as the annual movement of the sunrise point across the horizon. The movement of this point causes apparent "aberrations" in the positions of the stars (Andersen, *The Old Testament Pseudepigrapha* 1.111, second column of n. b).

75. Ibid.

76. Ibid., 127, second column of n. d.

77. Ibid., 110, n. 4a.

78. Ibid., 121, second column of n. g.

79. Ibid., 123, n. 13a.

80. Ibid., 128, n. b.

81. There are also two recensions of the Latin version, a Slavonic recension, and Coptic and Greek fragments (see Adela Yarbro Collins, "The Christian Apocalypses," *Semeia* 14 [1979] 84–85).

82. There is no mention of anyone sitting on the throne.

83. There is no mention of passwords as Isaiah and the angel are ascending; the motif appears only in the descent of the Beloved.

84. See the discussion above.

85. See, e.g., Irenaeus, *Against Heresies* 1.5.2, 1.24.3–7 (Latin) (cf. Bentley Layton, *The Gnostic Scriptures* [Garden City, N.Y., 1987] 420–25); *Against Heresies* 1.30.12 (cf. Culianu, *Psychanodia,* 9); Irenaeus, *Against Heresies* 2.30.6–7; Tertullian, *Against the Valentinians* 20.

86. Cf. T. Levi 3:4 with Asc. Isa. 9:37.

87. Cf. Apoc. Abr. 15:7 with Asc. Isa. 9:6.

88. Cf. Apoc. Abr. 19:3–7 with Asc. Isa. 7:14–15, 19–21, 24–27, 29–31, 32–37.

89. The motif of Paradise, as noted above, appears in 2 Corinthians, chapter 12, *The Life of Adam and Eve,* and 2 Enoch.

90. See the discussion by H. E. Gaylord in *The Old Testament Pseudepigrapha* 1.655–56.

91. Gaylord translates "the heaven was set fast" and refers to 1 Enoch 18:5 and 33:2, passages that say that heaven rests on the ends of the earth (ibid., 665 and n. 2a); H. M. Hughes and A. W. Argyle translate "where the vault of heaven was set" (*The Apocryphal Old Testament,* 904).

92. The Greek version reads "third heaven" (10:1), but it is evident that this reading is a mistake; see Gaylord, *The Old Testament Pseudepigrapha* 1.673, n. 10 a.

93.   Plutarch, *De facie in orbe lunae* 27–29; cf. *De genio Socratis* 590B.

94.   *De sera numinis vindicta* 563D.

95.   See the discussion by Culianu, *Psychanodia*, 41–46.

96.   *Pistis Sophia* 102, 126–27, 144; *Apocalypse of Ezra* (Greek) 1:7–8, 4:5.

97.   When Baruch and the angel enter the gates of the lower heavens, there is no indication that they travel upward in order to enter the relevant heaven.

98.   Layton, *The Gnostic Scriptures*, 447.

99.   Ibid., 453, n. 9 b.

100.   See the translation by Layton (*Gnostic Scriptures*, 457–58). Culianu argues that the order of the vices in *Poimandres* corresponds to the so-called Chaldean order of the planets (*Psychanodia*, 49).

101.   David Ulansey, *The Origins of the Mithraic Mysteries* (New York, 1989).

102.   In a marble relief of a tauroctony found in Rome, the planets are represented as seven stars beside Mithras's head, four on the left, three on the right: CIMRM 368 (M. J. Vermaseren, ed., *Corpus Inscriptionum et Monumentorum Religionis Mithriacae* [The Hague, 1956] 1.368). In a white marble low-relief, kept at Bologna, exact find-spot unknown, Mithras is depicted slaying the bull. On the vaulted upper border the raven and the busts of the seven planets are represented (CIMRM 693). In the center of a bronze plate (CIMRM 1727) found near the back wall of a small mithraeum in Brigetio (in Pannonia, what is now Hungary; CIMRM 1723) is Mithras slaying the bull. Behind his head, there are seven stars in the field. Below this and other scenes and separated from them by two horizontal lines are the busts of the seven planets with their attributes.

103.   CIMRM 239.

104.   The mosaic floor is CIMRM 240.

105.   CIMRM 287.

106.   CIMRM 288.

107.   Culianu, *Psychanodia*, 53–54.

108.   Bousset, "Die Himmelsreise der Seele," 263–64.

109.   Translation by Layton, *Gnostic Scriptures*, 175.

110.   Irenaeus, *Against Heresies* 1.30.5.

111.   Ibid., 7 (Layton, *Gnostic Scriptures*, 176).

112.   Ibid., 8 (Layton, *Gnostic Scriptures*, 177).

113.   Ibid., 9 (Layton, *Gnostic Scriptures*, 178).

114.   Ibid., 12 (Layton, *Gnostic Scriptures*, 179–80).

115.   Origen, *Contra Celsum* 6.21.

116.   Ibid., 6.22. See Ulansey, *Mithraic Mysteries*, 18–19.

117.   Ibid., 6.21.

118. CIMRM 299; cf. Ulansey, *Mithraic Mysteries,* 19.
119. Irenaeus, *Against Heresies* 1.1.1–1.8.5; see Layton, *Gnostic Scriptures,* 276–302.
120. Ibid., 1.5.2; translation by Layton, *Gnostic Scriptures,* 291.
121. See above.
122. See the discussion in Alexander, *The Old Testament Pseudepigrapha* 1.237.
123. Cf. the "seals" mentioned in the Naassene hymn quoted by Hippolytus (*Refutation of All Heresies* 5.10.2 = 5.5 [ANF 5.58]).
124. Irenaeus, *Against Heresies* 1.30.5; see above.
125. *Reality of the Rulers* 94.8–13; see the discussion by Alexander, *The Old Testament Pseudepigrapha,* 1.236.
126. *Reality of the Rulers,* 95.19–22.
127. Ibid., 95.13–21.
128. Ibid., 95.31–34.
129. Epiphanius, *Against Heresies* 26.9.6–9; see Layton, *Gnostic Scriptures,* 210–11.
130. It is preserved in Coptic, Arabic, and Latin; see E. Hennecke and W. Schneemelcher, *The New Testament Apocrypha* (Philadelphia, 1963) 1.430.
131. Bousset, "Die Himmelsreise der Seele," 150.
132. This work is also called the *Trimorphic Protennoia* or the *Triple Protennoia;* the passage quoted is 43.13–17; the translation is by Layton and the comments in brackets are from his notes (*Gnostic Scriptures,* 96).
133. See Francis Fallon, "The Gnostic Apocalypses," *Semeia* 14 (1979) 135–36.
134. On these see Culianu, *Psychanodia,* 28; on the order used in Babylonian astronomical literature of the Seleucid period and on a different, older, Neo-Babylonian order, see F. Rochberg-Halton, "Benefic and Malefic Planets in Babylonian Astrology," in E. Leichly et al., eds., *A Scientific Humanist: Studies in Memory of Abraham Sachs* (Occasional Publications of the Samuel Noah Kramer Fund 9; Philadelphia, 1988).
135. Translation by Layton, *Gnostic Scriptures,* 422–25; the comments are taken from his notes. He notes in addition that the name "Abrasaks" was widely used in Greek magic and astrology (425, n. 1.24.7.c).
136. Epiphanius, *Against Heresies* 26.6.6–9; see Layton, *Gnostic Scriptures,* 210. See also the discussion by Culianu (*Psychanodia,* 64, n. 47).
137. Irenaeus, *Against Heresies* 1.30–31.
138. On Ptolemy, see ibid., 1.1.1–1.8.5; on the Ophites, see Origen, *Contra Celsum* 6.24–38.

CHAPTER 5

Paul and the Beginning of Jewish Mysticism

Alan F. Segal

As the Dead Sea Scrolls sectarians knew, there are basically two kinds of people in the world: There are those who divide the world into two kinds of people and there are those who do not. The community at the Dead Sea were definitely a group of people who divided the world into two kinds of people. I think of myself as one who does not divide the world into two kinds of people. In this particular case, there are lumpers and splitters—those who put different materials together for comparison versus those who distinguish carefully between cases for contrast. I prefer not to choose between either camp, as I said, but for the purposes of the conference, Ioan Culianu asked me to serve as a kind of summarizer for the western pseudepigraphical and mystical traditions. It is not something that I take on easily. So I will jump over some of the differences between us as scholars of Western mysticism and ascent in order to address some of the underlying commonalities.

While contemplating Carol Zaleski's material on near-death experiences, I want to say that in a sense all Jewish mystics of this period—and especially Paul—thought of their experiences as "near death" experiences, not in a literal sense, but in a figurative sense. They saw their visionary ascent as an exact parallel to the voyage of the soul to heaven after death. Indeed, Paul explicitly says that his experience of Christ was like his death, followed by his rebirth in Christ. It is that identification of the mystic with the figure in heaven that I want to investigate, so as to show that the language that Carol mentions in chapter 17 is part of the mystical tradition of the West.

JEWISH MYSTICISM

That Jewish mysticism has a history is due to Gershom Scholem. When all the modern Jews were saying that Judaism was a religion of reason, more reasonable than Christianity they thought, hence more able to deal with the modern world, Scholem pointed out that they were forgetting—trying desperately to forget—a lively tradition of Jewish mysticism. That history includes Merkavah mysticism, classical Kabbalah, and Hasidism. Moshe Idel added to and corrected Scholem's history by pointing out the experiential aspect of Jewish mysticism. He noted that altered states of consciousness, ecstasy and not just fanciful cosmology, if you will, was part of Jewish mystical tradition from the beginning.[1]

It is Merkavah mysticism that I want to consider here. But it is clear to me that what we call "Jewish mysticism" grew out of a separate phenomenon, apocalypticism, the tail-end of the prophetic movement that claimed the world is going to end abruptly.

All Jewish mysticism, indeed even the doctrine of resurrection itself, depends on a very peculiar passage in Daniel, chapter 12, the only apocalyptic work accepted into the Hebrew Bible:

> At that time shall arise Michael, the great prince who has charge of your people, And there shall be a time of trouble, such as never has been since there was a nation til that time; but at that time your people shall be delivered, every one whose name shall be found written in the book. And many of those who sleep in the dust of the early shall awake, some to everlasting life, and some to shame and ever-lasting contempt. And those who are wise shall shine like the brightness of the firmament; and those who turn many to righteousness, like the stars for ever and ever. (Dan. 12:1–3)

We often gloss over the rather peculiar aspects of this prophecy in Daniel. In it, it says that two kinds of people will be resurrected— the very good, and the very bad (not the usual understanding). More interesting to me is the idea that the maskilim, those who are wise, will shine as the stars in heaven, *yazhiru ke'zohar haraqi'a*—this is literally where *Zohar*, the principal book of Jewish mysticism, gets its name. Essentially this document tells us that those who make themselves wise will become stars, but it actually means that the good people on earth will become angels. Angels in heaven and stars are equated. The history of Jewish mysticism is deeply concerned with the experience of becoming a star. But that is precisely what Paul tells us. We must wait to see how this takes place.

I want to underline three aspects of this Jewish mystical spirituality and show how it is fundamental to Paul's experience. The first aspect of the Jewish mystical experience is *angelophany*—the vision of a principal angelic mediator who, like the angel of the Lord in Exodus, carries the name of God or somehow participates in God's divinity. All the passages describing the Glory of the Lord, especially Eze. 1:26—the human figure on the throne in Ezekiel's vision—are pulled into this angelic figure, making a consistent figure of a principal angelic mediator. This mediator figure can be called a variety of different names—Yahoel, Melchizedek, and even the Son of man—and, as I have tried to show in *Paul the Convert*, it was the figure that Paul saw and with whom he identified the crucified Christ. So for Paul, the figure was the traditional one except, as he says in 2 Cor., it has the face of Jesus.

The second aspect of this tradition that is important to the study of Paul is *transformation*. In the Jewish mystical tradition, adepts or heroes or patriarchs can be transformed or subsumed into the mediator figure. This is more or less the equivalent of becoming an angel or becoming a star, which is the exact point of Daniel, chapter 12. The most obvious example of this phenomenon, though by no means the only one, is Enoch, who is transformed into the Son of man in 1 Enoch 71. I would submit that what is narrated there is the very experience of being made a star, which is also narrated in Daniel, chapter 12. From a historical point of view, the problem with this tradition is that chapter 71 of Enoch cannot be proven to be pre-Christian. Most scholars believe it to be pre-Christian, but that is not the same thing as proof.

However, this is only the prologue, for Merkavah mysticism involved apocalyptic visions of a violent end to the enemies of God, not quiet contemplation. Also, it was the active desire to journey to heaven and see what was there. One could go to heaven and not only at the end of one's life—some people actually went while alive. This is the third aspect of the tradition I want to highlight here—*ascent*. In fact, the importance of going during one's life, you might say, was to prove that one was going after death. It was a kind of eschatological verification (pace Hick).

Here is an example: In the ninth century, Hai Gaon recounts that the journey to view this divine figure was undertaken by mystics who put their heads between their knees (the posture Elijah assumed when praying for rain in 1 Kings 18:42),[2] reciting repetitious psalms, glossolalic incantations, and mantralike prayers, which are recorded in abundance in the hekhalot literature:[3]

> When he seeks to behold the Merkabah and the palaces of the angels on high, he must follow a certain procedure. He must fast a number of days and place his head between his knees and whisper many hymns and songs whose texts are known from tradition. Then he perceives the chambers as if he saw the seven palaces with his own eyes, and it is as though he entered one palace after another and saw what is there. And there are two *mishnayoth* which the tannaim taught regarding this topic, called *Hekhaloth Rabbati* and *Hekhaloth Zutreti*.

The Gaon is aware of the mystical techniques for heavenly ascent and describes them as "out-of-body" experiences during which the adept ascends to heaven while his body stays on earth. It is even possible that he understands the entire journey as an internal, intrapsychic one, but that is not entirely clear.[4] The hekhaloth texts themselves sometimes mention the transformation of the adept into a heavenly being, whose body becomes fire and whose eyes flash lightening, a theme that is repeated in the Paris Magical Papyrus.[5]

MERKABAH AND ITS PREDECESSORS

Though it would be impractical here to review all the detailed work currently underway on apocalyptic and Merkabah mysticism, its relationship to Christianity and Paul's writing can be briefly summarized. Basically the central issue of Jewish mysticism was the relationship between human beings and an enormous angelic human figure manifesting God. The figure is generally called "God's Glory" or his "Kabod." The relationship was one of absorption, as we shall see.

The Angel of the Lord

Let us first see who the figure is. In the Bible, God is sometimes described in human form. In other places, like Exod. 23:21f., an angel is mentioned who has the form of a man and who carries within him or represents "the name of God." The human figure on the divine throne described in different ways in Ezekiel, chapter 1,

Daniel, chapter 7, and Exodus, chapter 24, among other places was blended into a consistent picture of a principal mediator figure who, like the angel of the Lord in Exodus, chapter 23, embodied, personified, or carried the name of God, YHWH, the tetragrammaton. We shall see that this figure, greatly elaborated by Jewish tradition, becomes a central metaphor for the Christ in Christianity. To see how, we must trace its history in Judaism.

Several Jewish traditions discuss the *eikon* or image of God as Adam's prelapsarian appearance, an especially glorious and splendid form which humanity lost when Adam sinned, since humanity is described as made in "the image and form of God" in Genesis 1:26: בצלמנו כדמותנו. The same "image and form of God" is thereafter associated with God's human appearance in the Bible or the description of the principal angel of God who carries God's name. Most significantly, the human figure on the Merkabah that Ezekiel describes is called "the appearance of the likeness of the glory of the Lord" (mareh demut ke'vod YHWH). Thus, God's Glory or Kabod can become a technical term for God's human appearances.[6]

It seems likely that this enigmatic human appearance of God, discussed with appropriate self-consciousness in the Bible, is related to the so-called the Son of Man, which is not a proper name. The heavenly Son of Man appears in the vision in Dan. 7:13 in which an Ancient of Days appoints a human figure ("one like a son of man") to execute justice in the destruction of the evil ones. This human figure is best understood as an angel.[7] Later on in Daniel, resurrection is promised both for the faithful dead and for the most heinous villains, who will be resurrected so that they may be sentenced to eternal perdition. *Hamaskilim* (המשכילים) or "those who are wise," apparently the elite of the apocalyptic group, will then shine as the stars in heaven (Dan. 12:3). This scripture essentially states that the leaders will be transformed into angels, since the stars were identified with angels in biblical tradition (e.g., Job 38:7).

The preeminence of this angel is due primarily to the description of the angel of the Lord in Exodus. Exod. 23:20–21 states: "Behold, I send an angel before you, to guard you on the way and to bring you to the place which I have prepared. Give heed to him and hearken to his voice, do not rebel against him, for he will not pardon your transgression; for my name is in him." The Bible expresses the unique status of this angel by means of its participation in the divine name.[8] Thereafter in Exodus 33:18–23, Moses asks to see the Glory (כבוד) of God. In answer, God makes "his goodness" pass in front of him but He cautions, "You cannot see my face; for man shall not see me and live. . . . Behold, there is a place by me where you shall stand upon the rock; and while my glory passes by I will put you in a cleft of the rock, and I will cover you with my hand until I have passed by; then I will take away my hand and you shall see my back; but my face shall not be seen." Yahweh himself, the angel of God, and his Glory (כבוד) are melded together in a peculiar way, which suggested to its readers a deep secret about the ways God manifested himself to humanity.

Let us look at the more philosophical expression of these issues in more detail. The Septuagint, the second century B.C.E. translation of the Hebrew Bible into Greek, identifies the figure on the throne in Ezek. 1:26 with the form (eidos) of man. This term has a philosophical history starting in Plato's Parmenides 130C, where eidos means the idea of man. Because of Plato's fortunate use of language, Hellenistic Jews like Philo could reunderstand the phrase "form of man," describing man's resemblance to God in Gen. 1:26 and also occuring in biblical theophanies like Ezek. 1:26, as referring to the Platonic eidos or idea of man, which inevitably meant for Platonists the unchanging immortal idea of man that survives death. So for Hellenistic Jewish mystics like Philo, the figure of man on the divine throne described in Genesis, Exodus, Ezekiel, Daniel, and the Psalms (and which formed the basis of the "Son of man" speculation) was also understood as the ideal and immortal man. His immortality and glorious appearance was something Adam possessed in the garden of Eden and lost when he sinned.[9] Paul, as we shall see, uses all these traditions to good advantage. In this form, the traditions are centuries older than Christianity.

In the Hellenistic period many new interpretations of this passage appeared. Foremost among the various names given to this angel in various Jewish sects and conventicles is Yahoel in the first-century apocalyptic work, The Apocalypse of Abraham. The name Yahoel illustrates one interpretation of carrying the divine name, since it is a combination of the tetragrammaton and a suffix denoting angelic stature. Yahoel appears in chapters 10–11, where he is described as the one: "in whom God's ineffable name dwells." Other titles for this figure included Melchizedek, Metatron, Adoil, Eremiel, and preeminently "the Son of Man." For instance, Melchizedek appears at Qumran, in the document called 11QMelch, where he is identified with the "elohim" of Ps. 82:1, thus giving us yet another variation on the theme of carrying the name of God. Metatron is called YHWH hakaton, or YHWH Junior, and sits on a throne equal to God's in 3 Enoch 10:1.[10] Typically, the name of the angel varies from tradition to tradition. Thus, Michael is God's "mediator" and general (archistratēgos, 2 Enoch 33:10, T. Dan. 6:1–5, T. Abr. 1:4, cf. *The Life of Adam and Eve* 14.1–2). Eremiel appears in the Apocalypse of Zephaniah 6:1–15, where he is mistaken for God. In The Ascension of Isaiah 7:2–4, an angel appears whose name cannot be given.

Chief angelic mediators appear all over Jewish literature of the first several centuries.[11] The chief angelic mediator, which we may call by a number of terms—God's vice-regent, His wazir, His regent, or other terms expressing his status as principal angel—is easily distinguished from the plethora of divine creatures, for the principal angel is not only head of the heavenly hosts but sometimes participates in God's own being or divinity.

The rabbis most often call God's principal angel Metatron. The term *Metatron* in rabbinic literature and Jewish mysticism is probably not a proper name but a title adapted from the Greek word metathronos, meaning "one who stands *after* or behind the throne." If so, it represents a rabbinic softening of the more normal Hellenistic term, synthronos, meaning "one who is *with* the throne," sharing enthronement or acting for the properly throned authority. The rabbis would have changed the preposition from one connoting equality (*syn-*, "with") to one connoting inferiority (*meta-*, "after or behind") in order to reduce the heretical implications of calling God's principal helping angel his *synthronos,* his equal regent on the throne.[12]

Transformation

Alongside these traditions lies the stranger but more relevant notion to Christianity in some apocalyptic-mystical groups that certain heroes can be transformed into angels as part of their ascension. This may easily be the most puzzling part of the mystic traditions, but, in view of Paul's mysticism, it is the most important to summarize.[13] Amazingly, some patriarchs are exalted as angels. In the Testament of Abraham, chapter 11 (Recension A), Adam is pictured with a terrifying appearance and adorned with glory upon a golden throne. In chapters 12–13 Abel is similarly glorified, acting as judge over creation until the final judgment. Second Enoch 30:8–11 also states that Adam was an angel: "And on earth I assigned him to be a second angel, honored and great and glorious."[14] In the *Prayer of Joseph*, found in Origen's commentary on John 2:31, with a further fragment in *Philocalia* 23:15, Jacob describes himself as "an angel of God and a ruling spirit" and claims to be the "first-born of every living thing," "the first minister before the face of God," "the archangel of the power of the Lord, and the "chief captain among the sons of God."[15]

Another important and rarely mentioned piece of evidence of the antiquity of mystical speculation about the Kabod is from the fragment of the tragedy *Moses* written by Ezekiel the Tragedian.[16] There, in a document of the second century B.C.E. or earlier Moses is depicted as seeing a vision of the throne of God with a figure seated upon it. The figure on the throne is called "*phos gennaios*" (a venerable man), which is a *double entendre* in Greek, since *phos* can mean either "light" or "man" depending on the gender of the noun.[17]

The surviving text of Ezekiel the Tragedian also hints at a transformation of an earthly hero into a divine figure when he relates that the venerable man (*phos gennaios*) handed Moses his sceptre and summoned him to sit upon the throne, placing a diadem on his head. Thereafter the stars bow to him and parade for his inspection. Since, as we have seen, throughout the biblical period the stars are thought to be angels (see, e.g., Job 38:7), there can be no doubt that Moses is here depicted as being leader of the angels and hence above the angels. This enthronement scene with a human figure being exalted as a monarch or divinity in heaven resembles the enthronement of the "Son of man"; the enthronement helps us understand some of the traditions that later appear in Jewish mysticism and may have informed Paul's ecstatic ascent. The identification of Jesus with the manlike appearance of God is both the central characteristic of Christianity and understandable within the context of Jewish mysticism and apocalypticism.[18]

Philo speaks of Moses as being made into a divinity (*eis theon*) in several places (e.g., *Sacrifices* 1–10; *Moses* 1.155–58). In exegeting Moses' receiving the Ten Commandments, Philo envisions an ascent, not merely up the mountain, but to the heavens, possibly describing a mystical identification between this manifestation of God and Moses by suggesting in his *Life of Moses* and *Questions and Answers on Exodus* that Moses attained to a divine nature through contact with the *logos*. In *Questions and Answers on Exodus* 1.29, 1.40, Philo writes that on Sinai Moses was changed into a divinity. In *Life of Moses* 1.155–58, he says that God placed the entire universe into Moses' hands and that all the elements obeyed him as their master; then God rewarded Moses by appointing him a "partner" (*koinonon*) of his own possessions and gave into his hand the world as a portion well fitted for his heir (1.155). In the *Sacrifices of Cain and Abel* 8–10, Philo refers to Deut. 5:31 as proof that certain people are distinguished by God to be stationed "beside himself." Moses is preeminent among these people for his grave is not known, which for Philo apparently means that Moses was transported to heaven.

Much of our evidence is later than Paul. But one apocalyptic mediator clearly predates Paul, and that is the Enoch portrayed in the Enochic literature, now known to be widespread in Judaism through the Dead Sea Scrolls.[19] Enoch is a primeval hero of the Bible whose death is not mentioned. Instead, Gen. 5:18–24 twice relates that Enoch walked with God and then disappeared, for "God took him."

The Parables of Enoch contains several references to angelic transformation. In chapter 39, Enoch ascends to heaven while reciting hymns and blessings as do the Merkabah mystics; there he is overcome with the splendor and glory of the throne rooms. His face changes on account of the vision, which evidently reflects the experience of the prophecy that "those who are wise shall shine as the stars" (Dan. 12:3), because 1 Enoch 62:15 states that the elect shall shine as stars and be clothed with garments of glory.

Most importantly, at the end of The Parables of Enoch, chapters 70–71, Enoch is mystically transformed into the figure of the "son of man" on the throne: "My whole body mollified and my spirit transformed" (1 Enoch 71:1).[20] This is an extraordinarily important event, as it underlines the importance of mystic transformation between the adept and the angelic vice-regent of God, giving a plausible explanation of how the sectarians that produced the visions in Daniel expected to be transformed into stars. Indeed, it is possible to say that 1 Enoch 71 gives us the experience of an adept undergoing the astral transformation prophesied in Dan. 12:3 albeit in the name of a pseudepigraphical hero. And, if that is true, Paul gives us the actual, confessional experience of the same spiritual event, with the Christ substituting for the Son of man. In both cases, the believer is subsumed into the body of a heavenly savior and becomes a kind of star or celestial immortal.

Whatever the intention of the author of Enoch, which may be construed in any number of ways, the relationship to Paul's experience is extremely important.[21] Like Enoch, Paul claims to have gazed on the Glory, whom Paul identifies as the Christ. Like Enoch, Paul understands that he has been transformed into a more divine state, which will be fully realized after his death. Like Enoch, Paul claims that this vision and transformation is somehow a mystical identification. Like Enoch, Paul claims to have received a calling, his special status as intermediary. Paul specifies the meaning of this calling for all believers, a concept absent from the Enoch texts that we have, although it may have been assumed within the original community.

Yet complete surety about the history of this tradition is elusive. Paul does not explicitly call the Christ the "Glory of God." And because the Parables (1 Enoch, chapters 37–71) are missing from the Dead Sea Scrolls, we cannot date them accurately. As opposed to the earlier Enoch material, they *may* date to the first century or later and may be influenced by Christianity, since they are extant only in the Ethiopic Version of Enoch, the official canon of the Ethiopian Christian church. Yet, whatever the date of 1 Enoch chapters 70–71, there is no doubt that the stories of Enoch ascensions in 1 Enoch, chapter 14, antedated Paul and would have influenced any of his conceptions about heavenly journey.[22] Furthermore, as long as the date of 1 Enoch chapters 70–71 cannot be fixed exactly and as long as evidence of the Dead Sea Scrolls remains ambiguous, Paul himself remains the earliest author explicitly expressing transformation in Judaism. If his discussion of transformation can be related to apocalyptic mysticism in Judaism, he also becomes the only Jewish mystic of this period to relate this personal experience confessionally.

The theme of angelic transformation usually accompanies a heavenly journey. It becomes especially important in later Kabbalah, but it is sparsely attested in first-century Judaism. Since we have no rabbinic works that can be firmly dated to the first century, Paul's confessional reports are extremely important, though usually overlooked, as evidence for dating Merkabah mysticism.[23] Thus, Paul provides important information about first-century Judaism and Jewish mysticism, equally important to the use that Jewish texts have found in establishing the meaning of Christian texts. Indeed, Paul's letters may be more important to the history of Judaism than are rabbinic texts for establishing the meaning of Christian scriptures.

Second Enoch, extant only in Slavonic, is a further extension of the Enoch legend, most probably through a Christian recension, since Torah does not figure in the story at all. Yet, the possibility of a Semitic, possibly even a Jewish *Vorlage,* especially in the shorter version, cannot be ruled out. In 2 Enoch 22:7, Enoch is transformed during a face-to-face encounter with the Lord into "one of his glorious ones"—in short, an angel; but note the use of glorification language to characterize angelic status. Immediately afterwards, God decrees: "Let Enoch join in and stand in front of My face forever," thus explaining for us the rabbinic term "Prince of the Presence," which is normally applied to Metatron. Then Enoch is transformed:

> And the LORD said to Michael, "Go, and extract Enoch from [his] earthly clothing. And anoint him with my delightful oil, and put him into the clothes of my glory. And so Michael did, just as the Lord had said to him. He anointed me and he clothed me. And the appearance of that oil is greater than the greatest light, and its ointment is like sweet dew, and its fragrance myrrh; and it is like the rays of the glittering sun. And I looked at myself, and I had become like one of his glorious ones, and there was no observable difference. (2 Enoch 22:8–10, recension A)

Here, the transformation is affected through a change of clothing. The clothing appears to function as or symbolize Enoch's new immortal flesh for Enoch, as they are immortal clothes emanating from the throne room, not from earth. This is a significant parallel with Paul's future glorification of the mortal body in 2 Cor. 5:1–10.[24] One might even say that Enoch has been put *in* the body of an angel, or that he is *in* the manlike figure in 1 Enoch, chapter 71. This may explain Paul's use of the peculiar terminology *in Christ.*

The Ascension of Isaiah also focuses on ascent and heavenly transformation. In chapters 6 through 11, usually attributed to a Christian hand, the famous theophany of Isaiah, chapter 6, is understood to be a heavenly journey during which the prophet sees God. The prophet is taken through each of the seven heavens, stopping to view the glorious figure seated on the throne of each heaven. When he worships the figure in the fifth heaven, he is explicitly warned not to worship any angel, as the rabbis warn not to commit the crime of assuming "there are two powers in heaven." Instead, Isaiah is told that his throne, garments, and crown await him in heaven (7:22). All those who love the Most High will at their end ascend by the angel of the Holy Spirit (7:23). At each heaven, Isaiah is glorified the more, emphasizing the transformation that occurs as a human travels closer and closer to God (7:24); effectively he becomes one of the angels. According to the other angels, Isaiah's vision is unprecedented; no one else has been vouchsafed such a complete vision of the reward awaiting the good (8:11–13). But Isaiah must return to earth to complete his prophetic commission before he can enjoy the rest that awaits him in heaven.[25]

The climax of the story is angelic transformation, but the stated purpose of the journey in these early apocalyptic texts is usually theodicy—to understand God's justice. The journeys begin after a crisis of human confidence about God's intention to bring justice to the world, while the result of the journey is the discovery that the universe is indeed following God's moral plan. Thus the ancient scriptures about God's providence is true and the evil ones who predominate on earth, even oppressing God's saints, will soon receive the punishment that they richly deserve.

In 2 (Syriac) Baruch, the theme of angelic transformation sounds loud and strong. This book is widely believed to have been influenced by Christianity, but it is variously dated from the first century to the third. Second Baruch 51:3ff. portrays a gradual transformation of all believers into angelic creatures, as the process of redemption is fulfilled:

> Also, as for the glory of those who proved to be righteous on account of my law, those who possessed intelligence in their life,

and those who planted the root of wisdom in their heart—their splendor will then be glorified by transformations, and the shape of their face will be changed into the light of their beauty so that they may acquire and receive the undying world which is promised to them. . . . When they therefore will see that those over whom they are exalted now will then be more exalted and glorified than they, then both these and those will be changed, these into the splendor of angels and those into startling visions and horrible shapes; . . . For they will live in the heights of that world and they will be like the angels and be equal to the stars. And they will be changed into any shape which they wished, for beauty to loveliness, and from light to the splendor of glory. . . . And the excellence of the righteous will then be greater than that of the angels.[26]

Here is a true fleshing out of the visions of Daniel. The evil ones are transformed into the terrible beasts of the Daniel vision, while the righteous are explicitly transformed into stars.

In chapters 3–15 of the later Merkabah tract now called 3 Enoch (its Hebrew name is *Sefer Hekhaloth*), the man Enoch is transformed into Metatron. Metatron bears a striking resemblance to Moses in Ezekiel the Tragedian's play. For instance, God makes a throne for Enoch-Metatron in 3 Enoch (10:1). He gives him a special garment of Glory and a royal gown (12:1–3); God makes him ruler over all kingdoms and all heavenly beings (10:3); all the angels of every rank, and the angels of the sun, moon, stars, and planets, fall prostrate when Enoch sits on his throne (14:1–5); he knows the names of all the stars (46:1–2; see Ps. 147:40);[27] God reveals to him all the secrets of heaven and earth so that Enoch knows past, present, and future (10:5, 11:1, cf. 45:1; 48 [D]:7); God calls him YHWH ha-katon, another interpretation of Exod. 23:21 (12:5).[28] Of course, the date of these documents is far too late to be of specific guidance for Paul.[29] Whatever one's scholarly inclination about the dating of Daniel or the earliest son of man traditions, there is no doubt that this angelic figure, the figure that the Bible sometimes calls the Kabod (כבוד) or the principal angel of God, is pre-Christian and is a factor in Paul's description of Christ.[30]

There is adequate evidence, then, that many Jewish mystics and apocalypticists sensed a relationship between the heavenly figure on the throne and important figures in the life of their community. The roots of this tradition are pre-Christian. Furthermore, Jewish scholars have overlooked Christianity as evidence for the existence of these traditions in first-century Judaism. Paul did not have to be a religious innovator to posit an identification between a vindicated hero and the image of the Kabod, the manlike figure in heaven, although the identification of the figure with the risen Christ is obviously a uniquely Christian development.

Paul's experiences are, when seen in this light, not unique so much as characteristic of Jewish mystical thought. Indeed, they give us good evidence that the mystical ascent of adepts to heaven was already known in the first century. Paul is the only Jewish mystic to report his own personal, identifiably confessional mystical experiences in the fifteen hundred years that separate Ezekiel from the rise of Kabbalah.

PAUL'S USE OF MYSTICAL VOCABULARY

Paul himself gives the best evidence for the existence of ecstatic journeys to heaven in first-century Judaism, with his report in 2 Corinthians.[31] We begin with heavenly ascent. Although the account of Paul's ecstatic conversion in Acts is a product of Luke's literary genius, Paul gives his own evidence for ecstatic experience. In Galatians, chapter 1, Paul claims that he did not receive the gospel from a human source. And in 2 Cor. 12:1–9, he describes an experience that transcends human ken:[32]

> I must boast; there is nothing to be gained by it, but I will go on to visions and revelations of the Lord. I know a man in Christ who fourteen years ago was caught up to the third heaven— whether in the body or out of the body, I do not know, God knows. And I know that this man was caught up into Paradise— whether in the body or out of the body, I do not know, God knows—and he heard things that cannot be told, which man may not utter. On behalf of this man, I will boast, but on my own behalf I will not boast, except of my weaknesses. Though if I wish to boast, I shall not be a fool, for I shall be speaking the truth.

As in Galatians, chapter 1, Paul calls this experience an *apokalypsis* (an apocalypse, a revelation). Just as in Acts and Galatians, chapter 1, the actual vision is not described. Unlike the text Acts and Galatians, chapter 1, however, this passage is a confessional description of a vision, or possibly two different ones, depending on whether the paradise visited in the ascension can be located in the third heaven.[33] Thus, the vision is both mystical and apocalyptic.[34] The vision ought to be seen in the context of first-century Jewish apocalypticism.

Paul's inability to decide whether the voyage took place in the body or out of the body is firm evidence of a mystical ascent and shows that the voyage has not been clearly interiorized as a journey into the self, which later becomes common in Kabbalah. Furthermore, since the rabbis proscribed the discussion of these topics except singly, to mature disciples, and only provided they had experienced it on their own (מבין מדעתו, M. Ḥag. 2.1), the rabbinic stories interpreting the Merkavah experience often take place while traveling through the wilderness from city to city when such doctrines could easily be discussed in private. This is precisely the scene that Luke picks for Paul's conversion.

It is significant that in 2 Corinthians, chapter 12, when Paul talks about mystical journeys directly, he too adopts a pseudepigraphical stance. He does not admit to the ascent personally. Apart from the needs of his rhetoric, rabbinic rules also forbid public discussion of mystic phenomena. A first century date for this rule would explain why Paul would not divulge his experience *in his own name* at that place. It would also suggest why Jewish mystics consistently picked pseudepigraphical literary conventions to discuss their religious experience, unlocking the mystery behind the entire phenomenon of pseudepigraphical writing. But none of the standard discussions of this incompletely understood phenomenon discuss Paul's confession or the Mishnah here.[35] Again, Paul may be giving us hitherto unrecognized information about Jewish culture in the first century that is unavailable from any other source.

When Paul is not faced with a direct declaration of personal mystical experience, he reveals much about the mystical religion as it was experienced in the first century. Paul himself designates Christ as the image of the Lord in a few places: 2 Cor. 4:4, Col. 1:15 (if it is Pauline), and he mentions the *morphē* of God in Phil. 2:6.[36]

Christ is not explicitly given the title *the Glory of God* in the New Testament.[37] However, there are several New Testament passages in which *doxa* (glory) and, more relevantly, *the* glory is attributed to Christ or the Son. In James 2:1, it is possible that we should translate the text to read "our Lord Jesus Christ, the Glory." Paul himself repeatedly uses the term *glory* to refer to Christ. In Phil. 3:21 Paul speaks of Christ's "Body of Glory" (*soma tes doxes*) to which the believer's body is to be conformed.[38] He thinks of Christ as the Lord of Glory (1 Cor. 2:8). Through the glory of the father, Christ was raised from the dead (Rom. 6:4). God makes known the riches of glory in or through the exalted Christ (Rom. 9:23, Phil. 4:19, see also Eph. 1:18, 3:16, Col. 1:27). The gospel that Paul preaches, which features the death, resurrection, and return of the Christ is called the "gospel of glory" (2 Cor. 4:4, 1 Tim. 1:11, see also Col. 1:27). Other passages bearing on this theme would include 1 Cor. 2:8, describing Christ as "the Lord of Glory," and the doubtfully Pauline Heb. 1:3: "He reflects the Glory of God and bears the very stamp of his nature, upholding the universe by his word of power." In Eph. 1:17 "the God of our Lord Jesus Christ, the Father of the Glory" appears. Some of these references, of course, merely describe the brilliance of vision.

Even more interestingly, Paul describes the "Glory of the Lord" (2 Cor. 3:16–4:6) in the very places where he describes his own conversion, which he also uses as a pattern for experience by which other believers come to be in Christ. As an heir of Christ, the believer shares the glory of Christ (Rom. 8:17), which eclipses any suffering that may have been experienced in the believer's life (Rom. 8:18, 2 Cor. 4:15–17). This exchange of suffering for glory will occur at Christ's coming, according to Col. 3:4. Paul himself talks of the faithful being changed or transformed into the "image of Christ" (Rom. 8:29, 1 Cor. 15:49), which again resembles Ezekiel's language of "the appearance of the likeness of the Glory of the Lord" (Ezek. 1:28, cf. 70). Central to Paul's Christian experience is the transformation of believers at the apocalypse. More importantly, Paul anticipates the technical terminology of the transformation of believers into angels in Jewish mysticism.

Paul's longest discussion of these themes occurs in an unlikely place in 2 Cor. 3:18–4:6. Here he assumes the context rather than explaining it completely:

> And we all, with unveiled face, beholding the glory of the Lord, are being changed into his likeness from one degree of glory to another; for this comes from the Lord who is the Spirit. Therefore, having his ministry by the mercy of God, we do not lose heart. We have renounced disgraceful, underhanded ways; we

refuse to practice cunning or to tamper with God's word, but by
the open statement of the truth we would commend ourselves to
every man's conscience in the sight of God. And even if our
gospel is veiled it is veiled only to those who are perishing. In
their case, the god of this world has blinded the minds of the
unbelievers to keep them from seeing the light of the gospel of the
glory of Christ, who is the likeness of God. For what we preach is
not ourselves, but Jesus Christ as Lord, with ourselves as your
servants for Jesus' sake. For it is the God who said, "Let light
shine out of darkness," who has shone in our hearts to give the
light of the knowledge of the glory of the Lord in the face of
Christ. (2 Cor. 3:18–4:6)

For now, the main point must be the usually unappreciated use
of the language of transformation in Paul's works. In 2 Cor. 3:18
Paul says that believers will be changed into Christ's likeness from
one degree of glory to another. He refers to Exodus, chapters 33
and 34, where Moses' encounter with the angel of the Lord is
narrated. Earlier in that passage, the angel of the Lord is described
as carrying the name of God (Exod. 23:21). Moses sees the Glory
of the Lord, makes a covenant, receives the commandments upon
the two tables of the law and, when he comes down from the
mount, the skin of his face shines with light, as the Bible states
(Exod. 34:29–35). Moses thereafter must wear a veil, except when
he is in the presence of the Lord. Paul assumes that Moses made an
ascension to the presence of the Lord, was transformed by that
encounter, and that his shining face is a reflection of the encounter.
    Thus, Paul's term, "the glory of the Lord" must be taken both
as a reference to Christ and as a technical term for the Kabod
(כבוד), the human form of God appearing in biblical visions. In 2
Cor. 3:18 Paul says that Christians behold the Glory of the Lord as
in a mirror and are transformed into his image.[39] For Paul, as for
the earliest Jewish mystics, to be privileged enough to see the
Kabod or Glory of God is a prologue to transformation into His
image. Paul does not say that all Christians have made the journey
literally but compares the experience of knowing Christ to being
allowed into the intimate presence of the Lord. However, we know
that he has made that journey.
    It is very difficult not to read this passage in terms of Paul's
later description of the ascension of the man to the third heaven
and conclude that Paul's conversion experience also involved his

identification of Jesus as the "image" and "glory of God," as
the human figure in heaven, and thereafter as Christ, son, and
savior. Or at least this is how Paul construes it when he recalls
it. In Phil. 2:6, the identification of Jesus with the form of God
implies his preexistence. The Christ is depicted as an eternal aspect of divinity that was not proud of its high station but con-
sented to take on the shape of a man and suffer the fate of men,
even death on a cross (though many scholars see this phrase as a
Pauline addition to the original hymn). This transformation of
form from divinity is followed by the converse, the retransfor-
mation into God. Because of this obedience God exalted him
and bestowed on him the "name which is above every name"
(Phil. 2:9). For a Jew this phrase can only mean that Jesus received the divine name Yahweh, the tetragrammaton YHWH,
understood as the Greek name *kyrios,* or Lord. We have already
seen that sharing in the divine name is a frequent motif of the
early Jewish apocalypticism where the principal angelic mediator
of God is or carries the name Yahweh, as Exodus, chapter 23,
describes the angel of Yahweh. Indeed the implication of the
Greek term *morphē,* "form," is that Christ has the form of a
divine body identical with the Kabod, the glory, and equivalent
also with the *eikon,* for man is made after the *eikon* of God and
thus has the divine *morphē* (or in Hebrew, [דמות]). The climax
of Paul's confession is that "Jesus Christ is Lord to the glory of
God the Father" (Phil. 2:11), meaning that Jesus, the messiah,
has received the name Lord in his glorification and that this
name, not Jesus' private earthly name, is the one that will cause
every knee to bend and every tongue confess.[40]

In paraphrasing this fragment from liturgy, Paul witnesses that
the early Christian community directed its prayers to this human
figure of divinity along with God (1 Cor. 16:22, Rom. 10:9–12,
1 Cor. 12:3)–all the more striking since the Christians, like the
Jews, refuse to give any other god or hero any veneration at all.
When the rabbis gain control of the Jewish community they vociferously argue against the worship of any angel and specifically
polemicize against the belief that a heavenly figure other than God
can forgive sins (b. Sanhedrin 38b), quoting Exod. 23:21 promi-
nently among other scriptures to prove their point. The heresy
itself they call believing that there are "two powers in heaven." By
this term the rabbis largely (but not exclusively) referred to Chris-

tians who, as Paul says, do exactly what the rabbis warn against—worship the second power.[41]

Concomitant with Paul's worship of the divine Christ is transformation. Paul says in Phil. 3:10 "that I may know him and the power of his resurrection and may share his sufferings, becoming like him (*summorphizomenos*) in his death." Later, in Phil. 3:20–21, he says: "But our commonwealth is in heaven, and from it we await a Savior, the Lord Jesus Christ, who will change (*metaskēmatisei*) our lowly body to be like (*summorphon*) his glorious body, by the power which enables him even to subject all things to himself." The body of the believer eventually is to be transformed into the body of Christ.

Paul's depiction of salvation is based on his understanding of Christ's glorification, partaking of early Jewish apocalyptic mysticism for its expression.[42] In Rom. 12:2 Paul's listeners are exhorted to "be transformed" (*metamorphousthe*) renewing of your minds." In Gal. 4:19 Paul expresses another transformation: "My little children, with whom I am again in travail until Christ be formed (*morphōthē*) in you! This transformation is to be effected by becoming like him in his death (*summorphizomenos to thanatō autou* [Phil. 3:10]).

Alternatively, Paul can say, as he does in Gal. 1:16 that "God was pleased to reveal His Son in me (*en emoi*)." This is not a simple dative but refers to his having received in him the Spirit, in his case through his conversion. Being *in Christ* in fact appears to mean being united with his heavenly image. The same, however, is available to all Christians through baptism. This is not strange, since apocalyptic and mystical Judaism also promoted *tebilah* (טבילה), ritual immersion or baptism as the central purification ritual preparing for the ascent into God's presence. The Jewish ritual of purification for coming into the divine presence and proselyte baptism has been transformed by Paul's community into a *single* rite of passage, though it does not thereby lose its relationship to its source. Dying and being resurrected along with Christ in baptism is the beginning of the process by which the believer gains the same image of God, his *eikon*, which was made known to humanity when Jesus became the Son of man—that human figure in heaven who brings judgment in the apocalypse described by Daniel.

Paul's conception of the risen body of Christ as the spiritual body (1 Cor. 15:43) at the end of time and as the body of Glory

(Phil. 3:21) thus originates in Jewish apocalypticism and mysticism, modified by the unique events of early Christianity. The meaning of Rom. 8:29 can be likewise clarified by Jewish esoteric tradition. There, Paul speaks of God as having "foreordained his elect to be conformed to the image of his Son" (proōrisen summorphous tēs eikonos tou uiou autou). Paul uses the genitive here rather than the dative as in Phil. 3:21, softening the identification between believer and savior. But when Paul states that believers conform to the image of his Son, he is not speaking of an agreement of mind or ideas between Jesus and the believers. The word *summorphē* itself suggests a spiritual reformation of the believer's body into the form of the divine image. Paul's language for conversion develops out of mystical Judaism.

Of course, the mystical experience of conversion is not only with the *risen* Christ but with the *crucified* Christ. The most obvious relationship between the believer and Christ is suffering and death (Rom. 7:24, 8:10, 13). By being transformed by Christ, one is not simply made immortal, given the power to remain deathless. Rather, one still experiences death as the Christ did and, like him, survives death for heavenly enthronement. This is a consequence of the Christian's divided state. Although part of the last Adam, living through Spirit, the Christian also belongs to the world of the flesh. As James Dunn has noted: "Suffering was something *all* believers experienced—an unavoidable part of the believer's lot—an aspect of experience as Christians which his converts shared with Paul: Rom 5:3 ('we'); 8:17f ('we'); 2 Cor. 1:16 ('you endure the same sufferings that we suffer'); 8:2; Phil. 1:29f. ('the same conflict which you saw and now hear to be mine'); 1 Thess. 1:6 ('imitators of us and of the Lord'); 2:14 ('imitators of the churches of God in Judea: for you suffered the same things'); 3:3f. ('our lot') 2 Thess. 1:4ff."[43]

Thus, the persecution and suffering of the believers is a sign that the transformation process has begun; it is the way to come to be *in* Christ. Paul is convinced that being united with Christ's crucifixion means not immediate *glorification* but *suffering* for the believers in this interim period. The glorification follows upon the final consummation. The connection between suffering and resurrection has been clear in Jewish martyrology; indeed the connection between death and rebirth was even a prominent part of the mystery religions as well. But the particular way in which Paul makes these connections is explicitly Christian.

Paul's central proclamation is: Jesus is Lord and all who have faith have already undergone a death like his, so will share in his resurrection. As we have seen, this proclamation reflects a baptismal liturgy, implying that baptism provides the moment whereby the believer comes to be "in Christ." Christianity may have been a unique Jewish sect in making baptism a central rather than a preparatory ritual, but some of the mystical imagery comes from its Jewish past.

Paul's letters are the very first witness to Jewish mysticism, in a personal and confessional way. Paul tells us in his own language just what it feels like to be transformed into the Glory of God, to become a star, as it were. Paul is the only Pharisee to leave us his writings and the only Jewish mystic in the first century to do so. And when we look at Paul's writing we discover not so much a systematic theology as the memoirs of a man who has had overwhelming visions which he describes as death in life, bringing him a new life in the body of his savior.

NOTES

1. Moshe Idel, *Kabbalah: New Perspectives* (New Haven, 1988).

2. The term often used to describe merkabah mystics, "the descenders into the chariot" (*yordei merkabah;* יורדי מרכבה), seems to me best understood as referring to this position (pace Gruenwald).

3. See *Otsar Ha-Geonim*, ed. B. Lewin, on *Ḥagigah,* (Jerusalem, 1932) *Teshuvoth,* 14–15. Trans. Idel.

4. I cannot agree with David Halperin in *The Merkabah in Rabbinic Literature* (New Haven, 1980) that the Gaon totally misunderstands the Ezekiel traditions on the basis of mysticism of his own day. Apocalypticism is well known to be a highly exegetical enterprise, as Lars Hartman pointed out in 1966 in his *Prophecy Interpreted: The Formation of Some Jewish Apocalyptic Texts and of the Eschatological Discourse Mark 13 par.* (Lund, 1966). Halperin's distinction between the exegetical character of rabbinic comment on Ezek. 1 and the apocalyptic-mystical does not hold. Both groups use the themes exegetically; both may have understood them mystically and sought to reproduce the experience.

5. Gershom Scholem, *Major Trends in Jewish Mysticism* (New York, 1941) and Morton Smith, "Some Observations on Hekhaloth Rabbati," in A. Altmann, ed., *Studies and Texts,* vol. 1 (Cambridge, Mass., 1963). Also see the Jewish Christian evidence, for instance, Ps.-Clem. Hom. 17.16. See Jarl Fossum, *The Name of God and the Angel of the Lord* (Tübingen, 1985).

6. See Carey Newman, *Paul's Glory-Christology, Tradition and Rhetoric* (Leiden, 1992), for a sound analysis of the Hebrew Bible references to the Kabod (glory).

7. Matthew Black, "The Throne Theophany Prophetic Commission and the 'Son of Man': A Study in Tradition-History," in Robert Hamerton-Kelly and Robin Scroggs, eds., *Jews, Greeks, and Christians: Religious Cultures in Late Antiquity* (Leiden, 1976) 57–73; Christopher Rowland, "The Vision of the Risen Christ in Rev. 1:13ff.: The Debt of an Early Christology to an Aspect of Jewish Angelology," *Journal of Theological Studies* 31(1980) 1–11; and Jarl Fossum, "Jewish Christian Christology and Jewish Mysticism," *Vigiliae Christianae* 37(1983) 260–87.

8. See on a related theme, James Charlesworth, "The Roots of Christology: The Discovery of the Hypostatic Voice," *Scottish Journal of Theology* 39(1986) 19–41.

9. See G. Quispel, "Gnosticism and the New Testament," in P. Hyatt, ed., *The Bible in Modern Scholarship* (Nashville, 1965) 252–71, and Fossum, *Name*, 278.

10. Of course, 3 Enoch must be seen as a late document. See F. J. Horton, *The Melchizedek Tradition: A Critical Examination of the Sources to the Fifth Century* A.D. *and in the Epistle to the Hebrews* (Cambridge, 1976); P. J. Kobelski, *Melchizedek and Melchireša* (Washington, D.C., 1981); S. F. Noll, "Angelology in the Qumran Texts," (PhD. dissertation; Manchester, 1979); G. Quispel, "Gnosticism and the New Testament," in J. P. Hyatt, ed., *The Bible and Modern Scholarship* (Nashville, 1965) 252–71; "The Origins of the Gnostic Demiurge," in P. Granfield and J. A. Jungman, eds., *Kyriakon: Festschrift Johannes Quasten* (Münster, 1970) vol. 1, 272–76.

11. See my *Two Powers in Heaven* (Leiden, 1977) 182–219; Peter Schaefer, *Rivalitaet zwischen Engeln und Menschen: Untersuchungen zur rabbinischen Engelvorstellung* (Berlin/New York, 1975) 9–74; H. B. Kuhn, "The Angelology of the Non-Canonical Apocalypses," *Journal of Biblical Literature* 67(1948) 217–32; F. Stier, *Gott und sein Engel im Alten Testament* (Münster, 1934).

12. See Saul Lieberman, "Metatron, the Meaning of his Name and his Functions," Appendix in Ithamar Gruenwald, *Apocalyptic and Merkavah Mysticism* (Leiden, 1980) 235–41, esp. 237–39.

13. For the growing consensus that apocalypticism implies visionary or "mystical" experience as well as secret knowledge of the end of time, see Christopher Roland, *The Open Heaven: A Study in Apocalypticism in Judaism and Early Christianity* (New York, 1982). See James H. Charlesworth, "The Portrayal of the Righteous as an Angel," in George W. E. Nickelsburg and John J. Collins, eds., *Ideal Figures in Ancient Judaism:*

Profiles and Paradigms (Septuagint and Cognitive Studies 12; Chico, Calif., 1980); Idel, *Kabbalah: New Perspectives,* which stresses the theme of transformation but does not consider the Pauline corpus.

14.   Translated by F. I. Andersen in James H, Charlesworth, ed., *The Old Testament Pseudepigrapha* (Garden City, N.Y., 1983) 1.152.

15.   J. Z. Smith, "The Prayer of Joseph," in J. Neusner, ed., *Religions in Antiquity Essays in Memory of Erwin Ramsdell Goodenough* (Leiden, 1968) 253–94. See A. M. Denis, *Fragmenta Pseudepigraphorum quae Supersunt Graeca Una Cum Historicum et Auctorum Judaeorum Hellenistarum Fragmentis* (Leiden, 1970) 61–62.

16.   See Gilles Quispel, "Ezekiel 1:26 in Jewish Mysticism and Gnosis," *Vigiliae Christianae* 34(1980) 1–10; his review of J. Frickel, *Hellenistische Erloesung in christlicher Deutung* (Nag Hammadi Studies 19; Leiden, 1984) in *Vigiliae Christianae* 39(1985) 196–99; also his "Gnosis," in M. J. Vermaseren, ed., *Die orientalischen Religionen in Roemerreich* (Leiden, 1981) 413–35; see also C. R. Holladay, "The Portrait of Moses in Ezekiel the Tragedian," *Society of Biblical Literature Seminar Papers 1976* (Missoula, Mont., 1976) 447–52; H. Jacobson, "Mysticism and Apocalyptic in Ezekiel's Exagoge," *Illinois Classical Studies* 6(1981) 272–93; P. W. van der Horst, "Moses' Throne Vision in Ezekiel the Dramatist," *Journal of Jewish Studies* 34(1983) 21–29, and "Some Notes on the Exagoge of Ezekiel," *Mnemosyne* 37(1984) 354–75.

17.   See *The Exagoge of Ezekiel,* ed. Howard Jacobson (Cambridge, 1983) 54–55 (lines 68–69). Jacobson denies that there is any mystical content to the book. But this is not the best conclusion from these traditions. For one thing, those scholars who most vociferously deny mystical content of these traditions seem to have no idea what mysticism meant in the first century, importing instead some ananchronistic twentieth century definition of mystical experience. R. G. Robertson has pointed out, if only in passing, the relevance of this passage to the "son of man" figure in his translation of Ezekiel the Tragedian for *The Old Testament Pseudepigrapha* 2.812 (see note b2).

18.   See Alan F. Segal, *Two Powers;* also Jarl Fossum, who has resumed all the known evidence in a most complete and scholarly fashion in his book, *Name* (see n. 5); L. Hurtado, *One God, One Lord: Early Christian Devotion and Ancient Jewish Montheism* (Philadelphia, 1988).

19.   The Enoch literature is possibly as old or older than the Daniel "son of man" traditions in which it participates. M. A. Knibb, *The Ethiopic Book of Enoch* (Oxford, 1978).

20.   Translated by E. Isaac in *The Old Testament Pseudepigrapha* 1.50.

21.   Another unemphasized aspect of the journey motif is that it is a

kind of travel narrative, purporting to be the actual experience of a trust-worthy patriarch of the profoundly moral structure of the cosmos con-firming the biblical account, which reassures the righteous of their final reward.

22. See M. A. Knibb, "The Date of the Parables of Enoch: A Criti-cal Review," *NTS* 25(1979) 345–59; also J. T. Milik, *The Books of Enoch: Aramaic Fragments of Qumran Cave 4* (Oxford, 1976). Though Milik and Black's dating of hekhalot literature has been criticized, the book does contain a good summary of the scholarship on the problem until their publication. (See also Ephraim Isaac, in *The Old Testament Pseudepigrapha* 1.6–7, who dates the Parables to the late first century. Hence, he believes that the Parables may be post-Christian). According to J. Charlesworth, the SNTS Pseudepigrapha session in Paris virtually unanimously agreed—including Matthew Black but still excluding Milik—that the Parables are very early. I realize that I am dating the Parables later than most scholars do. But I feel that this conservative dating is necessary on account of the lack of any fragments from the Parables in the Dead Sea Srolls, in spite of Qumranic appreciation for Enochian literature. Therefore, although Milik's late dating of the Para-bles may be too extreme, a post-Christian date seems prudent, as a meth-odological necessity, until some new positive evidence for the early date of the Parables appears. For scholarly opinion in print, see Knibb's review of Milik, "On the Date of the Parables of Enoch: A Critical Review" *New Testament Studies* 25(1979) 345–59; M. E. Stone, "The Book of Enoch and Judaism in the Third Century B.C.E.," *Catholic Biblical Quarterly* 40(1978) 479–92; G. W. E. Nickelsburg, "Enoch, Levi, and Peter: Recip-ients of Revelation in Upper Galilee," *JBL* 100(1981) 575–600. Of course, if the Parables are pre-Christian as many scholars now believe, my case is measurably stronger. I am dating these texts late only as a control of my own enthusiasm. The evidence from Paul satisfies me that the transformation motif originates before the first century within Judaism.

At the NYU conference on the Dead Sea Scrolls, and in private con-sultation, the late Morton Smith claimed that he had found a text that would firmly anchor these experiences to the first century and to Qum-ran, thus necessarily with a long prehistory. In 4QMª of the Dead Sea Scrolls found at Qumran, Morton Smith saw evidence to translate this passage:

[El Elyon gave me a seat among] those perfect forever,
a mighty throne in the congregation of the gods.
None of the kings of the east shall sit in it
and their nobles shall not [come near it].
No Edomite shall be like me in glory.
And none shall be exalted save me, nor shall come against me.

> For I have taken my seat in the [congregation] of the heavens,
> and none [find fault with me].
> I shall be reckoned with the gods
> and established in the holy congregation.

(See the essay by John J. Collins in this volume and Eileen Schuller, "A Hymn from a Cave Four *Hodayot* Manuscript: 4Q427 7 i+ii," *JBL* 112(1993) 605–28). If Smith is correct, there is evidence that the mystics at the Dead Sea understood that they were one in company with the angels, whom they call the "*bny elohim*," and that they must have achieved this through some rite of translation and transmutation. If this is so, ought we to count The Wisdom of Solomon 5:5–8 as a similar passage?

23.   Paul's experience of the third heaven *may have* transformed him proleptically into an angelic creature, as Enoch was transformed in his heavenly journey. Paul may thus attain to the title apostle, in the same way as many other "angelic" figures did, by literally becoming God's—or, in this case, the Christ's—messenger on earth.

24.   See James Tabor, *Things Unutterable: Paul's Ascent to Paradise in its Greco-Roman, Judaic, and Early Christian Contexts* (Lanham, Md., 1986) 84–85.

25.   Tabor, *Things Unutterable*, 85–86.

26.   Translation by A. F. J. Klijn in *The Old Testament Pseudepigrapha* 1.638.

27.   Josephus reports that the Essenes knew all the names of the angels.

28.   Van der Horst, "Moses' Throne Vision in Ezekiel the Dramatist," 24–25.

29.   See P. S. Alexander, "The Historical Setting of the Hebrew Book of Enoch," *Journal of Jewish Studies* 28(1977) 156–80. He dates the material to the fourth century but suggests that these chapters are much earlier. He may be right, but because it it uncertain Paul still remains the earliest sure witness to this material.

30.   See now Carey Newman, *Paul's Glory*, especially chap. 6.

31.   Terence Callan, "Prophecy and Ecstasy in Greco-Roman Religion and in 1 Corinthians," *NovT* 27(1985) 125–40. Callan shows how Paul wished to limit the term *ecstasy*. Prophecy for Paul is not ecstatic, in that it need not be accompanied by trance. Therefore our use of it, though proper, remains an *etic* term.

32.   See the new book by James Tabor, *Things Unutterable*, (above, n. 24) based upon the author's 1981 University of Chicago dissertation. Tabor illustrates his contention that this mystical experience is meant to be taken very seriously as a part of Paul's religious life. Although Paul means to criticize those who make claims on the basis of their spiritual gifts, this is not merely a strange corner of Paul's universe, and it is

certainly not a parody of an ascent, in the tradition of Lucian's *Death of Peregrinus*.

33. Paradise or the Garden of Eden was often conceived as lying in one of the heavens, though the exact location differs from one apocalyptic work to another. See Martha Himmelfarb, *Tours of Hell: An Apocalyptic Form in Jewish and Christian Literature* (Philadelphia, 1983). Second Enoch, for example, locates them in the third heaven. But 2 Enoch may have been influenced by Paul's writings, even though the shorter version mentions worship in the Temple in a way that suggests it is still in existence, thus antedating 70 C.E.

34. In different ways, the close relationship between mysticism and apocalypticism has been touched upon by several scholars of the last decade, myself included. See my *Two Powers*; Ithamar Gruenwald, *Apocalyptic and Merkavah Mysticism* (Leiden, 1979); and now especially Christopher Rowland, *The Open Heaven: A Study of Apocalyptic in Judaism and Early Christianity* (New York, 1982); Jarl Fossum, *Name*. The Pauline passage is also deeply rooted in Jewish and Hellenistic ascension traditions, which imposed a certain structure of ascent on all reports of this period. Mary Dean-Otting, *Heavenly Journeys; A Study of the Motif in Hellenistic Jewish Literature* (Frankfurt-New York, 1984); Ioan Petru Culianu, *Psychanodia 1: A Survey of the Evidence of the Ascension of the Soul and its Relevance* (Leiden, 1983). Culianu also published a more general work, *Expériences de l'Extase: Extase, ascension et récit visionnaire de l'Hellénisme au Moyen Age* (Paris, 1984), introduction by Mircea Eliade. The verb ἁρπάζω in Greek and its Latin equivalent *rapto* is sometimes shared with pagan ascensions (*sol me rapuit*, etc.), but als probably initially denotes both the rapture of the vision and the specific heavenly journeys of Enoch (לקח = μετεθηκεν) and Elijah (עלה = ανελήφθη). Similar ascensions can be seen in apocalyptic literature, for instance 1 Enoch 39:3, 52:1, and 71:1–5 as well as 2 Enoch, chapters 3, 7, 8, 11, and 3 Baruch, chapter 2. In rabbinic literature the word denoting the journey is often איתנגיד. Paul's reference to the third heaven confirms the environment of Jewish apocalypticism and mysticism.

35. The most recent good analysis of pseudepigraphal writing is David G. Meade, *Pseudonymity and Canon: An Investigation into the Relationship of Authorship and Authority in Jewish and Earliest Christian Tradition* (Tübingen, 1986). Mystical notions are not even mentioned.

36. In this section, I am particularly indebted to Gilles Quispel, "Hermetism and the New Testament, Especially Paul," *ANRW* 2.22 (forthcoming).

37. The older methodology of tracing Christological titles to the

exclusion of exegetical developments is tendentious anyway. See Donald Juel, *Messianic Exegesis* (Philadelphia, 1987).

38. G. Scholem has asked whether this phrase ought to be identified with the Merkabah term *guf hashekina,* "the body of Glory," which we find in the Merkabah texts. See *Von der mystischen Gestalt der Gottheit* (Zurich, 1962) 276, n. 19. But Scholem did not exploit the implications of this perceptive intuition. On the history of the term *glory,* see now Carey Newman, *Paul's Glory,* especially chapter 6.

39. The use of the mirror here is also a magico-mystical theme, which can be traced to the word *eyyin* (עין) occurring in Ezekiel 1. Although it is sometimes translated otherwise, *eyyin* probably refers to a mirror even there, and possibly it refers to some unexplained technique for achieving ecstasy. The mystical bowls of the magical papyri and Talmudic times were filled with water and oil to reflect light and stimulate trance. The magical papyri describe spells that use a small bowl that serves as the medium for the appearance of a god for divination: e.g., PGM 4.154–285 in Hans Dieter Betz, ed., *The Greek Magical Papyri in Translation, Including the Demotic Spells* (Chicago, 1986) 40–43, PDM 14.1–92, 295–308, 395–427, 528–53, 627–35, 805–40, 841–50, 851–55, in Betz, ed., *Magical Papyri,* 195–200, 213, 218–19, 225–26, 229, 236–39. The participant concentrates on the reflection in the water's surface, often with oil added to the mixture, sometimes with the light of a lamp nearby. Lamps and charms are also used to produce divinations, presumably because they can stimulate trance under the proper conditions. The *Reuyoth Yehezkel,* for instance, mention that Ezekiel's mystical vision was stimulated by looking into the waters of the River Chebar. It seems to me that Philo appropriates the mystic imagery of the mirror to discuss the allegorical exposition of scripture. See *The Contemplative Life* 78 and Dieter Georgi, *Die Gegner des Paulus im 2. Korintherbrief* (Philadelphia, 1986) 272–73. Also Schulz, "Die Decke des Moses," *Zeitschrift für die neutestamentliche Wissenschaft* 49(1958) 1–30. Paul's opponents then look into the mirror and see only the text. But because Paul and those truly in Christ actually behold the glory of the Lord, they have a clearer vision of the truth.

40. The bibliography on the Pauline and post-Pauline hymns in Phil. 2:6–11 and Col. 1:15–20 appears endless. See E. Schillebeeckx, *Jesus: An Experiment in Christology* (New York, 1979); M. Hengel, "Hymn and Christology," in E. A. Livingstone, ed., *Studia Biblica* 1972, 173–97, reprinted in *Between Jesus and Paul: Studies in the Earliest History of Christianity* (Philadelphia, 1983) 78–96; J. Murphy O'Connor, "Christological Anthropology in Phil. 2:6–11," in E. Dinkler, ed., *Zeit und Geschichte, Dankesgabe an Rudolf Bultmann* (Tübingen, 1964)

263–93, esp. 291 for bibliography. As David Balch reminds me, Käsemann emphasizes that Paul's metaphoric use of the body and its separate parts is characteristic of paraenetic sections, emphasizing the relationship between the believer and the risen Lord. See Schweitzer in *Theological Dictionary of the New Testament* 7(1971) 1073.

41.   See my *Two Powers*, 33–158, esp. 68–73.

42.   Scholars like Kim who want to ground all of Paul's thought in a single ecstatic conversion experience, which they identify with Luke's accounts of Paul's conversion, are reticent to accept this passage as a fragment from Christian liturgy, because to do so would destroy its value as Paul's personal revelatory experience. But there is no need to decide whether this passage is originally Paul's, hence received directly through the "Damascus revelation," since ecstatic language normally is derived from traditions current within the religious group. Christian mystics use Christian language, Muslim mystics use the languages developed for mysticism in Islam, and no mystic is ever confused by another religion's mysticism. See R. C. Zaehner's *Hinduism and Muslim Mysticism* (New York, 1969); Steven Katz, ed., *Mysticism and Philosophical Analysis* (New York, 1978). In this case the language is not even primarily Christian. The basic language is from Jewish mysticism, though the subsequent exegesis about the identification of the Christ with the figure on the throne is Christian; the vision of God enthroned is the goal of Jewish mystical speculation.

43.   James D. G. Dunn, *Jesus and the Spirit: A Study of the Religious and Charismatic Experience of Jesus and the First Christians Reflected in the New Testament* (London, 1975).

CHAPTER 6

The Practice of Ascent in the Ancient Mediterranean World

Martha Himmelfarb

In the ancient Mediterranean world the boundary between human-ity and the divine was widely understood as permeable. A variety of literature, from the apocalypses and the hekhalot texts to the lives of holy men like Jesus and Apollonios of Tyana, shows us human beings crossing that boundary. In many of these works the transition from mortality to immortality is achieved through as-cent to heaven.

The question I would like to address here is whether we can move from the realm of literature to the realm of practice. Phenom-ena like the use of ascent in claims on behalf of various holy men and the institutionalization of ascent in the ritual for the apo-theosis of the Roman emperors make it clear that many people in antiquity believed ascent to be possible. Do we have evidence to suggest that Jews, Christians, or others developed practices de-signed to achieve such ascents?

In his article "Ascent to the Heavens and the Beginning of Christianity," Morton Smith gathers accounts of and references to heavenly ascent in ancient Judaism and its environment from bibli-cal times.[1]

> The unusual frequency and importance in Palestinian literature
> of these stories of ascent led several scholars to conjecture that
> there must have been some sort of pious practice—meditation, or
> prayer, or whatever—that centered on the theme and perhaps led
> the imaginative to believe that they, too, experienced the sort of
> heavenly ascents they read and wrote of.[2]

123

For Smith these conjectures have been confirmed by the Dead Sea Scrolls' references to the presence of angels in the midst of the sect, although he admits that the Scrolls contain no explicit references to techniques for ascent. For the nature of those techniques, he appeals to the somewhat later Mithras Liturgy and hekhalot texts. The Scrolls are seen as offering evidence for the use of such techniques in the first century; further evidence appears in the letters of Paul.[3]

The scantiness of the evidence should not surprise us:

> We have to recognize that all these bits of evidence concern what was presumably secret teaching about which no explicit reports were likely to be preserved. So what is preserved must be only the tip of the mountain of revelation. Hence we can fairly conclude that one or more techniques for ascent into heaven were being used in Palestine in Jesus' day, and that Jesus himself may well have used one.[4]

As the concluding sentence of this passage makes clear, the availability of techniques for ascent in the first century is crucial to Smith's program of understanding Jesus as a magician.[5] As usual, Smith offers many persuasive insights along the way to a provocative conclusion. But I must confess to being troubled by the form of his argument: we cannot expect accounts of techniques for ascent, since such techniques are esoteric; thus even when we do not find any hints of them, we are entitled to assume that they exist.

Here I propose to look again at some of the evidence Smith treats. It seems to me that some rather different conclusions are required. My interest in the question of practices for ascent grows out of my work on the apocalypses, where ascents and visions are sometimes associated with ascetic practices, but not with elaborate rituals like those the magical papyri direct for various purposes.

The only ascent from the magical papyri I knew before writing this as a conference paper was the famous Mithras Liturgy, PGM 4.475–829. Of course the Mithras Liturgy is hardly a typical magical text; its most recent editor, Marvin W. Meyer, sees it as a product of "Mithraism on the fringe, a Mithraism preoccupied with individualism, syncretism, and magic."[6] Morton Smith has pointed to its parallels to the hekhalot literature,[7] and I have been impressed by many points of contact with the ascent of the Apocalypse of Abraham.[8] The goal to be achieved by ascent, immortalization, is very much like the goal of ascent in the hekhalot texts and the apocalypses. In some significant ways the liturgy appears to have more in common with those bodies of literature than with the corpus of magical papyri, which are concerned primarily with more practical ends. Still it offers a very impressive ritual for ascent.

The ritual is provided only after the description of the ascent. One stage involves an elaborate recipe for obtaining the "ointment of immortalization." It centers on a sun-scarab, which is fed a special cake that causes it to die. The scarab is then preserved in rose oil while the celebrant recites a spell over it for seven days. On the seventh day the scarab is buried, together with myrrh, Mendesian wine, and fine linen, in a bean field (750–72). Later, however, the text reports that the god rejects the ointment in favor of a different use of the scarab (791–98).

The ascent is achieved apparently without benefit of the oil. After three days of purity, at the right astrological moment, the celebrant licks off the eight-letter name he had written on a persea leaf with the juice of the *kentritis* herb, honey, and myrrh (777–91).

Until I sat down to write this paper I assumed that the Mithras Liturgy was the tip of the iceberg, or in Smith's phrase, of "the mountain of revelation," only one of many techniques for ascent to be found among the magical papyri.[9] Perhaps my suspicions should have been aroused by the fact that the Mithras Liturgy is cited over and over again in discussions of ascent in the ancient world without reference to other magical ascents and that it is the only magical papyrus Smith refers to in support of his claim for techniques of ascent.[10] In fact, the process of reading through the magical papyri reveals that the Mithras Liturgy is the only instance of ascent in the magical papyri.[11]

I do not wish to deny that there is further evidence for techniques for ascent in contexts related to the magical papyri. Smith points out that the *Chaldean Oracles* suggest a practice for ascent. As Hans Lewy reconstructs it, the practice involves preparatory purification, interment to represent death, and the use of a magical formula to enable the initiate to breathe in the rays of the sun.[12] The role of the rays of the sun is reminiscent of the Mithras Liturgy, where the initiate is also instructed to breathe in the rays of the sun as he begins his ascent (PGM 4.538). Further, the magical papyri contain instructions for achieving immortality or divinity, which is frequently the goal of ascent, by means other than ascent, although even these are not very common. (The only one I can point to is PGM 4.154–221.) Altogether, then, the magical papyri offer little to support a view that techniques for heavenly ascent were widely practiced. The best explanation I can offer for this fact is that the eminently practical practitioners of magic did not view heavenly ascent as a very practical undertaking.

Disappointed by the magical papyri, let us turn to the hekhalot texts. From Scholem[13] to Idel,[14] these texts have been represented as containing instructions for ascent to heaven,[15] and, as I have noted, they serve Smith as models for the kind of techniques he claims were in use in the first century. Yet the evidence of the hekhalot texts is far from unequivocal.

To begin with, recent scholarship has pushed ascent away from the center of the hekhalot texts—quite rightly in my view. The work of Peter Schäfer and David Halperin in particular has challenged Scholem's view of the hekhalot literature with a more complete picture of the variety of the contents of these texts.[16] It has emphasized especially the volume and significance of the adjurations of angels for a range of purposes, of which the most important is the mastery of the Torah.

Still the fact that the ascents of the hekhalot texts no longer look as central as they once did should not eliminate the instructions for ascent from our consideration. These instructions fall into two large categories: songs to be sung to achieve ascent (Hekhalot Rabbati, Ma'aseh Merkavah) and seals to be shown to the angels guarding the gates of the palaces (Hekhalot Zuṭarti, Hekhalot Rabbati, the Ozhayah fragment from the Geniza).[17]

The songs for ascent are of two kinds. One group consists mainly of hymns that conclude with the trishagion. These appear in both Hekhalot Rabbati and Ma'aseh Merkavah, and their efficacy lies in the fact that they form part of the heavenly liturgy. By reciting them with the angels, the visionary takes his place among the angels.[18] Carol Newsom suggests a similar understanding of the function of the Songs of the Sabbath Sacrifice from Qumran.[19] Such a view also underlies parts of the synagogue liturgy.[20] The hekhalot hymns under discussion would be at home in the synagogue liturgy, and some of them are actually found there. If recitation of such songs constitutes a technique for ascent, then it is no exaggeration to say that all Jews who recited the prayers of the synagogue used such techniques—but surely that would rob the idea of a technique for ascent of any content.

The other group of hymns, which appears at the end of Ma'aseh Merkavah, consists of hymns containing God's twelve-letter name. These are not the ordinary hymns of the synagogue and might more properly be considered to represent a magical technique, although they are not accompanied by any ritual actions.[21] The hekhalot texts do prescribe ascetic practices like fasting and immersion as preparation, not for ascent, but for other activities like the adjuration of angels.[22] These preparations are far less elaborate than the rituals of the magical papyri.[23]

The other type of instructions, the seals or passwords to be given to the angelic doorkeepers to allow the visionary to proceed on his ascent, do not cause the ascent; they are called upon when the journey is already underway. The instructions for confronting terrifying ordeals at the gate of the sixth palace, which appear in the works with seals, also assume that the ascent is in progress.[24]

Of the three hekhalot works with seals, only Hekhalot Rabbati preserves instructions for undertaking the ascent. Relative to the rituals of the Mithras Liturgy, they are extremely simple: "When a man wishes to descend to the chariot, he should call on Suryah the Prince of the Presence and invoke him one hundred twelve times by Ṭoṭrosy'ay YVY, who is called Ṭoṭrosy'ay Ṣurṭaq . . . ," and so on—a list of ten or fifteen names, varying from manuscript to manuscript (no. 204).[25] It is worth noting that, like the songs, this ritual consists entirely of words.

The opening of the Ozhayah fragment is lost, and thus the absence of instructions for starting on the ascent does not necessarily indicate that there never were such instructions. Hekhalot Zuṭarti, however, is extremely interesting in this regard. It culminates in the words the lucky mystic is to use in requesting power over the angels for any purpose he desires, a goal more magical than Scholem attributed to the ascents. Although it lacks instructions for how to undertake the ascent, the instructions for using the seals conclude: "Repeat this mishnah every day after prayer" (no. 419).[26]

In case we miss the point, a similar procedure is laid out in more detail a few paragraphs later by R. Aqiba: "A heavenly voice from beneath the throne of glory told me, 'I have instituted this blessing three times a day in the court above and the court below for my beloved, who troubles himself with descent and ascent to the chariot. I will love and redeem the household in which it is repeated'" (no. 423).

It appears, then, that Hekhalot Zuṭarti does not provide instructions for ascent because none are necessary. The user of this text does not need to follow Aqiba on his difficult and dangerous journey. He can experience the journey vicariously and achieve its benefits by reciting the deeds of the great worthies of a bygone era.

These instructions for recitation are, I believe, the only such instructions associated with ascent, but similar instructions appear in relation to other aspects of the hekhalot literature.[27] One set of instructions for adjuring the Prince of the Torah, for example, includes the direction to recite "this midrash of the Prince of the Torah" three times daily after prayer in conjunction with fasting and other ascetic practices (no. 300). It should be noted that in a passage following the institution of the practice of recitation of the mishnah in Hekhalot Zuṭarti, R. Aqiba tells us that the recitation is to take place after the mystic has fasted for forty days and is in a state of sexual purity; this recitation is accompanied by rituals of purification. Further, the mystic is to place his head between his knees as he recites (no. 424).[28]

This understanding of the way in which the hekhalot texts were to be used has the advantage of taking seriously their pseudepigraphic attributions to great rabbis of the past. Rather than attempting ascent on his own, the mystic recites the deeds of these pious heroes and thus shares in the benefits ascent confers. The recitation undoubtedly constitutes a ritual, but not for ascent.[29]

The hekhalot texts, then, are hardly more fertile a source of techniques for ascent than the magical papyri. Such techniques exist in these bodies of literature, but they are by no means widespread. Thus Smith's claim that such techniques, though unmentioned, stand behind the Dead Sea Scrolls and other literature of the turn of the era loses its plausibility.

Let me now suggest a different model for understanding ascent in the ancient Mediterranean world: rapture, that is, being taken up to heaven at God's initiative. This is the understanding of ascent of two of the earliest writers to discuss ascent in their own names,[30] the apostle Paul and the Manichean teacher Baraies, whose words are preserved in the Cologne Mani Codex.[31] Baraies quotes from five otherwise unknown ascent apocalypses, attributed to antediluvian patriarchs, and from Paul's second letter to the Corinthians, with its famous account of an ascent to the third heaven.[32]

For Baraies, the ascents are "raptures," that is, the visionary is taken up at God's initiative. Two of the passages Baraies cites from the apocalypses use the verb *harpazo*,[33] as does Paul's text, twice (2 Cor. 12:2, 4). Thus I must disagree with Smith and Alan Segal, who see the passage in 2 Corinthians as evidence for the use of techniques of ascent in the first century.[34] Not only is there no allusion to a technique of any kind, but Paul actually calls the experience rapture.

"Rapture," as a model of understanding, also fits rather well the ascents of the apocalypses that have come down to us, despite the infrequency of *harpazo* or equivalents in these texts. The only examples I could find of such verbs appear in the Similitudes of Enoch and the Ascension of Isaiah. In the Similitudes, which is preserved only in Ethiopic, one of Enoch's tours of heaven is introduced thus: "And at that time clouds and a storm-wind carried me off from the face of the earth . . ." (1 Enoch 39:3).[35] There is no suggestion here of any preparation for the ascent nor even a hint about the setting in which the ascent takes place. This absence is related to the form of the Similitudes, which in my view constitutes a reworking of the Book of the Watchers and is difficult to understand without reference to the Book of the Watchers. The concluding chapters of the Similitudes describe ascents in a somewhat similar fashion. First Enoch's name is "lifted" to God's presence (70:1); then in the final chapter, usually understood as a later addition, Enoch's spirit is "carried off" (71:5). The Ethiopic of the Ascension of Isaiah says that Isaiah's "spirit was caught up into heaven" (6:10); the clause is missing in Latin and Slavonic.

I suspect that the reason for the infrequency of such expressions in the apocalypses is that they are unsuitable for the process of describing layers of heavens, which is so important to many ascent apocalypses. As we see in 2 Corinthians, rapture takes the hero directly to his destination, in that case, the third heaven; there is no opportunity to describe the contents of other heavens. The Similitudes of Enoch contains only a single heaven, and there are no indications of a plurality of heavens in the apocalypses Baraies cites, although the quotations are far too brief to permit any conclusions. The Ascension of Isaiah with its seven heavens is the exception. Here we get a description of each heaven in turn as Isaiah ascends.

Now I turn to the material in the apocalypses that might be considered to hint at techniques for ascent. The most common activity in which the seer is engaged immediately before the ascent is mourning, sometimes expressed through weeping. Second Enoch describes Enoch in bed weeping as the angels come to lead him through the heavens (1:2); the cause of the tears is never explained. In the Testament of Levi, Levi grieves over the sins of humanity before his ascent (2:3–4), while in 3 Baruch, Baruch weeps and mourns the destruction of Jerusalem (1:1–3). It should also be noted that several of the visions in Daniel, 4 Ezra, and 2 Baruch are preceded by mourning and weeping, sometimes at the command of God or an angel.[36]

The Book of the Watchers, from the third century B.C.E., is the oldest of the ascents, dated earlier than the period discussed here. But it is of interest for us because it was so influential. The Book of the Watchers places Enoch at a holy site for his ascent; the ascent takes place in a dream after Enoch falls asleep reciting the petition of the fallen Watchers, whose fate is the subject of the words God will address to him in heaven (1 Enoch 13:7–8). While this is not exactly mourning, it presents a certain parallel to Levi's contemplation of the sins of *humanity* in the Testament of Levi, which elsewhere shows the influence of the Book of the Watchers.[37]

Moshe Idel has recently argued that weeping constitutes a technique for inducing mystical experience in Jewish tradition and cited 2 Enoch, 4 Ezra, and 2 Baruch as our earliest evidence for the practice.[38] As these examples show, if weeping is in fact a technique in the apocalypses, it is an all-purpose technique, good for producing ascent or visions. Furthermore, in Daniel, 4 Ezra, and 2 Baruch, mourning is associated with fasting. This combination of ascetic practices seems to me to suggest preparatory rites of purification, intended to make the practitioner worthy of revelation, rather than techniques for producing revelations.

Nor did Baraies think such preparation incompatible with his understanding of rapture. From an otherwise unknown Apocalypse of Enoch, Baraies quotes a passage in which Enoch describes himself mourning and weeping before his ascent: "I am Enoch the righteous. My grief is great and tears pour from my eyes for I have heard the blame coming from the mouth of the impious. . . .

[Seven angels] put me in a chariot of wind and carried me off to the ends of the heavens" (58–59).[39]

Other ascents offer further instances of ascetic preparations, though without mourning and weeping. In the Apocalypse of Abraham, God commands Abraham to undertake a limited fast before his ascent; Abraham goes beyond God's command and neither eats nor drinks for forty days and nights (9:7, 12:1). The influence of the biblical depiction of Moses at Sinai is obvious here, and this behavior too suggests preparation for a vision rather than a technique for producing one.

At first glance the Ascension of Isaiah appears to be the most promising apocalypse in the search for a practice designed to produce ascent. This work consists of two parts, a Martyrdom of Isaiah, generally understood as a Jewish work of perhaps the first century B.C.E., and a Christian ascent, which also circulated separately. Thus the Martyrdom's picture of Isaiah as the head of a group of prophets who lead an ascetic life in the wilderness (2:7–11) is not an integral part of the ascent. Still the author of the ascent chose to represent Isaiah seated in the midst of a group of followers as he undertakes the ascent (6:1–5), thus appropriating aspects of the setting of the Martyrdom for the ascent.

Yet the description of the way the ascent begins excludes the possibility of a practice designed to produce it. As Isaiah exhorts Hezekiah about the truth, the assembled company hears a door open and the voice of the Holy Spirit speaking (6:6).[40] Isaiah begins to prophesy, but he suddenly falls silent as his spirit ascends to heaven (6:10–11). Thus the trance overtakes the prophet as he is in the midst of preaching; beyond the ascetic regimen attributed to Isaiah in the Martyrdom, there are no preparations preceding the ascent, and there is certainly no ritual that could be construed as a technique.

This passage provides the clearest example of the relationship of ascetic practice to ascent in the apocalypses. Most of the ascents imply some sort of ascetic regimen on the part of the visionary. But if the regimen is necessary for the ascent, it is certainly not sufficient. Either the visionary needs to be in a state of readiness produced by ascetic practice to receive the revelation, or ascetic practice marks the visionary as worthy of ascent. But ascent is understood in the apocalypses as coming at God's initiative, as prophecy comes to the biblical prophets; indeed, ascent in the apocalypses can be seen as growing out of the prophetic claim to stand in the divine council.[41] Rapture is not a bad description for this understanding of ascent.

Finally let me consider the Apocalypse of Zephaniah, which is of particular interest for this discussion. The opening of this work has been lost, but the hero of the ascent appears to be a dead soul. Thus his ascent is automatic, and no practice is required to achieve it. The ascent of the righteous dead is presupposed by many of the apocalypses, most notably by the Ascension of Isaiah, where Isaiah sees the exalted status of the righteous dead (chap. 9) and is informed that his great distinction is that he was able to ascend while still alive (8:11). This suggests the coexistence of two different understandings of ascent in the world of the apocalypses, the automatic ascent of the righteous after death and the rapture of the visionary priveleged to ascend during life.

I must confess that I had hoped that investigating the availability of techniques for ascent in the ancient world would provide some hints about the possibility that the experiences of the pseudepigraphic heroes of the apocalypses were in fact experienced by their authors. Some recent studies take this possibility very seriously. I think here especially of Michael Stone's claim that 4 Ezra, an apocalypse without ascent, represents the author's own highly emotional experience of conversion from one understanding of the meaning of the fate of Israel to another, a conversion difficult to justify in logical terms.[42] What is more, Stone suggests that the author of the work may have served his small community as a prophet in much the way Ezra serves the people of Israel in 4 Ezra.[43]

Despite the appeal of such an approach, I am not inclined to read the ascent apocalypses as reflecting the author's experience in any but the most indirect way, as any author's experience is reflected in his writing. My reasons have to do primarily with the highly literary nature of these works and the way in which the ascents are integrally related to the narratives of which they form a part.[44] I had thought that the absence of techniques for ascent in the apocalypses might be taken as further encouragement to read the apocalypses as literature rather than as mystical diaries.

But as we have seen, the absence of techniques of ascent leaves the apocalypses in the mainstream of ancient accounts of ascent. Thus the style of ascent attributed to the pseudepigraphic heroes of the apocalypses reflects the style of ascent the author took as standard based on the expectations of his contemporaries. In other words, I need to make my case for the literary nature of the apocalypses on other grounds.

In conclusion, I would suggest that while techniques for ascent were not unknown, the dominant understanding of ascent in ancient Jewish and Christian literature is of a process initiated not by the visionary but by God. Further, the idea of ascent was so powerful that in some times and places reciting accounts of ascent was believed to offer tangible benefits. Finally, although I have not made the case in any detail here, I believe that the apocalypses show us that simply reading about ascent had a kind of power as well.

NOTES

1. Morton Smith, "Ascent to the Heavens and the Beginning of Christianity," *Eranos-Jahrbuch* 50(1981) 403–29.

2. Ibid., 411.

3. Ibid., 411–15.

4. Ibid., 415.

5. This program is carried forward in Morton Smith's books, *Cement of Alexandria and a Secret Gospel of Mark* (Cambridge, Mass., 1973), and *Jesus the Magician* (San Francisco, 1978).

6. *The "Mithras Liturgy"* (Missoula, Mont., 1976) viii. For the discussion of the Mithras Liturgy below, I follow Meyer's more recent translation in H. D. Betz, ed., *The Greek Magical Papyri in Translation, Including the Demotic Spells* (Chicago, 1986) 48–54.

7. Morton Smith, "Observations on Hekhalot Rabbati," in Alexander Altmann, ed., *Biblical and Other Studies* (Studies and Texts 1; Cambridge, Mass., 1963) 158–60.

8. These are discussed in chap. 3 of my book, *Ascent to Heaven in Jewish and Christian Apocalypses* (New York, 1993).

9. This assumption is widely shared. See, e.g., Rachel Elior in her interesting review of David Halperin's *The Faces of the Chariot: Early Jewish Responses to Ezekiel's Vision* (*Numen* 37[1990] 233–49): "Heavenly ascents are ubiquitous in the literature of late antiquity and magical texts expressing cognate ideas and practices may be found throughout the Greek magical and theurgical literature" (242).

10. "Ascent," 409.

11. This generalization derives from the texts included in Betz, ed., *Magical Papyri,* which includes papyri and demotic material not found in

Preisendanz, *Papyri Graecae Magicae,* and from Robert W. Daniel and Franco Maltomini, *Supplementum Magicum* vol. 1, (Abhandlungen der rheinisch-westfälischen Akademie der Wissenschaften; Papyrologia Coloniensia 16; Opladen, 1990).

12. Smith, "Ascent," 409; Hans Lewy, *Chaldean Oracles and Theurgy: Mysticism, Magic, and Platonism in the Later Roman Empire* (Cairo, 1956) 177–226. Smith's claim for Apollonios of Tyana (409) is also a bit overblown; Apollonios does not claim that the Indians used a technique for ascent, but only that they were able to ascend (Philostratos, *Life of Apollonios* 6.11), and Apollonios accomplishes his ascent at death, when no technique is necessary (8.30).

13. Gershom Scholem, *Major Trends in Jewish Mysticism* (New York, 1941) 49–54.

14. Moshe Idel, *Kabbalah: New Perspectives* (New Haven, 1988) 88–91. Idel cites part of the passage from Smith, "Ascent," quoted above on the availability of techniques for ascent in Jesus' Palestine (89).

15. In the interests of full disclosure I must confess that my article "Heavenly Ascent and the Relationship of the Apocalypses and the *Hekhalot* Literature" (*Hebrew Union College Annual* 59[1988] 73–100) also treats the hekhalot texts as containing instructions for ascent, contrasting this aspect of their genre to the narrative of the apocalypses.

16. Schäfer's groundbreaking publication of manuscripts of the hekhalot texts has made this progress possible: Schäfer in collaboration with Margarete Schlüter and Hans Georg von Mutius, *Synopse zur Hekhalot-Literatur* (Texte und Studien zum antiken Judentum 2; Tübingen, 1981). Schäfer has also published the geniza materials in *Geniza-Fragmente zur Hekhalot-Literatur* (Texte und Studien zum antiken Judentum 6; Tübingen, 1984). Schäfer's essays on the hekhalot literature through 1986 are collected in *Hekhalot-Studien* (Texte und Studien zum antiken Judentum 19; Tübingen, 1988). David J. Halperin's recent book, *The Faces of the Chariot: Early Jewish Responses to Ezekiel's Vision* (Tübingen, 1988), consists in large part of his reading of the hekhalot literature; he has also published a number of articles on the subject.

17. With the exception of the Ozhayah fragment, these hekhalot texts are printed in *Synopse.* The Ozhayah fragment appears in *Geniza-Fragmente.*

18. Himmelfarb, "Heavenly Ascent," 91–96.

19. Carol A. Newsom, *Songs of the Sabbath Sacrifice: A Critical Edition* (Atlanta, 1985) 17–18, 61–72.

20. The correspondence between heavenly liturgy and earthly is made explicit in the *qedushah,* the sanctification that forms part of the public recitation of the *'amidah.* The *qedushah* takes its name from the trishagion of Isa. 6:3. The introductory words of the *qedushah* for most

services run, "Let us sanctify your name in the world as they sanctify it in the exalted heavens."

21. Himmelfarb, "Heavenly Ascent," 95–96.

22. This is Schäfer's observation in "Gershom Scholem Reconsidered: The Aim and Purpose of Early Jewish Mysticism," 12th Sacks Lecture, Oxford, 1986, reprinted in *Hekhalot-Studien*, 277–95. Schäfer's formulation is more cautious. He writes, "As far as I can see, the great majority of these preparatory rites, if not all of them, are connected to the adjuration ritual and not, as Scholem maintained, to the heavenly journey" (284).

23. See the example cited by Schäfer in "Scholem Reconsidered."

24. On these instructions, Himmelfarb, "Heavenly Ascent," 80–91.

25. All parenthetical references to units of the hekhalot literature refer to Schäfer, *Synopse*. The spelling of the names differs from manuscript to manuscript; I follow MS Oxford 1531.

26. I am deeply indebted to Halperin's discussion of the repetition of the mishnah in Hekhalot Zuṭarti in his review of Schäfer's *Synopse*, "A New Edition of the Hekhalot Literature," *JAOS* 104(1984) 549–51.

27. Schäfer, "Scholem Reconsidered," 293–94.

28. Halperin, "New Edition," 550–51, suggests that this passage is the source of Hai Gaon's famous description of the practice required for the journey to the merkavah. If so, Halperin points out, Hai Gaon did not get the passage quite right, for it describes a procedure, not for inducing ecstatic ascent, but for reciting an account of ascent and thus obtaining its benefits.

29. "The Merkavah mystic to whom the Hekhalot literature is addressed does not expect to ascend to heaven in ecstasy and makes no claim to have done so. Rather, by means of magical and theurgic practices he repeats the heavenly journey of his heroes, Moses, Ishmael and Aqiva. This is the point where the heavenly journey and adjuration meet. Like adjuration, the heavenly journey is a ritual, so to speak a liturgical act. The texts are instructions, formulas which can be passed on and repeated as often as desired. In the truest sense of the word, they are the 'Mishnah' of the Merkavah mystics" (Schäfer, "Scholem Reconsidered," 294).

30. I have not included John of Patmos as a third such writer, since Revelation consists of visions rather than a journey through heaven. Still, though his account of the inauguration of his vision does not use the verb *harpazo*, it fits our category, for John is invited into heaven: "After this, I saw, and behold, a door opened in heaven, and the first voice, which I had heard speaking to me like a trumpet, said, "Come up here, and I will show you what must come to pass. At once I was in the spirit, and behold, a throne stood in heaven . . ." (Rev. 4:1–2). The verb *harpazo* does ap-

pear in Rev. 12:5 when the child of the woman clothed with the sun is taken up to heaven. I would like to thank Professor Adela Yarbro Collins for pointing this out to me.

31.   The Codex is now available with German translation and notes in Ludwig Koenen and Claudia Römer, eds. and trans., *Der Kölner Mani-Kodex: Über das Werden seines Leibes* (Abhandlungen der rheinisch-wesfälischen Akademie der Wissenschaften; Papyrologica Coloniensia 14; Opladen, 1988). Parenthetical references are to pages of the Mani Codex.

32.   Most scholars assume that Paul is here speaking of himself. In "Ascent," however, Smith maintains that Paul is referring to Jesus (425–29). I find Smith's position convincing, but my argument does not rely on the identification of the one who ascends in this passage.

33.   Apocalypse of Enosh (53); Apocalypse of Shem (54).

34.   Smith, "Ascent," 414–15; Segal, *Paul the Convert: the Apostolate and Apostasy of Saul the Pharisee* (New Haven, 1990) 36. While Segal makes a compelling case for the importance of traditions associated with Ezekiel's chariot vision for understanding Paul's thought (34–71), he does not confront the absence of such traditions in the ascent of 2 Corinthians, chapter 12. On the lack of relationship between 2 Corinthians, chapter 12, and merkavah tradition, see Schäfer, "New Testament and Hekhalot Literture. The Journey into Heaven in Paul and in Merkavah Mysticism," in *Hekhalot-Studien*. A particularly powerful point in my view is that the revelation in the ascent in 2 Corinthians involves hearing rather than seeing ("New Testament," 238, 247).

35.   Trans. M. A. Knibb, in H. F. D. Sparks, ed., *The Apocryphal Old Testament* (Oxford, 1984).

36.   Dan. 9:3, 10:2–3, 4 Ezra 3:1–3, 5:20 (angelic command in 5:13), 6:35 (angelic command does not mention weeping, 6:31), 9:27 (angelic command does not mention weeping), 9:24–25; and 2 Bar. 6:2, 9:2, 35:1–5.

On the subject of ascetic preparations for visions, Michael E. Stone, "Apocalyptic—Vision or Hallucination?" *Milla wa-Milla* 14(1974) 47–56, especially 55–56.

37.   George W. E. Nickelsburg, "Enoch, Levi, and Peter: Recipients of Revelation in Upper Galilee," *Journal of Biblical Literature* 100(1981) 575–600.

38.   Idel, *Kabbalah*, 76–77. See also Daniel Merkur, "The Visionary Practices of Jewish Apocalyptists," in L. Bryce Boyer and Simon A. Grolnick, eds., *The Psychoanalytic Study of Society* 14 (Hillsdale, N.J., 1989) 125–34.

39.   "Carried off" is *anaphero*.

40.   Compare Rev. 4:1–2.

41.   See Martha Himmelfarb, "From Prophecy to Apocalypse: *The Book of the Watchers* and Tours of Heaven," in Arthur Green, ed., *Jewish Spirituality* vol. 1, *From the Bible through the Middle Ages* (New York, 1986) 149–51.

42.   *Fourth Ezra: A Commentary on the Book of Fourth Ezra*, (Hermeneia; Minneapolis, 1990) 30–33. For other examples of recent works that take seriously the possibility that the apocalypses reflect the experiences of their authors, Merkur, "Visionary Practice"; Christopher Rowland, *The Open Heaven: A Study of Apocalyptic in Judaism and Early Christianity* (New York, 1982) 214–47.

43.   *Fourth Ezra*, 42, 428–31.

44.   I discuss this point in greater detail in my book *Ascent to Heaven*.

CHAPTER 7

Mystical Descents

Guy G. Stroumsa

Ioan Couliano, whose memory we honor, studied in his *Psycha-nodia* the *ascensus* or *anabasis* of the soul after death in various trends in ancient religious thought.[1] I wish to offer here some reflections on the *descensus ad inferos,* or, more precisely perhaps, the idea of *katabasis* in the history of religions in antiquity.

I

Ascent and descent are obviously complementary notions in the vocabulary of religious experience. Both are used, in various literatures of the ancient world, in two essentially different senses. One reads, first, about the descent from the heavens to the earth of a deity or savior who comes in order to reveal himself to mankind and offer salvation to those willing to recognize him or believe in him. This *descensus,* often conceived as being secret (in order to avoid those evil powers that rule the earth), is called "*absconditus.*" After revealing himself, his mission accomplished, the savior can return to the heavens in an *ascensus gloriosus.*[2] In a different pattern, various mythologies of the ancient Near East describe a descent of the god to the underworld.[3] Side by side with the descent and ascent of the savior, we find numerous descriptions, in different cultural and religious contexts, of a descent of the soul to the earth (in order to become incarnated within a body) and of its ascent back to heaven after death. Another pattern, of the soul's descent to the underworld, whether it is called Hades, She'ol, or Amente, is also to be found in various contexts.

Although the two metaphors of descent and ascent (of the soul or of a deity) are clearly related to one another, ascents seem to have elicited more research than have descents.[4] This fact can probably be explained, at least in part, by the much more prominent role of ascent in mystical language. The idea of a mystical descent, in particular, seems to be a rather strange phenomenon, still only partly understood. It is perhaps nowhere illustrated as clearly as in those hieratic Hebrew texts of late antiquity that we have come to call "hekhalot literature" and that represent the first strata of the Jewish mystical tradition. These texts describe the ecstatic experience and mystical visions of the *yordey merkavah*, those who "descend to the Chariot," a reference to the vision of the Chariot in Ezekiel, chapter 1.[5] Despite some new studies, the puzzling metaphor of descent and its original meaning are still defying scholars.[6] I hope to be able to suggest here a way to understand them better.

II

Salmoxis, the mythical Thracian hero cherished by Romanian historians of religion, seems to have been the first person whose *katabasis* was recorded in the annals of history. Herodotus recounts how he descended into an *andreion*, (underground chamber) which he had made, living there for three years (*katabas de katō, es to katagaion oikēma, diaitato ep' etea tria*).[7] Herodotus does not tell us what Salmoxis did or saw during his underground sojourn. But in this *andreion*[8] he instructed the best among his countrymen, telling them "that they should go to a place where they would live for ever and have all good things."[9] It may be noted that the verb used is *anadidaskein,* a rather rare verb that seems to indicate a special kind of teaching, implying perhaps repetition, or memorization of an esoteric content.[10] In any case, the story of Salmoxis clearly retains strong shamanistic elements. As we know, by the seventh century B.C.E. archaic Greek shamanism had already been deeply influenced by Scythian and other traditions.[11]

Pythagoras too, when he came to Crotona, descended into a subterranean dwelling that he had made (*kata gēs oikiskon poiēsai*) according to Diogenes Laertius, who reports a story told by Hernippus. When he finally came up, "withered and looking like a skeleton," he declared to the assembly that "he had been down to Hades, and even read out his experiences to them."[12]

But this is not the only experience of Pythagoras that involves a *katabasis* experience. While in Crete, the philosopher, together with Epimenides, had gone down into the cave of Ida.[13] The fact that Pythagoras would have undergone initiation to the Idean dactyls is not surprising. The Ida cave, indeed, was famous as the place of the oldest attested mystery warrior band and had served as a cult cave since the Minoan times.[14] However, since the character of the cults conducted in the cave was secret, few texts have reached us that tell about what took place there. Porphyry, on his side, describes both the ascetic preparation that Pythagoras underwent prior to his *katabasis* into the cave and the ritual cycle of three times nine days that he spent there, then making offerings to Zeus and finally seeing the god's throne (*etos thronon etheasato*), as it is spread annually with leaves.[15]

The "culmination," if one may mix metaphors, of the *katabasis* in the vision of a divine throne is a significant trait, which should be emphasized here, since a similar vision of the divine throne (the *kisse ha-kavod*) also forms the acme of the vision of the Jewish mystics, the *yordey merkavah*.[16] Visions of the god seated on his throne are found in different religious traditions and might well offer a background in which to see anew the Jewish texts. Already in apocryphal and pseudepigraphic texts such as 1 Enoch or the Testament of Levi, the rapture can end in the vision of God seated on his throne of glory.[17] A central place is reserved to Moses' vision of the divine throne by Ezechiel the Tragedian in his *Exagogē*, a play on the Exodus from Egypt written in Hellenistic Alexandria. Pieter van der Horst has shown that the biblical references in the play can be fully understood only in reference to hekhalot literature, particularly the Hebrew Book of Enoch (3 Enoch).[18] There was no doubt a long Israelite and Jewish tradition of reference to and speculation upon the divine throne. Yet, it would seem illegitimate to study the development of this tradition as if it had remained untouched by the overwhelming presence of similar visions of divine thrones in Greek and other literatures and religions.[19]

III

A whole literature with Orphic tendencies, which developed in the Pythagorean tradition, emphasized Orpheus's *katabasis eis Aidou*.

This *katabasis* is attested since the fifth century in literary works that have been described as "apocalypses avant la lettre."[20] This literature seems to have been one of Virgil's main sources in his classic description of Aeneas's visit to the underworld in Book 6 of the *Aeneid*.[21]

Under the empire, the literary importance of *katabaseis* grew, and they seem to have become particularly fashionable. As is well known, Aeneas's visit to the underworld offers a clear parallel to the *Nekyia,* the evocation of the dead in order to know the future, described in Book 11 of the *Odyssey.* Aeneas checks out the vast cavern on the hilltop protected by Apollo; it is the secret dwelling of the Sibyl. The description of Aeneas's visit includes visions of the god and references to the Sibyl's "secret utterances."

The *Isis Book* in Apuleius's *Metamorphoses* provides another *locus classicus* on the esoteric character of the vision of the gods encountered during the infernal voyage:

> Thou shalt understand that I approached near unto hell, even to the gates of Proserpine, and after that I was ravished throughout all the elements. . . I saw likewise the gods celestial and the gods infernal, before whom I presented myself and worshipped then. Behold now have I told thee, which although thou hast heard, yet it is necessary that thou conceal it [*quamvis audita, ignotes tamen necesse est*].[22]

During the first centuries of the common era, the descent into Hades, which remained a literary *topos* throughout antiquity, became commonly used for descriptions of the good life. In Lucian's parody of the *katabasis* genre, for instance, a text written in the tradition of Menippean satire, the hero goes down to Hades in order to see how one should live, lead by his reluctant guide, the wise wondermaker Mithrobarzanes.[23]

The most famous description, however, of a *katabasis* into the underworld dating from the empire is probably Pausanias's report of the descent into the crypt of Trophonius at Lebadeia.[24] We deal here with a direct testimony, describing in detailed fashion the trance and the terror with which the inquirer of the oracle is seized in the course of his descent. After he has set his mind on the descent, and after various preparations have been made by the priests, he is brought down by a rope and descends into the earth through an artificial hole. "The inquirer at the oracle is led at night into a vaulted chamber from which a whirlwind miraculously carries him through a small aperture above the ground." Walter Burkert, whose summary of Pausanias I quote here, follows Nilsson in believing that the theatrical elaboration, including, perhaps, mechanical elements, is a product of the imperial age.[25] In many places, there seem to have existed "subterranean installations which presented the Underworld in physical form."[26] Such caves (*megara,* sing. *megaron*) or chambers (*adyta,* sing. *adyton*) were places of worship, "into which offertory gifts were lowered."[27]

Another indication of the widespread role of caves in the religious psyche under the empire comes from the Mithraic cult. The Mithraeum is a cave, which mirrors the cosmos, while the killing of the bull represents the "esoteric philosophy" of these mysteries.[28]

"The classical world was full of holy places," we are reminded by Robert Markus.[29] Among these holy places, pagan holy caves held a place of honor. Speaking of the persistence of subterranean pagan piety in late antiquity, Robin Lane Fox mentions Eusebius's report that Constantine sent emissaries into "every pagan temple's recess and every gloomy cave," adding: "Their mission was apt, but impossible. Not even the entire army could have covered each cave of the Nymphs, the many caves which claimed Zeus' birthplace, the underground shrines of Mithras, the caves of Cybele and Attis or the many cavernous entries to Hades. Long after Constantine, the old Cretan caves still drew pagan visitors."[30]

In his *Life of Isidore,* Damascius tells us of a water stream and an abyss attracting pilgrims, both men and women, as late as in the fifth century. The passage has been recently studied in great detail by Michel Tardieu.[31] The stream, identified by Damascius as the Styx, is actually the Yarmuk, and the location of the place described is not far from Bostra. It is not a *katabasion,* but Damascius's choice of words recalls those used to describe katabaseis to caves. He speaks about the "holy fear" felt by the pilgrims during their descent into the abyss and about their offerings to the deity and the sacred oaths they swear.[32]

As a last example of this phenomenon, which was very widespread until late antiquity, I want to mention the text of a Greek magical papyrus. This text, a "charm of Hekate Ereschigal against fear of punishment," was analyzed by H. D. Betz. It contains, as Betz has shown, liturgical spells of a *katabasis* ritual from the mystery cult of the Idean dactyls: "I have been initiated, and I went down into the [underground] chamber of the Dactyls, and I saw the other things down below."[33]

But the shamanistic traits of the earlier *katabaseis* have disappeared here, and the descent into Hekate's realm has been transformed into a metaphor. To summarize the traits encountered in the various *katabasis* texts, we might point out, at least, the following: the descent is the prelude to a vision, it has an esoteric character, and it must be preceded by an ascetic preparation.

IV

It would be a mistake, however, to think that the experience of *katabasis* remained limited to pagan cults and literature. Extrapolating from the mention of the open tombs at the death of Jesus (Matt. 27:52), Christian exegesis developed very early the theme of Jesus' descent into hell between his death and his resurrection. The purpose of Jesus' infernal voyage would have been to teach the saints of the Old Testament, who had not had an opportunity to hear his message on earth. Despite various doubts as to its reality (for instance by Abelard, Erasmus, or Calvin), the *descensus ad inferos* was decreed an article of faith by the Council of Trent.[34]

The motif of Christ's *descensus ad inferos* obviously offers very close similarities to some Gnostic conceptions, and Christ's descent may also be at the root of some major Gnostic conceptions.[35] The motif is found in different domains of early Christian literature, perhaps nowhere as clearly as in the Syriac milieu. We find the theme of the Savior's *descensus* in the Manichaean *Psalms of Thomas,* which are extant only in Coptic but were written in Aramaic, and in the works of the two great writers of the fourth century, Aphrahat and Ephrem.[36] The clearest, and the best known, literary evidence from early Christianity on Christ's *descensus,* however, is the apocryphal Apocalypse of Peter, where Jesus gives an affirmative answer to a question about whether he had preached to the dead (chap. 41). It is to the credit of Albrecht Dieterich that he recognized in his *Nekyia* the connections between this text and the pagan tradition of *katabasis.*[37] Dieterich recognized that the new text, found in the sands of Akhmim, should be read against the background of the esoteric chthonic cults (*chtonische Geheimkulte*) of antiquity, a tradition going back to the time of Eleusis and Delphi, if not earlier, as showed by Aristophanes' testimony in *The Frogs.* For Dieterich, the *Apocalypse of Peter* reflected a Christianized version of "Orphic-Pythagorean Hades books," of a *nekyia* going back to archaic Greece.[38] Dieterich was right in what he saw, but, as Martha Himmelfarb has convincingly argued, he ignored much that could have been of direct relevance to his work. In particular, he turned "a nearly blind eye to Jewish sources, [which might have reflected] an expression of a certain kind of history-of-religions anti-Christian (and Jewish), pro-Greek feeling."[39] According to Himmelfarb, "what Dieterich fails to see is that the various motifs in the Apocalypse of Peter, whatever their origin, have been shaped in consciousness of a Jewish and Christian tradition."[40]

In contradistinction to Dieterich, Isidore Lévi did make the claim of direct literary connections between Jewish texts and Greek traditions. In particular, he pointed out that the *Revelation of Joshua ben Levi* was an apocalypse "derived from Pythagoras' *katabasis*."[41] Lévi's work, however, was marred by various sweeping and dubious statements, and his insights seem to remain ignored by most scholars to this day. Lévi, moreover, would not know the hekhalot literature that has become familiar since Scholem's groundbreaking studies "put them on the map of scholarship," as it were.

V

For Scholem, who was the first in the last generation to devote much thought to hekhalot literature, *yrd* was a puzzling, even paradoxical root in connection to the description of mystical or ecstatic experience finding its acme in heavenly vision. Indeed, the rationale for the use of *yrd* in some of the hekhalot texts remained unknown to him. It must be said that the poor preservation of the texts makes their study extremely difficult and renders any conclusions aleatory. This state of affairs was recently changed for the better, however, thanks to both the Synoptic edition and the concordance of hekhalot literature edited by Peter Schäfer.[42]

New research can now be conducted on philological ground less shaky than before, leading to more secure, or at least less speculative, conclusions. Annelies Kuyt was thus able to publish recently a remarkable article on the term *yarad* and its semantic field in the hekhalot texts.[43] Speculation on the meaning of *yarad* has been rife. It has been suggested that the semantic reference of the verb in Mishnaic Hebrew is "to go in," as much as "to go down."[44] The expression *yarad la-merkava* has also been seen as similar to *yarad lifne ha-teva*, that is, "he came down to the altar" [where the Torah is read in a synagogue].[45] The expression *yorde merkavah* has also been compared to that for those who navigate the sea, *yorde ha-yam*.[46] Yet another explanation, involving reference to theurgic praxis, has been suggested by Ithamar Gruenwald.[47] None of these explanations, however, seems to have been accepted as strong enough to carry conviction.

I propose to recognize the root *yrd*, as it is used in the context of the descent into the *merkavah*, as a linguistic calque of *katabasis*, the widely used term for the descent to the underworld, a theme known since the dawn of Greek civilization and one that had under the Roman Empire lost most of its shamanistic features to become a choice metaphor for the mystical voyage ending in the vision of the divine world and palaces, or even of the divinity itself, usually seated upon its throne of glory. As we have seen in these pages, the idea of a descent into the divine realm was so widespread in antiquity that there is no reason to ignore the possibility that it was used also by Jews in order to describe their own mystical experiences.

It may seem surprising that no one among the students of early Jewish mysticism appears to have thought of studying its vocabulary and praxis in the context of similar or parallel phenomena and spiritual experiences in the ancient world.[48] To be sure, parallels from diverse or even disparate cultural, religious or linguistic backgrounds do not by themselves explain phenomena, and we should be particularly careful when dealing with esoteric traditions, which by their very nature have left us few secure traces. By no means do I want to suggest that the hekhalot texts reflect a religious experience identical, or even similar to, that of the Greek *katabasis* rituals.[49] Yet in seeking to understand the religious praxis of late antique Judaism, there is no reason a priori to ignore patterns of behavior or traditions of belief current in the *Umwelt* in which Judaism flourished.

VI

In late antiquity, both Augustine and Plotinus seem to reflect a major paradigmatic shift, which was transforming the language of mystical expression and its basic metaphors. In antiquity, as we have seen, the search for the secrets of the universe had retained at least some of the basic metaphors stemming from its shamanistic heritage. This search was now forgotten, and the soul's adventure became her attempt to merge with the divinity. The esoteric trends that can still be detected in the earliest strata of Christian thought disappeared after the fourth century, while the vocabulary of the ancient mysteries was in some cases reused to describe the mystical experience.[50] The *unio mystica,* or rather the *way* leading to it, would usually be perceived, from now on, essentially through two different but combined metaphors, one the metaphor of going up, or ascent, and the other that of going inside, or interiorization. Augustine expressed this identification of the two metaphors better than anyone else in a lapidary formula: "*Intus Deus altus est,* the God within is the God above," he writes, thus widely disseminating in the religious mentality of the West a fundamentally Plotinian metaphor about the mystical ascent.[51] In the new thought patterns emerging from this transformation, the earlier metaphor of descent into the underworld retained no clear function, and its *Fortleben* was more literary than religious, directly linked as it was to Virgil's role model in European medieval literature. This influence, up to Dante, cannot be overemphasized.[52] In later religious thought, indeed, the *descensus ad inferos* seems to play a less and less significant role. Was this paradigmatic change initiated by the transformation in attitudes to the cosmos at the time? More precisely, is the demonization of the cosmos, or the more and more strongly perceived negative attitude to this earth, as a place of demons, ruled by the Prince of Evil, responsible for the insistence on the soul's duty to ascend to heaven?[53] Or does the new lack of enthusiasm for the discovery of the secrets of the universe, deemed perverse *curiositas* by Augustine, explain the refusal to investigate the entrails of the earth? And does this refusal stem from the growing conception of Hell as an underground, wicked place? It is impossible to deal with this complex issue here, but it would appear that all these facts did play a role in the transformation that seems to have taken place in late antiquity. It stands to reason to postulate that the same shift of perceptions should be called upon to explain what seems to be a similar shift of vocabulary within the Jewish tradition.

Noting some uncertainty about the use of the descent and of the ascent metaphors to describe the mystical experience in the texts, Gershom Scholem thought that the original term was 'alyia la-merkava (ascent into the charriot) and that for some reason, 'alyia became changed into yerida (descent). According to Scholem, yarad would have replaced 'alah, and the ascent would have been transformed into a descent, later in the development of this literature, around the year 500 C.E. According to him, "in the early literature, the writers always speak of an 'ascent to the Merkabah', a pictorial analogy which has come to seem natural to us."[54] By his own admission, Scholem was unable to account for the reasons for this change. On the basis of her rigorous analysis of the texts, Kuyt, however (who mentions at the outset of her article Scholem's puzzlement about the term yarad), presents a very strong case against Scholem's view of things and shows that yarad, not 'alah, appears to have been the original term describing the outward journey to the merkava in the hekhalot literature.[55] She thus argues for a later transformation of yarad into 'alah. However, she is unable to propose a clear reason for the use of this word.

The above reflections on the use of the descent metaphor in the Jewish mystical literature of late antiquity—as a linguistic calque from katabasis, and on the reasons for its transformation into the ascent metaphor—are offered not as the conclusions of an exhaustive study but mainly as a suggestion for further research.

NOTES

1. I. P. Culianu, *Psychanodia 1: A Survey of the Evidence Concerning the Ascension of the Soul and its Relevance* (Leiden, 1983). This work is based upon Culianu's French thesis, published as *Expériences de l' extase: extase, ascension et récit visionnaire de l'hellénisme au moyen age* (Paris, 1984).

2. This mythical pattern of descent and ascent of the savior stands at the basis of the so-called myth of the *salvator salvandus* cherished by the *Religionsgeschichtliche Schule*. See C. Colpe, *Die religionsgeschichtliche Schule: Darstellung und Kritik ihres Bildes vom gnostischen Erlösermythus* (Göttingen, 1961).

3. For traces of such mythologies in the literature of ancient Israel, see, for instance, A. Cooper, "Psalm 24: 7–10: Mythology and Exegesis," *Journal of Biblical Literature* 102(1983) 37–60.

4. See, for instance, A. F. Segal, "Heavenly Ascent in Hellenistic Judaism, Early Christianity and their Environment," *Aufstieg und Nie-*

dergang der Römischen Welt 2, 23,2. 1333–94. Although Segal speaks about the "mythical structure of *katabasis* and *anabasis*," his study concentrates much more on the latter than on the former. Oddly enough, the article does not refer to the *yordey merkavah*.

For a very rich catalogue of descent experiences in the ancient world, see the bulky work of J. Kroll, *Gott und Hölle: der Mythos von Descensuskampfe* (Studien der Bibliothek Warburg 20; Leipzig/Berlin, 1932). Kroll's extensive research shows that the *descensus* is usually linked to an *ascensus*. See also Ganschinietz, "*katabasis,*" *Pauly Wissowa Real-Encyklopädie* 10. 2, 2359–2449 (1919). See further J. E. Ménard, "Le *descensus ad inferos,*" in *Ex Orbe Religionum: Studia . . . Geo Widengren Oblata* (Leiden, 1972) 296–306. For a folklore approach, see A.-L. Siikala, "Descent into the Underworld," *Encyclopedia of Religion* 4, 300–304. On the shamanistic character of the "ascent of the soul," in ancient literature, see C. Colpe, "Die 'Himmelreise der Seele' as philosophie- und religionsgeschichtliches Problem," in E. Fries, ed., *Festschrift für Joseph Klein zum 70. Geburtstag* (Göttingen, 1967) 85–104.

5. For an introduction to this literature and its problems, see in particular G. Scholem, *Jewish Gnosticism, Merkavah Mysticism and Talmudic Tradition,* 2nd ed. (New York, 1965), and for a clear presentation, I. Gruenwald, *Apocalyptic and Merkavah Mysticism* (Leiden, 1980). The careful philological work of Peter Schäfer and his students has transformed the field. For a presentation of the texts, see P. Schäfer, "Tradition und Redaktion in Hekhalot Literatur," in his *Hekhalot-Studien* (Tübingen 1988) 8–16. In contradistinction to Scholem and other early students of this literature, Schäfer insists on its magical core, rather than on the heavenly vision. See his "The Aim and Purpose of Early Jewish Mysticism," in *Hekhalot-Studien,* 277–95.

6. The most thorough work, with references to previous studies, is A. Kuyt, "Once Again: *yarad* in Hekhalot Literature," *Frankfurter Judaistische Beiträge* 18(1990), 45–69. See now her *The 'Descent' to the Chariot: Towards a Description of the Terminology, Place, Function, and Nature of the Yeridah.*

7. Herodotus 4.95 Cp. F. Hartog, "Salmoxis: Le Pythagore des Gètes ou l'autre de Pythagore," *Annali della Scuola Normale Superiora di Pisa,* Cl. di lett. e fil. 8(1978) 15–42, who gives the basic discussion. On Salmoxis and early Thracian religion, see further M. Eliade, *Zalmoxis, the Vanishing God: Comparative Studies in the Religions and Folklore of Dacia and Eastern Europe* (Chicago, 1972). Eliade points out (p. 24) that Strabo (7.297ff.) does not mention an "underground chamber," but a cave on mount Kaganoion.

8. On this term, see Hartog, "Salmoxis," 26: "En Crète, le terme désigne le local public où se réunissaient les membres des hétairies. . ."

Eliade, *Zalmoxis*, 24, notes that the underground chamber is reminiscent of the rooms in which the ritual banquets of the secret religious societies took place.

9.   Herodotus 4.95; I quote the LCL translation.

10.   Hartog, "Salmoxis," 28, notes that *redoceo, iterum doceo, edoceo*, are given by the *Thesaurus*. Cp. the Hebrew term *mishna*, i.e. *deuterôsis*, "second teaching," which seems to imply also the idea of a 'deeper', i.e. esoteric teaching, not imparted to all, and perhaps also of an oral teaching, learned by heart. These terms and the history of their semantics deserve further study.

11.   This recognition is due especially to the seminal work of K. Meuli. See, for instance, his "Scythica," *Hermes* 70(1935) 121–76, quoted by Culianu, *Psychanodia 1*, 26.

12.   Diogenes Laertius, *Lives of Eminent Philosophers*, II. On the nature of Pythagoras's *katabasis* and its relationship to religious beliefs, see W. Burkert, "Das Proömium des Parmenides und die *katabasis* des Pythagoras," *Phronesis* 14(1969) 1–30. For Burkert, Pythagoras behaved as the hierophant in a Demeter cult of Asia Minor, while the rites emphasize the secret of death and the belief in reincarnation.

13.   Diogenes Laertius, 8.2–3.

14.   W. Burkert, *Greek Religion in the Archaic and Classical Age* (Cambridge, Mass., 1987), 48, 280. On the cultic role of caves in antiquity, see P. Saintyves, "Essai sur les grottes dans les cultes magico-religieux et dans la symbolique primitive," appendix to J. Trabucco, trans., Porphyre, *L'antre des nymphes* (Paris, 1918) 35–262.

15.   Porphyry, *Life of Pythagoras*, 17 (Paris, 1982). For an English translation, see M. Smith and M. Hadas, *Heroes and Gods: Spiritual Biographies in Antiquity* (New York, 1965) 112–13. See further I. Lévi, *La légende de Pythagore de Grèce en Palestine* (Bibliothèque de l'Ecole des Hautes Etudes, 250; Paris, 1927) 28ff.

16.   See for instance D. J. Halperin, *The Faces of the Chariot* (Tübingen, 1988).

17.   See, for instance, 1 Enoch 14; 8–18, T. Levi 2:7. For further O. Schnitz, "*Thronos*," in *Theological Dictionary of the New Testament* 3, 160–167. On these texts and their influence upon the crystallisation of Gnostic mythology, see F. T. Fallon, *The Enthronement of Sabaoth: Jewish Elements in Gnostic Creation Myths* (Nag Hammadi Studies, 10; Leiden, 1978) 39ff.

18.   P. W. van der Horst, "Moses' Throne Vision in Ezechiel the Dramatist," *Journal of Jewish Studies* 34(1983) 21–29, especially 24. See also the commentary of H. Jacobson, *The Exagoge of Ezekiel* (Cambridge, 1983) 89–97.

19. For a rich analysis of *thronosis* in initiation in Greek religion, see A. D. Nock, "A Cabiric Rite," *American Journal of Archaeology* 45(1941) 577–81, reprinted in his *Essays on Religion and the Ancient World*, vol. 1 (Oxford, 1972). For a general background, see A. Hug, "*Thronos*," *Pauly Wissowa Realenzykopädie*, 2d ser., 6 A, 613–18 (1935).

20. R. Turcan, "La catabase orphique du papyrus de Bologne," *Revue de l'Histoire des Religions* 150(1956) 136–72.

21. See P. Boyancé, *La religion de Virgile* (Paris, 1963) 454ff.

22. Apuleius, *Metamorphoses* 9.23, *in finem*. I quote the translation of J. Gwyn Griffiths, *Apuleius of Madauros, the Isis Book (Metamorphoses, Book XI)* (Leiden, 1975) 296–301.

23. Lucian, *Menippus, or the Descent into Hades*, 5–6 (IV, 84–85). The text describes the purifying rites undergone by Menippus. Note that the hero comes back to earth through the sanctuary of Trophonius, in Lebadeia. Before his trip to the underworld, Menippus had undertaken an ascent to heaven, in order to discover the truth about the nature of the universe.

24. Pausanias, *Description of Greece* 9.39.

25. Burkert, *Greek Religion*, 115 and notes 46–47. See Burkert, *Lore and Science in Ancient Pythagoreism* (Cambridge, Mass., 1972) 154, which refers to M. P. Nilsson, *Geschichte der griechischen Religion*, vol. 2 (3rd ed.; Handbuch der Altertumswissenschaft; Munich, 1967) 450. See also Plutarch, *De Genio Socratis (Moralia 7)* 589F–593A, where Timarchus is said to have descended into the crypt of Trophonius, where he remained underground for two nights and a day in order to know the nature of Socrates' sign. On Plutarch's knowledge of Orphic *katabaseis*, see Y. Vernière, *Symboles et mythes dans la pensée de Plutarque: essai d'interprétation religieuse des Moralia* (Paris, 1977), especially 286. On p. 289, Vernière refers to the testimony of Clearchus's *Peri Hupnon*, according to which Aristotle would have been taught the new doctine of the other world by a Jewish sage. But she reads in Josephus, *Contra Apionem* 1.22 more than the text allows: Josephus does not quote enough for us to know what the Jewish sage told Aristotle. She also points out that Clearchus is the first author to give a clear ascentional character to the infernal journey.

On Plutarch's initiatic experience, see Y. Vernière, "Initiation et eschatologie chez Plutarque," in J. Ries and H. Limet, eds., *Les rites d' initiation* (Louvain-la-Neuve, 1986) 335–52.

26. Burkert, *Lore and Science*, 155.

27. On *megara*, see P. Chantraine, *Dictionnaire étymologique de la langue grecque*, s.v. "megaron." Chantraine points out that the word may

well be a loan word from a semitic origin, referring to Hebrew *me'ara*, "cave." See also Liddell, Scott, and Jones, *Greek-English Lexicon*, s.v. "megaron."

28.   See Walter Burkert, *Ancient Mystery Cults* (Harvard, 1987) 83–84.

29.   Markus, *The End of Ancient Christianity* (Cambridge, 1991) 139.

30.   R. Lane Fox, *Pagans and Christians* (Harmondsworth, 1986) 673. The text of Eusebius is *Vita Constantini* 3.57.4. For other examples of cultic caves under the empire, see also D. E. Aune, *Prophecy in Early Christianity and the Ancient Mediterranean World* (Grand Rapids, Mich., 1983) 25–30.

31.   M. Tardieu, *Paysages reliques: Routes et haltes syriennes d'Isidore à Simplicius* (Louvain/Paris, 1990) 45–69.

32.   *Damascius, Vita Isidori Reliquiae,* Cl. Zintzen, ed., (Hildesheim, 1967) no. 199, 272–74. A reference was made to this text already by Ganschinietz in his thorough entry on *katabasis* in PW, 2.2, 2379–80.

33.   Translation in H. D. Betz, ed., *The Greek Magical Papyri in Translation, Including the Demotic Spells* (Chicago, 1986) 297–98. Cf. Betz's study of this text, "Fragments from a Catabasis Ritual in a Greek Magical Papyrus," *History of Religions* 19(1980) 287–95. Cf. my review of I. Gruenwald, *Apocalyptic and Merkavah Mysticism* in *Numen* 29 (1981) 107–9, where I refer to this text and suggest in a nutshell the argument developed here.

34.   See, for instance, "Descente de Jésus aux Enfers," *Dictionnaire de Théologie Catholique,* vol. 4, 565ff. The importance of the conception in early Christianity is emphasized by O. Rousseau, "La descente aux Enfers, fondement sotériologique du baptême chrétien," *Recherches de Sciences Religieuses* 40(1952) 273–97. See also O. Michel, "Der aufsteigende und herabsteigende Gesandte," in W. Weinrich, ed., *The New Testament Age: Essays in Honor of Bo Reicke* (Macon, Ga., 1984) 335–336. See further W. Bieder, *Die Vorstellung von der Höllenfahrt Jesu Christi* (Zurich, 1949), *non vidi.* For the early Christian tradition and the polemics with Gnostic conceptions, see A. Orbe, S. J., "El 'Descensus ad inferos' y san Ireneo," *Gregorianum* 68(1987) 485–522. C. H. Talbert, "The Myth of a Descending-Ascending Redeemer in Mediterranean Antiquity," *New Testament Studies* 22(1976) 418–39, argues that "the early Christian myth of a descending-ascending redeemer was taken over from Hellenistic Judaism."

35.   See for instance M. Peel, "The 'descensus ad inferos' in the *Teachings of Silvanus* (CG 7, 4)," *Numen* 26(1979) 23–49.

36.   References to texts and studies in *Der Kleine Pauly,* s.v. "katabasis."

37. A. Dieterich, *Nekyia: Beiträge zur Erklärung der neuent-deckten Petrusapokalypse* (Leipzig, 1893).

38. See M. Himmelfarb, *Tours of Hell: An Apocalyptic Form in Jewish and Christian Literature* (Philadelphia, 1983) 41.

39. Ibid., 44, n. 13.

40. Ibid., 67.

41. I. Lévi, *La légende de Pythagore*, 8. The *Revelation of Joshua ben Levi* was published by Jellineck, *Beit Ha-Midrash*, 2.48–51. In the Hebrew text, the hero looks for "hell and its treasures."

42. P. Schaefer, ed., *Synpose der Hekhalot-Literatur* (Tübingen, 1981); P. Schaefer et al., eds., *Konkordanz zur Hekhalot-Literatur*, 2 vols. (Tübingen, 1986, 1988).

43. A. Kuyt, "Once Again: *yarad* in Hekhalot Literature." On n. 9, Kuyt points out that the results of the article reflect her research toward her doctoral dissertation on the subject.

44. See for instance the expression *yarad le-gano*, "he came into his garden." The argument here seems somewhat weak, since it is of course difficult to know for sure that the going into one's garden did not imply an act of descent.

45. In ancient synagogues, the altar might well have been lower than the ground, instead of being elevated above it, as it is usually today. This has been proposed by Scholem.

46. D. J. Halperin, *The Faces of the Chariot: Early Jewish Responses to Ezekiel's Vision* (Tübingen, 1988) 226–27.

47. This understanding, reading *yarad* as a *hiph'il*, interprets the expression as a magic practice of the bringing down of the [divine] name. See Gruenwald, *Apocalyptic and Merkavah Mysticism*, 142ff. This suggestion is accepted by Rahel Elior in her edition of Hekhalot Zuṭarti, 60, comment on line 6. These references are provided by Kuyt, 64 and n. 132. On the occasion of my preliminary presentation of these findings at a seminar on magical texts led by Hans Dieter Betz at the Hebrew University of Jerusalem in December, 1990, my colleague Shaul Shaked suggested linking *yordey merkava* to the Hebrew expression for sailors: *yordei yam*, refering to Arabic *markab*, "ship" (cf. n. 46 above). The journey of the soul to the underworld was indeed perceived to have taken place in a ship in various ancient cultures. In Egypt, for instance, the soul goes on a journey in a vessel after death. One should also in this context refer to the vessel, or *okhèma* of the soul, through which it goes down from heaven at birth, and up again after the death of the body, in Neo-platonism; see E. R. Dodds, *The Greeks and the Irrational* (Berkeley, 1951) appendix 2; see further H. Lewy, *Chaldaean Oracles and Theurgy* (2nd ed., M. Tardieu; Paris, 1981).

48. A recent monograph on Hekhalot literature, M. D. Swartz,

Mystical Prayer in Ancient Judaism: an Analysis of the Ma'aseh Merkavah (Tübingen, 1992), has remarkably little to say about the term: "The term *yrd*, 'to descend,' is often employed in *Hekhalot Rabbati* and other texts to refer to the mystical journey" (84).

49. For a caveat on the use and misuse of thematic parallels in the study of merkavah literature, see P. Schäfer, "Einleitung," *Hekhalot-Studien* (Tübingen, 1988) 1–7.

50. On esoteric trends in early Christianity, see G. G. Stroumsa, *Savoir et salut: Traditions juives et tentations dualistes dans le christianisme ancien* (Paris, 1992) 127–43.

51. Augustine, *Homiliae in Psalmos* 130.12 (PL 37, 1712), quoted by Bernard McGinn, *The Foundations of Mysticism* (New York, 1991) 242. McGinn mentions (205) that Ambrose was the first Latin Christian writer to make the mystical paradigm of ascension available in the West, through his adaptation of Origenist and Plotinian mysticism. The equivalence of the two metaphors was well analyzed by P. Henry in his introduction to a new publication of MacKenna's classic translation of Plotinus's *Enneads*.

52. On the whole tradition, deemed by Cumont "littérature hallucinante" in *Lux perpetua* (Parix 1949) 245, see Dieterich, *Nekyia* (1894), and especially H. Diels, "*Himmel und Höllen Fahrten von Homer bis Dante*," *Neues Jahrbuch für klassische Altertum* (1932) 246–53.

53. See Culianu, *Psychanodia 2*, 22, which highlights the importance of Kroll's research in his *Gott und Hölle* on the new demonization of the universe in the early centuries of the common era, and its influence on the *katabasis* patterns.

54. G. Scholem, *Major Trends in Jewish Mysticism*, 3rd ed. (New York, 1961) 46–47. No discussion of the "descent to the Chariot" is found in N. Janowitz, *The Poetics of Ascent: Theories of Language in a Rabbinic Text* (Albany, 1989).

55. See Kuyt's conclusions, "Once again: *yarad* in Hekhalot Literature," 67–69.

CHAPTER 8

The Crown of Immortality: Toward a Redescription of Christian Martyrdom

Arthur J. Droge

On March 7, 203 c.e., a small group of North African Christians, victims of the persecution of Septimius Severus, were led into the amphitheater at Carthage to fight with wild beasts. Among them were Vibia Perpetua, twenty-two years of age, newly married and the mother of an infant son, Perpetua's slave girl Felicitas, two young men named Saturninus and Secundulus, a Christian slave named Revocatus, and a young catechumen named Saturus. Their deaths have been recorded in the famous *Acts of Perpetua and Felicitas,* written by an anonymous Christian of North Africa (perhaps Tertullian), allegedly from the martyrs' own words as recorded in the diaries that they kept in prison.[1]

This text is remarkable for many reasons, not the least of which is its vivid depiction of how some early Christians chose death rather than compromise their religious convictions. Despite the leniency and pleas of the Roman governor, Hilarianus, Perpetua remained unmoved. "Have pity on your father's grey head," the proconsul exhorted her, "have pity on your infant son. Offer the sacrifice for the welfare of the emperors" (6.3). Perpetua refused: "*Non facio.*" "Are you a Christian?" asked the governor. "*Christiana sum,*" was her reply (6.4). Whereupon Hilarianus passed judgment on all of them: they were condemned to the beasts as part of the games to be held in honor of the birthday of Geta, the emperor's younger son (6.6; cf. 7.9; 16.3).

We do not know how these Christians came to the attention of the Roman governor, whether they were hunted down as criminals or whether, like Jesus and so many other martyrs, they deliberately baited the authorities to arrest them. From the *Roman* point of view this was not a persecution; it was the *prosecution* of individuals deemed to be a threat to the state. But for Perpetua and her circle, this episode was a religious act par excellence. The night before she was to face the beasts Perpetua had a vision in which she realized "that it was not with wild animals that I would fight but with the Devil, but I knew that I would win the victory" (10.14). Victory, for Perpetua, signified immortality: death meant entry into life.

Saturus, too, had a vision. "We had died and put off the flesh, and we began to be carried toward the east by four angels. . . And when we were free of the world, we first saw an intense light. And I said to Perpetua (for she was at my side): "'This is what the Lord promised us'" (11.2–4). The angels brought them first to a luscious garden, where they were greeted by their fellow martyrs, and then before the throne of God himself (11.5–12.6). Saturus's vision concludes with an exultant Perpetua declaring, "Thanks be to God because I am happier here now than I was in the flesh" (12.7). So resolute were these martyrs that, in the words of the narrator, when "the day of their victory dawned, they marched from the prison to the amphitheater joyfully as though they were going to heaven with calm faces, trembling, if at all, with joy rather than fear" (18.1).

Throughout the *Acts* emphasis is placed on the *voluntary* nature of the martyrs' impending deaths. "We came to this of our *own free will*," Perpetua declared, "that our *freedom* should not be violated" (18.5). Even after being knocked down in the amphitheater by a "mad heifer," Perpetua modestly adjusted her tunic to cover her thighs, and then asked for a pin to fasten her hair, "for it [is] not right that a martyr should die with her hair in disorder, lest she seem to be mourning in her hour of triumph" (20.3–5). When the hostile crowd of onlookers demanded that the victims be brought out into the open, in order to witness their throats being slashed by the gladiator, "the martyrs got up and went to the spot *of their own accord . . .* , and kissing one another sealed their witness [*martyrium*] with the ritual kiss of peace" (21.7).

In the *Acts* there is not the slightest hint that these condemned Christians felt compelled in any way by their executioners. On the contrary, they embraced death willingly and in a manner that must have struck the Roman authorities, to say nothing of the modern reader, as utterly reckless. Lucian, an educated pagan of the second century, expressed what must have been a typical Greek and Roman attitude when he wrote of the Christians: "The poor wretches have convinced themselves, first and foremost, that they are going to be immortal and live forever, in consequence of which they despise death and even *willingly* give themselves over to arrest."[2]

Despite its condescending and condemnatory tone, Lucian's comment finds its mark, and, indeed, is confirmed by the account of Perpetua's own death.

> The others took the sword in silence and without moving, especially Saturus, who being the first to climb the stairway was the first to die. . . Perpetua, however, had yet to taste more pain. She screamed as she was struck on the bone; then she took the hand of the young gladiator and guided it to her throat. It was as though so great a woman, feared as she was by the unclean spirit, *could not be killed unless she herself was willing.* (21.8–10)

I want to use the *Acts of Perpetua and Felicitas* to reconsider the conventional understanding of Christian martyrdom, and I have chosen to begin with this particular account, not just because it has been called "the archetype of all later Acts of the Christian martyrs,"[3] but because it illustrates the ambiguity and complexity of the phenomenon of self-killing, whether understood positively as martyrdom or negatively as suicide.

In pursuit of this goal I shall argue four points, though not all with the same vigor: (1) early Christian fascination with martyrdom was inversely proportional to reality (that is, far more Christians committed apostasy than were executed for their religions convictions; and of those who were executed, it seems that a majority asked for it, or "volunteered"); (2) the early Christian martyr was more a literary creation and character than a historical figure; (3) however much Christian ideologies of martyrdom were informed by a dualistic (or utopian) cosmology, their power derived as much from a literary tradition with its roots in the Gospels' representations of the death of the Christ and, to a lesser extent, in Plato's depiction of the death of Socrates; and (4) Christians before Augustine failed to develop terminology and criteria for distinguishing between martyrdom and suicide.

The modern study of "martyrdom" either ignores or finds

problematic the many instances in which early Christians are said to have *volunteered* for martyrdom; that is, acted in a deliberately provocative way in order to be arrested and officially executed. Indeed, some of the more extreme cases in antiquity so strain the limits of the category, "martyrdom," that they have even been described, and condemned, by scholars as "suicidal." When does a martyr become a suicide? The standard answer states that, with few exceptions, only "heretics" sought out martyrdom, while the "orthodox," sensibly enough, condemned this kind of strident behavior. Insofar as suicide has been condemned in the West as an unpardonable sin and a crime punishable, paradoxically, by death, it is not so surprising that voluntary martyrdom has posed a problem for the historian of early Christianity.

Another look at the evidence, however, indicates the problem is more complex than the conventional understanding of martyrdom would suggest. The evidence that has survived reveals that "heretics" were not the only Christians who were portrayed as having given themselves up voluntarily. At Pergamum, on the coast of Asia Minor, two Christians named Carpus and Papylus stood trial before the Roman governor for refusing to offer sacrifices to the gods.[4] Their behavior was deliberately provocative, despite the efforts of the governor to persuade them to save their lives. "Sacrifice to the gods,' the proconsul exhorted them, 'and do not play the fool.' Carpus, with a gentle smile, said, 'May the gods be destroyed who have not made heaven and earth'" (9–10). The proconsul thereupon ordered Carpus and Papylus to be hung up and scraped with claws (23, 35). When the governor became annoyed at their extraordinary endurance, he finally ordered them to be burned alive. Although Carpus and Papylus had suffered much, they both "ran to the amphitheater that they might all the more quickly depart from the world" (36). A common motif in this and other *Acts* is that although their tortures were gruesome, the martyrs did not suffer, enjoying "anesthesia" and an "analgesic state."[5]

Papylus was nailed to the stake, and after the fire was brought near "he prayed in peace and gave up his soul" (*paredoken ten psychen*, 37). Like Jesus in the Gospel of John (19:30), Papylus died voluntarily and without pain. As Carpus was nailed down he laughed at the bystanders. When they asked why, Carpus mocked them and replied, "I saw the glory of the Lord and I rejoiced," then, uttering a prayer, he too "gave up his soul" (38–41). A woman named Agathonike, one of the onlookers, "saw the glory of the Lord, as Carpus said he had seen it. *Realizing that this was a call from heaven, . . .* she threw herself joyfully upon the stake. . . . And thus she gave up her spirit and died together with the saints" (42–47).

The death of Agathonike is especially worthy of note. On the basis of what the text says (or fails to say), it appears that Agathonike was not even a Christian but a pagan onlooker who was sparked off by the sight of Carpus's death.[6] Her voluntary act of self-destruction was spontaneous, yet well judged and ennobling: "She gave up her spirit and died together with the saints" (47).[7] We encounter a similar perspective on self-killing in Jewish tradition. There voluntary death could be seen as an act of sincere contrition and simultaneous transformation, enabling the individual (whether Jew *or* pagan) to atone for his sins and to attain eternal life.[8] But the most striking feature of Agathonike's death was her recognition of the "divine signal." Having seen the glory of the Lord, she realized that "this was a call from heaven" (42) and so threw herself into the fire. The echo of Plato's *Phaedo* is still being heard six centuries later. Agathonike is a Socrates gone mad.[9]

The analogy with Socrates is one that the Christians themselves were quick to notice. Justin, for example, compared Christians with Socrates, who "was accused of the very same crimes as ourselves."[10] Even so, Justin points out, "no one believed in Socrates so as to die for [his] doctrine, but in Christ . . . not only philosophers and scholars believed, but also artisans and people entirely uneducated, despising glory and fear and death."[11]

In the fourth century John Chrysostom argued that the Christian martyrs were far superior to Socrates, saying that in the first place, he could list "ten thousand" Christian martyrs for every Socrates the pagans could find and, in the second place, Socrates had no choice but to accept death, whereas the martyrs went to their deaths *willingly.*

> For not against their will did the martyrs endure, but of their will, and being free not to suffer. . . . This you see is no great wonder: that he whom I was mentioning drank hemlock; it being no longer in his power not to drink, and also when he had arrived at a very great age. . . . But show me someone enduring torments for godliness' sake, as I show you ten thousand every-

where in the world. Who, while his nails were being torn out, nobly endured? Who, while his joints were being wrenched asunder? Who, while his body was being cut in pieces, member by member? Who, while his bones were being forced out by levers? Who, while being placed on frying-pans without relief? Who, when thrown into a caldron? Show me these instances. For to die by hemlock is like falling asleep, even more pleasant than sleep. . . . But if certain of them did endure torments, yet of these too the praise amounts to nothing. For on some disgraceful occasion they perished: some for revealing mysteries; some for wishing to rule; others detected in the foulest crimes; still others did away with themselves rashly, fruitlessly, and foolishly, there being no reason for it. But not so with us. Of their acts, therefore, nothing is said, but our deeds flourish and increase daily.[12]

Christian martyrs are not only numerically superior to pagan martyrs (indeed, ten thousand to one!) but also nobler, more courageous, and above all *volunteers*.[13]

Were Christians really prepared to die in the manner and numbers Chrysostom claimed? Could it be that the importance placed on martyrdom by Chrysostom, the authors of the *Acts,* and those who avidly read these gory accounts was inversely proportional to their own chances of suffering martyrdom? In all probability, only a very small percentage of Christians actually died as martyrs. The counterpart to voluntary martyrdom was "voluntary apostasy," and the latter seems to have been far more common than the former. Cyprian tells us that during the Decian persecution (250) many of the Christians of Carthage "did not even wait to be arrested . . . or interrogated before they made their denial. . . . They ran to the market-place of their own accord, they hastened to death of their own will."[14] Note the reversal: to live as an apostate is to die; to die as a martyr is to live.

Martyrdom was believed to bring with it special privileges, above all the assurance of immediate salvation. "The martyrs bypassed the long delays, the intervals of cooling and refreshment, the minor corrections and discipline, the years of waiting in Abraham's bosom. They sped straight to Christ and his Father."[15] Martyrdom was a shortcut to immortality: *autoapotheosis.*

In addition to conferring immortality, martyrdom brought great publicity. The strident behavior of Christians like Carpus and Papylus made a noticeable impression on their pagan contemporaries. Agathonike was so moved by the "injustice" of their treatment and the miraculous spectacle of their execution that she was motivated to imitate them, and in doing so was converted. Justin too owed his conversion to the martyrdoms of Christians who were "fearless of death."[16] This is no doubt what Tertullian meant when he wrote to the governors of the empire, "Nothing whatever is accomplished by your cruelties, each more exquisite than the last. It is the bait that wins men for our school. We multiply whenever we are mown down by you; the blood of Christians is seed."[17]

It is a constant refrain of historians of early Christianity that voluntary martyrdom was condemned by the "orthodox." Even G. E. M. de Ste. Croix has fallen prey to such a view. In his important essays on the persecutions, de Ste. Croix correctly stresses the significance and prevalence of voluntary martyrdom. He argues persuasively that voluntary martyrdom was a factor that contributed to the outbreak of persecution and tended to intensify it when already in being. Nevertheless, de Ste. Croix maintains that "the heads of the churches, sensibly enough, forbade voluntary martyrdom again and again, and were inclined to refuse to these zealots the very name of martyr."[18] He states categorically that "voluntary martyrdom was officially condemned by the orthodox."[19] De Ste. Croix claims that there are references to the condemnation of voluntary martyrdom in "a dozen different sources," but he cites only six.[20] Whichever figure is correct, the overwhelming evidence supports the opposite conclusion: voluntary martyrdom was a widespread phenomenon, at least in fiction if not in fact. From the second century on, voluntary martyrdom was practiced and idealized by both "orthodox" and "heretic" alike, in the East as well as in the West. It is true that we find occasional references condemning voluntary martyrdom, mostly from those who fled in times of persecution, but there was no official, universally recognized judgment on the matter. Nor were the criteria on which these occasional objections were based clearly articulated.

Voluntary martyrdom was believed to be a *necessary* reenactment or imitation of the death of Christ. Like Christ, the Christian martyrs were victims—albeit in appearance—of a sinister alliance between pagans and Jews, orchestrated by Satan. But appearances could be deceiving, at least so the early Christians argued. The

Gospels revealed that Christ had not been executed as a criminal; rather, he went to his death of his own accord.[21] The pagans and Jews—even Satan—were little more than unwitting accomplices in his death. The same interpretation was applied the deaths of Christ's followers, as can be seen in the *Martyrdom of Pionius,* bishop of Smyrna, in about the year 250. "What these people [the Jews] forget," Pionius told his comrades in prison, "is that this 'criminal' [Christ] departed from life at his own choice" [*ho idia proairesei exagon heauton tou biou*].[22] "Thus," Pionius declared, "in obedience to my Teacher I choose to die" [*apothneskein hairoumai*].[23] Death was not forced on Pionius. Like Christ, he *chose* it. Refusing the appeals of the Roman authorities, Pionius said, "Light the fire and we shall climb upon it of our own accord."[24] "Many others have offered sacrifice," the proconsul objected, "and they are now alive and of sound mind. Why do you rush toward death?" "I am not rushing toward death," Pionius answered, "but towards life."[25] For Pionius, the categories of life and death had been turned inside out.

Sometimes Christians would go to their deaths either to provoke others to do the same, or to prevent others from committing apostasy. On their way to execution in c. 257, Agapius and Secundius, two North African bishops, stopped to exhort their fellow Christians to follow their example. "It was not enough," the narrator says, "that they were to devote their own precious blood to glorious martyrdom; they wished to make others martyrs by the inspiration of their own faith."[26] Before the sword struck their comrade Marianus he prophesied revenge on the pagans. His words, the narrator says, "sounded a trumpet call, as it were, to arouse his brethren to emulate his courage, so that in the midst of these temporal plagues the saints of God might grasp at the opportunity for a death that was precious and holy."[27] Marianus and his fellow martyr James believed, like Socrates in the *Phaedo,* that they had received the divine signal to depart. In the words of the narrator, they "*possessed the signs* they had always desired, the the divine choice had fallen on them. . . . They recognized that their footsteps had been guided by the providence of Christ to the very spot where they would receive their crowns."[28] Marianus and James are examples of those who responded to the call, and in doing so they became signals to many others who were provoked by the sight of Christians being tried, tortured, or executed.[29]

From the period of the Great Persecution (303–312/13) Eusebius preserves numerous accounts of individuals in Palestine either "volunteering" for martyrdom or killing themselves outright. The information Eusebius offers is geographically specific, and his statistics do not provide a reliable index of the numbers of Christians who died for their religion. But the evidence, such as it is, suggests that very few Christians were *sought out* by the Roman authorities. As de Ste. Croix has shown, "nearly twice as many (if not more) were volunteers."[30]

One famous "volunteer" was Euplus. On April 29, 304, he stood outside the governor's chamber in the city of Catania, Sicily, and shouted, "I want to die; I am a Christian." Calvisianus, the governor, replied, "Come in, whoever it was who shouted out." Euplus entered the council chamber, carrying copies of the forbidden Gospels. Following an interrogation, Euplus was tortured and executed. "So it was," the narrator of his martyrdom says, "that the blessed Euplus received the unfading crown."[31]

In the following year Eusebius describes how a rumor spread that Christians would be thrown to the beasts as part of a festival at Caesarea. While the Roman governor was en route to the amphitheater, he was met by six Christians, young men, who demanded to be thrown to the beasts with their comrades. The governor and his entourage were overcome by astonishment at their request. The six men were arrested, but they were not thrown to the beasts as they had requested: the governor had them beheaded.[32]

In the Thebaid in Upper Egypt, Eusebius says he was an eyewitness to the execution of "many" Christians "in a single day." His description goes into great and gory detail, but it reveals that most of the martyrs were volunteers. "It was then that we observed a most marvelous eagerness and a truly divine power and zeal in those who had placed their faith in the Christ of God. For as soon as sentence was pronounced against the first one, some from one quarter and others from another would leap up to the tribunal before the judge and confess themselves Christians, . . . receiving with joy and laughter and gladness the final sentence of death."[33] Far from condemning such behavior, Eusebius praises these "volunteers" for their courage and endurance.

Admittedly, some Christian leaders disapproved of such conduct. Clement of Alexandria, for example, criticized those Christians whose fascination with voluntary martyrdom led to theatrical displays.

> We blame those who have rushed on death, for there are some who are really not ours but share only the name, who are eager to hand themselves over in hatred against the creator, athletes of death. We say that these men take themselves out without witness [*exagein heautous amartyros*], even if they are officially executed. For they do not preserve the characteristic mark of faithful witness, because they do not know the real God, but give themselves up to a futile death, as the Gymnosophists of the Indians to useless fire.[34]

There is much more to Clement's evaluation of martyrdom than this passage indicates and space allows. It is sufficient to note that his distinction between two forms of self-killing—literally, "witness" and "without witness"—is polemical. Clement was condemning the actions of men he considered heretics: "those who are really not ours but share only the name." Heretics, by definition, cannot believe or act in an acceptable manner, or, in Clement's terms, as the "true Gnostic" believes and acts. Depending on the perspective or commitment of the critic, the act of self-killing could be evaluated positively, as an authentic witness, or negatively, as a vain death—or worse, as the equivalent of self-murder. Like Augustine two centuries later, Clement would not allow the "heretics" to appeal to their martyrs as justification for the authenticity of their beliefs.

Clement's denunciation of voluntary martyrdom was by no means universally recognized, and his call for restraint seems to have gone unheeded. In addition to individuals who volunteered for martyrdom, Eusebius reports a number of instances of Christians who deliberately killed themselves. At Alexandria a year before the Decian persecution, an angry mob assaulted an elderly woman named Apollonia, threatening to burn her alive if she did not recite with them their "blasphemous sayings" (*ta tes asebeias kerygmata*). According to Eusebius, Apollonia asked for some time to think it over, and "as soon as she was left alone she eagerly threw herself into the fire and was consumed."[35] Describing the persecution of Diocletian in Nicodemia, Eusebius reports that "men and women leaped upon the pyre with a divine and unspeakable fervor." Far from condemning these Christians, Eusebius calls them "martyrs" and says that "they were perfected by fire."[36]

At Antioch, also during the Great Persecution, Eusebius tells of a woman and her two daughters who opted for "flight to the Lord" rather than be raped by their captors.

> She exhorted both herself and her daughters that they ought not to submit to listen to even the least whisper of such a thing, and said that to surrender their souls to the slavery of demons was worse than all kinds of death and every form of destruction. So she submitted that to flee to the Lord was the only way of escape from it all. And when they had both agreed to her opinion, and had arranged their garments suitably around them, on coming to the middle of their journey they quietly requested the guards for a little time for retirement, and threw themselves into the river that flowed by. Thus they became their own executioners.[37]

We cannot be certain that the stories Eusebius and other Christian writers relate are historical. The accounts of the death of Perpetua, Carpus, Agathonike, and the other Christian martyrs are probably no more or less historical than Plato's description of the death of Socrates, Cicero's account of the death of Cato, or even the Johannine version of the death of Jesus. That some early Christians died for their beliefs cannot be disputed. Nor can it be denied that some gave themselves up voluntarily. But in the first three centuries only a very small percentage of Christians were executed for their religion. The evidence indicates that far more chose flight or committed apostasy. Nonetheless, the ideal of martyrdom enjoyed an importance that belied the relatively insignificant number of actual martyrs. Of interest to us, therefore, is not so much what the early Christians did as how their actions were described, imagined, and evaluated by their fellow Christians and contemporaries.

The martyrs are portrayed as going to their death in one of three ways: as a result of being sought out, by deliberately volunteering to die, or by actually taking their own lives. On the basis of the evidence that has survived, it would appear that the majority of Christian martyrs chose death by the second and third means. But even in those cases where individuals "waited" for the persecutors to arrest them, the emphasis is placed on their willingness to embrace death. Like Jesus, they went to execution "of their own accord."

Behind every description of martyrdom lay the example of Jesus. Martyrdom was believed by many to be a necessary reenactment of his death and to hold out the prospects of a similar reward: "the crown of immortality." The authors of the Gospels described the death of Jesus as divinely ordained. He went to death in willing obedience to God. Those who preserved and revered the memory of the martyrs explained their deaths in the same way. Both the martyrs themselves and even some of their critics emphasized the importance and necessity of a divine signal or command. Only when such a sign had been given could martyrdom be justified. Plato had said much the same thing about the death of Socrates, and it is tempting to think that the early Christians were familiar enough with the Socratic tradition on voluntary death to apply it to their martyrs. With a few authors—Clement, for example—we can establish a direct link with the *Phaedo,* but not in most cases. It may be, as Rudolf Hirzel has suggested, that the early Christians arrived at the same conclusion independently.[38] In any case, the problem of voluntary death was evaluated by Christians in terms similar to those used by Plato.

As important as the requirement of a divine sign was thought to be, it did not solve the problems of definition and evaluation. To state it in Foucaultian terms: the early Christians failed to "problematize" voluntary death, despite considerable debate and polemical squabbling. They recognized an ambiguity in the act of self-killing and attempted to force a distinction between "martyrdom" and "self-murder," but they never developed a language of problematics or criteria of evaluation. There was no agreed-upon definition of what constituted *martyria* (witness), nor was there a pejorative term (like *suicide*) to denote its negative counterpart. A further complication was the appeal to the divine sign. How was the "sign" to be recognized, and what was the criterion to determine that it was "divine"? Insofar as these questions were left unanswered, the debate about voluntary death never went beyond polemic to problematization.

The condemnation of voluntary martyrdom was a factor of self-definition and self-justification. Clement denounced the heretics of his day as having killed themselves "without witness" (*amartyros*). Clement's judgment was not a description of self-killing; it was an evaluation of the act, an expression of self-definition vis-à-vis the proximate other: those who falsely claimed the name "Christian." Heretics qua heretics could not be authentic martyrs.

That was a title reserved only for Clement's "Gnostic." Once the categories of "orthodoxy" and "heresy" are removed, however, it becomes impossible to distinguish between authentic and inauthentic "witness"—between, if you will, "martyrdom" and "suicide." And that problem is still with us.

NOTES

1. The precise day and year of the martyrdoms have been disputed. For convenience I have given the traditionally accepted date. On this, see T. D. Barnes, "Pre-Decian *Acta Martyrum*," *Journal of Theological Studies* 19(1968) 522–23. For the Latin text and English translation of this and other acts, I have followed H. Musurillo, *The Acts of the Christian Martyrs* (Oxford Early Christian Texts; Oxford, 1972).

2. Lucian, *The Death of Peregrinus* 13.

3. Musurillo, *Acts of the Christian Martyrs* xxv.

4. *The Martyrdom of Carpus, Papylus, and Agathonike* survives in Greek and Latin recensions. I cite from the Greek recension. Eusebius (*Church History* 4.15.48) refers to these three martyrs immediately after Polycarp and Pionius, who are dated to the reign of Marcus Aurelius. Some scholars, however, prefer a date in the reign of Decius. See the discussion in Musurillo, *Acts of the Christian Martyrs* xv.

5. See, among many examples, Blandina in *The Martyrs of Lyons* 18, 56; and Sanctus in Eusebius, *Church History* 5.1.22.

6. At least she is not referred to as a Christian according to the Greek recension of the *Martyrdom*. In the Latin recension she has become a condemned Christian, no doubt to explain her otherwise "suicidal" behavior to a later (post-Augustinian) age. Cp. the forced explanation of Johannes Quasten, *Patrology* 1:183: "It seems that the Acts in their present [Greek] form are incomplete. Agathonice has been condemned like the other two. This part of the text is missing, so that she *appears* to have committed suicide" (emphasis added).

7. Note the meaning of her name: "Noble Victory." Agathonice conquers death by dying.

8. Jew: *b. Ketuboth* 103b; pagan: *'Abod. Zar.* 18a.

9. This is but one of a large number of similar examples of voluntary martyrdom. See further G. E. M. de St. Croix, "Aspects of the 'Great' Persecution," *Harvard Theological Review* 47(1954) 83, 93, 101–3; idem, "Why were the Early Christians Persecuted?" in M. I. Finley, ed., *Studies in Ancient Society* (Past and Present Series; London, 1974) 235–36, and Robin Lane Fox, *Pagans and Christians* (New York, 1987) 441–45.

10.   Justin, *Second Apology* 10.5. The crime, according to Justin, was the introduction of new deities and refusal to worship the gods recognized by the state (i.e., "atheism").

11.   Ibid., 10.8.

12.   John Chrysostom, *Homilies on 1 Corinthians* 4.7.

13.   Note that Chrysostom misinterprets Socrates' "compulsion" (*Phaedo* 62c) to mean that he had no choice but to accept death. This is a sharp break with Plato's view that Socrates drank the poison willingly.

14.   Cyprian, *On the Lapsed* 8. For a similar response in Alexandria also during the persecution of Decius, see Dionysius's letter to Fabius, preserved by Eusebius, *Church History* 6.41.12. Eusebius reports that during the persecution of Diocletian Christian leaders "hid" and "thousands" of bishops offered sacrifice (8.2.1; 8.3.1).

15.   Fox, *Pagans and Christians*, 435 (with important refs., 751, n. 8).

16.   Justin, *Second Apology* 12.1.

17.   Tertullian, *Apology* 50.13; cf. *Acts of Perpetua and Felicitas* 17.2–3; *Martyrdom of Pionius* 7.1. On the importance of martyrdom for conversion, see the famous discussion by A. D. Nock, *Conversion: The Old and the New in Religion from Alexander the Great to Augustine of Hippo* (Oxford, 1933) 187–98.

18.   De Ste. Croix, "Why were the Early Christians Persecuted?" 234.

19.   De Ste. Croix, "Aspects of the 'Great' Persecution," 83.

20.   De Ste. Croix, "Why were the Early Christians Persecuted?" 234, referring to "Aspects of the 'Great' Persecution," 83, n. 40.

21.   See esp. John 10:18: "No one takes [my life] from me, but I lay it down of my own free will. I have power to lay it down, and I have power to take it again." Cf. Mark 8:34–35 par.; Luke 9:51; Matt. 26:52–54.

22.   *Martyrdom of Pionius* 13.7 See Fox, *Pagans and Christians*, 469–92, which presents a convincing case for dating the *Martyrdom* to the reign of Decius. Fox's entire discussion is excellent, except on one point. He asserts that "Pionius shared the Church's execration of suicide, a death, naturally, which was quite distinct from martyrdom" (480). This claim is anachronistic and without textual support. On the contrary, Pionius insists that Jesus was not executed by the Jews, but "departed from life at his own choice." In other words, Jesus' death, like Pionius's, was *voluntary.*

23.   *Martyrdom of Pionius* 4.7.

24.   Ibid., 18.2. Pionius will not allow himself to be compelled.

25.   Ibid., 20.3, 5. The Roman governor implies that Pionius is mad. This is what Augustine will say of the Donatist martyrs.

26.   *Martyrdom of Marianus and James* 3.5.

27. Ibid. 12.8.

28. Ibid. 2.3.

29. On "secondary martyrdom," see, for example, Lucius, in Justin, *Second Apology* 2.19; Agathonike, in *Martyrdom of Carpus, Papylas, and Agathonike* 42–47 (Greek); Vettius Epagathus, in *Martyrs of Lyons* 9; a crowd, in *Acts of Cyprian* 5.1; a bystander, in *Acts of Marianus and James* 9.2–4; Philoromus, in *Martyrdom of Phileas* 7.1–3.

30. De Ste. Croix, "Aspects of the 'Great Persecution,'" 102. According to Lactantius, some Roman governors boasted of not having executed any Christians (*Divine Institutes* 5.11). Many governors simply looked the other way.

31. *The Martyrdom of Euplus* 1–2 (Greek).

32. Eusebius, *The Martyrs of Palestine* 3.2–4.

33. Eusebius, *Church History* 8.9.5; cf. his similar description of the martyrs of Lyons and Vienne (5.1.9–11).

34. Clement of Alexandria, *Stromateis* 4.17.1.

35. Eusebius, *Church History* 6.41.7.

36. Ibid., 8.6.6.

37. Ibid., 8.12.3–5; cf. 8.14.16–17: a Roman aristocratic woman killed herself rather than be outraged.

38. Rudolf Hirzel, "Der Selbstmord," *Archiv für Religionswissenschaft* 11(1908) 473–74.

CHAPTER 9

Abathur: A New Etymology

Nathaniel Deutsch

The origin of the name Abathur has long puzzled scholars of Mandaean religion. According to Wilhelm Brandt, the name Abathur
may be read as a contraction of the Mandaic words *aba* (father)
and *uthra* (divine being, similar to angel).[1] Thus, *Aba dUtrê* (father
of the uthras) > Abathur. The etymology of Abathur as "father of
the uthras," that is, the progenitor and ruler of a host of angelic
beings, is ellipitically supported in a passage from the *Ginza Raba*,
where Abathur is refererd to as B'haq-Ziwa but calls himself the
"father of the uthras":

> B'haq-Ziwa shone by himself, and he held himself to be a mighty
> one. He held himself to be a mightly one and abandoned the
> name that his father had called him by. And he spoke: "I am the
> father of the uthras. The father of the uthras am I, I made shkinas
> for the uthras."[2]

Against this explanation, many scholars have supported
an Iranian etymology.[3] According to this position, the name
Abathur is based on the reconstruction Abathur = *aβa(g)tur[a]*,
combining the two "Iranian" words *aβa*, "he that has," and *tura*,
"balance, scale," meaning "the one with the scale." However, as
Svend Pallis has pointed out, the word *tura* does not exist in Iranian and was only reconstructed by Andreas on the basis of the
Sanskirt noun *tula*, "lever, beam," and the verb *tulayati*, "to
weigh."[4] In addition, the word *aβa* appears only in Neo-Persian,
indicating that the name Abathur would date from 800 C.E., which
is extremely unlikely.[5] Despite these linguistic difficulties, an Indo-
European origin for the name Abathur has been granted some
legitimacy by a parallel drawn between Abathur and an Iranian

"prototype" called "Rashnu razishta," both of whom are characterized as weighing human souls. As Kurt Rudoloph, one of the current champions of an Indo-European origin, has noted: "Das an den Seelenaufstieg anschließende Seelengericht durch den 'Waagemann' Abathur hat sein Vorbild in dem Rashnu razishta."[6] It must be added, however, that although Abathur is explicitly identified with "Rashna uRast" in the *Ginza Raba*, this occurs in a passage of late provenance.[7]

In place of the unsatisfying Mandaean and Iranian reconstructions, I would like to propose a new etymology for the name Abathur. Rather than indicating the "father of the uthras" or the "one with the scale," the name Abathur may reflect a combination of the words *aba*, "father," and *thur(a)* or *thor(a)*, = "bull." Thus, the name Abathur should be read "Father Bull." Although one would expect a final aleph in the Mandaic (and generally Aramaic) word for "bull," the name Abathur may preserve an older Aramaic or northwest Semitic form, *thôr*, which lacks the definate article ending, aleph.[8] In any case, personal names often do not conform to standard morphological patterns. Indeed, even if the form were originally Mandaic, it is possible that the final vowel dropped out, just as it does in the other hypothetical reconstructions we have cited: *Aba dUtrê* > Abathur and *aβa (g) tur[a]* > Abathur. If this linguistic observation were the only evidence for the reconstruction "Father Bull," it would be a weak argument, indeed. However, there is an intriguing matrix of associations between Abathur and another divine figure known by an epithet remarkably close to "Father Bull," namely, the Canaanite god El.

In a number of passages, El is referred to as *tôru 'il abuhu*, "Bull El his father."[9] In these passages, the "son" in question is the storm god Baal. The name Abathur looks remarkably like a metathesis of the epithet *tôru 'il abuhu*. Other evidence for a correlation between Abathur and El as "bull" gods is found in the *Diwan Abathur*, a Mandaean text. In a list of the seven secret names of Abathur, we find the name Tauriel or Taurel, which literally means "Bull-El": "And Abatur putteth on its robes, (he) whose name is Kanfiel, he whose name is Bhaq, he whose name is Hazazban, he whose name is Nsab, his name is Tauriel.[10] (These are) the seven secret names of Abatur."[11] At this point, the connection between Abathur and El is based solely on two linguistic parallels. Yet, this hardly exhausts the associative matrix between the two figures.

In addition to their epithets, Abathur and El share two common functions: father of the lesser gods (including the demiurge) and judge. In the hierarchy of Mandaean deities, Abathur is the third god, following the "Great Life" (*haiye rabbe*) and the first emanation Yoshamin. As the *Qolasta* (or *Canonical Prayer Book of the Mandaeans*) states: "The First Life [Great Life] is anterior to the Second Life [Yoshamin] by six thousand myriad years and the Second Life anterior to the Third Life [Abathur] by six thousand myriad years and the Third Life more ancient than any 'uthra by six thousand myriad years."[12] Although Abathur is third among the gods who inhabit the World of Light (*alme d'nhura*), he is the most powerful deity in the physical cosmos, whose creation he sets into motion by gazing into the "black" or "turbid" waters which form the lower boundary of the World of Light. By gazing below, Abathur commits an act of extreme hubris and even rebellion, for the proper focus of the emanated beings is on the Great Life, above. As punishment for his "sin," Abathur is exiled from the World of Light and enthroned at its entrance. Like Sophia in the western Gnostic mythos, Abathur's gazing results in the creation of the demiurge of the physical cosmos, who is called Ptahil. Abathur's creation of Ptahil is described in the *Ginza Raba* as follows:

> I. Abathur arose, opened the gate (of the World of Light) and gazed into the black waters; and immediately his counterpart was formed in the black waters. Ptahil was formed and ascended to the boundary.[13]

In addition to creating the demiurge of the physical universe, Abathur also fathers the numerous divine beings called "uthras"—a function noted above.

Turning to El, we find a similar profile. In a number of passages, El is explicitly called "*'abu bani 'ili*,"[14] "father of the gods," an epithet that parallels Abathur's title as "father of the uthras." Just as Abathur creates Ptahil, who in turn creates the physical world, El fathers Baal, who is the demiurge proper in Canaanite mythology. The distinction between El as a "god of theogony" and Baal as a "god of cosmogony" is articulated clearly by Frank Cross in his book *Canaanite Myth and Hebrew Epic:* "'El is creator, the ancient one whose extraordinary procreative powers have populated heaven and earth, and there is little evidence that his vigor has flagged. Myths of 'El perceive creation as theogony. Myths of

Ba'l view creation as cosmogony."[15] As we have seen above, the same distinction between creation as theogony and creation as cosmogony may be applied to Abathur and Ptahil, respectively.

Besides performing their common function as father of the gods, Abathur and El are both enthroned as judges. In numerous passages, Abathur is characterized as a judge:

> Then Hibil Ziwa went and said to Abatur, "Arise! set up thy throne in the House of Boundaries and take over sovereignty. And sublimate that which is sound (good) from that which is base when Man's measure is full and he cometh and is baptized in the Jordan, is weighed in thy Scales, is sealed with thy Seal and riseth up and dwelleth in thy world."[16]

Likewise, El is described as an enthroned judge:

> 'El is enthroned with 'Attart ⟨of the field⟩;
> 'El sits as judge with Haddu his shepherd,
> Who sings and plays on the lyre. . .[17]

As Cross has noted: "The exercise of authority by 'El over his council suggests that his role is more that of a patriarch, or that of the judge in the council of a league of tribes than the role of a divine king." Similarly, Abathur is primarily characterized as a judge, rather than a king, although Abathur may aspire to a royal function.[18]

Besides these linguistic and functional parallels, there is another association between Abathur and El that mut be noted. Perhaps the most striking connection between the two figures is not a direct parallel but a common tie to a third figure. More explicitly, a "triangle" may exist among the figures of El, the "Ancient of Days" in Daniel, chapter 7, and Abathur. Cross has already noted the parallel between El and the Ancient of Days or *atiq yomin*.[19] Both figures sit in judgement, and both are called by epithets that stress their ancient age. In Ugaritic sources, El is called both *mélek 'ôlam*, "eternal king," and *malku 'abu shanima*, "king father of years."[20] The similarity between these epithets and the name *atiq yomin*, combined with the themes of enthronement and judgment, have led Cross to theorize that the author of Daniel, chapter 7, revalorized ancient Canaanite motifs in order to create the figure of the Ancient of Days: "The text of Daniel 7 is of particular interest. The apocalyptist utilized for his eschatological vision an old mythological theme: 'El sitting in judgment in his court. The identity of the Ancient One is transparent."[21]

While the figure of El clearly influenced the Ancient of Days in Daniel, chapter 7, the exact relationship between the apocalyptic figure and Abathur is less obvious, although a number of striking parallels exist between the two figures. The important parallels between the Ancient of Days and Abathur are: (1) Abathur's enthronement as judge, (2) the epithet *atiqa*, "ancient," which is commonly attributed to Abathur, and (3) the description of the myriad of angelic beings who serve before Abathur. The *Ginza Raba* states that surrounding Abathur were: "Thousand upon thousand with their eyes upon him, and ten thousand upon ten thousand stand before him [at his service],"[22] while Dan. 7:10 reads, "Thousands upon thousands served him and ten thousand upon ten thousand stood before him." In addition to this detail, the most common epithet for Abathur is "Abathur, the ancient, high, hidden, and guarded" or simply "Abathur the Ancient." In Mandaic, the word for ancient is *atiqa*, precisely the word employed in *atiq yomin*, the figure who sits on the throne in Dan. 7:9. Therefore, Abathur is linked to the figure in Dan. 7:9–10 by appearance, name, and even by function, for just as Abathur sits in judgement, so does the figure in Dan. 7:10, that is, "the judgement was set and the books were open."

The parallels between Abathur and the *atiq yomin* may be explained by the direct influence of Daniel, chapter 7, on Mandaean theology or by positing that both Daniel, chapter 7, and Mandaeism drew on common sources. In any case, we have seen other features linking Abathur and El that are independent of the common connection with the Ancient of Days from Daniel, chapter 7. As Frank Cross and John Collins[23] have noted, the revitalization of ancient mythological elements is a characteristic feature of apocalyptic writings in general, with the parallels between El and the Ancient of Days being only one example. The possibility that Mandaeism also produced a reemergence of Canaanite mythological motifs, including those related to Abathur, is a topic that must be examined more closely, as must the links between Mandaeism and Apocalypticism. Thus, while it is clear that Abathur and the Ancient of Days are both influenced by the Canaanite deity El, it is unclear whether Abathur is also directly influenced by the figure of the Ancient of Days, or whether both figures incorporate common apocalyptic or preapocalyptic imagery.

Obviously, the view that Abathur's profile as enthroned judge depends, at least partially, on Canaanite and Jewish sources runs contrary to the standard opinion of a Persian origin for Abathur. According to Kurt Rudolph, the figure of Abathur reflects two profiles: (1) weigher and judge of souls and (2) creative light creature. These dimensions are combined in what Rudolph calls "ein typisch 'synkretistiches' Produkt der mandäischen Mythologie."[24] Rudolph adds that Abathur's identity as weigher and judge of souls belongs to the oldest Iranian stratum of Mandaeism, while Abathur's function of demiurge stems from the Jewish or "semi-Jewish (gnostic) world."[25]

In light of the striking parallels between the descriptions of Abathur, El, and the *atiq yomin* in Dan. 7:9–10, the conclusion of Rudolph (et al.) concerning the Iranian origin of Abathur's identity as weigher and judge of souls may have to be amended. Either the Mandaeans had already created an "Abathur like" figure before arriving in Babylonia and western Iran, basing it in part on Dan. 7:9–10 and/or other sources, or the figure of Abathur was originally based on a combination of Jewish and Iranian elements. In this scenario, the Mandaeans or a group of proto-Mandaeans may have employed Canaanite and Jewish imagery as an original element in the creation of Abathur or in order to "fill in" the portrait of a preexisting figure, which the Mandaeans derived from Persian religion. The possibility that the Mandaeans employed Dan. 7:9–10 in either creating or, if he already existed in some form, portraying Abathur is strengthened by the fact that Dan. 7:9–10 is written in Aramiac, probably in an eastern dialect, which, in any case, would have been comprehensible to Mandaic speakers.

Besides these historical questions, there is a compelling phenomenological issue that must be addressed; namely, what is the underlying significance of the adoption of El as a prototype or *Vorbild* for the figure of Abathur? The solution to this problem lies in the distinction between Abathur and the Great Life. As we have already noted, the Great Life is the highest god in the Mandaean "pantheon." A perfect being of light, the Great Life does not create (for this would compromise its perfection) but emanates. The first and second emanations of the Great Life are Yoshamin and Abathur, respectively. Abathur compromises the unity of the Pleroma by gazing into the turbid waters of chaos, an act the produces the demiurge. For his impudence, Abathur is exiled from the Pleroma and enthroned at its entrance, a vantage point that allows him complete knowledge of the world and its inhabitants. In addition,

Abathur takes on the capacity of weigher and judge of souls as well as that of leader of myriad uthras (divine beings). In Abathur's fallen incarnation, he is known as "Abathur-Muzania" (Abathur of the Scales). Yet, even after his exile, Abathur retains an incarnation (*dmuta*) in the World of Light and is called Abathur-Rama (Abathur the Exalted). Only in the eschaton will the two incarnations of Abathur be united, along with the rest of the Pleroma.

The figure of Abathur is a hybrid, composed, quite literally, of two distinct *ontoi*. On the one hand, Abathur is a creature of light, who dwells in the Pleroma, and on the other, he is a judge, enthroned outside (albeit, at the entrance) of the World of Light. As a being of light, Abathur is a dimmer reflection of the Great Life, since as the light is emanated, its quality decreases. It is well known that in Gnosticism, and as we have seen, in Mandaeism, a distinction is made between the highest god and the demiurge. Because in both Gnosticism and Mandaeism the highest god is a perfect being of light, and therefore "perfectly" transcendent, the act of creating the demiurge must fall to an intermediary divine being, who bridges the gap between the Pleroma and the physical cosmos. In Gnosticism, this divine being is a mother, Sophia. In Mandaeism, the creator of the demiurge is a father, Abathur, who is also enthroned as the judge of the world. Likewise, in Canaanite mythology, El is both the father of the demiurge and an enthroned judge. Thus, in El, the Mandaeans found a ready-made prototype for a wisened god of judgment and father of the demiurge.

The revolution of Mandaeism was the creation of a perfect god, whose transcendence precluded any contact with the physical world. Yet, at this phenomenological stage Mandaeism encountered two dilemmas: how was the world created and how is it judged? In order to solve these problems, Mandaeism revitalized the ancient mythological dynamic between a god of theogony/ judge (El > Abathur) and a god of cosmogony/divine warrior[26] (Baal > Ptahil). As noted by Cross, the Hebrew god Yahweh represents the integration of the defining features of El (the father of the gods and judge) and Baal (the divine warrior and demiurge of the cosmos). In Abathur and Ptahil, we discover a Yahweh deconstructed on a symbolic, if not a literal, level.

While Yahweh is a synthesis of the dialectic between El and Baal, Abathur represents an incomplete synthesis of a new dialectic between El (or an El-like god) and the Great Life. Incomplete, because Abathur has a split-personality: Abathur-Muzania and Abathur-Rama. Abathur manifests the ontological and functional features of both a transcendent being of light and an immanent creator and judge. In doing so, he bridges the physical and philosophical chasm between the Pleroma and the physical cosmos. It is quite likely that even if a figure such as El had not already existed to serve as a prototype, his characteristic features would have been invented in the figure of Abathur.

NOTES

This work is dedicated to Ioan Couliano, my teacher and friend, who opened my eyes to a multiplicity of worlds. Ioan taught me that only through reason *and* imagination can we approach truth.

1. Wilhelm Brandt, *Die Mandäische Religion* (Leipzig, 1889) 51.

2. Mark Lidzbarski, *Ginza. Der Schatz oder das große Pouch der Mandäer.* (Göttingen, 1925) 97.

3. For discussions of the etymology of the name Abathur, see M. Lidzbarski, *Das Johannesbuch der Mandäer* (Giessen, 1915) XXIX and Kurt Rudolph, *Theogonie, Kosmogonie und Anthropogonie in den mandäischen Schriften* (Göttingen, 1965) 122–23. Both scholars base their views on Andreas's artificial Iranian etymology.

4. Svend Pallis, *Mandaean Studies* (Amsterdam, 1974) 111.

5. Ibid. Pallis's position is supported by Rudolph Macuch, who writes in his *Handbook of Classical and Modern Mandaic* (Berlin, 1965) 211, n. 156, that "Andreas' artificial etymology (cf. Brandt, *Jüdische Baptismen,* 147; Lidzbarski, *Jb,* xxix) doubted by Nöldeke (ZA 1916, 157) and refuted by Pallis (Mandaen Studies (cf. note 4) 111–14) is made still more improbable by the pronunciation of the name . . ."

6. K.Rudolph, *Die Mandäer I. Prolegomena: Das Mandäerproblem* (Göttingen, 1960) 124.

7. M. Lidzbarski, *Ginza,* 284.

8. In fact, the Ugaritic word for "bull" is *thôr,* which lacks a final vowel except as a case ending. This is not to imply that the name Abathur preserves an archaic Ugaratic form, but it does indicate a potential transition from an older form which lacked a final aleph (= definate article), to one which incorporated it.

9. Cp. A. Herdner, *Corpus des tablettes en cunéiformes alphabétiques* (Paris, 1963) 3.5.43.

10. Geo Windengren has already noted the parallel between Tauriel and El. Cf. Geo Widengren, "Die Mandäer," in Geo Widengren, ed., *Der Mandäismus* (Darmstadt, 1982) 59.

11. E. S. Drower, *Diwan Abatur* (Vaticano, 1950) 7. All of these names are clearly Semitic in origin (as "Abathur" itself may be, *contra* Rudolph, et al.) and one of them, Kanfiel, appears in the hekhalot literature as the name of an angelic being in Genizah Fragment 21, 2b in Schäfer's edition.

12. E. S. Drower, *The Canonical Prayer Book of the Mandaeans* (Leiden, 1959) sec. 1, p. 1.

13. M. Lidzbarski, *Ginza*, 174.

14. *Corpus des tablettes en cunéiformes alphabétiques*, 32.1.25, 33, etc.

15. Frank Cross, *Canaanite Myth and Hebrew Epic* (Cambridge, Mass., 1973) 43.

16. *Diwan Abatur*, 1–2.

17. *Canaanite Myth*, 21, as quoted from the "Rephaim" cycle, *Corpus des tablettes en cunéiformes alphabétiques*, 20–22.

18. In fact, in "Abathur's Lament" or "Abathurs Klage," Abathur is sometimes called "King of the Shkintas," although Abathur is described as unfairly usurping this position. "Abathur's Lament" comprises sections 70–72 of Lidzbarski, *Das Johannesbuch der Mandäer*, 232–34.

19. *Canaanite Myth*, 16.

20. Ibid., cf. notes 23 and 24 for Ugaritic texts.

21. Ibid., 17.

22. M. Lidzbarski, *Ginza*, 195.

23. John Collins, *The Apocalyptic Imagination* (New York, 1984).

24. K. Rudolph, *Theogonie, Kosmogonie und Anthropogonie*, 138.

25. Ibid.

26. Like Baal, who struggles with Mot and Yam before he creates the world, Ptahil must combat the forces of chaos.

Medieval

CHAPTER 10

The Imagination of Death in Jewish Spirituality

Michael Fishbane

The love of God even unto death itself is a widespread and multi-faceted ideal in Judaism—recurring throughout its two millennia history in ever new and revitalized forms.[1] Two main types can be discerned: the act of martyrdom, whereby the faithful commit their life in witness to the wholehearted love of God in their souls; and the quest for spiritual perfection, whereby the philosopher or mystic (and even the scrupulous adherent to the law) directs total attention to God and longs to cleave to the divine reality with such intensity as to die to his self and this world. The patterns and practices of both types vary; but since they are expressive of two fundamentally different religious acts, rarely overlap. For surely the ideal of spiritual perfection indicated by the exhortation "to love the Lord your God, to walk in His ways, and to cleave to Him" (Deut. 11:22) is distinct from the desire to "love the Lord your God with all your heart and with all your soul" (Deut. 6:5)—when the devoted commitment of one's soul means a martyrological death, as an ancient and influential rabbinic interpretation put it (*Mishnah Berachot* 9.5). If the first ideal thus advocates an ongoing religious praxis, cumulative over one's lifetime and guided by the commandments (as interpreted in ethical, mystical, or philosophical ways), the second counsels an ever-present readiness for the ultimate commitment. Indeed, while imbued with normative characteristics (in terms of proper performance), martyrdom is a disruptive and one-time religious act. Given these clearly distinct patterns, it will therefore be of interest to observe how the two types have been correlated and, even more, how the routine of ritual practice has provided substitutes for the martyrological ideal. Hereby, the most perfect and ultimate act of religious love is incorporated into everyday observance—transforming the merits of the *mitzvot* (commandments) with the symbolism of (self-)sacrifice.

A striking early expression of this paradox is the interpretation of the biblical command "you shall love the Lord your God with all your heart and with all your soul" found in the rabbinic midrashic compilation of *Sifrei Deuteronomy* (32).[2] We have already alluded to the absolutizing explanation of this ideal in the Mishnah, according to which the duty to love God "with all your soul" means: "even if He takes your soul." Love of God is here defined as a total commitment—unto death. To reinforce this point, the commentary in the *Tosefta*[3] and *Sifrei* supplement the Mishnah's laconic remark with a quotation from Ps. 44:23 (often cited in martyrological contexts): "For Your sake are we killed all day long (and regarded as sheep for the slaughter)."[4] At first sight the value of this prooftext seems merely to support the point with another scriptural source—with the notable merit of providing a verbal tally to the Torah text (cf. "*all* day long"; "*all* your soul"). But on closer inspection the new testimony is odd. For although the passage from Psalms articulates the people's ideal of death for God's sake, the locution is extreme. This being so, it is doubtful if anyone (including the psalmist) would think to take the hyperbole literally —unless there was another purpose in mind.

It would thus seem that Rabbi Simeon ben Menasia must have had some ulterior motive when he took the words "all day long" at face value and asked (in the *Sifrei*): "Now is it really possible for a person to die *all day long?*" Put this way, the interjection has no answer. The sage knew this, of course, and undoubtedly meant the question as a rhetorical foil to his ensuing solution: "[Thus this Scripture] can only mean that the Holy One, blessed be He, regards the righteous as if [*ke'ilu*] they are killed every day." At first glance, this explanation seems merely to replace one conundrum with another. For what can *it* mean? And how does it explicate the first half of the verse (where the psalmist says that he is "killed all day long")? The first clue towards an answer lies in the phrase "we are regarded as sheep for the slaughter." From his explanation, it is clear that Rabbi Simeon has reinterpreted the passage in a complex manner. First of all, he understands God to be the implied subject of the verb *regarded* (i.e., "we are regarded *by God*"), so that the verb takes on a specific theological resonance; second, he reinterprets the particle *as* so that it marks not a simile but a hypothetical comparison ("as if"); and finally, he applies both revisions (in the second phrase) to the opening words. The result is a transformation of the martyrological ideal—a routinization of it, so to speak—such that the righteous are meritoriously regarded by God as if they die daily. But what is it about the righteous or their behavior that connects them to dying? Here it seems that Rabbi Simeon is drawing upon a whole range of rabbinic teachings in which the task of the pious is to "conquer his [evil] *yetzer*"—that is, his inclination to follow instinct and desire rather than God's word. In one notable dictum, the struggle would seem to require the actual death of desire; for after teaching that "the righteous are ruled by their good inclination," R. Yosi the Galilean adduces a verse from Ps. 109:22, "For I am poor and needy, and my heart is slain [*ḥalal*] within me." Like the other prooftexts found in this passage, it is clear that this one is also used to portray an aspect of the religious psychology. Compared with the other types (the average and evil persons), the righteous individual is considered one who overcomes his baser self and "kills" his evil heart—thus becoming a true servant of God. It is thus just some such notion of a righteous person's ability to sacrifice base desire for God's sake that links their action to martyrdom, and so we confidently construe R. Simeon's remark to suggest that if martyrdom be regarded as the acceptance of death *in extremis* for the love of God (the first midrashic interpretation), killing one's evil *yetzer* may correspondingly function as the daily expression of such supreme devotion. Psychological strife thus provides the drama of personal perfection, and slaying the evil inclination is the perpetual combat whereby the devotee offers "all" his soul to God.[5]

The striking point here is that Rabbi Simeon is not simply concerned to reiterate the rabbinic injunction about slaying false desire or even to say that the one who does so is truly righteous. His intent is rather to innovate and say that such devoted behavior is a ritual substitute for martyrdom; indeed, that true piety is "considered" by God to be "like" death "all day long." The psalmist's hyperbole is thus strategically literalized by the sage in order to serve as the "precedent" for a more normative mode of self-sacrifice. In a cultural context where martyrological devotion had become a standard of perfect love of God, the connection of such acts with the routine performance of rabbinic piety transfigured the latter and gave it new sanctity. Indeed, says the sage, God regards the righteous "as if" they died for His sake: "as if" being considered the real thing.

Before proceeding further, it will be instructive to focus a bit more on other ancient rabbinic use of the term *ke'ilu* (as if, like)— for this will provide further proof of the self-conscious transfer of ritual acts from one sphere to another; not their mere simulation (as might be expected), but their actual reconfiguration. Indeed such transfers reveal much about Judaism and how it transformed "historical impossibilities" into viable avenues of religious performance. The case of the Temple and the sacrificial service may provide an important instance; for while much is often made of the dictum of R. Yoḥanan be Zakkai, who consoled the post-destruction generation with the teaching that acts of ethical devotion serve as the true sacrificial atonement acceptable to God (*'Avot de Rabbi Nathan* A, chap. 4), this comfort hardly contends with the central spiritual need for ritual purification and forgiveness. In fact, Rabbi Yoḥanan's saying was in its time but one dictum among many, and its triumphant recounting by contemporary historians or theologians may say more about modern proclivities to find ethical replacements for old practices than about the deep anxieties such dicta were meant to assuage. Accordingly, we should cast a more serious eye on those ancient sayings that address the concrete need for atonement in the absence of the Temple cult. A collection of interpretations at the end of the talmudic tractate of *b. Menaḥot* (110a) is particularly notable in this regard, for each one invokes the expression *ke'ilu* (as if) in order to note the functional equivalent of Torah study and the ancient Temple service. The first two are fairly general: "scholars who devote themselves to the study of Torah wherever they are," or "at night," are considered "as if" they "burnt and presented offerings" to God or "were occupied with the Temple service." The third more precisely specifies that "scholars who are occupied with the laws of the Temple service" are considered "as if the Temple were built in their days." But it is the fourth and fifth paragraphs that connect the performative benefits of study with the transformative effects of sacrifices in a detailed way.

Resh Laqish said, What is the significance of the verse, "This is the law for the burnt-offering, for the meal-offering, for the sin-offering, and for the guilt-offering"? (Leviticus 7:37).—It teaches that whoever occupies himself with the study of the Torah is as if [*ke'ilu*] he were offering a meal-offering, a sin-offering, and a guilt-offering. Rabba asked, Why then does the verse say, "*For* the burnt-offering, *for* the meal-offering"? It should rather have [simply] said, "a burnt-offering, a meal-offering"! Rather, said Rabba, [this formulation] means that whoever occupies himself with the study of Torah needs neither burnt-offering, nor meal-offering, nor sin-offering, nor guilt-offering. Rabbi Isaac said, What is the significance of the verse, "This is the law of the sin-offering" (Leviticus 6:18); and "This is the law of the guilt-offering" (7:1)?—They teach that whoever is occupied with the laws of the guilt-offering is as if [*ke'ilu*] he were offering a guilt-offering.

The rhetorical cast of these interpretations should not obscure their exhortatory force nor especially the expiatory function of study that is proclaimed for Jews who lived after the destruction of the Temple and its service. Surely this reflects the ideals of the class of scholars who make these points; but just as surely does it betoken the changing notion of service (*'avodah*) that was then at work in Judaism. No longer the sacrificial service of the Shrine but now the devoted service of the heart (in prayer) and mind (in study) are proclaimed as *the very means* of reparation between the individual and God. A more lapidary formulation found in *b. Megillah* 31b makes this point at the conclusion of a "dialogue" between God and Abraham. The latter asks how Israel can be protected from punishments due to sin when the Temple service does not exist, and he is told: "I [God] have already established for them 'an order of sacrifices,' [so that] whenever they read from them I consider [Israel] as if [*ke'ilu*] they make a sacrifice before Me—and I forgive all their sins"! But other acts of substitution could be included, as well. It may suffice here simply to mention the poignant petition of Rav Sheshet who, after a penitential fast, prayed "that my fat and blood which has diminished (through fasting) be as if [ke*'ilu*] I sacrificed them on the altar before You, and You favored me (with forgiveness)."[6] And then too there is the assertion that even if one brings only his "self" (or "soul") before God in penitence, "it would be as if [*ke'ilu*] he sacrificed a soul." These teachings give added weight to Rabbi Simeon's teaching, presented earlier, and we surely miss their living spirituality if they are reduced to mere hyperbole. Imitative replacements of the sacrificial service (through fasting and penance and study) are thus deemed serious spiritual means to the same end. Performing these substitutions, the worshipper was occupied daily with the Temple service itself—and was to receive its divine benefits. Here too, "as if" is like the real thing.

By the High Middle Ages, this attitude had entered into the order of prayers and was canonized by codes prescribing and describing liturgical practice—a sure sign that even if the talmudic dicta once had a hyperbolic aura, they were long since understood and actualized as effective behaviors in the daily service of God. Thus, in one of the earliest works on halakhic practice—the *Sefer ha-Manhig* of R. Avraham ben Natan Hayarḥi of Lunel (c. 1155–1215)—the author first refers to the obligation to recite the biblical rules of daily sacrifices [*parashat temidin*] every day and then adds: "and these are accounted before God in place of an offering [*u-bimqom qorban hen neheshavim lifnei ha-maqom*]; as it is stated: 'We shall pay the fruit [*peri!*] of our lips' "[7] Following this Sefardi tradition, Abudarham (fourteenth cent.) states that the rabbis ruled regarding the recitation of "the sacrifices more than other topics since whoever recites these with intention [*kavanat ha-lev*] it is as if [*ke'ilu*] he offered them [in sacrifice]."[8] But the concern was also well-established in the Ashkenazi rite. Thus by the thirteenth century R. Zedekiah b. Avraham Ha-Rofe (of Italy) refers to the daily recitation of the *tamid*-sacrifice in his *Shibbolei Ha-Leqet* as something "required" [*ve-tzarikh . . . liqrot*];[9] and the saintly R. Eleazar b. R. Yehudah (of Worms) comments on the words "to sacrifice to Me" in the *tamid*-service, saying: "The *tamid* should always be performed; and if one should object and say that it is [now] annulled [because of the Temple's destruction], one may answer this [with the biblical verse:] 'Instead of bulls we shall pay [the offering of] our lips' and [with the rabbinical dictum:] 'Prayer has been established in lieu of sacrifices.' "[10]

Gradually, statements that stressed the substitution of verbal recitation for sacrifices were incorporated into the prayer book and became an explicit petition interleaved with the paragraphs recounting the actual sacrifices. Thus by the sixteenth century R. Moshe ibn Makhir (of Safed) notes that after reciting the *tamid*-sacrifice the worshipper says, "May the words of our lips be deemed worthy and acceptable as if [*ke'ilu*] we offered the *tamid*-sacrifice at its appointed time." Similarly, R. Yosef Karo ruled that after reciting the ancient sacrificial prescriptions [concluding with *parashat ha-'olah*] one should say: "May it be your will that this be deemed worthy and acceptable as if [*ke'ilu*] I offered the *'olah*-sacrifice."[11] These phrases recur in the Ashkenazi rite, along with a more explicit account of the atoning purpose of this prayer. Thus, just before reciting the rules of sacrifice, one is bidden to add:

> May it be your will, O Lord our God and God of our ancestors, that You have mercy upon us and forgive all our sins, and grant us atonement for all our iniquities, and wipe away all our transgressions; and that you build the Temple speedily in our day that we may office you the daily [*tamid*-] sacrifice, that it provide atonement for us . . .

II

The preceding materials indicate, in a most striking manner, the importance of ritual substitutes in normative Jewish practice. Through the term *ke'ilu,* moreover, they underscore the paradox at hand—for this expression is at once a highly self-conscious indicator of the difference between the rabbinic recitations and sacrificial performance *and* a deliberate defense of their similarity. Indeed, given the sacramental nature of sacrifice, such replacements are nothing short of remarkable: words replace deeds in all their erstwhile efficacy. No mere "imitation of an action," they are, rather, new actions and new recitations. In the course of time, this process was extended to included martyrdom as well—thereby reversing in a paradoxical manner the singular saying of R. Simeon ben Manasiah. For if that sage had replaced the martyr's death with acts of righteous devotion to divine service, later generations returned to the former ideal of perfect love but sought to ritualize it through recitation! In its various patterns, such a ritual development reveals further dimensions of our overall theme.

We can find, contemporary with the canonization of the liturgical recitation of the order of sacrifices for the daily atonement of sins, a similar development of the sources stemming from *Sifrei Deuteronomy* 32. Whatever the prehistory, it is striking to read the instructions for reciting the *Shema* (Deut. 6:4–6) that Rabbi Moshe de Leon provides in *Sefer ha-Rimmon,* his thirteenth-century commentary on the commandments. Concerned to inculcate the proper mental and spiritual "intentions" (viz., focus) in the worshipper, de Leon first refers to the mishnaic and midrashic understanding of the phrase "with all your soul" as meaning "even if He takes your soul" and then adduces the following:

> Every person who loves his Creator, whenever he reaches the verse "and you shall love (etc.)" in the recitation of the *Shema*, should direct his mind and thoughts towards the love of his Maker, as if [*ke'ilu*] he were giving up his soul for His sake in love, with absolute sincerity, and accepting death upon himself. And it is obligatory upon each person to resolve [lit., determine; *ligmor be-nafsho*] this matter daily. And this is like what (the sages meant when) they said, "For your sake we are killed all day long, and regarded as sheep for the slaughter." And how splendid if he employs this intention daily in the love of his Maker, and to devote his soul for His sake, as we have said; and He, may He be blessed, wants intention [in worship].[12]

Here we have a spiritual intention concerning martyrological devotion during prayer, long before the supposed shift from effects of concrete performance (during the Crusades) to their spiritual enactment (during the sixteenth to eighteenth centuries).[13] What is more, this valuable document already employs the word (*ke'ilu*) to mark the meditative act involved. As distinct from contemporary and later uses of the "as if" formula to indicate projective visualizations of the given Name (and other matters),[14] de Leon counsels a mental focusing of intent—a projection of will, performed daily. The goal is thus to enact the commitment to die, as an expression of absolute loving devotion. And while nothing further is said here regarding actual martyrological practice, it is clear from de Leon's theosophical introduction that such a "death-act" has more practical, theurgical benefits. In the first place, he strongly remarks that the commitment of human love is a pillar that sustains the universe,[15] even as it is a means of restoring one's divine nature to its transcendental Source.[16] And finally, drawing on a discussion of the capacity of joyful service to draw forth heavenly blessing from the supernal gradations (of divine Being), de Leon goes on to speak of the "holy martyrs" who "accepted death in love, through the mystery of joy"; for this caused supernal joy to descend upon them while cleaving to God in love—such that "they were joyful in their sufferings"![17] Alluding to Rabbi Akiba's celebrated theology of "the sufferings of love" (*b. Berakhot* 5a),[18] the text invokes the model of Akiba, who accepted his tortuous death with a resolute spirit and who, because of his great attachment to God while reciting the *Shema* at his death, "*did not feel his torture!*" Intense love may thus lead to the transcendence of pain—as the contemporary sage Rabbi Meir of Rothenberg attested (and with the same idiom, *gomer be-da'ato*).[19] For de Leon, then, the proper practice of the daily *Shema* is as much a preparation for saintly death as it is a credo of living love of God. The ritual recitation functions as an interiorization of death, to the degree that the true devotee is already in life a spiritual martyr in deed.

This interpretation of the *Shema* recitation as a meditation on martyrological death recurs throughout the Middle Ages—and beyond. Particularly influential was the annotation of the celebrated sixteenth-century talmudist Rabbi Joel Sirkis to Rabbi Jacob ben Asher's monumental code, the *'Arba'ah Turim.*

> When one recites the *Shema* one should have the intention to accept upon oneself the yoke of the Kingdom of Heaven, to be slain for the sanctification of the Name . . . This is what is meant by "with all your soul"—even if He takes your soul . . . With this intention one will recite it with fear and trembling.[20]

But the issue comes up in other sixteenth-century documents and genres. Thus Rabbi Eliezer Azikri counsels in his spiritual guidebook, *Sefer Ḥaredim,* that one should resolutely intend to die a martyr while reciting the *Shema,* so that if the event should come to pass he would devote himself to God "in joy"—and this prayerful resolution "would be accounted (*neḥeshav*) to him as if (*ke'ilu*) he devoted himself in fact."[21] Such a point achieved a summary formulation by the eighteenth-century kabbalist and moralist Rabbi Moshe Hayyim Luzzatto in his spiritual guidebook, *Derekh ha-Shem.* He said:

> One of the conditions associated with this commandment [of reciting the *Shema*] is that each person mentally resolve [*gomer be-da'ato*] to devote his soul for the sake of God's Unity and willingly undergo all manner of sufferings and types of death for the sanctification of his Name—and [such a resolve] will be accounted [*neḥeshav*] as if [*ke'ilu*] he did the deed in fact, and was slain for the sanctification of the Name. [Such a resolve,] moreover, has great consequences for the benefit of the creation and the more general rectifications.(4.4.5).

Several matters are intertwined here. Beginning with the traditional emphasis on the meritorious benefits accruing to the individual
worshipper who determines to die a martyr while reciting the
Shema, the passage ends with a reference to the greater boon be-
falling creation and the overall redemption. Indeed the meditative
act not only produces a ritual exchange of thought for divine merit
but has a theurgical effect on the fragments of fallen existence
awaiting rectification. Put differently, but in the linguistic spirit of
Luzzatto's formulation, the intense human resolve to sacrifice oneself for divine Unity actually influences the restorative unification
of all Being. Self-sacrifice thus stands in the center of world-
restorative actions, actually replacing the ancient Temple as the site
of ritual at-one-ment. Indeed, Luzzatto says, the mental resolve to
suffer and die for the sanctification of God's name is not only like
the real occurence of such actions, but even actualizes cosmic dimensions as well. Verbal proclamation and mental resolve thus
combine as two sides of a performative utterance—with divine
effect.

The pattern of spiritual intention that recurs throughout these
sources involves a readiness for martyrdom while reciting the
Shema. While this recitation may have ritual value in imitating the
myth of Rabbi Akiba's passion (when he reportedly died with this
proclamation on his lips[22]), the recitation per se has no effective
function. For just such efficacy of martyrdom through a recitation
about martyrdom, we must turn to a source on the late Middle
Ages—the *Yosef 'Ometz,* a collection of liturgical and other practices written by Rabbi Yosef Yuzpa Hahn Noyrlingen (1570–
1635), who witnessed the Fettmilch massacres. Citing a passage
from "Rabbi Yosselman Rosheim, the great Court Jew" (d. 1554),
in which the rules of martyrology are mentioned along with a
stirring exhortation to fulfill the commandment,[23] Hahn goes on
to urge his readers to learn the rules well so that there be no danger
of dying unnecessarily—for then one would be guilty of suicide
and not praiseworthy for sanctifying God's name in love.[24] It
has been argued that this emphasis on study is one facet on a
seventeenth-century transformation in the meaning of Jewish martyrdom, the others being an absence of contemptuous resistance of
Christianity (common in the twelfth-century martyrologies) and a
new emphasis on ritual spiritualization of the sanctification.[25]

The argument is not without difficulty since, in the first case, considerations of the proper conditions for "putting one's life at risk" were long a part of the talmudic curriculum and its post-talmudic annotators and decisors.[26] Indeed, study of these "rules of sanctification" constituted an authentic part of rabbinic piety, vitally concerned with knowing the commandments and their proper performance. The very fact that notice of such behavior—not to mention a precis of related rules[27]—is prescribed in a book whose genre conforms with others dealing with customs and ritual should give double pause. And if the matter of genre is significant here, it must also temper any inference about active resistance to be drawn from *Yosef 'Ometz*. For it hardly helps to compare twelfth-century chronicles with a seventeenth-century book of ritual instructions. Indeed if one were to turn to the chronicles of Hahn's day, such as the *Yevein Metzula* of Rabbi Nathan Neta Hanover, one can find many exhortations of religious constancy and defiance. The case in Tulczyn may stand for many. According to the chronicler, the great scholars of that city "urged the holy people to sanctify the Name and not to change their faith. [And] all of them replied: 'Hear O Israel, the Lord is our God, the Lord is One! As there is but One in your hearts, so is there but One in our hearts.'" And when the enemy came and proclaimed, "Whoever wishes to change his faith and remain alive, let him sit under this banner," none answered, and many were killed mercilessly.[28]

The third contention bears directly on our subject. For it claims that the focus on ritual performance reflects a decisive spiritualization of martyrology—a shift from concrete action (real death) to mental substitution at a time when Christianity was no longer the same aggressive threat to the Jew that it had been in medieval Europe. But we must be careful not to misjudge this interior ritualization of self-sacrifice during normal circumstances. Hahn's discussion is instructive.

> In addition to this [foregoing] reason [for learning the rules of martyrdom], there is, in my opinion, a greater one: that a person should learn those laws upon which the foundation of our faith depends; for [their very name proves this, since] they are called "[the laws for the] sanctification of the Name." Accordingly, whoever studies them in all their details and devotes himself in love for the sanctification of his great Name, then this theoretical

recollection and acceptance will be considered as a deed in fact—in accordance with what the sages have said concerning whoever studies the [biblical] portion of sacrifices . . . and the wise among the kabbalists assert likewise . . . For there are indeed a number of commandments which certain persons will never be obligated to perform, and these will be accounted in his favor if he (but) studies their laws and affirms to fulfill them if necessary . . . This acceptance will be deemed a deed in fact. In just this way did the sages expound the [biblical] verse, "For Your sake are we killed all day long" in the [Midrash] *Sifrei* [saying], "And is it conceivable that one be killed every day? Rather then (the sense is) that should one accept upon himself daily to sanctify his great Name [then] it will be accounted as [if he were] a sheep [led] to the slaughter"; see *Sefer Ḥaredim* 17, which cites the *Zohar* that everyone should accept upon himself self-sacrifice [*mesirut nafsho*] for the sanctification of the Name through elongating the work "One" [in the *Shema*], and also when he recites "with all your heart and all your soul."[29]

In a document of such import, it would be unwise to conclude that the substitutions for martyrdom indicated here are merely historical displacements—without concrete religious value. For one thing, Hahn cites the old rabbinic dictum from *b. Menaḥot* 110a that vaunts the merit for studying the laws of sacrifice after the destruction of the Temple. Clearly, in this serious context one can hardly imagine that it was perceived as a mere homiletical hyperbole; much more does it seem to provide precise proof that vicarious substitution has an ancient rabbinic precedent. What is more, there is no doubt that the medieval kabbalists themselves already took this dictum seriously, as Hahn clearly notes—and the reason he gives is significant: substitution is necessary to enable one to fulfill all the commandments—even those like sacrifice, which would otherwise be impossible to perform owing to historical circumstances. That is to say, though the commandment to sanctify God's name is one of the positive duties of the Halakha, there are various conditions attached to the physical performance of this commandment (even in times of persecution) such that one may never have the opportunity to show self-less devotion to God and thus observe *all* the *mitzvot*. For the traditional Jew this was no light matter. And so we find Hahn drawing on the ancient Midrash, the thirteenth-century *Zohar*, and the sixteenth-century *Sefer Ḥaredim*—all for the purpose of teaching that one may also fulfill the *mitzvah* of sanctifying God's name through the proper

recitation of the *Shema;* that is, if one recites the opening proclamation of Unity and the succeeding determination to love God
(with "all your soul") with absolute sincerity. Since the operative
clause "with all your soul" was undoubtedly understood in the
Akiban sense—namely, "even if he takes your soul," the requirement is that one should recite the prayer *as if (ke'ilu)* one were
giving up his soul at that very moment (and also intending to do so
in fact, circumstances permitting). Performed this way, the verbal
utterance would fulfill the physical *mitzvah.*

What are the theological reasons for this remarkable turn? One
particularly significant explanation occurs in another portion of
the *Yosef 'Ometz* passage adduced above. After Hahn comments
that one who studies the laws of sanctification of the name has the
merit of one who has actually performed the commandment, he
adds: "And the wise of the Kabbalists taught likewise." The rest of
the remark continues as follows:

> [And the wise of the kabbalists taught likewise] in response to a
> problem raised in connection with the transmigration of souls.
> For they [the kabbalists] said that a person could not acquire
> perfection without fulfilling [all of] the 613 commandments; and
> were he to omit even one of the commandments of God his
> supernal garment would be wanting, and he would have to re-
> turn to the round of rebirth until he had performed all 613
> commandments. Against this, it was objected: "Now surely there
> are a number of commandments that a person might never have
> the opportunity to perform." And they [the kabbalists] an-
> swered: "If one were to study such laws, and determine to fulfill
> them if the occasion should arise . . . this (theoretical) accep-
> tance would be accounted a deed in fact."

This text transports us into the world of mystical metempsychosis
—of the transmigration of souls—in which one must perform perfectly all the commandments to be released from the cycle of rebirth. According to this kabbalistic notion, found variously in the
Zohar (but of great antiquity; cf. Ascension of Isaiah 8:14f; 9:1–5,
36–40), each completed commandment adds a piece to the supernal garment that a person weaves upon his astral body.[30] Failure to
fully cloth one's heavenly alter ego results in a deficit that returns
the earth-bound soul to the travails of rebirth. It was therefore
necessary for those who accepted this kabbalistic tradition to find
a means for performing *all* the commandments. For the *mitzvah* of
sanctification of God's name, the solution provided was ritual

study of the rules of martyrdom and proper martyrological meditations during prayer.

The kabbalistic theosophy underpinning this concern for ritual
perfection was clearly articulated by Hahn's contemporary, R. Isaiah Horowitz of Prague. In his masterwork, the *Shnei Luḥot ha-
Berit,* Horowitz noted the mystical tradition that each of the 613
commandments of Jewish observance is related to a different part
of the Supernal Anthropos—a spiritual structure in the highest
realm that is also the archetype for the human anthropoidal configuration on earth. Accordingly, one of the mysteries of the commandments performed by mortals is the capacity of these acts to
repair (and rebuild) the heavenly form while perfecting the earthly
self.[31] Individual and cosmic eschatology are thus interdependent
and absolutely dependent upon the human performance of every
divine law—even those that are physically precluded by spatial
setting (e.g., not living in the land of Israel), historical occasion
(e.g., martyrdom), or social event (e.g., levirite marriage or writing
a bill of divorce). So what could one do under such circumstances?
Developing an older solution, R. Horowitz offered a profound reinterpretation and combination of the ancient idea that recitation of
the sacrifices was like their performance with the new notion of
"spiritual preparation" [*hakhanah*].[32] This last has two historical
aspects: the period of the Patriarchs and that of Sinai.

The first aspect of *hakhanah* is pre-Sinaitic and concerns the
question of how the patriarchs achieved spiritual perfection, since
they lived before Sinai and thus did not have the concrete commandments to perform. Horowitz's answer is that they realized the
commandments in a wholly interior way, through "the power of
their preparation [*hakhanatam*]; that is, they were absolutely attached [*devukim be-takhlit ha-devekut*] to the Creator, may he be
blessed, and were joyfully prepared [*mukhanim*] to fulfill his will
in whatever He might command them . . . And this preparation
[*hakhanah*] was *like* the actual deed [*ke-ma'aseh be-fo'al*]." What
is more, through the strength of their "absolute preparation" [*takh-
lit ha-hakhanah*], these saints realized through the commandments
they did perform the entirety of 613 commandments—for the totality was "included" [*kelulim*] in each and every *mitzvah.* After
Sinai [the second, historical phase], when the 613 commandments
were revealed, pious people practiced what they could do in fact
[*be-fo'al*] and remained prepared to fulfill all of the command-

ments joyously—so that "what one cannot fulfill [in fact] is [accounted] as if [*ke'ilu*] he [actually] fulfilled [it], since he is prepared [to do so]" through study of the Torah for its own sake. "Thus even though one may not fulfill (a commandment) because it is unavailable to him to do so, but he is [nevertheless] prepared [*mukhan*] to fulfill it then [the commandment] is accounted to such a one as if [*ke'ilu* he fulfilled it—because he brought the deed to actuality by the power of this preparation [*hakhanah*]."

For R. Isaiah Horowitz, the capacity of the individual to fulfill the commandments through mental preparation is "a very great mystery" [*rav hu sod ha-hakhanah*], and he goes on to invoke the ancient rabbinic dictum that "whoever occupies himself with the portion of sacrifices is [accounted] as if [*ke'ilu*] he offered the sacrifices [themselves]" (cf. *b. Menaḥot* 110a). The emphasis remains here on personal perfection, as it does on several occasions when the author takes up this powerful theme.[33] Indeed, on several occasions the capacity of thought, study, and recitation to even repair ruptures in the supernal Godhead brought about by human sin is dramatically presented in terms precise liturgical formulations.[34] Now the efficiency of the substitute not only beseeches divine atonement but mystically induces a unification of the divine name, and thus divinity itself. Reciting the holy Torah can now achieve the highest theurgical ends. If the mystic has lost the Temple, he has gained the capacity to rebuild the cosmos—no mean substitute.

III

As we have seen, one way that a simulation of death-in-love was enacted in Jewish ritual was by intending martyrdom in one's mind while reciting the liturgy (of *Shema*). A more physical procedure is the penitential practice of *nefilat 'apayim*, a bodily gesture of simulated prostration performed in the morning and afternoon daily service—immediately after the public repetition of the *'Amidah* prayer, the central standing prayer of the liturgy. Depending upon customary procedure, the worshipper first recites a confession and the thirteen attributes of divine mercy, or immediately enacts the prostration rite and a psalm. In ancient rabbinic times, according to talmudic tradition (cf. *b. Megillah* 22a), it was customary for one to lie physically prostrate and request divine mercy. This abject act of humility and self-nullification was commuted to the more symbolic gesture of leaning to one side while seated—to the right side in the morning (because the phylacteries are worn on the left arm) and to the left in the afternoon, according to Ashkenazi custom.[35] At this point, either Psalm 6 (in the Ashkenazic rite) or 25 (in the Sephardic and kabbalistic rite) is recited.[36] On Mondays and Thursdays the Ve-Hu Raḥum penitential is added as well.

Various explanations for the *nefilat 'apayim* rite are found in the sources. They reflect different spiritual dimensions and various modes of self-nullification or death enactment—ranging from the moral piety found in R. Baḥye ben Asher's comments to Num. 16:22 to the mystical rites found in the *Zohar* and subsequent sources. We shall focus on a selection from the latter material— since the mystical rites reveal profound spiritual exercises in which the enactment of death is a rebirth of the soul. This holds whether the penitent is imitating a cosmic event, theurgically effecting it, only in a state of utter rapture.

A number of striking discussions of the *nefilat 'apayim* rite occur in the *Zohar* and refer to its performance just after completing the major prayer of the morning service, the *ʿAmidah* (standing prayer). In one passage, the recitation of the *ʿAmidah* brings about a conjunction of the masculine and feminine dimensions of God— and "in shame" before this cosmic coupling, the worshipper falls forward and covers his face while focusing his mind on the birth of souls resulting from this Holy Union (2.128b–129a). The purpose of this physical and mental exercise is to undergo a cycle of death and rebirth, insofar as the worshipper "devotes his soul" to the feminine dimension—and by thus cleaving to her when she is "taking" other souls, may be reborn anew (2.200b). Accountingly, the expression of shame in this scenario induces a spiritual (rather than psychological) transformation of the worshipper, a change that results from cleaving to the divine during its process of regeneration.

In other cases, it is precisely the readiness or resolve to die during the rite of *nefilat apayim* that is decisive for the worshipper; that is, the penitent physically expresses the intention to die at the hands of the Shekhina, the feminine aspect of God, who is symbolized by the Tree of Death. The process is as follows. During the upright *ʿAmidah* prayer the mystically minded is supposed to be physically attached to the masculine principle known as *Tif'eret*, the vertical column of the divine hierarchy that helps link the upper feminine grade with the lower one (*Malkhut;* Shekhinah). This masculine aspect is also symbolized by the Tree of Life. Accordingly, when the worshipper detaches his meditative attention from *Tif'eret* at the conclusion of the *'Amidah,* he must immediately acknowledge the feminine side of Death, that he not die altogether.[37] "It is thus necessary for a person—immediately upon concluding the *'Amidah*—to regard himself as if [*ke'ilu*] he departed from the world" (3.120b). This is done through the mimetic act of *nifilat 'apayim,* whereby he falls face forward and (through reciting Psalm 25) redeposits his soul with the same feminine aspect of God with which he deposits it at night—but now not in a temporary way "but as one who actually [*vada'i*] departs from the world" (3.121a)

Functioning at several levels, this ritual process is at once an integration (within the worshipper) of the opposites of life and death; a unification (for God's sake) of the Tree of Life and Death; and a human attachment to the divine Tree of Death for the sake of renewed life. This latter point is vital; for as the *Zohar* states, "The secret [i.e., mystical] explanation [of this rite] is that there are sins which remain unatoned for until a person departs from the world, as is said, 'This sin will not be expiated until you die' (Isa. 22:14). Thus [the worshipper] should give himself truly over to death, and devote his soul to that (other) 'place'—not as a [temporary] deposit [of the soul] as [done] at night, but as if he actually [*vada'i*] departed from this world." Absolute sincerity is thus essential for this atonement to "work"; no dissembling of death is allowed. The absence of the letter *vav* (numerically, six) from the acrostic in Psalm 25 is said to hint at this as well, since the principle of 'Life' and the gradation of *Tif'eret* are symbolized by this letter (and number)—and the worshipper must abandon these for "Death" after the *'Amidah* prayer (3.121b). Moreover, the letter *quf* is missing as well—to teach that the worshipper should not dissemble death like the (proverbial) monkey (*qof*) who pretended to be dead when a serpent (*ḥivta'*; punning on *life,* symbolic of the Shekhinah) came to kill it. Only loving sincerity assures divine favor and the forgiveness of sins.[38] In his Hebrew work *Sefer ha-Rimmon,* de Leon mentions these letters but demythologizes the explanation, even as the zoharic notion of succumbing to the dark side of "Death" is neutralized.[39]

A more far reaching mythic understanding of the *nefilat*

'apayim rite was taught centuries later by the most daring trans-
former of zoharic traditions—the Holy Lion, R. Yitzhaq Luria
Ashkenazi (sixteenth cent.).[40] In his view, the worshipper (in the
ideal sense—for the task requires consummate skill and is filled
with spiritual danger) performs a heroic journey into the cosmic
realms—releasing souls trapped in the husks of Gehenna and bearing them aloft through the four divine worlds, where they help
effect a conjunction of masculine and feminine elements in the
supernal spheres.[41] As a result of the holy prayers of Israel, these
souls are purged and transformed into *mayim nuqvin*—the female
waters (viz., the fertilizing fluids of the heavenly realm that can be
inseminated by masculine aspects of Wisdom). The worshipper
collects these waters, raises them to the (masculine) gradation of
Ze'ir Anpin in the highest world (*Atzilut;* Emanation).[42] It is here
that drops of mercy have secreted from higher aspects of this anthropomorphic configuration, as a result of previous prayers in the
liturgy. They now enter the generative principle called "*Ze'ir Anpin,*" which is "Jacob," who unites with "Rachel" his beloved.
Remarkably, all this is achieved through a consummate act of spiritual intention, as the worshipper first imagines himself physically
hurled from the exalted world of *Atzilut* (which he has attained
through the *'Amidah* prayer, just concluded) to the nethermost
realm of *Asiyah* (the world of Making) and then concentrates upon
his ascension with the transfigured souls. The act of *nefilat 'apayim*
is thus conceived here as a real fall into the divine abyss and, as
such, is fraught with danger. Luria therefore cautions his reader
not to preform these intentions unless he is truly righteous and can
withstand contact with evil. For there are those who barely escape
with their own souls intact, while others never ascend. Such souls
are transfigured by their own acts of imagination and remain in
this dimension of "world."[43] In these cases the shamanic descent is
aborted, and an act of salvation ends in spiritual suicide.

In the course of other elaborations of the worshipper's journey,
Luria speculates that the redemptive goal is for the adept to join
the three aspects of his soul (life force; spirit; super-soul) to the
corresponding aspects of lost souls in each of the three lower
worlds, and thence to raise them to the gradation of *Ze'ir Anpin* in
the fourth world through the mystery of the *mayyin nuqvin*. In a
more complex alternative, the performer of the *nefilat 'apayim* rite
is bidden to take only the soul aspect called "life force" from the

fivefold configuration of souls in each of the three lower worlds—each ensemble of five being labeled *en toto* by one of the three main terms for soul.[44] Such arcana mark the perilous siege of entrapped fragments of divinity that the worshipper intends to redeem for the sake of the Godhead itself. As an act of self-devotion (*mesirat nefesh*), it borders on the spectacular; but it is not the spectacular itself. This exalted position is reserved for devotion unto death in the course of reciting the *Shema*—in the (twice) daily liturgy or during the (unique) act of martyrological sanctification of the name. Luria thus conceives a hierarchy of death-devotions that dominate the intentions and imagination of the Jew at prayer.[45]

Of the two main types of *mesirat nefesh* unto death, the ritual of *nefilat 'apayim* is the type performed by the righteous, who in their reparation of souls activate a syzygy in the lower reaches of the Godhead (*Tif'eret* and *Malkhut* in the highest world—activating a well of saving waters, which flow upward from the feminine (the womb of the righteous in heaven) and downward from the masculine gradation. This temporary conjunction is the result of the enacted death of the worshipper, who is "as if departed from the world." Its liturgical rubric is "To You (*'eleykha*), Lord, I raise my soul" (Ps. 25:1); that is, the adept raises his soul only to the hypostatic gradation of "Lord" (the masculine dimension of *Tif'eret*)—no further.[46] By contrast, through the martyrological intention of the *Shema* recitation in the liturgy, the worshipper activates a higher syzygy (the supernal Father and Mother, *Ḥokhmah* and *Binah*); for he now intends to die in fact, and, in accord with the key verse "For Your sake [*'aleykha*] we are killed all day long" (Ps. 44:23), actually goes "to the One who is above You" [*'alehkha;* i.e., to *Ḥokhmah,* who is above *Tif'eret*].[47] This produces a more permanent union in the supernal realm—all the more so when the recitation of the *Shema* accompanies an actual martyrdom.

In the practice of the Holy Lion, the adapt engages in shamanic flights to resure soul's from permanent "death." The mystical task therefore, while prostrate and "as if" dead in the *nefilat 'apayim* rite, is to be so spiritually focused as to accomplish the siege perilous—the descent into the realms of death itself in order to revive and unify the Godhead. If this is an ecstatic state, it yet remains one of astonishing inner awareness. The mystic is only outwardly deathlike; inwardly, he is all clarity for the sake of the holy reparations to be done. A more permanent union is reserved, as we noted, for recital of the *Shema* with the intention to die intact. Such recitations, we may assure, confirmed this theology through the ecstatic deaths of the worshippers. They were then "as if" dead in the body and mind alike.

Given this hierarchy, and the centrality of Luria's model for later mystics, it is all the more astonishing that Rabbi Dov Ber (the son of Rabbi Shueur Zalman of Liadi) reversed the spiritual gradation of the two rites in his powerful tract on ecstasy, the *Quntres ha-Hitpa'alut*.[48] There are many complex psychological and spiritual features of this book, which is complexly ordered and calibrated by a profound mystic intent on removing any possibility of self-delusion in worship.[49] What is important in this context is that Dov Ber puts the "death" achieved in the *nefilat 'apayim* rite on a higher plane than recitation of the *Shema*. Indeed, elaborating a gradation of states in his *Sha'ar ha-Teshuvah veha-Tefillah*,[50] the *nefilat 'apayim* rite is also superior to the ecstatic state achieved during the *'Amidah* prayer.[51] The differences are as follows: In the *'Amidah*, the worshipper may achieve only a temporary nihilation of the self—and no permanent "cessation of one's entire essence" (*'atzmuto*). Unless the former (*'Amidah*) stage is the basis for a deeper penetration in the divine Whole, the worshipper will gradually return to mundane reality and self-centeredness.[52] Only the *nefilat 'apayim* rite brings one to the state of supernormal consciousness that Dov Ber desires. Here the adept may be "absorbed [*nikhlal*] into the supernal Reality"—becoming One with it (*ve-hayu le-'ahadim*) that any trace of former separation is erased;[53] this deep *unio mystica* is deemed a permanent "bonding" (*hit-qasherut*) with God, an annihilation of the self into "the actual divine Reality" (*mahut 'eloqut mamash*).[54]

The superiority of the *nefilat 'apayim* state to that induced by the *Shema* recital reveals another dimension of this exalted level of mystical death in the thought of Dov Ber. For though this master recognized the spiritual heights possible through contemplating martyrdom while reciting the *Shema*, and lauded those who were able to prepare for such a death in the liturgy and withstand its terrors in actuality,[55] the advantage of the *nefilat 'apayim* practice lies precisely in its conjunction of the theoretical and actual. Recalling the old zoharic rubric that one should consider himself "*as if*" dead when performing *nefilat 'apayim*, Dov Ber says that "this is no mere act of imagination (*shi'ur*) but an 'actual seeming' [*dami mamash*]"; that is, when one truly gives oneself to death in the ritual, such that the merest "trace" of life is left, "this is no mere semblance (of death) produced by the imaginative faculty (*koaḥ ha-meddameh*]—but verity itself."[56] In such a state, that aspect of the worshipper's divine soul known as "*yeḥidah*" ascends on high and he is virtually dead to this world, having entered a near-comatose state of "deep sleep" (*nirdam*). At this level of expiration, the ecstatic is insensate to himself and all pain—an intriguing link in the old chain that taught that persons truly cleaving to God do not feel the tortures of their martyrdom.

One final document will conclude the theme: bringing the topics of imagination, martyrdom, substitutions, and recitation into one final ensemble. Indeed it teaches a spiritual practice of uncompromising intensity—one that attempts to bring life and death into the most fateful fusion for the sake of inner perfection. The text is the so-called *Tzeṭl Qoṭon* of the great nineteenth-century Hasidic master, the Tzaddik, Rabbi Elimelekh of Lizensk.[57] Following common Hasidic custom, with roots in roots in the medieval moral literature and beyond, Rabbi Elimelekh provides a list of spiritual practices (a kind of interior *regimen vitae*), which the adept is urged to study and internalize. The first two directives are of direct pertinence to our present discussion.

> 1. Whenever a person is not engaged in Torah study, and particularly when alone in his room or unable to sleep at night, let him think of the positive duty of "and I shall be sanctified among the people of Israel" (Lev. 22:32). And let him imagine in his soul and visualize in his mind "as if" (*ke'ilu*) a great and awesome fire burned before him up to the heart of heaven; and that he, for the sake of the sanctification of the Name, And the Holy One, blessed be he converts good thought into deeds (in his sight), so that the worshipper need not sit idly but may (even at such times) fulfill positive commands of the Torah.
> 2. A person should also think of the foregoing (meditation of death) during the 1st verse of the *Shema* and the 1st blessing of the *'Amidah*. And he should also intend the following: (that) even

if the gentile nations persecute him terribly, and rake his flesh to force him to deny God's Unit—heaven forbid!—he shall endure these torments and never cower to them. And he shall visualize in his mind "as if" (ke'ilu) they were doing the foregoing to him, and in that way (he shall) properly fulfill the recitation of the Shema and 'Amidah prayers.

The work continues with the stark advice to have similar thoughts and intentions while eating, or engaged in sexual intercourse, or during any other physical pleasure.

With this regimen, the imagination of death has absorbed the totality of one's life—filling the spaces of solitude, insuring the validity of prayer, and even neutralizing essential acts of human satisfaction. For Rabbi Elimelekh, the ruins of the heart must be sanctified through sacrificial discipline. In this way the old martyrological ideal is transformed: God is not simply or only "sanctified among [be-tokh] the children of Israel," but "within" their very being. A purified inwardness thus supplements public resistance as the way to sanctify the name. In a remarkable counterpoint to the meditative practice revealed by Maimonides near the close of his Guide for the Perplexed (2.51), in which the philosopher tells his discipline to meditate on the Shema and the perfection of God when one is in bed and alone, the mystic substitutes an awesome visualization of a martyrological consummation for rational contemplation. So much must the visualization of a sacrificial death play a central roll that the worshipper seeks to annihilate his human will in the fire of this imagination. In this way, the intention to die (the "good thought") will become a deed in fact and all the "positive commands of the Torah" will be performed. Fear of persecution is thus transferred in this document into a sublime readiness to die—a readiness that is meant to purify the heart and glorify God. Visualizing the death of the self-as-martyr becomes the utter transformation of that sacrifice: for now the spiritual training is to be a witness to one's own death. In a bitter revenge against cruel history, the perfected soul is a substitute for itself.

NOTES

1. A full discussion of this complex theme can be found in my book, The Kiss of God: Spiritual and Mystical Death in Judaism (Seattle,

1993). Portions of my discussion are drawn from chapter 3 there. The broader ideal of love of God in Judaism has been discussed by G. Vajda, *L'amour dieu dans la théologie juive du moyen age* (Paris, 1957).

2. See the L. Finkelstein edition (New York, 1969), 55.

3. 6.7 (line 37, in the edition of S. Lieberman, *Tosefta: Zera'im* (New York, 1955), 35.

4. See for example *Mekhilta de-Rabbi Ishmael, de-Shira* 3; Horowitz-Rabin edition (Jerusalem, 1960), 127.

5. The combat motif is quite common. Compare two sayings of Rabbi Resh Lakish: "One should always incite the good inclination against the evil one [and Rashi glosses: 'He should wage war against the evil inclination) . . . If he conquers him, fine, if not, let him study Torah . . ." (*b. Berakhot* 5a]; and, "A person's [evil] *yetzer* gathers strength each day, and seeks to slay him . . . ; and were it not that the Holy One, Blessed by He comes to his aid, he would not overcome it" (*b. Qiddushin* 30b).

6. *b. Berakhot* 17a.

7. *Sefer Ha-Manhig,* ed. Y. Raphael (Jerusalem, 1978), I (*dinei tefillah* 1), 36f. (Hebrew pagination) the ruling follows *Sefer Ha-Orah* (par. 12): *qorban hashvinan le-hu* (note *ad* 1.36). The scriptural citation from Hosea is remarkable: while it accords with the main sense of the Massoretic text, the reading *peri* (fruit) instead of *parim* (bulls) is similar to the Septuagint *karpon* (fruit).

8. *Abudarham Ha-Shallem* (Jerusalem, 1959), *Seder shaharit shel hol,* 48.

9. *Sefer Shibbolei Ha-Leqet Ha-Shallem,* ed. S. Buber (Vilna, 1886), 2. R. Zedekiah's brother, R. Benjamin, is cited as having written "that the recitation of the *tamid*-service is obligatory [*hovah*]."

10. In *Perushei Siddur Ha-Tefillah La-Rokeah,* ed. R. Moshe Hirschler and R. Yehudah Alter Hirschler (Jerusalem, 1992), 2.16; on 35, R. Eleazar justifies the custom by citations from Hosea 14:3 and *b. Megillah* 31b.

11. *Shulhan Arukh, Orah Hayyim,* 2.

12. *The Book of the Pomegranate: Moses De Leon's Sefer Ha-Rimon,* ed. E. R. Wolfson (Atlanta, 1988), 225f.

13. So J. Katz, in his influential essay "*Beyn TaTeNU le TaH TaT,*" in S. Baron, ed., *Yitzhak Baer Jubilee Volume,* (Jerusalem, 1960), 318–37.

14. See, for example, R. Menahem Recanati, *Peirush 'al ha-Torah* (Venice, 1548), fol. 77 c–d. For a full discussion, see my *The Kiss of God* (n. 1 above), chap. 1.

15. *Sefer ha-Rimmon,* 41f.

16. Ibid., 39f.

17. See ibid., 43f; the earlier reference to joy is on 37f.

18. Cf. *b. Berakhot* 61b and *j. Soṭah* 5, 20c.

19. See his *Tashbetz* (Cremona, 1557) para. 415; and in his *Responsa* para. 517. For fuller discussion, with other examples, see my *The Kiss of God*, chap. 2.

20. *Bayit Ḥadash* to *Ṭur, Oraḥ Ḥayyim* sec. 61.

21. (Zolkiew, 1804), 20b.

22. See the sources noted above, n. 18, and the discussion in *The Kiss of God*, chap. 2, where the historicity of this account is analyzed and its role as a mythic model considered.

23. (Frankfurt-am-Main, 1922) no. 482.

24. Ibid., no. 485.

25. See n. 13, above.

26. Cf. *M. Baba Qamah VIII. 6* and *b. Sanhedrin* 74b; also, *Tos. Baba Qama* 91a, s.v., "ve-lo'," and the *Pisqei Tosaphot, Baba Qama, Ha-Ḥovel* no. 215; Maimonides, *Mishnah Torah, Hilkhot Yesodei Ha-Torah* 5. 6–7.

27. *Yosef Ometz*, no. 486.

28. The *Yevein Metzula* Chronicle was first printed in Venice, 1653, and repeatedly thereafter. The popular Lvov edition, 1851, is unpaginated; the present episode occurs on 7a. On this theme, cp. the defiant resistance of R. Samson ben Pesah of Ostropol—one of the martyrs of the Chmielnicki persecutions (1648). See the penetrating analysis of this saint's life and death by Y. Liebes, "Mysticism and Reality: Towards a portrait of the Martyr and Kabbalist, R. Samson Ostropoler," in I. Twersky and B. Septimus, eds., *Jewish Thought in the Seventeenth Century* (Cambridge, Mass., 1987) 221–55.

29. *Yosef Ometz*, no. 485.

30. Cp. *Zohar* 1.66a, 224a–b; 3.69a. On the whole subject, see G. Scholem, "Ḥaluqa De-Rabbanan," *Tarbiz* 24 (1955) 297–306.

31. *Shnei Luḥot ha-Berit* vol. 2, pt. 1 (*Torah She-Bekhtav*) 1c–d.

32. Ibid.; and see the discussion of this source and older sources in Green, *Devotion and Commandments: The Faith of Abraham in Hasidic Tradition* (Cincinnati, 1989) 39–59.

33. Cf. *Shnei Luḥot Ha-Brit* vol. 1, pt. 2 (*Taʿanit, Meʿinyan Ha-ʿAvodah*), 45a.

34. Ibid., vol. 2, pt. 2 (*Torah She-Beʿal Peh*) 23b. A variation of this recitation, in a more condensed form recurs in R. Nathan Hanover's slightly later (1662) collection of prayers called *Shaʿarei Tziyyon;* cf. the Pisa, 1789, edition, 95a–96a.

35. The rite is not performed during Sabbath and Holy Festivals, certain minor feast days and fasts, and various other occasions varying from a day to a month, depending upon custom. These times are listed in the Codes, like the *Shulḥan Arukh, Oraḥ Ḥayyim*, 131.5–7.

36. See simply the gloss of Rabbi Moses Isserles to the *Shulḥan Arukh,* 131.1.

37. See also the comments of I. Tishby, *Mishnat ha-Zohar* (Jerusalem, 1975), 2:275.

38. *Zohar Ḥadash, Terumah,* R. Margoliot ed. (Jerusalem, 1979), 42a.

39. Y. Liebes, *Ha-Mashiaḥ shel ha-Zohar,* in *Ha-Ra'ayon ha-Meshiḥiy be-Yisrael* (Jerusalem, 1982), 177f., n. 311, makes the case for the demythologized *qof;* while Wolfson, *Book of the Pomegranate,* 84, note *ad* line 1, transfers his point to the larger issue of self-devotion without being specific. The discussion of the missing letter appears in *Sefer ha-Rimmon,* Wolfson ed., 84f.

40. *Sha'ar ha-Kavvanot, 'Inyan Nefilat 'Apayim* (Jerusalem, 1989), pt. 1, 301b–314b. This includes five interpretations.

41. See Interpretation *(Derush)* 1, 301b–302b.

42. The *Ze'ir Anpin* is the zoharic equivalent of the six lower gradations (from *Tiferet* to *Yesod*), not including the final gradation of *Malkhut,* or the Shekhina. In *Ze'ir Anpin* the divine qualities of mercy, justice, and compassion are in balance.

43. See the whole discussion in *Derush* 2, 301a–305a.

44. See *Derush* 3, 305a–307b.

45. See *Derush* 53, 310b–314b; and on *'Inyan Kavvanat Keriy'at Shema, Derush* 5, 137b.

46. This stasis is marked by the terms *dayyeka* and *mamash,* "precisely"; see *'Inyan Kavvanat Keriyat Shema, Derush* 5, 137b.

47. Here, too, the key term *'aleykha* is marked by *dayyeka* and *mamash;* see ibid., 137b and 310a.

48. The tract is published under the title, *Liqquṭei Be'urim* (Warsaw, 1868), with a commentary by R. Hillel of Paritch.

49. For a full discussion see my *The Kiss of God,* chap. 3.

50. Published in two parts in Shklov (1817, 1818); reprinted as one volume entitled *Sha'arei Teshuvah* (Zhitomer, 1864). I have used the later edition (reprint; Brooklyn, 1983), where pt. 1 is *Sha'arei Tefillah.* For an earlier examination of *nefilat 'apayim* in this work, see the discussion of N. Lowenstein, "Self-sacrifice of the Zaddik in the Teachings of B. Dov Ber, the *Mittler Rebbe,*" in A. Rapaport-Albert and S. Zipperstein, eds., *Jewish History: Essays in Honor of Chimen Abramsky,* (London, 1988) 465–71. His larger concern is with the central role of self-sacrifice in early Hasidic thought; cf. *Communicating the Infinite* (Chicago, 1990), 55–56, 90–97, 127–28.

51. *Sha'arei Teshuvah,* 1, 42b–43b; the prooftext used is again cited at 44a and developed. It seems that Dov Ber was strongly influenced by his father, Rabbi Shneur Zalman, who in his *Seder Tefillot* (Kopyst, 1831; 4th ed., Brooklyn, 1986) 21a, begins with the same verse and

distinguishes the superiority of the *nefilat apayim* ritual from the ecstatic states to be achieved during the recital of the *Shema* and the *ʿAmidah*. Dov Ber follows his father in his analyses. Several other important borrowings will be pointed out below (see nn. 52–53, 56). This filiation of ideas has not been recognized in Loewenthal's consideration.

52.   R. Shneur Zalman, *Seder Tefillot*, 81c–82d, treats at length the theme of "astonishment" from Gen. 24:21 as the basis of being opened to a new (initial) level of spiritual consciousness. Dov Ber follows him in this, and in one of the analogies.

53.   R. Shneur Zalman, *Seder Tefillot*, 26a, already uses the image of glue in connection with spiritual bonding; and the striking reuse of Ezek. 37:17, "ve-hayu le-aḥadim mamash" [they shall be One in actuality], 26d (var., 26a), to convey the *unio mystica* involved. He also speaks of the mystical state as one of absorption, saying "when the soul and body are totally absorbed [*be-hikkalel*] in the Unity of God they shall be One in actuality."

54.   See 45c; here and elsewhere the term *mamash* is repeated, often in conjunction with the recitation of Psalm 25. This derives from Lurianic models; see above, and nn. 37–38.

55.   Ibid., 45d–46c.

56.   Ibid., 46c–d. See also R. Shneur Zalman, *Seder Tefillot*, 26a–d, where the oxymoron of being "as if" (*keʾilu*) death and "actually" (*mamash*) dead is developed to show that in the *nefilat ʾapayim* rite one actualizes martyrdom and achieves a truer level of adhesion to God.

57.   It is found at the beginning of his *Noam Elimelekh* (Kracow, 1896) and in collections of spiritual practices.

CHAPTER 11

Weeping, Death, and Spiritual Ascent in Sixteenth-Century Jewish Mysticism

Elliot R. Wolfson

In the sixteenth century, in the wake of the expulsion of the Jews from Spain in 1492, a spiritual renaissance of sorts took shape in a small community in the Galilean town of Safed in northern Palestine. In a wonderfully written essay, full of both learning and pathos, Solomon Schechter captured the mystical animus of this community of kabbalists, preachers, poets, and moralists.[1] To be sure, there is historical evidence that from at least the latter part of the thirteenth century Safed was a center for Jewish mystical activity, and indeed many of the trends that informed the leading kabbalists in the sixteenth century find their expression in sources deriving from authors inhabiting that city at earlier times.[2] One can, therefore, legitimately speak of a continuity of mystical traditions in that locality. Moreover, the view espoused by Scholem that only in Safed of the sixteenth century do most of the mystical rites described in earlier texts, principally the *Zohar,* become enacted in the realm of performative ritual,[3] has been challenged by recent scholarship that has focused more on the wider range of human experience and behavior to which the earlier textual sources attest as well as on the possibility that behind the fictional fellowship described in zoharic literature is an actual group of mystics who lived and functioned as a society.[4] Thus it is no longer sufficient to view the history of Kabbalah in a linear fashion as a transformation from esoteric doctrine (*torat ha-sod*) to a living religious teaching (*torat ḥayyim*). Still, something distinctive occurred in the sixteenth century, a confluence of socioeconomic, political, and

religious factors (including, of course, an intensified messianic enthusiasm that may have erupted on account of the expulsion of
Jewry from the Iberian Peninsula at the end of the fifteenth century
and the consequent migration of Jews to North Africa, Italy, and
the Ottoman Empire[5]) resulting in the formation of a major center
of Jewish mystical activity at this time and in this place. The impact
of this circle on world Jewry was decisive, especially in the area of
religious customs (*minhagim*), many of which were either instituted or transformed in light of kabbalistic principles.

One of the characteristic features of the spiritual revival initiated by the kabbalists in Safed was a renewed interest in the cultivation of revelatory experiences or mystical illumination.[6] Thus, in
striking contrast to the general trend in the history of Jewish mysticism to avoid writing first-person accounts of mystical experiences,[7] we find a proliferation of reports of dreams and angelic
visitations in the sixteenth century.[8] Various examples could be
given to illustrate this point, but here I will only mention some of
the better known ones: the *Maggid Mesharim* of Joseph Karo,
which is the record of his conversations with his angelic mentor
(*maggid*);[9] the *Sefer Gerushin* of Moses Cordovero, the record of
the forced banishments of the kabbalists which resulted in inspired
exegesis;[10] the *Milei de-Shemaya* of Eleazar Azikri, a book of
ethical-pietistic teachings rooted in heavenly revelations;[11] and the
Sefer ha-Ḥezyonot of Ḥayyim Vital, the mystical diary that registers his many visions of angels, the prophet Elijah (in different
forms), and communications with souls of departed saints.[12] There
is, additionally, sufficient evidence to show that the idea of an
ecstatic journey of the soul to the heavenly realms, known from the
ancient apocalyptic and hekhalot literature as well as from classical works of medieval kabbalah (e.g., the *Zohar*), was once again
appropriated as a desired goal of the *via mystica* by the sixteenth-
century kabbalists.[13] In this material the ascent is referred to as
ʿaliyyat neshamah, thus conveying the belief that the soul under-
goes the heavenly journey and ecstatically leaves the body. As will
be discussed more fully below, it is evident that these older traditions concerning ascent are recast in light of contemporary theosophical assumptions, but the fact nevertheless remains that these
mystics demonstrated a keen interest in the spiritual journey to
other realms of being, an interest that colored their theosophical
systems in a fundamental way.

The interest in the cultivation of ecstatic experience is also attested by the fact, noted by various scholars,[14] that Abraham Abulafia's meditative method of inducing the prophetic state by the technique of permutation and combination of Hebrew letters informed many of the kabbalists in sixteenth-century Safed, including Judah Albotini, Moses Cordovero, and Ḥayyim Vital. There is yet another vantage point that allows us to appreciate the centrality of revelatory experience in the sixteenth-century mystical revival. As has been noted in the scholarly literature, in the history of Judaism—especially of the apocalyptic and mystical varieties, but in more normative sources as well—there is a long-standing tradition that upholds inspired exegesis or pneumatic interpretation as a legitimate mode of reading Scripture. Rather than representing distance from God or a substitute for direct revelation, the interpretative process (*midrash*) is predicated precisely on a reenactment of the state of prophetic inspiration or revelation characteristic of the text in its compositional layer.[15] In the specific case of Vital there is sufficient textual evidence to support the view that he posited a clear nexus between prophecy (understood by him to entail mystical or contemplative illumination) and comprehension of the secrets of Torah.[16] (Needless to say, Vital draws upon earlier sources, some of which he cites explicitly in the fourth part of his *Sha'are Qedushah*.) The human capacity to understand mysteries of Torah is related proportionally to the prophetic influx that one receives from one's soul-root in the sefirotic realm.[17] The point is epitomized in the following passage from *Sha'ar Ruaḥ ha-Qodesh,* which underscores the significance of the meditative practice of contemplative unifications (*yiḥudim*)[18] as a higher form of worship than normative Torah-study, for these unifications facilitate communion with the departed souls of the righteous and the drawing down of the efflux of light from the supernal realm, although the ultimate purpose of this mystical praxis is not realization of personal spiritual fulfillment but rectification of the upper realms of being:

> Know that if the souls of these righteous ones who were mentioned are revealed to a person who is from the root of their soul, his comprehension increases wondrously . . . Know that if a person who has begun to unify these unifications abstains from unifying he brings about great harm . . . for he causes those souls who wanted to be united with the person to withdraw and

be separated from him. Do not say that the engagement with [study of] Torah is greater and it is not appropriate to abolish it, for the matter of the unifications that has been mentioned is greater than the engagement in [study of] Torah, for he unifies the upper worlds. [This activity] is called engagement in [study of] Torah and unification; it is all one. Even if the souls are not revealed to him well he should not worry nor cease from the unification. His intention should not be only to dray down to himself that soul but rather to rectify the upper worlds.[19]

In the parallel passage in *Sha'ar ha-Yiḥudim*, which represents part of the corpus of Vital edited by Jacob Zemaḥ, the illuminative nature of this praxis is emphasized as well:

> Know that the one who knows how to unify the upper unifications but abstains from performing them causes those righteous ones who want to be impregnated[20] by him to assist him in the [study of] Torah and the [fulfillment of the] commandments to withdraw from him and he brings about great harm upon himself . . . The reason is that involvement with the unifications is greater than engagement with the Torah for the unification is engagement with the Torah. Further, he who unifies the worlds merits a great reward. Thus it is good to unify these unifications constantly every day, for this will help him more than engagement with Torah. Moreover, by means of this he will draw down upon himself the souls of the righteous who want to be impregnated by him for they very much desire these unifications for they too are unified and cleave to that unification, and a great light extends to them. From that great light which extends to them on account of that unification they divide and give a portion to the person who performs the unification, and they reveal to him the mysteries of Torah, and especially if the person intends to elevate them by the secret of the female waters.[21]

The concluding statement alludes to the fact that a consequence of the technique of *yiḥudim* is the heavenly ascent of the adept in consort with the soul of the righteous that he has brought down through contemplative meditation. Both souls function as the "female waters" (*mayim nuqvin*)[22] that rise to stimulate the unification of the lower male and female aspects of the Godhead (*Ze'eir 'Anpin* and *Nuqba' di-Ze'eir*), a motif to which I shall return below.

It is well known that, according to Vital, the authority accorded to his master, Isaac Luria, derived from the fact that he received his Kabbalah from Elijah through the Holy Spirit (*be-ruaḥ*

ha-qodesh 'al pi 'eliyahu).[23] That Luria's knowledge of theosophic
matters was attained through a revelation of Elijah (*gilluy 'eliyahu*)
is considered to be the greatest of his spiritual or mantic powers.
On one level the revelation of Elijah, an idea found in earlier
rabbinic and mystical texts, is meant to legitimate or privilege
Luria's teachings when compared to other kabbalistic trends of
sixteenth-century Safed. Thus, in the introduction to his *Sha'ar ha-
Haqdamot*, Vital relates that from Naḥmanides, who lived in the
thirteenth century, until Luria in the sixteenth, there were no authentic kabbalists, for all kabbalistic works composed during this
period were based on speculation rather than an oral reception
from a master.[24] (For Luria, of course, the *Zohar* was a work of
R. Simeon bar Yoḥai, and therefore it belonged to the second century.) Luria revived the "tradition" for he received kabbalistic secrets directly from the mouth of Elijah, as did R. Simeon according
to the *Zohar*[25], as well as some of the first known kabbalists according to the chain of tradition (*shalshelet ha-qabbalah*) reported
by various kabbalists living in the latter part of the thirteenth and
early part of the fourteenth century.[26] Yet, on another level, as may
be gathered from Vital's writings, the motif of the revelation of
Elijah indicates that Luria received esoteric matters in an inspired,
indeed ecstatic, state of mind. Thus Vital, in the introduction to his
large anthology of Luria's teachings, duly warns the reader that the
"sermons and the words themselves in this composition of mine
attest and declare that deep and wondrous words such as these are
not in the power of the human intellect to compose, if not by
means of the influx of the Holy Spirit through Elijah, blessed be
his memory."[27] This accords well with the view of Vital, mentioned above, that one can comprehend mystical secrets only to the
extent that one receives the prophetic influx from above. In one of
the introductions published in his *'Eṣ Ḥayyim*, Vital cites the following in the name of Luria: "Whenever a person is occupied with
this wisdom [i.e., Kabbalah] with all [of his] concentration and
strength, and [he is scrupulous with respect to] the fulfillment of
the commandments, and he is on guard against any sin, even if he
is a servant or the son of a maidservant, the Holy Spirit rests upon
him and Elijah the prophet, may his memory be blessed, is revealed
to him, and [this revelatory state] does not cease as long as he is
involved with it."[28] In a similar vein Solomon Shlomeil of Dresnitz
relates in the first of his five extant letters (written in 1609) that the

secrets revealed by Luria "could not be comprehended by any being except by means of the appearance of the Holy Spirit from above and through Elijah, blessed be his memory . . . Even though there is no prophet or seer after the destruction [of the Temple] the spirit of the living God is not prevented from hovering upon those who are worthy of it."[29] Both Luria and Vital function as the prototype for the mystic visionary, as numerous examples are offered to show that when they studied or expounded kabbalistic truths they had revelatory or ecstatic experiences. To cite in this context one illustration: in *Sefer ha-Hezyonot* Vital reports that one Sabbath morning he was delivering a sermon in a synagogue in Jerusalem, and a certain woman, Rachel, the sister of R. Judah Mishan, related that the whole time that Vital was expounding the text she saw a pillar of fire above his head (from other passages it is evident that the pillar symbolizes the Presence) and Elijah to his right helping him out. When Vital completed the textual exposition, the pillar and Elijah vanished.[30] This incident is indicative of a larger assumption in Vital's worldview, namely, the activity of *derashah* is an occasion for revelatory experience, including especially the appearance of Elijah.

Here I would take issue with a comment of R. J. Zwi Werblowsky, who utilized Rudolf Otto's distinction between mysticism and theosophy to characterize the nature of ecstatic experience formulated in the sixteenth-century kabbalistic literature. That is, according to Werblowsky, ecstatic experiences cultivated by kabbalists served only as a means for gnosis or esoteric knowledge. Generalizing from this observation Werblowsky contests the view expressed by Gershom Scholem that "under the cover of the bewildering and often bizarre theosophical speculations of the kabbalists there hides a genuinely mystical life."[31] Werblowsky offers the following critique, focusing primarily on Lurianic Kabbalah: "The fact remains, nevertheless, that the discursive and even dialectical elements are so prominent in kabbalistic literature that we may almost speak of an intellectualistic hypertrophy . . . More often than not kabbalistic literature is less the record of the *cognitio experimentalis dei* than the substitution of a theosophical *pilpul* for the halakhic one of the rabbinic lawyers."[32] Scholem's formulation is closer to the mark, although he himself was not always consistent on this point.[33] It is misconceived to isolate in the kabbalistic tradition in general, and in Lurianic Kabbalah in particular, theosophic gnosis from mystical ecstasy. In my estimation Vital is clear on this issue: study of Kabbalah is commensurate with prophetic illumination. More than that, the literature of the kabbalists, especially the disciples of Luria, is precisely what Werblowsky says it is not, namely, the record of their experiential knowledge of God. To the outsider it may appear that the Lurianic texts are an exercise in kabbalistic dialectics, a thicket of theosophical ruminations that conceal the living face of divine reality. However, to the initiate these texts constitute the map of the divine world such that textual study itself provides the occasion for mystical illumination.

In the remainder of this study I would like to concentrate on one specific ecstatic technique, that of weeping, which appears a number of times in the writings of Vital. This technique, as I will presently show, is viewed as a means for either comprehension of esoteric wisdom or heavenly ascent that occurs specifically while one is asleep. At the outset it behooves me to acknowledge that Moshe Idel has recently discussed weeping as a mystical technique in Jewish texts from apocalyptic sources to Hasidism of the eighteenth and nineteenth centuries.[34] More specifically, Ideal distinguishes two types of weeping in the relevant literature: "mystical weeping," which involved the "effort to receive visions and information about secrets as the direct result of self-induced weeping," and "theurgical weeping," which "intended to induce weeping above—internal processes within the Divine triggered by the shedding of human tears."[35] Within that framework Idel discusses some of the relevant material in sixteenth-century Kabbalah, including the works of Vital.[36] I do not intend to go over the entire historical range that Idel has already covered but will concentrate rather on the sixteenth-century material, for there are aspects of the weeping technique in this body of literature that still need to be explained and located within a broader phenomenological and hermeneutical context. Whereas Idel approaches the topic diachronically, as part of his grand effort of reconstructing ideas in Jewish mysticism on the basis of intertextual links, I am attempting a synchronic analysis in order to shed further light on the phenomenon as it presented itself in Safed.

Let me begin by citing the key text from Vital's *Sha'ar Ruaḥ ha-Qodesh*:

> The matter concerning a person's comprehension of wisdom [i.e., kabbalistic lore] entails several conditions. The first condition is silence. One should limit one's speech as much as is possible, and one should not sing any idle song. This is the meaning

of [what the rabbis], blessed be their memory, said: "A fence around wisdom is silence."[37] The second condition is that with respect to every word and every matter in the Torah or the *Zohar* that one does not understand, one should think [about them] and weep over them, and as much as one can, one should augment one's weeping. This [tradition] is from R. Abraham ha-Levi [Berukhim] who heard it from the Rabbi [Isaac Luria], blessed be his memory. Moreover, [with respect to] the ascent of the person's soul (*'aliyyat nishmat ha-'adam*) at night after he lays down to sleep, he should not meander about in the follies of this world, but rather immediately he should ascend to the place that is appropriate for him. All this depends on weeping, he should weep during the time of sleep, and sleep from the weeping.[38]

It is evident that two separate traditions (both of which ultimately may be derived from zoharic literature[39]) are conflated in Vital's text, the one, attributed to Abraham ben Eliezer Halevi Berukhim, concerning weeping as a propaedeutic for comprehension, and the other, apparently his own, which links weeping to the nocturnal ascent of the soul separated from the body.[40] Interestingly enough, in his aforementioned survey of weeping as a mystical technique in Jewish sources, Idel notes that weeping results in (1) revelatory or visionary experience, occasionally of the chariot, and (2) comprehension of esoteric matters. It is no accident that Vital adds to the first tradition the one that underscores the connection between weeping and heavenly ascent. Indeed, as I will set out to illustrate, the mechanics of the two are quite similar.

The tradition reported in the name of Abraham ben Eliezer ha-Levi Berukhim is repeated with some slight modification in a second passage in *Sha'ar Ruaḥ ha-Qodesh*: "R. Abraham ha-Levi, may God protect and preserve him, told me that my teacher [i.e., Luria], blessed be his memory, gave him advice to attain comprehension, and it is that he should not make idle conversation, and that he should rise at midnight and weep over [his] lack of knowledge. He should study much *Zohar* alone, in a rapid reading without going into too much depth."[41] In one of the introductions to *Sha'ar ha-Haqdamot* Vital combines the various views that were circulating amongst the disciples of Luria:

Comprehension of wisdom (*hassagat ha-ḥokhmah*): The first condition is that one should limit his speech and be quiet as much as is possible so that he will not produce idle conversation, in accordance with the saying of the rabbis, blessed be their memory, "A fence around wisdom is silence." Furthermore, another condition: concerning every matter of Torah that you do not understand you should weep over it as much as you can. Also the nocturnal ascent of the soul to the supernal world, so that one does not wander about in the vanities of the world, depends on one's going to sleep through weeping and in bitter sadness, especially to comprehend wisdom for nothing prevents wisdom more than this. Moreover, with respect to man's comprehension there is nothing that helps like purity and ablution[42] so that a person will be pure all the time.[43]

In yet another version of this tradition, extant in manuscript, weeping as a means to attain mystical gnosis (*hassagat ha-ḥokhmah*) is placed in the context of both prayer and study: "The second condition: in all your prayers, and in every hour of study, in a place that is difficult for you, where you cannot understand or comprehend your studies (*ḥokhmat ha-limmudim*[44]) or some secret, arouse yourself to bitter weeping until your eyes shed tears, and the more you can weep, you should do so. Increase your weeping for the gates of tears are not closed[45] and the supernal gates will be opened to you."[46] The juxtaposition of these different motifs, weeping, prayer, and the comprehension of secrets, is attested as well in the following account of Luria given by Solomon Shlomeil of Dresnitz:

> He would tell his students that he would cry as many tears as the [number of] hairs of his beard with respect to each and every secret that was revealed to him from heaven. Similarly, when he wanted to reveal a secret to his disciples they did not want to give him permission until he prayed countless prayers and cried as many tears as the [number of] hairs on his head.[47]

Finally, this tradition is mentioned in another context, the *Shaʿar ha-Yiḥudim:* "I have found in a manuscript of R. Ḥayyim Vital: It is good for the one who wants to apprehend [wisdom] to increase his silence as much as is possible, as well as his weeping on every matter that he does not know . . . Each night he should also place a stone under his head and contemplate the Tetragrammaton [spelled YWD HH WAW HH = 53] which numerically equals [the word] *'even* [i.e., stone = 53]."[48] The placing of a stone under one's head in order to meditate on the divine name is related to a well-known magical technique in Jewish sources, the dream-question (*she'elat halom*):[49] by placing a parchment with God's name under one's head one could adjure the angel of dreams to answer a query posed in the waking hours.[50] Knowledge of the name confers the capacity for receiving prophetic and visionary illumination.

The full force of the function of weeping in this context can be appreciated if we pause and consider the first specified condition to attain mystical comprehension, namely, silence or refraining from idle conversation.[51] The notion that silence is a prerequisite for the attainment of esoteric truths is expressed, for instance, in the kabbalistic-ethical compendium, *Reshit Hokhmah*, written by another sixteenth-century kabbalist, Elijah de Vidas, one of the students of Cordovero. Commenting on the same passage from the mishnah 'Avot mentioned by Vital, "a fence around wisdom is silence," de Vidas notes that "by means of one's silence one is removed from the six extremities [i.e., the six lower emanations], which are the voice and speech [respectively *Tif'eret* and *Shekhinah*], and ascends to the place of silence, which is thought, the secret of wisdom[52] . . . Another explanation of the matter is that when a person is silent he makes himself into a chariot for the place of silence, and he merits that secrets of Torah will flow upon him, for they are in silence, as permission is not granted for them to be revealed."[53] While the tradition of Abraham ha-Levi reported by Vital does not explicitly mention the theosophic transformation of the rabbinic idea that we find in the case of de Vidas, it is plausible to assume that this is precisely what underlies the former text as well. Silence, therefore, functions as a kind of magical device to draw down the influx from above, a process that Vital elsewhere, perhaps influenced by the anonymous Abulafian work written at the end of the thirteenth century, *Sha'are Ṣedeq*, calls "*hamshakhat ha-mahshavah*,"[54] drawing down of thought, by means of proper intentions and unifications (*kawwanot we-yihudim*).[55] It seems to me that in the teaching attributed to Abraham ha-Levi the silence also assumes a specifically magical role as a technique for drawing down the life force from the upper recesses of the Godhead.

This point is important, for it holds the key to understanding the significance of weeping in this context as well. That is, the weeping serves as the means by which the individual can directly effect the divine, specifically by opening up the highest channels to overflow in a way that parallels the shedding of tears below. This is alluded to in one of the formulations of Abraham ha-Levi's teaching to the effect that an increase of weeping opens the supernal gates, which may be interpreted as a reference to the upper emanations. In the case of some kabbalists, the *sha'are dim'ah*, gates of weeping, correspond to the forty-nine gates of *Binah* (understanding), the third emanation. Such a usage is found, for example, in the following comment from the unpublished part of Cordovero's encyclopedic work, *'Elimah Rabbati:*

> When a person desires to perform some unification . . . it should be by means of tears, for the heart does not cleave to the desire of the soul except through weeping. The tears are from the heart, therefore it is proper that when one unifies [the name of God] he should contemplate through weeping. The tears cause the cleaving of the person (*devequt ha-'adam*) . . . and he opens the gates of *Binah* . . . Therefore one must open the gates of weeping to open the gates [of *Binah*], and from there all the other gates are opened.[56]

For Cordovero, as in the other material that I have mentioned, the weeping serves simultaneously as a mystical technique and a theurgical device. It is virtually impossible in this context to keep the issues entirely distinct. In the case of the tradition reportedly going back to Luria, the weeping is presented as a means to attain mystical comprehension, but the latter is depicted as an opening up of the supernal gates. The comprehension of esoteric matters proceeds from an influx of divine light, an influx that can overflow only through the proper magical devices. In yet another context Vital explicitly states that the function of shedding tears below is to ameliorate the forces of divine judgment above. This is formulated, following the zoharic precedent, as a kabbalistic recasting of the rabbinic mythos concerning God's shedding two tears into the great sea when he recalls the suffering of Israel in exile.[57] According to Vital, the weeping below corresponds to the shedding of tears above from the supernal wisdom[58] to the lower wisdom, that is, the Presence symbolized as the great sea; hence, the talmudic gates of weeping, *sha'are dim'ah,* are identified as the aspects of *Neṣaḥ* (endurance) and *Hod* (majesty) within *Ḥokhmah* (wisdom).[59] From this context, then, we again see that the Lurianic kabbalist conceives of weeping as a theurgic means to open the highest channels of the sefirotic world.

There is another dimension here as well that is not openly stated but may be reconstructed on the basis of various other comments in the relevant literature. That is, the weeping of the eye symbolically displaces the seminal discharge of the phallus. Given the relative neglect of scholars to pay attention to the phallic symbolism of the eye in Lurianic Kabbalah (although, as I will show in more detail below, the eyes properly speaking represent not the phallus but rather the testes or at least an aspect of the upper dimension of the Godhead that corresponds to the latter), it seems to me warranted to enter here into a discussion exploring the various facets of this matter. As is the case with so many ideas and motifs in the complex Lurianic system, so too with respect to this particular symbol Luria and his disciples draw upon many earlier texts. The correlation of the eye and the phallus is an old one in Jewish sources, perhaps suggested by the fact that the word 'ayin connotes both the eye and a spring or fountain, the latter being a rather obvious phallic symbol.[60] The upwards displacement of the phallus by the eye, and the philological connection with 'ayin in the double sense of eye and spring, is attested in many rabbinic texts, both classical and medieval. Perhaps the most obvious example is found in the interpretation (attributed to R. Abahu) of Joseph's blessing in Gen. 49:22, "Joseph is a fruitful bough, a fruitful bough by a spring" (*ben porat yosef ben porat 'ale 'ayin*). According to the rabbinic reading, the blessing guarantees Joseph immunity against the evil eye.[61] The key expression 'ale 'ayin, "by a spring," is thus read 'ule 'ayin, "above the eye," that is, beyond the reaches of the evil eye (*'eina' bisha'*), which refers specifically to sexual desire.[62] This euphemistic usage of the word is implied in the talmudic dictum, "a person should not drink from this cup and cast his eye upon another cup."[63] The phallic symbolization of the eye also seems to underlie various rabbinic passages that deal with the seeing of the divine Presence,[64] especially the midrashic reading of Exod. 24:11, which contrasts the brazenness of the sons of Aaron, Nadab, and Abihu, who loosened their head-coverings and feasted their eyes upon the Presence, with the modesty of Moses, who hid his face in his visual encounter with the Presence.[65] As I have argued at length elsewhere, the act of gazing in this context likely implies some sexual activity with the eye functioning as a phallic symbol.[66] Drawing upon this midrashic motif, kabbalistic sources, particularly the zoharic and Lurianic materials, refer to the state of union between male and female potencies as a face-to-face glance (*histakkelut panim be-fanim* or *hashgaḥah panim be-fanim*).[67] A later attestation of the correlation of the eye and phallus is evident from the comment of Maimonides that semen is the "light of the eyes."[68] This correlation plays an instrumental role in several kabbalistic sources from the classical period of the development of Spanish Kabbalah in the thirteenth century. Here I will provide a modest sampling of the relevant references. The phallic symbolization is evident in a number of zoharic passages, of which I will mention one in this context:[69] the wise man, described as one who is filled with eyes, is said to cast his open eye (*peqiḥu de-ʿeinaʾ*)[70] upon the hidden secrets of Torah, which are revealed from beneath its garments, that is, the literal sense of Scripture.[71] As I have suggested elsewhere,[72] it seems that the open eye of the sage corresponds to the phallus (or fulfills a function that is phallic in nature) and the Torah, which is parabolically depicted as the beautiful maiden without eyes, is the feminine Presence. The casting of the open eye, therefore, is erotically charged for it bestows upon that which is seen. To cite one other example, Joseph Angelet comments as follows upon the verse, "The eyes of all look to You expectantly, and You give them their food when it is due" (Ps. 145:15):

> The "eyes of all" refer to the seven eyes[73] that are comprised within the attribute of All [*middat kol*], for the world stands upon seven pillars and all of them stand upon one Ṣaddiq [i.e., Yesod][74] . . . and the Ṣaddiq is called All, and all things comprised in him are called the "eyes of All" [which] "look to You expectantly," to that supernal anointing oil that flows from the brain, the most hidden of all that which is hidden, to the All. Then, "You give them their food when it is due." What is "when it is due" [*be-ʿitto*]? This refers to Ṣedeq [*Malkhut*] and she is filled like a container that is filled of all good things, and she overflows to the lower entities in accord with what is decreed in the supernal constellation [*mazzal*] for[75] children, livelihood, and sustenance derive from there.[76]

The seven eyes are thus seven attributes that are comprised within *Yesod*, which is designated as the All (*kol*). Further on in the same context, Angelet specifies the identification of the eye and *Yesod* more precisely: "He will be a 'fruitful bough by a spring' (Gen. 49:22), this refers to the eyeball (*ʿeina de-galgala*ʾ), for the whole sphere depends upon it. Thus he is the eye for all six [emanations], three from the right and three from the left, and he corresponds to the Sabbath, the seventh."[77]

The correlation of the eye and the phallus also underlies a theme repeated on various occasions in the zoharic literature to the effect that the punishment for the sin of onanism is not seeing the face of the divine Presence, that is, according to the principle of measure-for-measure, the eye substitutes for the phallus: the sin is committed through the latter and the punishment affects the former.[78] Based on these associations there develops within later kabbalistic literature the notion that the rectification of sexual sins (*pegam ha-berit*) is achieved through perfection of the eyes (*tiqqun 'einayim*), and especially through the shedding of tears. Thus, for example, de Vidas writes:

> All aspects of perfecting the eye (*tiqqune ha-'einayim*) . . . are rectification of the sign of the covenant (*tiqqun le-'ot berit*), for Joseph [symbolic of *Yesod*, the divine attribute that corresponds to the phallus] holds on to the eyes, as it is written, "Joseph is a fruitful bough, a fruitful bough by a spring" (Gen. 49:22) [the last words *'ale 'ayin* being here read as a reference to the eyes] . . . In particular, the semen is the light of a man's eyes, and since he sinned with respect to the semen, he sheds tears from his eyes, and the tears lessen the semen . . . for the tears too are the light of the eyes.[79]

Similarly, Eleazar Azikri writes that "the waters of the eyes atone for the semen spilled in vain."[80]

In neither the passage from Cordovero cited above nor the Lurianic material is the explicit connection made between weeping and the spilling of semen in vain, or, more generally, between the eye and the male genitalia. Nevertheless, it seems to me that some such correlation is tacitly implied by these texts: by weeping one cleaves to the sefirotic realm, and as a result of this cleaving the channels above—corresponding to the eyes below—are opened and overflow to the individual, enabling him to comprehend secrets that he did not comprehend before. It is through the weeping that one cleaves to the divine light and thereby receives the influx from above. That this explanation is valid can be supported by any number of texts in the Lurianic corpus that are predicated on a correlation of the eye and the male genitalia. Thus, for example, in *Sha'ar ha-Kawwanot* Vital offers the following explanation for the gesture of shutting the eyes[81] that is required when the *Shemaʿ*, the traditional proclamation of divine unity, is recited:

> Before you say "Hear O Israel [the Lord, our God, the Lord is one]" [Deut. 6:4] you should close your two eyes with your right hand and concentrate on what is written in the [zoharic section] *Sabbaʾ de-Mishpaṭim* [regarding] the beautiful maiden who has no eyes.[82] We have explained in that context that the meaning [of this expression] is Rachel, who ascends at this point [of the prayer] in the aspect of female waters in relation to the Father and Mother.[83]

To appreciate the complex symbolism underlying this comment it is necessary to bear in mind that, according to the Lurianic interpretation of the liturgical order, the mystical significance of the *Shemaʿ* is "to raise the female waters from the Male and Female to the Father and Mother so that the Father and Mother will be united and the [efflux of the] consciousness (*moḥin*) will come down to the Male and Female."[84] The worshipper thus joins the feminine hypostasis so that he may rise with her in the aspect of the female waters to facilitate the union of the lower two masculine and feminine configurations (*parṣufim*) in the Godhead, *Zeʿeir ʾAnpin* and *Nuqbaʾ di-Zeʿeir*, which, in turn, stimulate the union of the upper masculine and feminine configurations, the Father (*ʾAbbaʾ*) and Mother (*ʾImmaʾ*).[85] The latter union results in the overflowing of the male waters (*mayim dukhrin*) from *Zeʿeir ʾAnpin* to *Nuqbaʾ di-Zeʿeir* during the moment of coupling. What is most significant for this discussion is the fact that the male adept ritually covers his eyes to transform himself into that divine grade that is symbolized by the zoharic image of a beautiful maiden without eyes, namely, *Nuqbaʾ di-Zeʿeir*, the aspect of the configuration (*parṣuf*) that corresponds to the last of the ten *sefirot*, the *Shekhinah*. It may be concluded, therefore, that there is here a process of effeminization of the male, a motif that has not been sufficiently noted in discussions of Lurianic symbolism and ritual. Indeed, the whole question of sexual transformation in kabbalistic literature has not been adequately studied by scholars of Jewish mysticism. Yet, this thematic is critical for a proper assessment of the role accorded to gender and body symbolism in kabbalistic thought in general and Lurianic Kabbalah in particular. It lies beyond the concerns of this discussion to engage this important topic in full, but it is necessary to remark that the motif of the males becoming integrated in the female waters is part of this larger phenomenon of gender metamorphosis.[86] To be sure, the union of the righteous souls with the *Shekhinah* is facilitated by the fact that the former correspond to the male aspect of the divine par excellence, the *membrum virile*. However, once these souls enter into the *Shekhinah* they become integrated as part of her and constitute the female waters that further stimulate coitus in the divine realm. It is evident that the Lurianic teaching concerning the female waters is based on the physiological model of the vaginal secretions that the woman discharges during foreplay preceding sexual intercourse.[87] Again, for the immediate focus of this discussion it is essential to note that the assimilation of the male into the female is characterized as the male closing his eyes in emulation of the beautiful maiden without eyes. The ritual gains its mystical valence from the fact that the eyes function as a symbol for the male genitalia while still remaining eyes or, to put the matter somewhat differently, the eyes are the aspect in the head that function like the genitals in the lower region of the body. Hence, the female persona of the divine is depicted as the beautiful maiden without eyes for the latter function as the symbolic correlates of the masculine reproductive organs.[88] The male worshipper must partake of the character of the feminine by emasculating himself, a procedure that is ritually fulfilled through the shutting of the eyes. The interpretation that I have offered is confirmed by a second passage in *Sha'ar ha-Kawwanot* that deals more generally with the closing of the eyes during prayer. In this text Vital has imputed new theosophic valence to an established prayer-gesture that has as its purpose the augmentation of intention during worship:[89]

> You should shut and close your eyes during the morning and afternoon prayers only at the time of the *'Amidah* [the silent, standing prayer of eighteen benedictions] and in the evening prayer close your eyes during the whole prayer from the blessings of the recitation of *Shema'* until the [conclusion of the] *'Amidah*. The secret of the shutting of the eyes is alluded to in what is written in the [zoharic section] *Sabba' de-Mishpaṭim* . . . "Who is the beautiful maiden who has no eyes?" The explanation of this passage is that it is speaking about Rachel, the feminine of *Ze'eir 'Anpin*, for she is called the beautiful maiden . . . But she has no eyes for her [corporeal] stature (*shi'ur qomah*) is from the

chest and below of *Ze'eir 'Anpin*. There is no aspect of the eyes of *Ze'eir 'Anpin* corresponding to her to draw down from him to her the aspect of the eyes as well. But Leah has eyes according to the secret, "Leah had weak eyes" (Gen. 29:17), for the place of Leah is above in the place of the head of *Ze'eir 'Anpin* where there is an aspect of the eyes of *Ze'eir 'Anpin,* and from there their illumination goes forth in Leah who corresponds to them. He created and formed in her the aspect of the eyes as is not the case with respect to the lower Rachel.[90]

In still other places within the Lurianic corpus it is evident that the eyes represent the male potency. Thus, for example, this is the underlying symbolism of the ritualistic requirement to look at the cup of wine during the recitation of the *qiddush,* the prayer of sanctification of Sabbath. Building upon the rabbinic idiom cited above concerning the casting of one's eye upon a cup, which, as I have noted, has obvious sexual connotations in its original context, Vital applies this imagery to the specific rite of *qiddush:*

> In another pamphlet I have found that all this should be intended by the glance of his eyes upon the cup of wine, for by means of this he draws upon her the aspect of the crown as has been mentioned above.[91] In another pamphlet I have found [it written that] on the Sabbath when one casts his eyes upon the cup of wine as is known he should intend another, different intention from that of the week. He should intend the name Yah Adonai for five times Yah Adonai is numerically equal to *bat 'ayin*[92] concerning which the rabbis, may their memory be for a blessing, said "and one places one's eyes upon the cup."[93]

The masculine symbolization of the eyes is evident as well in the following anonymous Lurianic text:

> The female has nothing from the house of the father, for the father is not responsible for the sustenance of his daughter. However, in order that the matter not be trivial in his eyes, he gives her a dowry.[94] The matter concerns the fact that she [*Nuqba' di-Ze'eir*] has no eyes, but *Ze'eir* [*'Anpin*] glances with [his] eyes upon his chest and from there the light is transmitted to her so that she has eyes.[95]

Implicit in the above passage is a motif that recurs in Vital's own writings: the ocular glance (*histakkelut ha-'ayin*) is endowed with generative power.[96] Thus, for example, in the description of the different parts of the face of the Primordial Anthropos (*'Adam*

Qadmon) and the respective senses to which they are correlated, it
is said that the glance of the eye (which corresponds to the *sefirah*
of *Ḥokhmah* and the soul of the soul, *neshamah la-neshamah*)
upon the other three aspects of soul that compose the ʿ*olam*
ha-ʿaquddim (*neshamah,* which corresponds to *Binah* and the ears;
ruaḥ, which corresponds to *Tiferet* and the nose; and *nefesh,*
which corresponds to *Malkhut* and the mouth) creates the vessels
of the points (*ha-kelim shel ha-nequddot*) that eventually shatter
because they were not potent enough to hold the lights that stream
forth from the eyes.[97] The aspect of the lights that emerge from the
eyes of the Primordial Anthropos emanate in an atomized form
and are thus designated the "world of points" (ʿ*olam ha-nequddim*),
also referred to as the "world of chaos" (ʿ*olam ha-tohu*) insofar as
the cataclysmic shattering of the vessels is said to occur at this stage
of the unfolding of the divine.[98] A special relationship, therefore,
pertains between the points and the eyes.[99] It would appear, moreover, that the former too function phallically in this mythical theosophy, that is, the *nequddim* (or sometimes referred to as *nequd-
dot*) represent the feminine potencies of the Godhead that emerge
from the phallus (if not, more specifically, the drops of semen
itself[100]) associated with the aspect of *Ḥokhmah* (symbolized by
the permutation of the Tetragrammaton, whose sum tallies 63).[101]
To underscore the generative power of the eyes, Vital provides the
following example: the ostrich hatches its eggs by looking at them.
This indicates that there is "actual power in the glance of the eyes"
(*koaḥ mamashit be-histakkelut ha-ʿeinayyim*).[102] Vital applies this
dynamic to the Godhead—by means of the glance the eyes produce
the sphere of being called the world of points:

> From the aspect of this glance of the eyes (*histakkelut ha-zeh shel
> ha-ʿeinayyim*) the points emerge. Through this you can under-
> stand what is written in the *Tiqqunim,* tiqqun 70[103] . . . con-
> cerning the form of the [name] YHWH depicted in the form of
> eyes through points,[104] according to the secret, "and their rims
> were covered all over with eyes" (Ezek. 1:18), for the aspect of
> the eyes is the points . . . The eye has an aspect of the final *he'*
> and the first *he'* [of the Tetragrammaton], and this is the secret of
> what is written in the *Tiqqunim* [regarding the verse] "I was
> asleep" (Cant. 5:2), corresponding to the final *he',* for with the
> abolition of the light of the points [the consequence is] "I am
> asleep," according to the secret of sleep. Further, "I am asleep,"

[the word] *yeshenah* [asleep] has the letters of *sheniyah* [the second], for *Ḥokhmah* is the first *he'* and it is second to *Keter*. It is known that the cantillation notes correspond to *Keter*, the vowel-points to *Ḥokhmah*, the crownlets to *Binah*, and the letters to the lower seven [*sefirot* from *Ḥesed* to *Malkhut*]. Thus, the eye is the aspect of *Ḥokhmah* that consists of the points, and this is the reason that the sages of the community are called the "eyes of the community."[105]

In the continuation of this passage Vital remarks that these points compose the aspect of the Edomite kings who died,[106] that is, the primordial forces of judgment that are also connected with the verse, "And the earth was unformed and void" (Gen. 1:2). "The earth," writes Vital, "is the final *he'* that is the aspect of the eye."[107] This implies not that the feminine aspect of the Godhead, symbolized by the earth, is the eye but only that it partakes of divine wisdom, which is, as I have indicated above, represented by the eye. Therefore, it is appropriate to apply the symbol of the eye to the final *he'* of the Tetragrammaton, which represents the female configuration of the Godhead. The roots of divine judgment lie within the eyes of the Primordial Anthropos, which constitute elements of *Ḥokhmah,* and they are expunged as the light-points that come forth from the eyes. This is also expressed in terms of the description of the circular nature of the lights that emerge from the eyes in contrast to the linear nature of the lights that emanate from other parts of the head, to wit, the ears, nose, and mouth.[108]

> In the beginning of the emanation the points emanated exclusively in the aspect of their circles (*'iggulim*) without the linear (*yosher*), and these are the aspect of the soul of the points (*nefesh shel ha-nequddim*) . . . Therefore they were shattered because they only emerged in the aspect of their soul, for they are circular, and they were incapable of receiving the supernal light. Consequently, there was the aspect of the death of the kings and their abrogation.[109]

When the shattering of the vessels will be rectified then the light again will stream forth from the eyes in the dual aspect of the circle and the line, the former corresponding to the lower aspect of the soul (*nefesh*) and the latter to the higher (*ruaḥ*). Hence, Vital characterizes the *tiqqun* by citing the following biblical texts: "God said: Let there be light, and there was light" (Gen. 1:3) and "Open Your eyes and see our desolation" (Dan. 9:18). The opening of the eyes represents the (masculine) overflow of the divine influx. That the emanation of the circular lights from the eyes involves a process that parallels or resembles the emission of semen is implied in the following comment of Vital: "With this you will understand how the eyes allude to Neṣaḥ and Hod for the light of Neṣaḥ and Hod of this 'Adam Qadmon went out from the eyes; thus Neṣaḥ and Hod allude to the eyes."[110] That is, the eyes correspond to the aspects of the divine, Neṣaḥ and Hod, that are generally depicted as the testes that generate the semen that pours forth from Yesod to the Shekhinah.[111] It follows, therefore, that the eyes must serve a similar function. The punctiform lights that come forth from the sockets of the eyes are thus comparable to the drops of semen, an interpretation that is enhanced by the connection made by Vital between those light-points and the letter yod.

I have embarked upon a rather lengthy digression to show that the eye and ocular activities in Lurianic Kabbalah assume a phallic or masculine character. It is beyond the scope of this chapter to discuss in any more detail the central importance of this symbol, but it should be evident from my remarks that it is indeed crucial for understanding several different facets of the complex Lurianic doctrine, especially and perhaps most importantly the myth of the breaking of the vessels. The significant point to emphasize is that it is necessary to grasp precisely such a symbolic nuance to appreciate the central motif of this study. Weeping is a substitution (and in some instances a rectification) for seminal emission[112] and accordingly facilitates the attainment of esoteric knowledge. Additionally, Vital advanced the idea that weeping is a means for ascent of the soul, 'aliyyat neshamah, during sleep, culminating in some vision of the supernal realm. It should be noted, parenthetically, that the correlation between weeping and ascent is found in a passing remark in Karo's Maggid Mesharim: "He [the celestial angel] said to me: if it is possible for you to shed tears during your prayer, it is well and good, at least on Monday and Thursday. You [thereby] remove the mark from your face and you ascend."[113] Karo draws here upon a rather common idea expressed in earlier Jewish pietistic and mystical texts that recommend weeping during prayer to enhance one's intention. But he goes beyond these sources by suggesting that the weeping during prayer results in an ascent. Moreover, Karo alludes to the notion that the weeping washes off the mark of sin from ones's face, an idea expressed in the Zohar based in part on the talmudic reading of Ezek. 9:4 to the effect that the wicked are marked by the angel Gabriel with the letter *taw* made from blood on their foreheads so that the angels of destruction could rule over them whereas the righteous are marked with a letter *taw* made from ink.[114] Thus, one zoharic passage asserts that "when a person transgresses any of the words of Torah, the Torah goes up and down, and places marks on the face of the person."[115] In relating a story about one such individual, the *Zohar* places the following statement in his mouth: "Each day I saw my face in a mirror, and I wept before the Holy One, blessed be He . . . on account of that very sin, and with those tears I washed my face."[116] This text served as the basis for a penitential custom among sixteenth-century kabbalistic authors, as is attested, for example, in de Vidas's *Reshit Ḥokhmah*.[117] One context is particularly note-worthy insofar as the matter is discussed in relation to the ascent of the soul:

> One should also intend to weep in order to wipe away those accusers who prosecute him, for the one who commits a transgression acquires one prosecutor.[118] When he imagines the ascent of his soul above [*yeṣayyer 'aliyyat nishmato le-ma'lah*], and several accusers denounce him and push him outside, it is appropriate for him to weep, mourn, and show embarrassment for his sins. By means of the tears his accusers are nullified . . . Therefore, it is appropriate to weep in the forehead and the face because the sins are inscribed there.

We have seen above that Vital similarly links weeping and the ascent of the soul; in his case, however, the ascent occurs specifically during sleep. Vital's discussion of weeping and ascent is placed within the framework of an older idea found in kabbalistic literature, especially popular in the *Zohar*, regarding the nocturnal ascent of the soul to its source in the divine world, culminating with a vision of the Presence.[119] The kabbalistic idea itself is based, in part, on earlier rabbinic passages that speak of God taking the soul from a person during sleep and returning it upon waking. The zoharic authorship associates this idea with two other rabbinic traditions: sleep is considered one-sixtieth of death, and upon death the soul has a vision of the Presence denied it while it was inhabiting the body. Vital, obviously aware of these traditions, feels no need to elaborate in great detail for they were fairly commonplace in his time, and he certainly would have assumed that his readership was familiar with them. We should not misread his reticence: his assertion that the *'aliyyat neshamah* occurs during sleep presupposes, in line with the rabbinic and kabbalistic traditions briefly alluded to above, that sleep is a prolepsis of death that is marked by a visionary experience of the *Shekhinah*. The weeping, then, is a kind of preparation for the spiritual ascent that occurs while one sleeps, a foreshadowing of death. The introduction of weeping in this context is the novel element in Vital's formulation. The import of the weeping as a mystical ritual can be appreciated only if one takes into account the function assigned to weeping in other discussions in Vital or related writings. It seems likely, as I have suggested, that the weeping substitutes for seminal emission; indeed, it may even be the case that for Vital, as for other sixteenth-century kabbalists, the weeping is a form of rectification (*tiqqun*) of this sin. Interestingly enough, in one context Vital remarks with respect to the sin of spilling semen in vain that "it is most severe for it prevents the ascent of the soul at night to its Lord."[120] While this statement too is clearly based on earlier sources, the fact is that Vital connects weeping and ascent, on the one hand, and the spilling of semen in vain and an obstacle to ascent, on the other hand.

By means of weeping, the soul ascends and opens the channels above, thereby creating an overflow to the lower realm. In this ascent the soul experiences separation from body, which may be likened to ecstatic death. It is noteworthy that a similar mystical conception of death is expressed elsewhere in the Lurianic writings. According to Vital, a person is to give his soul over in death to God (*mesirat ha-'adam nafsho la-mitah lifne ha-qadosh barukh hu'*) at two different intervals in the morning service, during the recitation of the *Shema*ʿ and the prayer of supplication, the *nefillat 'apayim* (prostration).[121] The latter is already mentioned in the *Zohar* as an occasion for ecstatic death, which is further depicted as unification with the *Shekhinah*, symbolized as the tree of death (*le-'itkannesha' le-gabbe ha-hu' 'ilana' de-mota'*).[122] Thus, for example, in the description of the *nefillat 'apayim*, found in the book, *Kanfe Yonah* by the sixteenth-century Italian kabbalist, Menaḥem Azariah of Fano, based on a work of the same name by one of Luria's disciples, Moses Yonah,[123] three elements death, ascent, and union converge:

> The secret [of the prostration] is that at that point [in the service], which is after the completion of the ʿAmidah [i.e., the eighteen benedictions recited in a standing posture] . . . he gives himself

over to death [*moser 'aṣmo la-mitah*], and he should consider it as if he were really dead. And when he recites [the verse] "To you, O Lord, I lift my soul" [Ps. 25:1], he should give his soul to the *Shekhinah*, for when the soul of the righteous one ascends, it elevates the female waters for [the sake of] the unification of *Tif'eret* and *Malkhut* . . . In the time of the prostration, which is the moment of unification, he should intend to raise the female waters with the ascent of his soul and spirit.[124]

The enactment of death thus results in the union of the soul with the *Shekhinah*. The soul thereby provides the arousal from below, symbolized as the female waters, which assist in the union of the male and female in the Godhead, signified by the overflow of the masculine waters from above. While there clearly are differences between the death experienced at night and the ritual enacted during the supplication prayer, it is not incorrect to draw some comparison between the two, as is done already in the case of the *Zohar*. Both experiences involve mystical union with the divine Presence, a union characterized in overtly sexual terms. This section of the liturgy corresponds to the secret of the emission of semen (*sod hazra'at ha-tippah*), in ibn Tabul's formulation,[125] or the *horadat ha-tippah*, according to Vital.[126] At this moment the *ṣaddiq* unites with the *Shekhinah:* the forces of eros and thanatos converge such that ecstatic union is a kind of dying. Mystical life is truly a being-toward-death.

We can gather still more information about the nocturnal ascent in Vital's thought if we consider a passage in his *Sha'are Qedushah*, which deals with the mechanics of prophecy (*'ekhut ha-nevu'ah*).[127] Vital notes that the separation or withdrawal (*hitpashshetut*) of the mind from the body or material sensations (a usage that goes back to earlier sources[128]), which is a means to attain the state of union (*devequt*) of the soul and its divine source, characteristic of prophetic illumination, is not "actual" as it is in the case of sleep when the soul goes out from the body, *'ein 'inyan ha-hitpashshetut ha-zeh . . . be-'inyene ha-nevu'ah we-ruaḥ ha-qodesh hitpashshetut mamashiyi she-ha-neshamah yoṣet mi-gufo mamash ke-'inyan ha-shenah.*[129] Prophecy, or the indwelling of the Holy Spirit, is distinguished from dream-visions by the fact that in the former case the soul is still in the body, and the individual therefore can only imagine that he ascends to the upper realms to unite with his soul-root. There is here a curious elevation of the imaginative faculty as the locus of the prophetic vision.

> Then the imaginative faculty causes his thoughts to imagine and conjure as if he ascended to the upper worlds [we-'az yahafokh koah ha-medammeh mahshevotav ledamot u-leṣayyer ke-'illu 'oleh ba-'olamot ha-'elyonim], to the roots of his soul that are there. And when his imagination [ṣiyyur dimyono] reaches his supernal source, images of the [divine] lights are engraved in his mind as if he imagined and saw them [we-huqqaqu ṣiyyure kol ha-'orot be-mahashavto ke-'illu meṣuyyar we-ro'eh 'otam], in the manner that the imaginative faculty forms images of matters of this world even though it does not [actually] see them.[130]

The ascent of the prophet is thus an imaginary one, a "contemplation as if," in the description of Werblowsky.[131] By means of the imaginary ascent, the soul elevates the light of the divine emanations to their supernal source, causing an abundance of light, which then overflows in a downward direction, eventually reaching the rational faculty, which then overflows to the imagination in which are formed images of the spiritual realities. While the latter part of this process is no doubt based on Maimonides' description of prophecy, as has been noted in the scholarly literature,[132] the former part is related to descriptions of the imaginative ascent found in earlier kabbalistic sources, indebted to Islamic and Jewish Neoplatonism as I have suggested elsewhere.[133]

Vital alternatively describes the ladder of ascent, the *scala contemplationis,* as the line that extends from the soul-root in the divine realm to the soul embodied on earth. (This description is based on a passage in the fifth chapter of the late-thirteenth-century anonymous kabbalistic treatise *'Iggeret ha-Qodesh,* which deals primarily with the mystical intention required during sexual relations. Vital himself cites the relevant text in the fourth part of *Sha'are Qedushah.*[134])

> The soul is like a very long branch, extending from the root, attached to the tree, until the body of man. That line extends continuously inasmuch as when a person desires to ascend to his source, the light of his thought, which is called *muskal* [that which is intellectually cognized], ascends from the *maskil* [that which intellectually cognizes], which is the rational soul [*nefesh ha-maskelet*], until the intellect [*sekhel*] itself, which is the supernal source of his soul. They are joined together and become one

through the [process of] intellection itself [*u-mitddabbeqim we-na'asim 'eḥad 'al yede ha-haskkalah 'aṣmah*], which is the influx that extends from the intellect [*sekhel*] to that which intellectually cognizes [*maskil*].[135]

Even though this contemplative process is an imaginative one, Vital is quick to point out that it serves as the basis for the kabbalistic idea of mystical intention in prayer and the theurgic implications of religious praxis. Indeed, if one denies the power of human thought to impact the nature of the divine emanations then the whole purpose of prayer and religious observance from the kabbalistic perspective is undermined.[136]

I have spent a fair amount of time describing the contemplative process for, in my estimation, something similar occurs when the soul ascends during sleep. Admittedly, in this case there is an "actual" ascent as opposed to one that is imagined. Nevertheless, the goal of the ascent is to open the upper channels of the divine, thereby creating an overflow of divine light that eventuates in some sort of vision. The sleep itself, characterized by a separation of body and soul, is a simulation of death and thus provides the context for the visionary experience. Just as weeping in the case of the tradition reported in the name of Abraham ha-Levi is a means to open up the supernal gates, so too in the case of the *'aliyyat neshamah*, the ascent of the soul.

To sum up: Vital's use of the weeping motif represents the crystallization of various mystical and theurgical tendencies in previous kabbalistic literature. More specifically, he blended together two traditions, the one concerning Torah study and the other the ascent of the soul, for in his mind the two processes involve the same dynamic. It is evident that he viewed weeping as a means for an ecstatic departure culminating in a spiritual vision. Focusing on Vital's discussion of the contemplative ascent in the case of prophecy, Werblowsky was led to conclude that Vital, "like many earlier kabbalists, knows no ecstasy *sensu stricto* because the soul does not leave the body behind except in the lowest form of inspiration, dreams. There is no real ascent or *Himmelsfahrt* of the soul such as was cultivated in some other systems."[137] Such a conclusion neglects to take into account the passage from *Sha'ar Ruaḥ ha-Qodesh* that has served as the basis for my remarks. That text clearly indicates that Vital did entertain the possibility of ecstasy in a strict sense, involving the soul's disengagement from the body.

This occurs through mystical study or the nocturnal ascent, but in either case weeping serves as the vehicle to induce the ecstatic experience.

NOTES

1. S. Schechter, *Studies in Judaism: Essays on Persons, Concepts, and Movements of Thought in Jewish Tradition* (New York, 1970) 231–97.

2. See M. Idel, *Studies in Ecstatic Kabbalah* (Albany, 1988) 91–101, esp. 95–96; and 103–69, esp. 122–40. See also G. Scholem, *Major Trends in Jewish Mysticism* (New York, 1954) 378, n. 14.

3. G. Scholem, *On the Kabbalah and Its Symbolism*, trans. R. Manheim (New York, 1965) 118–57, esp. 134.

4. On the shift in focus from the theoretical to the experiential in the study of kabbalistic documents, see M. Idel, *Kabbalah: New Perspectives* (New Haven, 1988) 74–111. Some of my previous studies too have focused on the experiential element underlying earlier sources. See, e.g., E. R. Wolfson, "Circumcision, Vision of God, Textual Interpretation: From Midrashic Trope to Mystical Symbol," *History of Religions* 27 (1987) 189–215; idem, "The Hermeneutics of Visionary Experience: Revelation and Interpretation in the Zohar," *Religion* 18 (1988) 311–45; idem, "The Mystical Significance of Torah-Study in German Pietism," *Jewish Quarterly Review* 84 (1993) 43–78. This orientation is most fully developed in my monograph, *Through a Speculum That Shines: Vision and Imagination in Medieval Jewish Mysticism* (Princeton, 1994). On the possibility that the mythical circle of R. Simeon bar Yoḥai in the *Zohar* reflects an actual group of mystics, see Y. Liebes, "How the Zohar Was Written," *Jerusalem Studies in Jewish Thought* 8(1989) 1–72 (in Hebrew); idem, "New Directions in the Study of the Kabbala," *Pe'amim* 50(1992) 160–61 (in Hebrew); E. R. Wolfson, "Forms of Visionary Ascent as Ecstatic Experience in the Zoharic Literature," in J. Dan and P. Schäfer, eds., *Gershom Scholem's Major Trends in Jewish Mysticism 50 Years After: Proceedings of the Sixth International Conference on the History of Jewish Mysticism* (Tübingen, 1993) 209–235. On possible earlier sources for the kabbalistic rituals enacted in Safed, see also the important comment of E. K. Ginsburg, *The Sabbath in the Classical Kabbalah* (Albany, 1989) 250, n. 238, regarding the need to investigate the "possible connection between the ritual adaptations of Byzantine-Turkish provenance and the full-blown ritual creativity of Safed Kabbalah."

5. See Scholem, *Major Trends*, 244–51; idem, *The Messianic*

Idea in Judaism and Other Essays on Jewish Spirituality (New York, 1971) 37–48; R. Elior, "Messianic Expectations and Spiritualization of Religious Life in the 16th Century," *Revue des études juives* 145 (1986) 35–49. This Scholemian thesis has been challenged by various scholars from different vantage points. See Y. Liebes, "The Messiah of the Zohar," in *The Messianic Idea in Jewish Thought: A Study Conference in Honour of the Eightieth Birthday of Gershom Scholem* (Jerusalem, 1982) 87– 236 (in Hebrew); Idel, *Kabbalah: New Perspectives,* 258–59; D. B. Ruderman, "Hope Against Hope: Jewish and Christian Messianic Expectations in the Late Middle Ages," in A. Mirsky, A. Grossman, and Y. Kaplan, eds., *Exile and Diaspora: Studies in the History of the Jewish People Presented to Prof. Haim Beinhart* (Jerusalem, 1991) 185–202.

6.   See R. J. Zwi Werblowsky, *Joseph Karo: Lawyer and Mystic* (Oxford, 1962) 38–83; L. Fine, "Recitation of Mishnah as a Vehicle for Mystical Inspiration: A Contemplative Technique Taught by Ḥayyim Vital," *Revue des études juives* 141(1982) 183–99; idem, "Maggidic Revelation in the Teachings of Isaac Luria," in J. Reinharz and D. Swetschinski, eds., *Mystics, Philosophers and Politicians* (Durham, 1982) 141–57; idem, "The Contemplative Practice of Yiḥudim in Lurianic Kabbalah," in A. Green, ed., *Jewish Spirituality from the Sixteenth-Century Revival to the Present* (New York, 1987) 64–98, esp. 86–94.

7.   See Scholem, *Major Trends,* 15–16, 36–37, 211–12. Notable exceptions from the earlier (i.e., pre-sixteenth century) material include the personal accounts of revelation by Abraham Abulafia and his disciples, e.g., the author of *Shaʿare Ṣedeq* (see Scholem, *Major Trends,* 119–55, esp. 147–55; M. Idel, *The Mystical Experience in Abraham Abulafia* [Albany, 1987] 73–178), the collection of angelic revelations of Jacob ben Jacob ha-Kohen, called *Sefer ha-ʾOrah* (see G. Scholem, *Kabbalah* [Jerusalem, 1974] 56; a synoptic, critical edition of the work has been prepared as a doctoral dissertation by my student Daniel Abrams), and the mystical diary of Isaac of Acre, *ʾOṣar Ḥayyim* (see E. Gottlieb, *Studies in Kabbala Literature,* ed. J. Hacker [Tel Aviv, 1976] 231–47, in Hebrew). Mention should also be made here of the anonymous work *Sefer ha-Meshiv,* which is predicated on revelatory experiences; see M. Idel, "Inquiries in the Doctrine of *Sefer ha-Meshiv,*" *Sefunot* 17(1983) 185–266 (in Hebrew). See also G. Scholem, "The Maggid of R. Joseph Taitazak and the Revelations Attributed to Him," *Sefunot* 11(1977) 69– 112 (in Hebrew).

8.   Cf. references cited above, n. 6; see also *Milei di-Shemaya by Rabbi Eleazar Azikri,* ed. M. Pachter (Tel Aviv, 1991) 22–23 (in Hebrew).

9.   See Werblowsky, *Joseph Karo,* 9–23, 257–86.

10.   Ibid., 50–55.

11.   The work has recently been published by M. Pachter; see reference above, n. 8.

12.   Cf. Ḥayyim Vital, *Sefer ha-Ḥezyonot*, ed. A. Z. Aescoli (Jerusalem, 1954); D. Tamar, "R. Ḥayyim Vital's Messianic Dreams and Visions," *Shalem* 4 (1984) 211–29 (in Hebrew). The appearance of Elijah is used as a sign of mantic power in later hagiographic literature as well as we find, e.g., in the case of Israel ben Eliezer, the Besht. Cf. *In Praise of the Baʿal Shem Tov* [*Shivhei ha-Besht*], ed. A. Rubenstein (Jerusalem, 1991) 76–77 (in Hebrew); *Hasidic Tales by Michael Levi Rodkinson*, ed. G. Nigal (Jerusalem, 1988) 45 (in Hebrew). See also the testimony of R. Solomon of Lutsk in his introduction to Dov Baer of Mezeritch, *Maggid Devarav le-Yaʿaqov*, ed. R. Schatz-Uffenheimer (Jerusalem, 1976) 2–3.

13.   See Idel, *Kabbalah: New Perspectives*, 88–96. See also Fine, "The Contemplative Practice of Yiḥudim," 92–93.

14.   See G. Scholem, "Eine kabalistische Deutung der Prophetie als Selbstbegegnung," *Monatsschrift für Geschichte und Wissenschaft des Judentums* 74 (1930) 285–290; idem, *Major Trends*, 277, 378, n. 14; Werblowsky, *Joseph Karo*, 38–39, 72–73; L. Fine, "Techniques of Mystical Meditation for Achieving Prophecy and the Holy Spirit in the Teachings of Isaac Luria and Ḥayyim Vital," Ph.D., Brandeis University, 1976, 101–11; Idel, *Studies in Ecstatic Kabbalah*, 95–96, 122–40; idem, *Kabbalah: New Perspectives*, 101–2.

15.   See D. Boyarin, *Intertextuality and the Reading of Midrash* (Bloomington, 1990).

16.   See Idel, *Kabbalah: New Perspectives*, 240–41. L. Fine, "The Study of Torah as a Rite of Theurgical Contemplation in Lurianic Kabbalah," in D. R. Blumenthal, ed., *Approaches to Judaism in Medieval Times*, vol. 3 (Atlanta, 1988) 29–40, analyzes other aspects of the rite of Torah-study in the teaching of Luria. On mystical illumination during prayer, see esp. comment of Ḥayyim Vital, *ʿOlat Tamid* (Jerusalem, 1907) 10a.

17.   Cf. *Shaʿar Ruaḥ ha-Qodesh* (Jerusalem, 1874) 9a–b.

18.   See Fine, "The Contemplative Practice of Yiḥudim," 64–98, esp. 86–87, where the author discusses the attainment of prophetic inspiration through the practice of these unifications.

19.   *Shaʿar Ruaḥ ha-Qodesh*, fols. 24a–b. Cf. *Shaʿar ha-Gilgulim* (Jerusalem, 1981) chap. 38, 329.

20.   On the doctrine of *ʿibbur* (impregnation) in kabbalistic writings, see G. Scholem, *On the Mystical Shape of the Godhead*, trans. J. Neugroschel and ed. J. Chipman (New York, 1991) 221–28, 234, 240, 306, n. 57.

21.   *Shaʿar ha-Yiḥudim* (Jerusalem, 1970) 3c–d. Cf. *Shaʿar ha-Kawwanot* (Jerusalem, 1963) 23a; and see the description in the first letter of Solomon Shlomiel of Dresnitz published in *Ha-ʾAri we-Gurav* (Jerusa-

lem, 1992) 8–9; cf. *The Toledoth ha-Ari and Luria's "Manner of Life"* *(Hanhagoth)*, ed. M. Benayahu (Jerusalem, 1967) 157, 262 (in Hebrew).

22.   The kabbalistic notion of the upper, masculine waters (*mayim dukhrin*) and the lower, feminine waters (*mayim nuqvin*) is based on an earlier aggadic motif. Cf. J. Theodor and Ch. Albeck, eds., *Midrash Bereshit Rabba: Critical Edition with Notes and Commentary*, 2nd ed., 3 vols. (Jerusalem, 1965) 13:13, p. 122, and other references cited in n. 4. It is possible that this motif reflects gnostic speculation. See A. Altmann, "Gnostic Themes in Rabbinic Cosmology," in I. Epstein, E. Levine, and C. Roth, eds., *Essays in Honour of the Very Rev. Dr. J. H. Hertz, Chief Rabbi . . . on the Occasion of his Seventieth Birthday*, ed. (London, n.d.) pp. 23–24.

23.   Cf. Hayyim Vital's introduction to *'Eṣ Ḥayyim* (Jerusalem, 1910) 5b; and see *'Eleh Toledot Yiṣḥaq*, in *The Toledoth ha-Ari*, 247–48. The revelation of Elijah to Luria is emphasized several times in the letters of Solomon Shlomiel of Dresnitz and the hagiographical literature based thereon; cf. *Ha-'Ari we-Gurav*, 5, 8, 12, 15, 37, 52, 69, and see extended discussion of this motif on 143, 148–50. See also *The Toledoth ha-Ari*, 154, 262. The importance of Elijah in the life of Luria is underscored as well by the legendary account of Elijah's presence at Luria's circumcision; see *Ha-'Ari we-Gurav*, 3–4; *The Toledoth ha-Ari*, 151–52. In the hagiographical tales concerning Luria it is also reported that while he was asleep he would ascend to the heavenly academies to learn esoteric matters. Cf. *Ha-'Ari we-Gurav*, 5–6; *The Toledoth ha-Ari*, 155, 164–65. On the perception of Luria as a prophet in subsequent literature, including in specific halakhic contexts, see sources cited in *Ha-'Ari we-Gurav*, 181–182. Symbolically, it may be of significance to note that, according to some texts, the aspect of the Holy Spirit corresponds to the emanation of *Yesod*, the *membrum virile* in the divine anthropos. See, e.g., Menaḥem Azariah da Fano, *Kanfe Yonah* (Korets, 1786) 3:8, 3b. On the superiority of the kabbalist to Elijah the Prophet, see the comment in the text extant in MS Oxford 1784, fol. 37a: "An explanation for why in the [section on] the Song of Songs in the *Zohar* at one time it says '[the matter] was decreed by the mouth of Elijah' and another time it says 'R. Simeon began to expound'. This is on account of the fact that Elijah is a prophet and he does not have the ability to open the wells of salvation of wisdom. But R. Simeon, whose level of wisdom was higher than that of the angels, had the power to open the wells of wisdom. Know that the angels cannot reveal the secrets of Torah for our wisdom is greater than their wisdom, and they reveal only the secrets of this world." For a different version of this text see *Kanfe Yonah*, 2:31, 43d–44a.

24.   *Sha'ar ha-Haqdamot* (Jerusalem, 1909) 4a–b.

25.   See, e.g., *Zohar Ḥadash*, ed. R. Margaliot (Jerusalem, 1978) 59c.

26. Cf. 'Eṣ Ḥayyim, 4b–d, 5a–c. For discussion of this chain of tradition in earlier kabbalistic sources, see G. Scholem, Origins of the Kabbalah, trans. A. Arkush and ed. R. J. Zwi Werblowsky (Princeton, 1987) 35–39, 238–43.

27. 'Eṣ Ḥayyim, 4c.

28. 'Eṣ Ḥayyim (Korets, 1782) 2c. Cf. the passage from Vital's introduction to Shaʿare Qedushah cited by Werblowsky, Joseph Karo, 66.

29. Ha-ʾAri we-Gurav, 15–16.

30. Sefer ha-Ḥezyonot, 6. In the incident that is reported right after this one the same woman was said to have seen a pillar of fire atop the head of Vital one Sabbath morning in Damascus when he was leading the congregation in prayer. On the nexus between prayer and the indwelling of the Presence in the case of Luria, cf. The Toledoth ha-Ari, 189. This topos is repeated in other hagiographical literature. See, e.g., In Praise of the Baʿal Shem Tov, 85–90.

31. Scholem, Major Trends, 15–16.

32. Werblowsky, Joseph Karo, 40.

33. See esp. Scholem's characterization of kabbalistic theosophy in Kabbalah 4: "Speculations of this type occupy a large and conspicuous area in kabbalistic teaching. Sometimes their connection with the mystical plane becomes rather tenuous and is superseded by an interpretative and homiletical vein which occasionally even results in a kind of kabbilistic pilpul (casuistry)."

34. Idel, Kabbalah: New Perspectives, 75–88.

35. Ibid., 76.

36. Ibid., 80–81. On the theurgical significance of weeping in Vital's writings, see also R. Meroz, "Redemption in the Lurianic Teaching," Ph.D., Hebrew University, 1988, 109, 125, n. 87 (in Hebrew).

37. Cf. M. ʾAvot 3:13.

38. Shaʿar Ruaḥ ha-Qodesh, 6a. Cf. Peri 'Eṣ Ḥayyim (Jerusalem, 1980) 353, and the statement from Jacob Zemaḥ's Naggid u-Meṣaveh cited by Idel, Kabbalah: New Perspectives, 313, n. 36. Cf. the anonymous work Ṭaharat ha-Qodesh (Jerusalem, 1989) 156, and Natan Shapira, Ṭuv ha-ʾAreṣ (Jerusalem, 1891) pt. 3, fol. 5a. Cf. G. Scholem, "The Shetar ha-Hitqasherut of the Disciples of the Ari," Zion 5(1940) 145 (in Hebrew). It should be noted that the emphasis on crying as a means for comprehension of secrets stands in marked contrast to the opposite notion also expressed in kabbalistic literature regarding joy and happiness as the necessary means to receive esoteric matters (echoing the rabbinic idiom that the Holy Spirit or Shekhinah only dwells upon one who is joyous; cf. P. Sukkah 5:1; B. Shabbat 30b; Midrash Tehillim 24:3, ed. S. Buber [Jerusalem, 1977] 204). See, e.g., Isaiah Horowitz, Shene Luḥot ha-Berit (Amsterdam, 1698) fol. 84b.

39. On weeping as preparatory for comprehension of esoteric

matters, see esp. *Zohar* 3:79a; other pertinent examples are cited by Idel, *Kabbalah: New Perspectives*, 313, n. 33. On the nocturnal ascent of the soul, see I. Tishby, *Mishnat ha-Zohar* (Jerusalem, 1975) 2:125–28, and my study on forms of visionary experience in zoharic literature cited above, n. 4.

40. On the connection of weeping, sleep, and a dream-vision, see Vital's own testimony in *Sefer ha-Ḥezyonot*, 42–47. Other examples of pietistic forms of weeping are evident in Vital's diary, but they are not specifically connected with visionary experience or mystical techniques. See, e.g., 32, 110.

41. *Shaʿar Ruaḥ ha-Qodesh*, 9d, cited by Benayahu, *The Toledoth ha-Ari*, 319. See also Fine, "The Contemplative Practice of Yiḥudim," 73.

42. Cf. *Shaʿar Ruaḥ ha-Qodesh*, 9c, where Vital reports that R. Israel Sagis heard from Luria that the best thing for comprehension of esoteric matters is ritual ablution (*ṭevilah*), which insures that a person is always pure. Cf. *Shaʿar ha-Miṣwot* (Jerusalem, 1978) 128, where Vital reports the same tradition in the name of one of the colleagues (*ḥaverim*) without further specification. In that context, moreover, the positive effects of ablution are linked especially to the impurities of nocturnal emission and onanism.

43. *ʿEṣ Ḥayyim*, 5d.

44. This is a technical term in medieval philosophical texts for the propadeutic sciences like mathematics and astronomy.

45. Cf. *b. Berakhot* 32b.

46. MS Oxford-Bodleian 1706, fol. 49b, cited by Idel, *Kabbalah: New Perspectives*, 86, 313 n. 36.

47. *Ha-'Ari we-Gurav*, 51.

48. *Shaʿar ha-Yiḥudim*, 4d. Cf. *Taharat ha-Qodesh*, 156. See also *Shaʿar Ruaḥ ha-Qodesh*, 6c, where the same technique is related to the ritual of fasting.

49. See J. Trachtenberg, *Jewish Magic and Superstition* (New York, 1939) 241–43; Werblowsky, *Joseph Karo*, 47–48; J. Bazak, *Beyond the Senses: A Study of Extra-Sensorial Perception in Biblical, Talmudical and Rabbinical Literature in Light of Contemporary Parapsychological Research* (Tel Aviv, 1968) 40 (in Hebrew).

50. According to another variant of this motif, extant in MS Oxford-Bodleian 1959, fols. 9b–10a, one should place the name of God on his head in the place where the phylacteries are worn and on the other side of the parchment write his request. He then sleeps and sees great wonders.

51. For discussion of this motif in select Jewish mystical sources, including some of the passages cited in the body of this paper, see M. Hallamish, "On Silence in Kabbalah and Hasidism," in M. Hallamish and A. Kasher, eds., *Dat we-Safah* (Ramat-Gan, 1982) 79–89 (in Hebrew).

52. For a later reverberation of this motif see the teaching of Dov Baer, Maggid of Mezeritch, discussed in R. Schatz-Uffenheimer, *Quietistic Elements in Eighteenth Century Hasidic Thought* (Jerusalem, 1980) 108 (in Hebrew), to the effect that through silence (as well as closing one's eyes) one can cleave to the world of Thought.

53. *Reshit Ḥokhmah*, Shaʿar ha-Qedushah, chap. 11 (Jerusalem, 1984) 2:272.

54. Cf. *Shaʿare Ṣedeq*, ed. Y. Parush (Jerusalem, 1989) 22.

55. *Shaʿare Qedushah* (Jerusalem, 1985) 3:6, 93.

56. MS JTSA Mic. 2174, fols. 164a–b.

57. Cf. *b. Berakhot* 59a; and see discussion in M. Fishbane, " 'The Holy One Sits and Roars': Mythopoesis and the Midrashic Imagination," *The Journal of Jewish Thought and Philosophy* 1(1991) 1–21.

58. Cf. *Shaʿar Ruaḥ ha-Qodesh*, 7d, where the tears are said to come forth from *Ḥokhmah* and *Binah*.

59. *Shaʿar Maʾamere RaSHBI* (Jerusalem, 1898) 7c. Cf. Meroz, "Redemption in the Lurianic Teaching," 109.

60. See, by contrast, D. J. Halperin, "A Sexual Image in Hekhalot Rabbati and Its Implications," *Jerusalem Studies in Jewish Thought* 6(1987) 117–32, who interprets a reference to the eyes of the celestial beasts in a key passage from Hekhalot Rabbati as symbolizing the vagina. The eye may, in fact, function as a bi-sexual symbol, depicting both the male and female genitals. The connection of seeing, or more precisely the opening of the eyes, and erotic desire may be implied in the narrative concerning Adam and Eve in the Garden of Eden; cf. Gen. 3:5, 6, 7. Such an interpretation of the opening of the eyes is emphasized by later rabbinic interpreters on these biblical texts. See, e.g., Shem Ṭov ben Judah ibn Mayon's supercommentary on Abraham ibn Ezra's commentary on the Torah, MS Oxford-Bodleian 228, fol. 17a; A. Roth, *Ṭaharat ha-Qodesh* (Jerusalem, 1974) 1:132. In this connection it is of interest to note an interesting parallel in an ancient Egyptian source between the eyes of Horus and the testicles of Seth. See J. Assmann, "Semiosis and Interpretation in Ancient Egypt," in S. Biderman and B. Scharfstein. eds., *Interpretation in Religion*, (Leiden, 1992) 95. Recent scholarship has noted that the correlation of the penis and the eye underlies the phallomorphic ocularcentrism prevalent in Western culture. See L. Irigary, *Speculum of the Other Woman*, trans. G. C. Hull (Ithaca, 1985) 47–48, 145–146; idem, *This Sex Which Is Not One*, trans. C. Porter (Ithaca, 1985) 25–26; M. Jay, *Downcast Eyes: The Denigration of Vision in Twentieth-Century French Thought* (Berkeley, 1993) 493–542.

61. This reading is attested as well by the frequent use of this verse in Jewish amulets from Late Antiquity up until the present, bestowing upon the wearer of the amulet protection from the evil eye. Cf. E. A.

Wallis Budge, *Amulets and Talismans* (New York, 1961) 219; T. Schrire, *Hebrew Magic Amulets* (New York, 1966) 114; J. Naveh and S. Shaked, *Amulets and Magic Bowls: Aramaic Incantations of Late Antiquity* (Jerusalem, 1987) 237; L. H. Schiffman and M. D. Swartz, *Hebrew and Aramaic Incantation Texts from the Cairo Genizah: Selected Texts from Taylor-Schechter Box K1* (Sheffield, 1992) 24, 121, n. 22.

62.   Cf. *b. Berakhot* 20a, 55b; *Soṭah* 36b; *Baba Meṣiʿa* 84a; *Baba Batra* 118b. For other targumic and midrashic sources where this reading of Gen. 49:22 is employed, see J. L. Kugel, *In Potiphar's House: The Interpretative Life of Biblical Texts* (New York, 1990) 92, n. 35; and see now M. Niehoff, *The Figure of Joseph in Post-Biblical Jewish Literature* (Leiden, 1992) 147–48. While the evil eye has other connotations in rabbinic literature, it is frequently associated with the libidinal drive. See below, n. 78. A similar claim can be made with respect to the more general rabbinic notion, *yeṣer ha-raʾ* (the evil will). For recent discussion cf. D. Biale, *Eros and the Jews From Biblical Israel to Contemporary America* (New York, 1992) 44–45.

63.   *B. Nedarim* 20b. Cf. *Leviticus Rabbah* 12:1 (interpreting Prov. 23:31).

64.   See, e.g., *Leviticus Rabbah* 23:14; *Esther Rabbah* 3:14. On the erotic nature of visionary experience, see M. Idel, "Sexual Metaphors and Praxis in the Kabbalah," in D. Kraemer, ed., *The Jewish Family: Metaphor and Memory* (New York, 1989) 202–3; my article on circumcision cited above, n. 4; and D. Boyarin, "'This We Know to Be the Carnal Israel': Circumcision and the Erotic Life of the God of Israel," *Critical Inquiry* 18(1992) 474–505, esp. 491–97. See also H. Eilberg-Schwartz, "The Problem of the Body for the People of the Book," in H. Eilberg-Schwartz, ed., *People of the Body: Jews and Judaism from an Embodied Perspective* (Albany, 1992) 17–46, esp. 30–33.

65.   Cf. *Leviticus Rabbah* 20:10, and parallels. The link between visual encounter and erotic experience also seems to be implied in the midrashic comment in *Deuteronomy Rabbah* 11:10 to the effect that "from the day that [God] was revealed to [Moses] at the bush he did not have intercourse with his wife."

66.   Wolfson, *Through a Speculum That Shines*, 42–43.

67.   See, e.g., *Zohar* 2:99a, 176b; 3:59b, 296a; *Zohar Ḥadash* 62c; Liebes, "The Messiah of the Zohar," 164, n. 273; *ʿEṣ Ḥayyim* 16:3, 49b.

68.   *Mishneh Torah*, Deʿot, 4:19.

69.   This is not to say that every occurrence of the word *eye* symbolically refers to *Yesod;* on the contrary, this symbol is multivalent in zoharic literature. For example, the word *bat ʿayin*, the pupil of the eye, can symbolize the *Shekhinah;* cf. *Zohar* 2:204a (and cf. 1:226a); *Tiq-*

qune Zohar, ed. R. Margaliot (Jerusalem, 1978) 11, 26b; 70, 126b. Cf. especially the passage of Cordovero, MS JTSA Mic. 2174, fols. 178b–179a, where the *bat ʿayin* is a designation of the *Shekhinah* and the light from which she receives the light of knowledge (*ʿor ha-daʿat*) is associated with the three central *sefirot, Ḥesed, Din,* and *Raḥamim.* When she receives the light she is the open eye and when she does not she is the closed eye. Also significant is the depiction of the eyes of the two divine configurations, *'Arikh 'Anpin* and *Zeʿeir 'Anpin;* cp. *Zohar* 3:129b–130a (*'Idra' Rabba'*), 289a (*'Idra' Zuṭa'*). In the case of the latter the eye is said to have no covering or eyelid and to be perpetually open. This position signifies the attribute of divine mercy characteristic of this particular aspect of the Godhead. See especially the commentary on the first passage mentioned above in David ben Yehudah he-Ḥasid, *Sefer ha-Gevul,* MS JTSA Mic. 2193, fols. 4b–6a, which highlights the phallic dimension of the open eye in the uppermost configuration of the divine.

70.   Cf. *Zohar* 3:147b where the "open eye" (*peqiḥa' de-ʿeina'*) is depicted as the source of blessing (related to Prov. 22:9; cf. *b. Soṭah* 38b) in contrast to the closed eye which is the source of curses (related to Num. 24:3). See also ibid., 187b, 211b. Cf. Moses Zacuto's introduction to his *Tiqqun Soferim,* MS Oxford-Bodleian 1890, fol. 1a: "Happy are you righteous ones, masters of faith, to whom have been revealed the secrets of secrets, the Book of Concealment, and you exist at the time that the eye of providence, the open eye that has no covering, has providence over you."

71.   *Zohar* 2:98b.

72.   E. R. Wolfson, "Beautiful Maiden Without Eyes: *Peshat* and *Sod* in Zoharic Hermeneutics," in M. Fishbane, ed. *The Midrashic Imagination* (Albany, 1993) 185–87.

73.   Cf. *Zohar* 3:136b–137a (*'Idra' Rabba'*).

74.   Cf. *b. Ḥagigah* 12b.

75.   Cf. *b. Moʿed Qaṭan* 28a.

76.   *Livnat ha-Sappir,* MS British Museum 27,000, fol. 135a.

77.   Ibid., fol. 135b. Angelet's description of *Yesod* as the seventh emanation, corresponding to Sabbath, which is the spring that stands in the middle of six other emanations, three from the left and three from the right, echoes the parable in *Sefer ha-Bahir,* ed. R. Margaliot (Jerusalem, 1978) sec. 159. For the development of this motif in select kabbalistic sources, see Ginsburg, *The Sabbath in the Classical Kabbalah,* 87–92.

78.   Cp. *Zohar* 1:57a, 69a, 219b; 2:214b; 3:90a; *Shushan ʿEdut,* ed. G. Scholem, *Qovez ʿal Yad,* n.s. 8 (1976) 353; E. R. Wolfson, ed. *The Book of the Pomegranate: Moses de Leon's Sefer ha-Rimmon* (Atlanta, 1988) 230 (Hebrew text). It is also relevant to note here that in Jewish sources the eye (together with the heart) is often signaled out as a major vehicle for sin in general and sexual promiscuity in particular. See

S. Schechter, *Aspects of Rabbinic Theology* (New York, 1961) 208, 214, 258. In several rabbinic texts it seems that the evil eye specifically refers to the libido. This is clearly the case in zoharic texts as well. Cf. references cited in Y. Paḥah, *'Ule 'Ayin* (Jerusalem, 1990) 51–54. It is thus perfectly sensible that later moralists focused on the blemish of the eye (*pegam ha-'einayyim*) and safeguarding the eye (*shemirat ha-'einayyim*) when discussing matters pertaining to sexual purity. A classic example of this can be found in *Ṭaharat ha-Qodesh*, 1:110–37. Consider also the *Quntres ha-'Ayin Ro'eh* (Pamphlet on the seeing eye), published by the Bratslav Hasidim (New York, 1982), which collects the relevant material of R. Naḥman of Bratslav regarding this issue.

    79. *Reshit Ḥokhmah,* Sha'ar ha-Qedushah, chap. 17.

    80. *Mile di-Shemaya* by Rabbi Eleazar Azikri, 109.

    81. A *locus classicus* for the ritual of closing the eyes during prayer in kabbalistic literature is *Zohar* 3:260b, where it is connected specifically with the prohibition of looking at the *Shekhinah*. Regarding this gesture during prayer, see E. Zimmer, "Poses and Postures During Prayer," *Sidra* 5(1989) 92–94 (in Hebrew). On shutting the eyes as a contemplative technique in kabbalistic sources, see also Idel, *Studies in Ecstatic Kabbalah,* 134–36. For discussion of some of the relevant sources and the reverberation of this motif in Hasidic texts, see Z. Gries, *Conduct Literature (Regimen Vitae): It's History and Place in the Life of Beshtian Hasidism* (Jerusalem, 1989) 220–22 (in Hebrew). See below, n. 89.

    82. Cf. *Zohar* 2:95a, 98b–99a. Concerning this motif see my study referred to above, n. 72.

    83. *Sha'ar ha-Kawwanot,* 21c; cf. *Peri 'Eṣ Ḥayyim,* 168.

    84. *Sha'ar ha-Kawwanot,* 20c. Cf. Y. Avivi, "R. Joseph ibn Tabul's Sermons on the *Kawwanot,*" in *Studies in Memory of the Rishon le-Zion R. Yitzhak Nissim,* ed. M. Benayahu (Jerusalem, 1985) 4:82–83 (in Hebrew).

    85. Cf. *'Eṣ Ḥayyim,* 29:2, fol. 84a; *Sha'ar Ma'amere RaSHBI,* 53a–b. See also *Sha'ar ha-Kelalim,* chap. 1, printed in *'Eṣ Ḥayyim,* fol. 5c. The work is associated with three of Luria's disciples, Moses Yonah, Moses Najara, and Joseph Arzin. According to Y. Avivi, however, the text was authored by Ḥayyim Vital on the basis of compositions written by the aforementioned kabbalists. See Meroz, "Redemption in the Lurianic Teaching," 90–91.

    86. Cf. *Sha'ar ha-Kawwanot,* 46d–47a.

    87. Cf. *'Eṣ Ḥayyim,* 39:1, fol. 112d; *Qehillat Ya'aqov* (Jerusalem, 1992) 3. This motif too is expressed in zoharic literature. See, e.g., *Zohar* 1:60b, 135a. The obvious gender symbolism associated with these cosmological waters, based on the model of orgasmic secretion, is drawn boldly in zoharic literature. See, e.g., *Zohar* 1:29b. For a more elaborate

discussion of the ritualized gender metamorphosis in zoharic and Lurianic texts, see E. R. Wolfson, " Crossing Gender Boundaries in Kabbalistic Ritual and Myth," in *Circle in the Square: Studies in the Use of Gender in Kabbalistic Symbolism* (Albany, 1995) 79–121, esp. 110–115.

88.   Cf. the marginal note of Jacob Zemaḥ in Ḥayyim Vital, *Mavo' She'arim*, 2:2:6 (Jerusalem, 1892) 8c according to which the eyes are said to correspond to the consciousness of knowledge that is in the head (*moaḥ ha-da'at she-ba-ro'sh*). Here too one sees the specific linkage of the eyes to a masculine potency, albeit displaced from the genital region of the body to the cranium. In that context the zoharic reference to the beautiful maiden without eyes is also mentioned. See below, n. 110.

89.   See references above, n. 81. In the Lurianic material one can still find evidence for the more standard kabbalistic approach to the closing of the eyes as a technique to enhance mental concentration. See, e.g., *Sha'ar Ruaḥ ha-Qodesh*, 42d, 46d; *Sha'ar ha-Kawwanot*, 4a (regarding Luria's own practice of shutting his eyes during the private and public recitation of the Eighteen Benedictions).

90.   *Sha'ar ha-Kawwanot*, 59c.

91.   That is, by looking at the cup of wine, which symbolizes the feminine Presence, the individual draws down the masculine overflow and thereby reunifies the divine androgyne. Significantly, this unification is depicted in terms of the coronation motif. The understanding of the recitation of *qiddush* as a marriage ceremony and act of divine coronation is expressed in earlier kabbalistic literature including the *Zohar*. See E. K. Ginsburg, *Sod ha-Shabbat: The Mystery of the Sabbath* (Albany, 1989) 32, 114–15, n. 150.

92.   This numerology is probably to be decoded in the following way: the name Yah Adonai equals 80, which is to be multiplied by five to get the sum of 400. To this figure one should add the number 2, which stands for the two names. The sum 402 is also the numerical value of the word *bat*, the first of the two words in the expression *bat 'ayin*, i.e., the pupil of the eye. For a variant explanation cf. *Peri 'Eṣ Ḥayyim*, 422. On the use of *bat 'ayin* as a symbol for the feminine Presence (see above n. 69), cf. the anonymous Lurianic text (see Meroz, "Redemption in the Lurianic Teaching," 93) extant in MS Oxford-Bodleian 1786, fol. 469b. See, however, the passage from this collection cited below at n. 95.

93.   *Sha'ar ha-Kawwanot*, 71d. On the requirement to look at the cup of wine during *qiddush*, see also *Kanfe Yonah*, pt. 4, sec. 6, 33d; MS Oxford-Bodleian 1784, fol. 25b. Cf. Jacob Joseph of Poloyonne, *Toledot Ya'aqov Yosef* (Korets, 1780), 130a.

94.   See, e.g., *b. Ta'anit* 24a.

95.   MS Oxford-Bodleian 1786, fols. 469a–b.

96.   See, e.g., *'Eṣ Ḥayyim*, 9:1, 40a, where the beginning of the

shattering of the vessels is linked to a defect in the glance of the eyes of the Father and Mother, i.e., in their union.

97. Cf. *'Eṣ Ḥayyim* 4:3, 18d–19a; 9:5, 45a–b.

98. Cf. ibid. 8:1, 34a–35a. See Scholem, *Major Trends*, 265–66; I. Tishby, *The Doctrine of Evil and the 'Kelippah' in Lurianic Kabbalah* (Jerusalem, 1942) 29–31 (in Hebrew); Meroz, "Redemption in the Lurianic Teaching," 239–45.

99. Cf. *'Eṣ Ḥayyim*, 4:1, 17d.

100. See Meroz, "Redemption in the Lurianic Teaching," 100, 155, 194–95. On the feminine character of the "points," see now Y. Jacobson, "The Aspect of the Feminine in the Lurianic Kabbalah," in *Gershom Scholem's Major Trends in Jewish Mysticism 50 Years After*, 247–48.

101. Cf. *'Eṣ Ḥayyim*, 5:1, 20b–d. And see the marginal note from Ḥayyim Vital cited in *'Eṣ Ḥayyim*, 6:5, fol. 27a: "All the reality of the matter of the points is in the secret of the *Nuqba'*, and the matter concerns the fact that they come from the power of the light that strikes and sparkles and returns from below to above."

102. Ibid., 8:1, 34b. Cf. *Milei di-Shemaya by Rabbi Eleazar Azikri*, 103. The view articulated by Vital is clearly based on earlier sources. See, e.g., Naḥmanides commentary to Lev. 18:19, ed. H. Chavel (Jerusalem, 1960) 2:104. Nahmanides asserts that a woman in the period of menstruation who looks at a clear mirror made of iron creates red drops in the mirror corresponding to the drops of blood. The glance of the woman thus has the power to produce an external reality that reflects her internal state of impurity.

103. *Tiqqune Zohar*, 127b.

104. Vital has in mind the ancient tradition regarding the mystical spelling of the Tetragrammaton with twenty-four points. See Scholem, *Origins*, 328–29.

105. *'Eṣ Ḥayyim*, 8:1, 34b.

106. Regarding this symbol in kabbalistic literature, see E. R. Wolfson, "Light through Darkness: The Ideal of Human Perfection in the Zohar," *Harvard Theological Review* 81(1988) 73–95.

107. *'Eṣ Ḥayyim*, 8:1, 34c.

108. On the image of circles and the straight line as the geometric principles of the emanation of light from the Infinite, see Scholem, *Kabbalah*, 136–37; M. Pachter, "Circles and Straightness—A History of an Idea," *Da'at* 18(1987) 59–90 (in Hebrew).

109. *'Eṣ Ḥayyim*, 8:1, 35b.

110. Ibid., fol. 35d. Cf. Ḥayyim Vital, *Mavo' She'arim* 3:7, 25a; *Kanfe Yonah*, 4:6, 33d. Cf. Moses Cordovero, *Pardes Rimmonim* (Jerusalem, 1962) 23:16, 34a, s.v., "'ayin."

111. See, e.g., *'Olat Tamid*, 52b.

112.   On weeping as equivalent to overflowing with possible sexual connotations, cf. *Sha'ar ha-Kelalim*, chap. 2, 6a: "The lower half of *Tif'eret* of *'Arikh 'Anpin* remained and *Neṣaḥ, Hod,* and *Yesod* of him were disclosed without clothing. This is [the meaning of] what is said, 'the lower waters weep,' that is, these three lower *sefirot*, which are *Neṣaḥ, Hod,* and *Yesod*, were disclosed, and their light was great insofar as they were more revealed than the light of the arms [*Ḥesed, Gevurah,* and *Tif'eret*] for they were concealed within *'Abba'* and *'Imma'*. This is the secret of 'Blessed be the glory of God from its place' (*barukh kevod YWHW mi-meqomo* [Ezek. 3:12])—the first letters [of each word spell] *b[o]khim* ('they are weeping'). This is [the meaning of] they were weeping, that is, they were more revealed than the light of the arms, for the first vessels were abolished and shattered, preventing the light from entering into them. To rectify this it was necessary for the Emanator to comprise the thighs of *'Arikh 'Anpin* in his arms; *Neṣaḥ, Hod,* and *Yesod* were within *Ḥesed, Gevurah,* and *Tif'eret*, three within three, and the lower half of *Tif'eret*, which was revealed, was contained within the upper half. *Neṣaḥ* was contained within *Ḥesed, Hod* within *Gevurah,* and the lower half of *Tif'eret* within the upper half of *Tif'eret*. When *Neṣaḥ, Hod* and *Yesod* rose to enter the arms, which are *Ḥesed, Gevurah,* and *Tif'eret,* all the lights of the broken vessels ascended with them."

113.   Joseph Karo, *Maggid Mesharim* (Jerusalem, 1990), 183.

114.   Cf. *b. Shabbat* 55a.

115.   *Zohar* 3:76a.

116.   Ibid., 75b.

117.   Cf. *Reshit Ḥokhmah*, Sha'ar ha-Yir'ah, chap. 9; Sha'ar ha-Teshuvah, chap. 5; *Toṣe'ot Ḥayyim*, chap. 18. See also Eleazar Azikri, *Sefer Ḥaredim* (Jerusalem, 1966) 55.

118.   Cf. M. 'Avot 4:11.

119.   See references above, n. 39.

120.   *Sha'ar ha-Kawwanot*, 56b.

121.   Ibid., 48a; cf. *Peri 'Eṣ Ḥayyim*, 298–99.

122.   Cf. *Zohar* 3:120b–121a. See also *Zohar* 2:200b; *Zohar Ḥadash* 42a; Wolfson, *The Book of the Pomegranate*, 83–84 (Hebrew text); Liebes, "The Messiah of the Zohar," 177–78. For a more detailed discussion of this motif, see M. Fishbane, *The Kiss of God: Spiritual and Mystical Death in Judaism* (Seattle & London, 1994) 107–20. On the thematic connection of death and sexuality, see g. Bataille, *Death and Sensuality: A Study of Eroticism and the Taboo*, trans. M. Dalwood (New York, 1962).

123.   See Scholem, *Kabbalah*, 424; M. Benayahu, "R. Moses Yonah from the Circle of the Ari and the First to Write His Teaching," in *Studies in Memory of the Rishon le-Zion R. Yitzhak Nissim*, 7–74 (in Hebrew);

Meroz, "Redemption in the Lurianic Teaching," 90. Avivi, "R. Joseph ibn Tabul's Sermons on the *Kawwanot*," 75, attributes the work to Moses Yonah and Moses Najara.

124. *Kanfe Yonah,* 1:61, 24c–d. Cf. *Shaʿar ha-Kelalim*, chap. 1, 5c.

125. Cf. Avivi, "R. Joseph ibn Tabul's Sermons on the *Kawwanot*," 87.

126. Cf. *Peri ʿEṣ Ḥayyim*, 294.

127. *Shaʿare Qedushah* 3:5, 88–92.

128. Cf., e.g., Naḥmanides' formulation in *Shaʿar ha-Gemul*, in H. Chavel, ed., *Kitve Ramban,* (Jerusalem, 1982) 2:299, cited by Vital in the fourth part of *Shaʿare Qedushah* (cf. *Ketavim Ḥadashim le-Rabbenu Ḥayyim Vital* [Jerusalem, 1988] 14); see also passages from Karo and Azikri discussed by Werblowsky, *Joseph Karo,* 61.

129. *Shaʿare Qedushah* 3:5, 89.

130. Ibid.

131. Werblowsky, *Joseph Karo,* 69.

132. Ibid., 70.

133. Wolfson, *Through a Speculum That Shines,* chap. 6.

134. Cf. *Ketavim Ḥadashim le-Rabbenu Ḥayyim Vital,* 18.

135. *Shaʿare Qedushah* 3:5, 91.

136. Ibid., 92.

137. Werblowsky, *Joseph Karo,* 69.

CHAPTER 12

PaRDeS: Some Reflections on Kabbalistic Hermeneutics

Moshe Idel

I

Jewish mysticism, like other forms of religious mysticism, was in a permanent search for objective validation; the personal experience, sometimes the mystical intuition, important as it might be for the spiritual life of the individual, strove also to anchor itself in the collective experience of the community, basically by resorting to a reinterpretation of the canonical writings.[1] Accordingly, the hermeneutic enterprise in Kabbalah—the most important medieval form of Jewish mysticism—is a main component of this mystical lore. Centered on the Bible much more than are the Christian mystics, and perhaps more even than are the Sufis, the kabbalists offered a plethora of mystical interpretations whose relationship to the already existing corpus of traditional nonmystical interpretations of the Scriptures had to be yet clarified.

The major expression of this attempt to establish an explicit scheme that will explicate the hierarchical relationship among the different types of Jewish exegesis is known by the acronym *PaRDeS*. As an acronym, it designates a fourfold system of exegesis, used mostly in Kabbalistic writings. **PaRDeS** stands for **P**[eshat], "plain meaning," **R**[emez] or "hint," sometimes designating allegorical explanations, **D**[erash] or "homiletic expositions" and finally **S**[od] or "secret," namely symbolic, interpretations. In the following I shall present some reflections about the background of the emergence of the fourfold hermeneutics as it was advocated by kabbalists and the significance of its structure; then I shall elaborate upon two subjects related to the kabbalistic level of this method: semantic indeterminacy, namely, the assumption that the biblical text has infinite meanings, and the formal determinacy concerned with the minutiae of the writing the Torah-scroll, which should be preserved intact.

There are two main explanations for the emergence of the **PaRDeS** type of exegesis among the kabbalists at the end of the thirteenth century: that of W. Bacher, who maintained that the Kabbalists adopted and adapted the Christian fourfold theory of interpretation,[2] and the view of Peretz Sandler, who argued that this exegetical system emergences as the result of an inner development starting with the twelfth-century Jewish exegesis.[3] At the beginning, Gershom Scholem adopted the theory of Bacher, though later he did not reject explicitly the view of Sandler.[4] I believe that Sandler did not make a very strong point; on the other hand, it is rather difficult to simply accept the Bacher-Scholem theory because of the simple fact, pointed out already by Sandler, and more recently by Frank Talmage and van der Heide, that the kabbalistic fourfold method does not correspond in crucial details to the Christian fourfold method.[5] Though it is always possible that one individual kabbalist will accept an alien type of exegesis, whether Christian or Muslim,[6] it seems to me unconvincing to assume that several kabbalists accepted, exactly at the same time and apparently independently, a very similar exegetical method. We must look for a common factor that will explain the concomitant resort of several kabbalists to these exegetical methods.

Can we accept as reasonable the explanation that independent kabbalists would accept, at the same time, an alien type of exegesis, without having in common more substantial factors? It seems that the obvious fact that kabbalists were those who exposed such a fourfold method is highly significant. **PaRDeS** stands, as we have already mentioned, for the four methods of exegesis. However, in the last quarter of the thirteenth century, when this system emerged, it designated methods that were applied, separately, in different types of Jewish literature. The plain sense was the main subject of the rich exegetical literature produced by the northern France school of exegetes in the eleventh and twelfth centuries. A voluminous homiletical literature had already been produced between the third century and the early Middle Ages.

Jewish philosophers had used allegorical interpretation since the eleventh century; it flourished in the thirteenth century. Finally, kabbalistic (i.e., symbolical-theosophical) interpretations of the Bible and other canonical Jewish writings were already known at the middle of the thirteenth century. The **PaRDeS** method incorporated a variety of types of Jewish literature that were already in existence when the first formulations of this system were articulated. The latest type of literature was Kabbalah, and it is no accident that the exponents of this mystical lore were those who first exposed the method of **PaRDeS**.

On the other hand, we have sufficient evidence to suggest that some of the kabbalists who proposed the **PaRDeS** or other systematic exegetical methods underwent a certain spiritual development before they became Kabbalists. There can be no doubt, as pointed out by I. Twersky,[7] that Isaac ibn Latif, Moses de Leon, Joseph Gikatilla, and Abraham Abulafia were interested in Jewish philosophy before they became kabbalists. It is obvious that they were well acquainted with the Bible and its plain interpretations as well as with the midrashic literature. Thus it seems indisputable that the personal spiritual development of some of those kabbalists who exposed the **PaRDeS** system, or similar ones, is highly relevant for the acceptance of such a peculiar method, even if such an acceptance was the result of an appropriation of a foreign method. Because of the emergence of the additional, mystical, type of Jewish literature in Spain, the peculiar biography, or curriculum, of some of the intellectuals also included Kabbalah; the other three bodies of literature were read in preparation for the study of the mystical lore. Consequently, in order to better understand the ascent of the systematic hermeneutics in Spanish Kabbalah, one must consider not only the possible alien sources but also the cultural framework within which the new hermeneutics emerged as well as the spiritual biographies of those kabbalists who articulated it.

Two related conclusions can be drawn from the above observations. First, kabbalists presented, as van Heide has already indicated, the fourfold method in a very specific manner in order to confer upon their mystical lore the privileged status of an exalted type of knowledge.[8] By including the other three nonkabbalistic types of interpretation in the fourfold system, the Kabbalists achieved two distinct, though complementary, results: they safeguarded a place of honor for their peculiar lore, preserving, at the same time, the modes of interpretation that were then traditional as necessary stages for the development of the ideal approach to the canonical texts. Jewish mysticism was not portrayed as an alternative to the already existing bodies of Jewish literature; it was conceived as their culmination. This inclusive character of the kabbalistic fourfold system of interpretation avoided the centrifugal tendencies characteristic of some non-Jewish types of mysticism.[9] This is true also in the case of Abraham Abulafia's sevenfold exegetical system. As we can easily guess, it is his peculiar sort of kabbalah, the ecstatic one, that is considered the source of the highest methods of interpretation. In the various expositions of his hermeneutics, Abulafia does not discredit or oppose the other kabbalistic types of interpretations, namely, the symbolical ones, but he posits his own mystical approaches to the text as superior to other versions of Kabbalistic interpretation.[10] Again we can see both the conservative and innovative character of the kabbalistic hermeneutic systems: it is always inclusive, allowing an important role to all the existing achievements of Jewish cultural creativity as preparatory approaches, while presenting the respective mode of interpretation that corresponds to the Kabbalistic system—in whose framework it was articulated—as the highest one. However, de facto, we may describe the specifically kabbalistic exegesis itself, according to the versions found in the different layers of the book of the *Zohar*, as integrating elements from all the other three sorts of exegesis. I would like to emphasize that the *Zohar* does not resort, systematically, to the four exegetical methods as separate types of interpretation but uses various elements together as part of the zoharic interpretation of the Bible.[11] There can be no doubt that the author or authors of the *Zohar* were aware of the contributions of the various layers of Jewish exegetical literature to the formation of the zoharic text.

The second conclusion, which derives from the first one, is that the nature of even some of the innovative types of Kabbalah is relatively conservative. Far from being ready to regard the previous stages of Jewish exegesis as obsolete or superfluous, the innovative kabbalists strove to integrate them into more comprehensive exegetical systems, safeguarding their importance and survival[12] even when some of these kabbalists, such as Abraham Abulafia, would consider the "lower" types of exegesis pertinent for the vulgus alone.[13] Kabbalists attempted to articulate their hermeneutics in concert rather than in conflict with the traditional one. This responsible attitude toward the spiritual heritage of Judaism ensured the special role of Kabbalah in those Jewish circles that were not identical with the proper kabbalistic groups.

Nevertheless, there are examples of discussions that posit Kabbalah as totally indispensable to proper interpretation of a text. A pun related to the word **PaRDeS** will easily exemplify it. Rabbi Hayyim Yoseph David Azulai (1724–1807) better known as HYDA', commented in his *Midbar Qadmut* as follows: Whoever believes only in the plain sense of the Bible, **Peshat,** is indeed a fool, as a permutation of the consonants of **PeShaT** "demonstrates": **TiPeSh.** Moreover, he continues, without the secret, namely the kabbalistic, interpretation, designated by the *S* in **PaRDeS,** the three first consonants of this word will form the word *PeReD,* namely an "ass."[14] Important as the first three methods may be for the accomplished kabbalist, they do not in themselves suffice for real understanding of the text. In fact, without knowledge of Kabbalah, the exegete is no more than an ass.

Notwithstanding the fact that the regular attitude to the "lower" ways of exegesis was not negative, a perusal of the vast kabbalistic interpretative literature conspicuously reveals that, in general, the kabbalists were not inclined to propose plain, homiletic, or allegorical interpretations of their own. Though acknowledging in principle the importance of the "lower" modes of interpretation, the Kabbalists did not conceive of themselves as obliged, religiously, to provide the whole range of explanations suggested by the **PaRDeS** system. Moreover, with the significant exception of Rabbi Bahiya ben Asher's *Commentary on the Pentateuch,* the kabbalists contented themselves with providing Kabbalistic commentaries par excellence and not compilations of heterogenous types of exegetical material.[15]

Let me address another facet of the **PaRDeS** method: according to several discussions dating after the late thirteenth century, the four methods correspond to the four Tannaitic figures who entered the Pardes, namely, a spiritual adventure from which only one person, Rabbi Aqiva, returned safely.[16] According to the talmudic story, and to its parallel in the hekhalot literature, three other figures, Ben Zoma, Ben Azzai, and Elisha ben Abuyah were damaged, in various degrees, by a spiritual adventure whose peculiar nature is rather obscure.[17] For our purpose it is important to emphasize the fact that Rabbi Aqiva, who corresponds typologically to the kabbalistic method of interpretation, was the only person who returned safely. Thus, at least implicitly, the kabbalistic method of interpretation was regarded as the single safe type of exegesis, whereas the other three involved, again implicitly, different sorts of dangers. Nevertheless, this correlation is to be understood not as recommending that the masses use kabbalistic exegesis but as emphasizing the elitist nature of this type of spiritual preoccupation. Although Rabbi Aqiva's safe return did propose a safe type of exegesis, the study of Kabbalah still involved some dangers that should not be overlooked. Thus the mystical type of hermeneutics was to be restricted to the very few, an assumption that was indeed characteristic of the whole history of Kabbalah.

Another interesting relationship was established between the four methods of exegesis and the four cosmic layers or worlds, designated in Kabbalah by the acronym 'by': 'Azilut, Beriy'ah, Yezirah, 'Asiyah. The *Sod* corresponds to the world of 'Azilut or Emanation; the *Derash* stands for the second one, that of Beriy'ah or Creation; the *Remez* corresponds to the world of Yezirah or Formation; and, finally, the *Peshat* stands for the lowest world, that of 'Asiyah or Making. According to Lurianic texts, neglecting of one of the senses of the Torah induced a certain damage in the corresponding cosmic level.[18] Thus, it becomes obvious that even the kabbalist should not disregard the lower types of interpretations. Explicitly, the kabbalistic onto-hermeneutics of the Torah led the mystic to the divine world of emanation. The PaRDeS system involved a certain version of *scala mentis ad Deum;* gradually immersing himself in the various aspects of the text, the kabbalist was, at the same time, fathoming the depths of reality: the Bible became a tool for metaphysical exploration. At the core of this text stood the divinity, or one of its manifestations, and the dynamism of the divine life could be extracted through explication of the rich secret meanings of the infinite divine text. The hermeneutic enterprise of the kabbalist brought him, according to the above ontological concord, to an experience of the Divine; exploring the text, the kabbalist entered another, higher spiritual domain.[19] A kabbalistic reading of the Torah apparently meant, at least for some of the Jewish mystics, more than a determination of a certain potential meaning of the text; by creating, or extrapolating, this significance, the kabbalist also experienced it. In other words, some of the important stages of Jewish mysticism envisioned mystical exegesis, not only as a manner of extracting novel significances from a text by propelling some theological or theosophical views into it, but also—and in some cases this was perhaps the main purpose of the enterprise—as a way of encountering deeper levels of reality.[20] The experiential aspects of kabbalistic hermeneutics is a subject that still deserves detailed study; some of its facets are reminiscent of the modern phenomenological type of reading, which emphasizes experiential understanding over the analytical "objective" approach.[21]

II

As mentioned above, the most elaborated hermeneutic systems of Kabbalah emerged during the last third of the thirteenth century. Some forms of fourfold exegetical systems, like those of Isaac ibn Latif, Joseph Gikatilla, Moses de Leon, the *Zohar* and *Tiqqunei Zohar,* and Bahiya ben Asher, on the one hand, and the sevenfold system of Abraham Abulafia, on the other, provide convincing evidence of a serious interest in techniques of interpretation exceeding that found in the earlier stages of kabbalah. Also writings of other kabbalists (such as Rabbi Joseph of Hamadan in the late thirteenth century and Rabbi Isaac ben Samuel of Acre at the beginning of the fourteenth century), though not expressing an explicit and systematic hermeneutics, present a vital concern with different types of esoteric methods of understanding the Scriptures. The common denominator of the intellectual formation of most of the aforementioned authors is the fact that, despite their good formation as kabbalists, none of them can be considered an important halakhic figure and it is far from clear whether their halakhic formation included in-depth studies of the legalistic literature. Moreover, to the extent I am acquainted with the biographies of these authors, none of them played any leading, or even any significant, role in the Jewish communal life. There is no evidence that any of these kabbalists were involved in the internal affairs of their communities. The innovative kabbalists[22] can be described as belonging to the secondary elite; that is, they were educated individuals who were in a continuous search for new types of thought and were uneasy with the authoritative philosophical theology of Maimonides or with the perception of Kabbalah by another great authority, Naḥmanides.

All this stands in sharp distinction to the role played by their contemporaries, the "primary elite" and kabbalists, who were leading figures in Catalonia and Castile at this time. So, for example, Naḥmanides in Gerona, Rabbi Shelomo ben Abraham ibn Adret in Barcelona,[23] Rabbi Moses ben Shimeon of Burgos, and Todros ben Joseph ha-Levi Abulafia in Toledo were accomplished kabbalists, active on the public plane as important legalistic figures or leaders of their communities; there is no evidence that any of these men were interested in systematic hermeneutics. I believe that this clearcut distribution into distinct groups, with the "secondary elite" interested and the "primary elite" disinterested in presentations of systematic hermeneutics, is highly significant for our understanding of the kabbalistic conceptions of hermeneutics.

The hermeneutic systems were closely related to novel approaches to the canonical texts; by applying the exegetical method, kabbalists were able to extract new kabbalistic views or elaborate upon the existing kabbalistic theories. This innovative type of Kabbalah constitutes a considerable departure from the dominant perception of Kabbalah as an ancient and precious esoteric lore, one to be transmitted and preserved without changes. In other words, the emergence of the fourfold exegetical method, as well as Abulafia's sevenfold exegetical system, coincides with the nascent innovative Kabbalah. From the vantage point of the history of Kabbalah, the understanding of the affinity between the **PaRDeS** types of interpretation and the creativity that characterizes the contemporary Kabbalah, is of paramount importance.[24] It would be an exaggeration to assume that all the previously unknown themes appeared as the result of hermeneutic activity. I have no doubt that we must attribute the plethora of unknown kabbalistic views to the surfacing of ancient mythologoumena as well—for reasons that are not always clear. However, I assume that we would better attribute to the hermeneutic processes substantial contributions to the much more variegated landscape that the late thirteenth century Kabbalah presents to scholars.[25]

III

It should be emphasized that the level of the *Sod*, or secret interpretation, was not restricted by the innovative kabbalists to one single type of exegesis. Though the prevalent sort of kabbalistic exegesis was the symbolic-narrative one,[26] there were also several other types of nonsymbolic approaches to the divine text.

1. A monadic understanding of the Hebrew language and implicitly of the Bible. According to this view, which has ancient sources and became, by the intermediary of the kabbalistic material, prevalent in Hasidism, each and every letter was conceived of as a universe in itself. The atomization of the semantic units into letters conceived as designating divine names, the entire system of *Sefirot,* and the whole alphabet, diminished the importance of the specific sequence of the letters in the Bible, in favor of the immersion by the kabbalists and, later on, by the Hasidim, in the inner world of the letters. It is as if the interpreter were contemplating the text using a microscope.[27]

2. A hieroglyphic, iconic, or ideogramic understanding of the whole biblical text as the picture of the supernal divine system. This view is closely related to the anthropomorphic view of God in the hekhalot literature and its metamorphoses in the kabbalistic view of the ten *Sefirot* as constituting an anthropomorphic structure. It is as if the exegete were using a telescope in order to see the whole text as one unit.[28]

3. Somewhat related to this hieroglyphic view is the kabbalistic understanding of the white forms of the letters as pointing to a higher reality, in comparison to that symbolized by the black forms of the letter. This view will be discussed below.

4. A variety of mathematical approaches to the text; these approaches include methods such as **Notariqon, Gematriah, Temurah, Zeruf 'Otiot,** and other variations on these exegetical techniques.[29]

The symbolic-narrative as well as the static-symbolic and the nonsymbolical types of interpretations allowed the Kabbalist a relatively free choice in his hermeneutic project. The accumulation of the various exegetical techniques in the late-thirteenth-century Kabbalah was fateful for its development. One of the views that is characteristic of some of the kabbalistic systems, designated in the following as innovative Kabbalah, is the claim that the Torah, being a divine text, is infinite and thus can yield countless meanings. This view, whose roots can be detected at the middle of the thirteenth century, was not accepted by the conservative kabbalists, namely those persons who did not adopt the method of **PaRDeS**. Nevertheless it recurs in the writings of the kabbalistic innovative hermeneuts. Through the mediation of Christian Kabbalah, this view could have influenced modern theories on the open text.

The central assumption of the kabbalistic understanding of the divine text, namely, that it is, like its author, infinite, could be supported better if it were possible to return to the text and reinterpret it mystically time and again.[30] Some of the innovative kabbalists assumed that it was possible to apply more than one kabbalistic type of interpretation at the same time; this implicitly meant that the text was understood to offer a whole range of mystical meanings simultaneously.[31] In other words, mystical interpretation was not to be understood as explicating the infinite meanings of the texts as part of an evolving historical process that assumed the accommodation theory of revelation or related types of adaptationist theories. Though indeed the Torah was sometimes described by kabbalists using theories of accommodation, as it has recently been shown by S. D. Benin,[32] even the lower, mundane manifestation of the Torah was conceived as being pregnant with an infinity of meanings. Regularly, the assumption that the divine message has accommodated to the peculiar period of time or level of evolution points to the revelation of one hidden meaning implicitly excluding the concomitant existence of other similar meanings. In the case of the kabbalistic theory, even in the cases when the theory of accommodation was indeed adopted for one reason or another, this fact did not vitally affect the coexistence of a plurality of symbolic or nonsymbolic messages in the same text for the same person. Moreover, the general impression is that innovative kabbalists, though sometimes using accommodationalist formulations, were not eager to acknowledge a lowering of the status of the Torah by attributing to it only one significance that alone would inform the religious life of a certain generation. I would say that Kabbalah preferred the assumption that an infinity of meanings is latent in the *Gestalt* of the divine text over the view, found in several Christian texts, that the process of interpretation alone is infinite.[33] According to the latter, each and every exegete is able to contribute his view to the exegetical tradition, whereas the text per se is only very rarely regarded as infinite in its significances.

Indeed it would be much more representative to say that, according to the kabbalists, the kabbalist is assimilated to the Torah rather than the reverse.[34] It is man that must accommodate himself to the infinite Torah rather than Torah to man. One example of such a process can be adduced from a Hasidic statement that also faithfully reflects the stand of the kabbalists:

> Out of your union [with God] [*Me-ḥamat ha-devequt shelkha*] you will be able to pass from the word *'Anokhi* alone to the entire Torah, because just as God, blessed be he, is infinite, also his word is infinite, and likewise you, if you will be united to God, blessed be he, will comprehend an infinite understanding too.[35]

IV

An interesting development in kabbalistic thought, which stems from some ancient Midrashic traditions, generated a special theosophical understanding of the nature of the written language and, implicitly, of the biblical text. According to some ancient Jewish traditions, the Torah was written white fire on the black fire on the divine body.[36] In thirteenth-century Castile, Rabbi Isaac ha-Kohen, the son of Rabbi Jacob ha-Kohen, expressed an interesting theory on the relationship between the white and the black configurations of the Hebrew letters. When discussing the aleph he wrote:

> The inner [form] stands for the Holy One, blessed be he, as He is hidden from the eye of any creature and His innerness [aspect] cannot be reached. The external form stands for the [external] world, which depends on the arm of the Holy One, blessed be He, as an amulet does on the arm of a powerful man.[37] And just as the inner form is the locus of the external form, so [also] is God the locus of the world, and the world is not the locus of God.[38] What I have mentioned to you that the white form in the Aleph stands for the level of Holy One, blessed be he, but not the black one, [which is] external. I have told you this by the way of a [great] principle, and as a great secret because the white form stands for the white garment, and our sages, blessed be their memory, said:[39] Whence was the light created? It teaches that the Holy One, blessed be He, was clothed Himself with a white garment, and the splendor of it [the garment] shone from one end of the world to another as it is said [Ps. 104:2] "Who covers himself with light as with a garment" and [Dan. 2:22] "and the light dwells with him."[40]

The inner form is the white space that is the locus of the black configuration of the letter. It is the inner form that is the most important one, as it is the soul that sustains the body. This last type of image is expressly used in the context of our passage and it reflects the Neoplatonic view of the soul as sustaining the body by the very fact that she surrounds it. Moreover, the white light is conspicuously identified with the divine light, which is described as the divine garment. All this is related to the divine arm, granted the anthropomorphic aspect is somewhat attenuated in this passage. Crucial for our discussion is the fact that the amorphous component of the letter is conceived as the paramount element, identical with a divine manifestation. Obviously the above discussion does not refer, as in the midrashic literature, to the Torah in its entirety and to its role in the creative process. However, it seems to include an even more striking factor: the primordial written version of the Torah pregnant is with a divine dimension—and so, too, are the Hebrew letters in general, independent of the stage of creation. Consequently, not only the primordial Torah but also, in principle, any Hebrew text has a divine status.

This discussion conclusively demonstrates that kabbalists moved from a theory of the Hebrew letters as part of the divine text to one on the status of Hebrew letters in general, thus they opened up the possibility to build up a much more comprehensive hermeneutics of texts. The nature of the white light, the space surrounding the letter, is compared to an emanation of the light stemming from the divine garment. This light is comparable to the white fire, corresponding to God's skin in some midrashic texts. In both cases the external appearance of God is involved in the constitution of the written text. However, in the above kabbalistic passage the light is preferred because it better serves the kabbalistic theosophy that is interested in the emanative process. As it can be shown also in other kabbalistic passages, the emergence of the text, or according to other kabbalistic discussions, of the articulated verbal aspect of language,[41] serves as a metaphor for the emanation;[42] the white fire of the Midrash, with its anthropomorphic connotations, would be less appropriate as an image of a pure spiritual emanation.

Nevertheless, in some kabbalistic fragments, we find a discussion of the nature of the letter yod.[43] Its numerical equivalence in the Jewish system of counting is ten. In those texts, the kabbalists assume that there is a black yod, sustained by a white yod. The white one, which is also a hidden one, is conceived of as symbolic of the ten supernal *Sefirot,* the ten *Ẓaḥẓaḥot,* or divine Luminosities, which serve as the static and hidden paradigms of the lower dynamic *Sefirot*.[44] The higher *Sefirot* are arranged, according to an esoteric teaching in the circle of kabbalists who wrote the above texts, as an anthropomorphic structure. Thus, the white fire is again emblematic of a divine anthropomorphic view. In late thirteenth or early fourteenth century some kabbalists returned to the ancient view of the Torah as written on the divine skin, which offers an interesting parallel to Derrida's "transcendental space of inscription," while employing a much more sophisticated theosophy.

V

Let me address the question of the significance of attributing such a great importance to the white parts of the text. We may distinguish between two different approaches to this matter. On the one hand, the ancient approach, basically an anthropomorphic theology, integrated the view of the white fire as pointing to the divine skin, and as such the divinity of the peculiar writing of the Torah scroll was ensured. On the other hand, the symbolic interpretation of the white fire has something to do with the assumption that the higher or inner level in the divine realm is made much richer by its very ambiguity. The written, namely, the limited, aspects of the text are the lower one, whereas the higher one, which reflects the divine essence, is less definite.

On first appearance, it seems strange that in the very period when the kabbalists built up their theory that infinite meanings are hinted at in the biblical text that the external, static aspect of the biblical text became so important. Since it was possible to confer upon the written part of the Bible such an unlimited range of interpretations, why bother about the *minutiae* of its manifestation? It seems that the theory of the infinite meanings of the biblical text was emphasized by kabbalists who were also anxious to stress the importance of the external facet of the Bible. I assume that the drastic relativization of the semantic aspect of the words required an absolutization of their manifest side. It is precisely an attempt to postulate the absolute underlying the ongoing flow of the meaning that contributed to the ascent of the importance of the substratum of the words. That is, when it became obvious that the authoritative significance of the Bible depends on subjective interpretation, the need for balance contributed to the emergence of an emphasis on the other aspects of the text. The limited aspect, the black fire, became unlimited as far as the senses of the text were concerned. The authority installed by the identification of the white with the divine permitted the Kabbalists to relate themselves to the Bible as the absolute text.

However, this "new" authority was consonant with that mystical authority which may be amorphous, expressing amorphous experiences. The view of the Torah as expressed in some late-thirteenth-century kabbalistic texts may suggest that the ultimate source and substratum of the Torah is amorphous, just as the highest aspect of the divine is in the encounter between God and man, whereas the limited, black part of the text, namely, the letters, is the communal, public manifestation of the divine in the external world.[45]

The retreat to the indeterminate aspects of the Bible, the white "forms" of the letters, probably answers the need to emphasize the uniqueness of the Hebrew formulation of the Bible, more than the necessity to relate to its grammatical *Gestalt*. The elevation of the Bible's external form, which includes the white parts, to such an exalted rank of importance secured special significance for the theosophical kabbalists' punctiluous observance of the *minutiae* of copying the biblical scroll. Simply studying Hebrew does not bring one to the innermost aspect of the Bible; one must accept the formal facets of its transmission, as formulated by the rabbinic regulations, to be able to fathom the subtle, almost imponderable, subtleness of the scroll, which points to the indeterminate Godhead. In the eyes of the kabbalists, the stress upon the importance of the white implicitly safeguarded the importance of the Hebrew Bible, even in an age when the study of Hebrew by Christians was already an achievement of Christian exegesis. Curiously, the hermeneutic freedom that the kabbalistic exegesis achieved by cultivating the polysemic, dynamic, symbolical approach to the biblical text has culminated with the apotheosis of the static, para-semantic, hieroglyphic facets of this text.[46] It was a scroll-fascination that emerged in exactly the same period when the free symbolic interpretations of kabbalists reached its apex. Over-emphasizing the stable and static aspects of the text, kabbalists strove to balance the great freedom that emerged from the relativization of the symbolic interpretation resulting from the ascent of the concept of the Bible as an open text. The equilibrium between extreme semantic fluidity and extreme structural stability, namely, the *Gestalt* of the external features of the text, allowed innovative developments without endangering the authority of the canonical text. It may well be that the eccentric exegetical devices that prevailed in the kabbalistic literature could flourish precisely because of the extreme canonization of all the details of the Torah scroll. The theosophical kabbalists resolved the problem of authority of the text versus exegetical creativity on the level of the kabbalistic hermeneutics; they did not rely on the three "lower" types of interpretation in order to safeguard the authority of the text. The kabbalists invoked the importance of the mystical relevance of the white aspects of the text in order to establish a stronger authoritative anchor for their symbolic-narrative interpretations.

The last phase of Jewish mysticism, Hasidism, was less interested in the external shape of the text; instead it emphasized the paramount importance of the vocal realization. The real letter, and text, was the oral one—a dramatic change in comparison to Kabbalah in general. Nevertheless, the idea of the infinity of the significances of the Bible recurs several times in Hasidic texts, where interestingly enough, Kabbalah was conceived as a very profound lore, which can scarcely be fathomed. To a certain extent, this mystical lore was put on a pedestal. One of the most arresting expressions of this attitude came from Rabbi Yehudah Leib ha-Cohen of Anipola, who maintained that even the plain sense of Kabbalah is unknown because of the vicissitudes of the Exile, *a fortiori* the *Remez, Derash,* and *Sod* of **PaRDeS**.[47] This formula, which played an inclusive role in the medieval period, was interpreted by this Hasidic master as an exclusive device. He saw it as pointing not only to the levels of the biblical text but to the depths of Kabbalah, especially the *Zohar,* itself. Kabbalah, which was meanwhile sanctified as a revealed lore, was to be explored by the same criteria as the Bible itself.[48] In Hasidism, the plain sense of the Bible as expounded by Rashi is regarded as the mystical level par excellence.[49] The symbolic level of interpretation is no more the forefront of exegesis in Hasidism, which focuses its expositions on the dissemination of a devotional, psychological interpretation of Judaism.[50] The neutralization of several important aspects of kabbalistic theosophy rendered superfluous the complex kabbalistic hermeneutics as exposed by the medieval innovative kabbalists.

NOTES

1. See Gershom Scholem, *On the Kabbalah and Its Symbolism* (New York, 1969) 5–32.

2. W. Bacher, "L'Exegese biblique dans le Zohar" *Revue des Etudes Juives* 22(1891) 33–46, esp. 37–40. See also idem, "Das Merkwort PRDS in der Juedischen Bibelexegese," *Zeitschrift fuer die alttestamentliche Wissenschaft* 13(1893) 294–305.

3. Peretz Sandler, "On the Question of **Pardes** and the Fourfold Method," in *Sefer Eliahu Auerbach* (Jerusalem, 1955) 222–35 (Hebrew). See also A. van der Heide, "**Pardes:** Methodological Reflections on the Theory of Four Senses" *Journal of Jewish Studies* 34(1983) 147–59.

4. Scholem, *On the Kabbalah,* 61: "I am inclined to agree with Bacher." However, several years earlier, Scholem's opinion was much more clearcut in favor of the Christian influence: "I have no doubt that this method [**PaRDeS**] was taken from the Christian medieval exegesis." (Gershom Scholem, *Explications and Implications: Writings on Jewish Heritage and Renaissance* [Tel Aviv, 1975] 249 [Hebrew]).

5. Frank Talmage, "Apples of Gold: The Inner Meaning of Sacred Texts in Medieval Judaism," in Arthur Green, ed., *Jewish Spirituality* (New York, 1986) 320; van der Heide, "Pardes," 154–55.

6. See Talmage, *Apples of Gold,* 349, n. 48; Moshe Idel, *Language, Torah and Hermeneutics in Abraham Abulafia* (Albany, 1989) 93 and 191, n. 52.

7. See Isadore Twersky, *Studies in Jewish Law and Philosophy* (New York, 1982) 208.

8. Van der Heide, "Pardes," 149.

9. See, e.g., the tension between the plain sense and the esoteric one in Isma'ili hermeneutics; There, the plain sense was regarded as Satanic! For kabbalistic examples of a similar tension see Moshe Idel, *Kabbalah: New Perspectives* (New Haven, 1988) 207–8.

10. Idel, *Language, Torah and Hermeneutics,* 82–124.

11. See Bacher, "L'Exegese biblique."

12. See, e.g., one of the most important discussion of the zoharic hermeneutics, the maiden parable, which was analyzed in detail by several scholars: See ibid. 36–38, Scholem, *On the Kabbalah,* 55–56, Talmage, "Apples of Gold," 316–17, Isaiah Tishby, *The Wisdom of the Zohar,* vol. 2 (Jerusalem, 1961) 370–71 (Hebrew), Idel, *Kabbalah: New Perspectives,* 227–29.

13. Idel, *Language, Torah and Hermeneutics,* 83–87.

14. *Midbar Qadmut* par. **Peh,** section Peshat (Jerusalem, 1962) fol. 49a, quoted in the name of R. Isaac Luria.

15. On Bahya's version of the fourfold method see Scholem, *On the Kabbalah,* 59, 62.

16. See, e.g., *Tiqqunei Zohar,* printed in *Zohar* 1:26b.

17. *Ḥagigah* fol. 15a. On the whole issue see Gershom Scholem, *Jewish Gnosticism, Merkabah Mysticism and Talmudic Tradition* (New York, 1965) 14–19.

18. See *Sha'ar ha-Yiḥudim* (Koretz, n.d.) fol. 33d; *Shulḥan 'Arukh le-ha-Ari* (Krakow, n.d.) fol. 26a, par. *Qeriah be-Ḥokhmat ha-Kabbalah.*

19. In the domain of the theosophical-theurgical Kabbalah a relevant example is the maiden parable mentioned above, note 12, and see also Idel, *Kabbalah: New Perspectives,* 223–24.

20. As to the experiential implication of a mystical interpretation of the Bible in ecstatic Kabbalah, see Idel, *Language, Torah and Hermeneutics,* xi, 101–9, 121–24.

21. See Wolfgang Iser, *The Act of Reading* (Baltimore, 1979) 10: "meaning is no longer an object to be defined, but is an effect to be experienced."

22. On this kabbalistic type, in opposition to the conservative Kabbalah, see Moshe Idel, "We Have No Kabbalistic Tradition on This" in Isadore Twersky, ed., *Rabbi Moses Nahmanides (Ramban) Explorations in His Religious and Literary Virtuosity* (Cambridge, Mass. 1983) 63–73, idem, *Kabbalah: New Perspectives,* 212–13, and the study mentioned in the following note.

23. See Moshe Idel, "NAHMANIDES: Kabbalah, Halakhah and Spiritual Leadership" (forthcoming).

24. On the last quarter of the thirteenth century as one of the most creative period of Kabbalah see Idel, *Kabbalah: New Perspectives,* 211–12.

25. Kabbalistic hermeneutics, especially the zoharic one, was treated recently in some of the studies of Elliot Wolfson, "By Way of Truth: Aspects of Naḥmanides' Kabbalistic Hermeneutic," *AJS Review* 14:2(1989) 103–78; idem, "Circumcision, Vision of God, Textual Interpretation: From Midrashic Trope to Mystical Symbol" *History of Religions* 27(1987) 189–215; idem, "Left Contained in the Right: A Study in Zoharic Hermeneutics," *AJS Review* 11:1(1986) 27–52; idem, "The Hermeneutics of Visionary Experience: Revelation and Interpretation in the Zohar," *Religion,* 18(1988) 311–45. See also Ithamar Gruenwald, "From Talmudic to Zoharic Homiletics," in Joseph Dan, ed., *The Age of the Zohar* (Jerusalem, 1989) 255–98 (Hebrew), and Daniel C. Matt, "*Matnita Dilan:* A Technique of Innovation in the Zohar," in Dan, *The Age of the Zohar,* 123–45 (Hebrew).

26. I propose to distinguish between the narrative symbolic interpretation, namely, those cases—very common in theosophical Kabbalah—where the biblical story was decoded as pointing to another, supernal story, and the static symbolism, when the external structure of the text functions as an iconic symbol of another supernal, entity. For more on this issue see Moshe Idel, "Midrashic versus Other Types of Jewish Hermeneutics—Some Preliminary Reflections," in M. Fishbane, ed., *The Midrashic Imagination* (SUNY, Albany, 1993) pp. 45–58.

27. On this issues see Moshe Idel, "Die Rezeption der Kabbala in der zweiten Haelfte der 18. Jahrhunderts," *Hebraeische Beitraege zur Wissenschaft des Judentums,* 1/2(1986) 147–51; idem, "Reification of Language in Jewish Mysticism," in Steven Katz, ed., *Mysticism and Language* (Oxford/New York, 1992). On the kabbalistic theory of language see Gershom Scholem, "The Name of God and the Linguistic Theory of the Kabbala," *Diogenes* 79(1972) 60–80, and 80 (1972) 164–94.

28. For an example of such a view see Moshe Idel, "The Infinity of the Torah in Kabbalah," in Geoffrey H. Hartman and Sandford Budick, eds., *Midrash, and Literature* (New Haven, 1986) 144–45. On indeterminacy in ancient Jewish exegesis see David Stern, "Midrash and Indeterminacy," *Critical Inquiry* 15(1988) 132–61. For more on the function of the ideogramic attitude toward the biblical text, as it was exposed by Nahmanides and those influenced by him, see the lecture of Haviva Pedaya delivered at the tenth Congress of Jewish Studies in Jerusalem, August 1989.

29. Those techniques were exposed in detail by the Ashkenazi Hasidim; see Joseph Dan, "The Ashkenazi Hasidic 'Gates of Wisdom,'" in G. Nahon, and Ch. Touati, eds., *Hommages a Georges Vajda* (Leuven, 1980) 183–89; and Ivan G. Marcus, "Exegesis for the Few and for the Many: Judah he-Hasid's Biblical Commentary," in J. Dan, ed., *The Age of the Zohar* (Jerusalem, 1989) 1–24. In Kabbalah they were adopted in Abraham Abulafia's hermeneutics: see Idel, *Language, Torah and Hermeneutics,* 95–119.

30. Cf. Idel, *Kabbalah: New Perspectives* 247–49.

31. That is obviously the case in Abraham Abulafia's hermeneutics, which includes, explicitly, three major types of kabbalistic exegesis; cf. Idel, *Language, Torah and Hermeneutics* 95–117. See also the sevenfold exegetical method of the anonymous author of *Sefer Tiqqunei Zohar;* cf. Tishby, *The Wisdom of the Zohar* vol. 2, 370.

32. Steven D. Benin, "The Mutability of an Immutable God: Exegesis and Individual Capacity in the Zohar and Several Christian Sources," in Joseph Dan, ed., *The Age of the Zohar* (Jerusalem, 1989) 67–86.

33. See Pier Cesare Bori, *L'Interpretazione infinita, L'ermeneutica cristiana antica e le sue transformazioni* (Bologna, 1987). I wonder whether the divergence between the assumption that the text is infinite

and that the interpretation is infinite does not reveal a basically different attitude to the nature of the divine text; with the kabbalists the text is much more divine in comparison to the conception of the sacred text in the Christian literature. Though there are some statements as to the infinity of the Scriptures also in Christian literature (see Talmage, "Apples of Gold," 319) they seem to be rare.

34.   On the identification of the Jewish mystic with the Torah see Idel, *Kabbalah: New Perspectives*, 243–46 and idem, *Language, Torah and Hermeneutics*, 80 and 186, n. 233.

35.   *Berit Abram,* by R. Joseph Moses of Zbarov (Brod, 1875) fol. 126d. See also Idel, *Kabbalah: New Perspectives*, 245–46; idem, "Universalization and Integration: Two Conceptions of Mystical Union in Jewish Mysticism," in M. Idel and B. McGinn, eds., *Mystical Union and Monotheistic Faith: An Ecumenical Dialogue* (New York/London, 1989) 45. On the human change in order to be able to receive the divine Wisdom, see Origen, *Patrologia Latina,* vol. 25, col. 627c.

36.   See Moshe Idel, "The Concept of the Torah in the Hekhalot Literature and Its Metamorphoses in Kabbalah," *Jerusalem Studies in Jewish Thought* 1(1981) 44–46 (Hebrew). For more on the repercussions of the theme of the two fires in the medieval treatments of the nature of the divine text see Scholem, *On the Kabbalah,* 49–50. Scholem assumed that the text of R. Isaac the Old was written at the beginning of the thirteenth century; however, for reasons I cannot elaborate here, the date of the text is no earlier than the end of the thirteenth century.

37.   Cf. *Babylonian Talmud, Sanhedrin* fol. 21b.; Idel, "Concept of the Torah," 43–44, n. 59.

38.   *Sefer Yezirah,* ed. Ithamar Gruenwald, in "A Preliminary Critical Edition of Sefer Yezira" *Israel Oriental Studies* 1 (1971) 157, par. 38.

39.   *Genesis Rabba,* 3, 4, ed. Theodor and Albeck, 19. An analysis of this Midrash is found in Altmann's study, mentioned below, note 42.

40.   *The Rationales of the Letters,* edited by Gershom Scholem, *Madda'ei ha-Yahadut* vol. 2 (Jerusalem, 1927) 201–2.

41.   See Idel, "Reification of Language in Jewish Mysticism," Katz, *Mysticism and Language* (Oxford University Press: New York, 1992) pp. 42–79.

42.   See Alexander Altmann, "A Note on the Rabbinic Doctrine of Creation," *Journal of Jewish Studies* 6/7 (1955–56) 195–206.

43.   See Moshe Idel, "Kabbalistic Material from the Circle of R. David ben Yehudah he-Hasid," *Jerusalem Studies in Jewish Thought* 2:2(1983) 174–75, 177 (Hebrew).

44.   Ibid., 173–88; idem, "Une figure d'homme au-dessus des sefirot (A propos de la doctrine des "eclats" de R. David ben Yehouda he-Hassid et ses developpements)" *Pardes* 7(1989) 131–50.

45.   I would like to mention that recently, some scholars of religion proposed to conceive of the different reports of the mystics as reflecting experiences of different aspects of the divine: the impersonal versus the personal; see A. D. Ewing, "Awareness of God" *Philosophy* 40(1965) 16–17; R. L. Patterson, *A Philosophy of Religion* (Durham, 1970) 502, John Hick, *An Interpretation of Religion* (New Haven, 1989). The affinity of the two aspects of the Torah to the two aspects of God in theosophical Kabbalah invites a comparison with the assumption of the aforementioned scholars as to the various experiences of the mystics.

46.   To be sure, in the talmudic-midrashic thought as well there was a conspicuous concern related to the precise writing of the Torah scroll; however, the major interest of the ancient Jewish sages was limited to the possible semantic mutations that may occur as the result of changes introduced by the copyists; see Scholem, *On the Kabbalah* (note 1 above) 39–40. The kabbalists, however, also added to this concern the metaphor of the Bible as the picture of God, namely the iconic-ideogramic facet. See note 26 above.

47.   *Or ha-Ganuz* (Jerusalem, 1981) fol. 3b.

48.   On some medieval examples of applying the exegetical devices employed for biblical interpretation to writings of the mystics see Moshe Idel, "On Symbolic Self-Interpretations in Thirteenth-Century Jewish Writings," *Hebrew University Studies in Literature and the Arts* 16 (1988) 90–96.

49.   See Idel, *Kabbalah: New Perspectives,* 238–39.

50.   See ibid. 150–53.

CHAPTER 13

Hekhalot and Mi'rāj: Observations on the Heavenly Journey in Judaism and Islam

David J. Halperin

In this discussion, I will examine certain parallels between Muslim narratives of the prophet Muhammad's visit to heaven (the *mi'rāj*), and the ascension traditions of rabbinic Judaism.

I intend the latter category to include the tales of heavenly ascent found in Talmud and midrash, which normally cast Moses as the ascending hero. I include also the strange texts known as "Hekhalot," which speak of the ascensions and revelations of Rabbi Akiba and Rabbi Ishmael, and which seem at times to instruct their readers how they too can experience such ascensions and revelations. The midrashic ascension stories, I have argued elsewhere, were shaped by popular preachers in the Palestinian synagogues of the third century C.E. It was they who inspired the development of the Hekhalot over the course of the next few centuries (Halperin 1988). These are the Jewish materials on which I will focus here, leaving to the side the older ascension traditions found in Jewish apocalyptic literature.

My primary Muslim source is a life of the prophet Muhammad written late in the seventeenth century by the powerful Shi'ite cleric Muhammad Bāqir b. Taqī al-Majlisī of Isfahan (1628–99 or 1700) (Brockelmann 1960, 326–27; Momen 1985, 316–17; Yann 1980, 42). Majlisī was author of the *Biḥār al-Anwār,* a massive collection of *ḥadīth* that fills more than one hundred printed volumes. On the basis of the materials in the *Biḥār,* Majlisī composed (in Persian)

269

the *Ḥayāt al-Qulūb,* a three-volume work of sacred history as the Shi'ites viewed it. The second volume, treating the life of the Prophet, was translated into English in 1850 by James L. Merrick under the title *The Life and Religion of Muhammad* (Majlisī 1982). The *mi'rāj* story found in this text will be the focus of our inquiry.

It will not have escaped the reader that this Muslim text was written at least a thousand years later than the Jewish sources to which I will be comparing it. It may well seem remarkable that I have chosen to deal with it and not with the much older sources (such as Ibn Isḥāq's *Life of the Prophet*) that also describe the *mi'rāj.* My reasons, and the justification for them, will become clear as the chapter progresses.

I

I shall begin by summarizing Majlisī's *mi'rāj,* dwelling on those points that I will presently compare with Jewish sources.

The miraculous beast Burāq carries Muḥammad from Mecca to Jerusalem; there the Prophet leads the assembled prophets in prayer. When offered vessels of milk, wine, and water from which to drink, he chooses the milk. The angel Gabriel, who accompanies him, approves this choice: it is a sign he and his community are rightly guided.

"Jibraeel now conducted me, said Mohammed, to the first heaven. There I saw Ismaeel, the angelic regent of that place, and lord of the meteors with which every shaytan is repelled from the celestial mansions. Under the orders of Ismaeel are seventy thousand angelic officers, each of whom commands a division of seventy thousand angels. Who is this with you? said Ismaeel to Jibraeel. Mohammed; replied my conductor. Has he appeared? Yes, said my guide. Ismaeel then opened the gate of heaven, and we exchanged salutations, and mutually implored divine blessings on each other, and he said, Hail and welcome! my worthy brother, and worthy prophet. The angels advanced to meet me, and all that saw me laughed for joy" (193). The feature of this passage that will mainly concern us is the name of the welcoming angel: Ismaeel, the Arabic form of "Ishmael."

In the first heaven, Muḥammad meets Adam, who welcomes him "as a worthy son and prophet" (193). As Gabriel leads him upward, they continue to meet his predecessor-prophets in each of the seven heavens. Jesus and John are in the second heaven, Joseph in the third, Idrīs (Enoch) in the fourth, Aaron in the fifth, Moses in the sixth, Abraham in the seventh. In Idrīs's heaven, the fourth, Muḥammad also sees "an archangel seated on a throne, under whose orders were seventy thousand angelic officers, each commanding a company of seventy thousand angels. [He is thus exactly parallel to Ismaeel.] Methought there was no angel greater than this. Presently Jibraeel bade him rise, which he did, and he will remain standing until judgment day" (195). Majlisī gives no indication of what this curious episode might mean. We will presently see that Jewish sources will help us understand it as well as its link to Enoch/Idrīs.

In the seventh heaven, Muḥammad finds the heavenly sanctuary (*bayt al-maʿmūr*). He prays there, "standing in advance of the angels, who were arrayed behind me as the prophets had been at Bayt-ul-Mukaddes [the Jerusalem sanctuary]" (198). God then imposes on the Muslims fifty daily prayers, which, at Moses's prompting, Muḥammad manages to reduce to five.

Majlisī goes on to relate a series of other traditions, which he does not integrate very well with the preceding. Their Shi'ite character is sometimes very marked, as when Muhammad sees the likenesses of ʿAlī, Ḥasan, Ḥusayn, and the rest of the Twelve Imams "all performing prayers in a sea of light." He seems actually to meet ʿAlī in heaven and speak to him. But Gabriel explains that "[t]his is not Aly . . . but an angel of the merciful God, whom he created in the likeness of Aly; and when those of us privileged to approach near the Deity wish to behold Aly, we visit this angel" (203). "A tradition declares," Majlisī adds, "that the similitude of Aly in the heavens was created of divine light. When Aly was martyred by Ibn-Muljem, his celestial likeness appeared wounded also, wherefore the angels visiting that similitude morning and evening, curse the assassin" (204). Note the detail of the angelic visitations; it is of some importance.

The most remarkable episode occurs near the end of Majlisī's account:

> The prophet in his ascension came to a river of light, which Jibraeel directed him to cross, adding it had never yet been passed by angel or prophet. Jibraeel said he bathed in it every day, and washed his wings, and that the Most High, of every drop which

fell from his wings, created an exalted angel having twenty thousand faces, and forty thousand tongues, each of which speaks a distinct language unintelligible to the rest. Passing that river, the prophet arrived at the curtains or partitions, which are five hundred in number, and between every two of which is the immense space of five hundred years' journey. Jibraeel directed the prophet to proceed alone, saying that he could advance no further. Another tradition says that the angel declared, if he should go the length of a finger-joint further, he should be consumed. The prophet now proceeded alone as far as God willed, where He proclaimed, I am Mahmood and thou art Mohammed; I separated your name from my own. Whoever unites with thee in love and obedience, I will come near him in favor and mercy; and whoever separates from thee, I will cut him off from my regard. Go down to my servants and inform them what honor I have conferred upon thee. I have given a vizeer to every prophet I have sent; thou art my apostle, and Aly is thy vizeer. (205–6)

II

The features of Majlisī's account that I have stressed are richly paralleled in talmudic, midrashic, and hekhalot sources.

Let us begin with the last passage quoted. The "river of light," from whose drops God creates angels, has its analogue in the "river of fire" (*něhar dî nûr*), which entered Jewish celestial lore from Dan. 7:10. The Babylonian Talmud (Ḥagigah 14a) claims that "every day angels are created from the *něhar dî nûr*, utter a song, and then pass from existence. So it is written: *New ones every morning, great is your faithfulness* [Lam. 3:23]." Palestinian midrashim say much the same.[1] *The Visions of Ezekiel*, a midrash on the seven heavens that is linked particularly closely to the ascension traditions, adds the detail that the angels bathe in the river: "As soon as they are fashioned, they stretch out their hands, take fire from the river of fire, and wash their lips and tongue."

The account of Moses's ascension in chapter 20 of *Pesiqta Rabbati* (Braude 1968; Friedmann 1963) has Moses "met" by the fiery river, whose name is given as Rigyon.[2] He crosses it successfully. The parallel midrash *Maʿayan Ḥokhmah* (Jellinek 1967, 1:58–61) adds here a brief description of the angels' ablutions in Rigyon, which the writer identifies with Daniel's *něhar dî nûr*. The ablution theme is developed still further in the hekhalot texts.[3]

There is an obvious difference in these parallel passages: Jewish texts speak of a river of *fire*, Majlisī of a river of *light*. We may account for the difference by recalling that Daniel's Aramaic word for "fire," *nûr*, also occurs in Arabic with the meaning "light." An Arabic speaker who heard the phrase *nĕhar dî nûr* might easily assume it meant "river of light"—especially if, as we will presently surmise, he had some predisposition of his own toward the idea of a "river of light" from which angels are created.

According to *Pesiqta Rabbati* and *Ma'ayan Ḥokhmah*, the angel Hadarniel serves as Moses' guide for part of his heavenly journey but leaves him when they reach the fire of the angel Sandalphon, out of fear "lest the fire of Sandalphon consume me." Gabriel, similarly, leaves Muḥammad after they have crossed the river of light, explaining that "if he should go the length of a finger-joint further, he should be consumed."[4]

God, according to Majlisī, proclaimed to the prophet that "I am Mahmood and thou art Mohammed; I separated your name from my own." (Both *Maḥmūd* and *Muḥammad* are passive formations from the root *ḥmd*, "to praise.") This theme, of a human being whom God raises to heaven and provides with a name fashioned from his own, is found also in the hekhalot literature.[5]

The angel Metatron, who appears in the hekhalot text known as "3 Enoch" as Rabbi Ishmael's celestial patron and guide, explains that he was once the human Enoch, son of Jared. The early chapters of 3 Enoch describe how God elevated him, gave him a throne like his own, and transformed him into a supreme angel: "and he called me, 'The lesser YHWH' in the presence of his whole household in the height, as it is written, 'My name is in him' [Exod. 23:21]" (3 Enoch, chap. 12 [Alexander 1983, 223–315]). Another text, again calling Metatron "lesser Yahweh," adds that he "has seventy names, which God took from his own name and gave to him, who is Enoch son of Jared" (Schaefer 1981, no. 76). And, in yet a third passage, God himself narrates the story considerably more briefly, adding the detail that "I put under his authority the seventy angels of the seventy nations" (Schaefer 1981, nos. 295, 405).

These numbers will recall (give or take a few zeroes) Majlisī's mysterious archangel, enthroned in the fourth heaven, "under whose orders were seventy thousand angelic officers, each commanding a company of seventy thousand angels." If we suppose that this archangel is Metatron, the details of his story will at once become clear to us. We will understand why he is located in the heaven of Idrīs (= Enoch). And we will understand why he is suddenly obliged to stand up, once we take into account the talmudic legend (Ḥagigah 15a) of how Rabbi Elisha ben Abuyah was led into heresy. "He saw Metatron, to whom permission had been given to sit one hour a day, to record the merits of Israel," and supposed that he was looking at a second divinity. "They brought out Metatron and flogged him with sixty fiery lashes. They said to him: Why, when you saw him, did you not rise before him?" 3 Enoch, chapter 16, gives a fuller account, presumably based on the Talmud, which is more in accord with Majlisī's. In that account Enoch-Metatron sat "upon a great throne at the door of the seventh palace, and I judged all the denizens of the heights." (Compare Majlisī: "Methought there was no angel greater than this.") When Elisha mistook him for a second deity, another angel, 'Anafiel, "struck me with sixty lashes of fire and made me stand to my feet."6

The angel Ismāʿīl also has seventy thousand times seventy thousand angels under his charge, and we may suspect that he, too, is somehow connected with Metatron. But how are we to interpret this connection? And how are we to understand his name? Ismāʿīl is of course a Qur'anic prophet, Ishmael. Yet it seems odd to find a prophet-name given to an angel. Had Majlisī (or, as we shall see, the other miʿrāj authors who speak of Ismāʿīl) wanted to have Muḥammad meet his prophet-progenitor in heaven, this would have provided no difficulty. Place could have been found in the seven heavens for Ishmael alongside Joseph, Aaron, and the rest. We must suppose that the prophet Ismāʿīl and the angel Ismāʿīl are altogether distinct and seek a different source for the latter.

Now, we have one hekhalot text that speaks of an angel Shĕmôʿēl (or, Shimʿîʾēl). It describes him, indeed, immediately before its account of the angels' ablutions in the river of fire, which I have discussed earlier. He is called Shĕmôʿēl because he stands each morning "at the windows of the lowest heaven, to hear [lishmôʿa] all the hymns and praises" sung by the Jews and to make them heard (mashmîʿa) in the realms above. Only then can the angels begin to sing their own praises.7

There can be no doubt that Shĕmôʿēl, who "stands at the windows of the lowest heaven," has contributed his name and something of his function to the Islamic Ismā'īl, gatekeeper of the lowest heaven. But the form of this angel's Arabic name, his prominence in the *mi'rāj* story (in the hekhalot texts, he is an utterly obscure figure), and his apparent link with Metatron all suggest that something else has played a role in his creation.

He was born, I suggest, when someone interpreted the angel Shĕmô'ēl as being one and the same as the celestial traveler of the Hekhalot, Rabbi Ishmael. The underlying logic seems to have been somewhat as follows: Enoch, long known as a holy man who had journeyed to the heavens, was transformed into the angel Metatron. In this form, he served as guide to Rabbi Ishmael, who repeated the journey Enoch had himself made long ago. Now Ishmael, too, has become an angel, Shĕmô'ēl; and a new heavenly traveller, Muḥammad, is approaching. Surely it will fall on Ishmael to do as Metatron had once done for him and receive the newcomer.

This hypothesis presupposes that some person, deeply immersed in both the letter and the spirit of the Hekhalot, can at the same time have venerated the prophet Muḥammad as the culmination of the Hekhalot's sequence of heavenly visitors. We will presently find ourselves imagining a way in which this might have happened.

Muḥammad himself eventually steps into the role of Metatron. He replicates, as we have already seen, Metatron's attainment of a name taken from God's own. He also leads the angels in prayer. This act, which of course points to his being as superior to the angels as he was to the prophets he led at Jerusalem, has its own analogues in the Hekhalot. A "living creature," whose name is Israel, stands in the middle of heaven to lead the angels in prayer (Schaefer 1981, no. 296); and another passage (Schaefer 1981, no. 390) hints at some connection between this being and Metatron.

If Majlisī's Muḥammad can step into the role of the celestial Israel in the Jewish tradition, his 'Alī takes the place of the celestial Jacob. Talmud, midrash, and Hekhalot share the belief that God has an image of the patriarch Jacob engraved on his throne. Talmud and midrash attach this belief to Gen. 28:12, which says that *angels of God were ascending and descending* the ladder that is placed beside the sleeping Jacob. They were *ascending*, the Talmud explains, to gaze on Jacob's celestial image; *descending*, to gaze on his terrestrial image.[8] Majlisī's claim, that there exists in heaven an angelic counterpart of ʿAlī whom the angels can visit when they want to look at ʿAlī, is surely a reflex of this Jewish conception.[9]

It is very striking that, when Majlisī refers to the *miʿrāj* in other contexts, these contexts normally describe how Muḥammad or ʿAlī debates the Jews, and they invoke the *miʿrāj* precisely in order to show Muḥammad's superiority over Moses.[10] We recall that Moses is the most prominent hero of the midrashic ascension traditions. By recasting elements of these traditions, with Muḥammad as protagonist, Majlisī (or his source) thus manages to beat the Jews on their own ground.

III

These parallels between Majlisī's *miʿrāj* and the Jewish ascension materials are both numerous and striking. Yet the time gap that separates the two objects of our comparison is enormous. We possess, moreover, accounts of the *miʿrāj* that derive from the early centuries of Islam, that are therefore only slightly later than the Jewish texts I have invoked. Do these early *miʿrāj* narratives also yield the parallels that I have described?

The answer, unfortunately, seems to be no. Many of the details of Majlisī's *miʿrāj* are of course familiar to us from the oldest sources, such as the ḥadīths in Bukhārī's *Ṣaḥīḥ*, and Ibn Isḥāq's *Life of the Prophet*. But these details have no analogue whatever in Jewish materials—Muḥammad's selection of the appropriate beverage, for example, or his meeting the prophets in the several heavens.

With two exceptions, which I will mention shortly, I have encountered none of the features I have discussed here in *miʿrāj* narratives earlier than Majlisī. They do not appear in Bukhārī nor in Ibn Isḥāq's *Life of Muḥammad;*[11] nor in the extended *miʿrāj* account that Ṭabarī (839–923) quotes in the name of Abū Hurayra (Renaud 1987);[12] nor in Maqdisī's tenth-century *Book of Creation and History* (Huart 1899–1903, 149–54 [French], 159–64 [Arabic]); nor in the sixteenth-century *miʿrāj* of Najm al-Din al-Ghaitī (Jeffery 1962, 621–39). Miguel Asín Palacios seems not to have found them in any version of the *miʿrāj* tradition (Asín Palacios 1961; Asín 1926). Michael Sells (1989) has noted a number of parallels between the hekhalot texts and the legend of the *miʿrāj* experienced by the mystic Abū Yazīd al-Bisṭāmī (El-Azma 1973;

Nicholson 1926); but these are not the ones that we have found in Majlisī.

Now, it is highly unlikely that Majlisī himself learned these details from Jews and introduced them into the *mi'rāj*. It would be hard to imagine any Muslim cleric of Safavid Persia seeking wisdom from the persecuted and segregated Jews (Fischel 1971); to imagine this of the ferociously intolerant Majlisī, notorious for his persecution of the Sufis (Brockelmann 1960, 326–27; Momen 1985, 316–17; Yann 1980, 42), would be all but impossible.[13] Yet it remains true that, on the basis of the evidence we have seen so far, these elements might have been introduced at practically any time down to about 1650.

There are several reasons, however, for thinking that the midrashic and hekhalot elements in Majlisī's *mi'rāj* date considerably earlier than Majlisī. To begin with, at least two of these elements turn up, outside the context of a sustained ascension narrative, in sources prior to Majlisī. Dā'ūd Qaysarī, a Sufi writer of the early fourteenth century, speaks of "a reliable tradition, which relates that when the Prophet saw the Angel Gabriel at the *Lotus of the Limit,* the Angel had six hundred wings; every morning and evening, he entered the river of Life; he came out shaking his wings, and out of the scattered drops God created countless Angels" (Corbin 1977, 45). Aside from the substitution of "life" for "light," this is recognizably the same as Majlisī's account of the "river of light."

The tenth-century Shi'ite theologian Ibn Bābūya quotes a series of ḥadīths that explain Muḥammad's name as taken from the divine name *Maḥmūd*. In two passages, the context of this claim is the Shi'ite belief (to which we shall presently return) that Muḥammad was a primordial being of light, preexistent in the loins of Adam and his successors. "God," Muḥammad is made to say in one ḥadīth, "did not cease to convey me from pure loins into pure wombs . . . till he made with me the covenant of prophecy . . . He led me up to his heaven, and he split off for me one of his names. My people are those who give praise [*al-ḥāmidūn*]; the Lord of the Throne is the Praised One [*maḥmūd*]; and I am Muḥammad" (Ibn Bābūya 1971, 52 [ḥadīth 2 of the chapter entitled "The Meaning of the Names of Muḥammad, 'Alī, Fāṭima, Ḥasan, Ḥusayn, and the Imāms"]).[14]

There are, moreover, two exceptions to the generalization that these "Jewish" details do not occur in *mi'rāj* narratives prior to

Majlisī. The *miʿrāj* account given by the Shiʿite Abū ʾl-Futūḥ al-Rāzī in his Qurʾān commentary (written in Persian about the year 1116 [Piemontese 1987]) shares Majlisī's claim that Gabriel could not advance beyond a certain point and therefore had to send Muḥammad on his way without him. Like Majlisī, Rāzī speaks of a plurality of "veils": there are seventy, each one a five-hundred-year journey thick (?), with another five-hundred-year journey between any two of them. The two authors disagree on the precise details of the system of "veils"; yet, in describing them, both share the significant figure of five hundred years (see above, note 4).[15]

The second exception is yet more important, in that it carries us back to within a century or so of the genesis of the *miʿrāj* traditions. This is the angel Ismāʿīl. Ibn Isḥāq knows him as the guardian of "one of the gates of heaven called the Gate of the Watchers . . . [U]nder his command were twelve thousand angels each of them having twelve thousand angels under his command" (Guillaume 1955, 185). Maqdisī, purportedly using Wāqidī as his source, says much the same, but with substantial multiplication of Ismāʿīl's troops (70,000 × 100,000).[16]

The name Ismāʿīl, if I have interpreted it correctly, reflects a profound and subtle interpenetration of hekhalot ascension motifs with those of Islam. It would be paradoxical to claim that this took place before the middle of the eighth century, without the Hekhalot leaving any other imprint on the *miʿrāj* traditions until centuries afterward. We must consider the possibility that the other features we have examined had also been introduced into the *miʿrāj* tradition by Ibn Isḥāq's time—that is to say, the middle of the eighth century—but were suppressed in the early sources.

IV

We will understand a possible motive for their suppression when we reflect that the ideas they convey are bound to have been particularly congenial to *Shiʿite* Islam.

Shiʿites have at times exaggerated the universal Muslim veneration for the Prophet Muḥammad into something approaching deification. They have done the same, and indeed still more, for ʿAlī (Moosa 1988). This tendency made its appearance early; Muslim heresiographers attribute belief in ʿAlī's divinity to his semi-legendary contemporary ʿAbdallāh b. Sabā, whom they represent as the founder of Shi'ism (Friedlaender 1909–10; Hodgson 1960–).[17] Had these early Shi'ites become aware of the Hekhalot's apotheosis of Enoch/Metatron, or of the midrashic and hekhalot traditions on the celestial image of Jacob, they surely would have found them to be welcome guides to how a community might grant divinity to a human being and yet remain monotheistic.

Uri Rubin has shown that both Sunni and Shi'ite Islam have conceived Muḥammad as the bearer of supernatural light (Rubin 1975). Yet this image is particularly prominent in Shi'ism. Majlisī (1982) follows a venerable Shi'ite tradition when he depicts Muḥammad as a primordial being of light, which God created long before the heavens and the earth and which he afterward placed in Adam's loins, thence to be transmitted from generation to generation until it finally reached the womb of Muḥammad's earthly mother (2–9). A variant of this belief (also shared by Majlisī) holds that Muḥammad, 'Alī, Fāṭima, Ḥasan, and Ḥusayn were once beings of light, superior to the angels, whom God had created from the clay beneath his throne (Rubin 1975, 98–102). Is it any wonder that Shi'ites, in particular, would have welcomed the discovery that the Jews taught the existence of a "river of light"—so they preferred to understand *nĕhar dî nûr*—from which God created angels every morning? Surely the midrashic doctrine would have seemed to confirm their own cherished beliefs.

The Shi'ites taught the doctrine of *waṣiyya*, "inheritance"; that is, the transmission of prophetic authority from one prophet to his successor, normally through a series of intermediate links. Rubin has shown that there were two theories of the prophetic *waṣiyya*. One, essentially genetic, represented Ishmael as having received prophethood from his ancestors going back to Adam and as having transmitted it to Muḥammad through his line of Arab descendants. The other had Ishmael transfer his authority to Isaac, who passed it on through a series of prophetic inheritors among the Jews and Christians, through Moses and Jesus down to Muḥammad (Rubin 1979).

Now, Enoch/Metatron's relation to Rabbi Ishmael might well have suggested to some Shi'ite thinkers the possibility of a third *waṣiyya*, reinforcing the genetic and prophetic ones. This was the *waṣiyya* of heavenly travelers, each welcomed in turn by his predecessor, each transformed in turn into an angelic being. By creatively reinterpreting the Hekhalot, by identifying the human Rabbi Ish-

mael with the angel Shĕmôʿēl, the unknown thinkers who Islamicized the Jewish tradition fashioned this new chain of divine authority, with Muḥammad at its end, now separated by only one
link from his ancestor Enoch. At the same time, they reinforced the
message that the older versions of the *miʿrāj* had already conveyed
when they showed Muḥammad welcomed into the heavens by his
prophetic predecessors.

In short, the most strikingly "Jewish" features of Majlisī's *mi-
ʿrāj* are precisely those that we may assume to have been of most
particular interest to the Shiʾites. This, taken together with Ibn
Isḥāq's knowledge of the angel Ismāʿīl, will permit the conjecture
that Shiʾite thinkers adapted and incorporated these features into
the older story of Muḥammad's ascension at some time prior to
Ibn Isḥāq's writing—that is, in the first century or so after
Muḥammad's death. Ibn Isḥāq and subsequent writers, correctly
perceiving their Shiʾite overtones, passed over them in silence. Only
the name Ismāʿīl, which seemed harmless to those who did not
understand the context out of which it had emerged, escaped their
censorship.

V

Orthodox Twelver Shiʾism, as it crystallized under the Abbasids
(Hodgson 1955), does not seem to have rushed to embrace these
once Jewish, later Shiʾite, elements of the *miʿrāj* tradition. At first
sight, this would seem to contradict the hypothesis I have just
advanced. A few passages in the Shiʾite classics, however, give a
clue to the reasons why Twelver orthodoxy distanced itself from
traditions that were part of its early heritage.

The Hekhalot celebrate an unabashedly humanlike deity. They
declare, furthermore, that humans (like Enoch/Metatron) may
achieve a status approaching the divine. Features of this sort were,
as we will see shortly, more prominent in the early Shiʾite *miʿrāj*
narratives than in Majlisī's version. Orthodox Twelvers, recoiling
from their "anthropomorphism" (*tashbīh;* literally, the "likening"
of God to his creatures), preferred to discard the stories in which
they appeared.

Thus, the great Shiʾite Qur'ān commentator Ṭabarsī (d. 1153)
speaks of a category of *miʿrāj* stories "whose literal meaning
cannot be authentic, and which can be interpreted only by the

most arbitrary and farfetched means; it is best that we do not accept them." In this category are "such stories as that Muḥammad openly addressed God; that he saw him; that he sat with him on his throne; and tales of that sort, whose literal meaning demands an anthropomorphic conception of God [*yūjibu ẓāhiruhu al-tashbīh*]." True to his word, Ṭabarsī (1986) ignores materials of this sort and repeats the conventional *mi'rāj* story that we know from Ibn Isḥāq and from Bukhārī's ḥadīths (609–11 [on sura 17:1–3]). Of the assertions Ṭabarsī rejects, the most radical—the claim that Muḥammad sat on God's throne—is not far removed from what the Jewish ascension traditions tell of Moses and Metatron (Halperin 1988, 320–21, 423–26).[18]

Ibn Bābūya, whom I have already quoted as an early witness to the belief that Muḥammad's name was split off from God's, insists that one cannot interpret the *mi'rāj* "in the manner of the anthropomorphizers" (*'alā mā yaqūlu al-mushabbihūn*) (Ibn Bābūya 1981, 175 [chap. 28, ḥadīth 5]). In a vivid anecdote, he gives an example of the sort of claim made by these "anthropomorphizers." Two visitors inform the Imām 'Alī Riḍā (765–818) that a story is circulating to the effect that "Muḥammad saw his Lord in the shape of a fortunate [?] youth, his age about thirty years; his feet were in greenness." Others, Riḍā is told, have claimed that God is "hollow to his navel, the rest of him solid [?]."[19] The Imām loudly demonstrates his horror at these blasphemies. "Whatever you have imagined," he tells his visitors, "you must imagine God as being something other than that." The stories they have repeated are the sort of thing one would expect from a *ghālī*, an "extremist" (Ibn Bābūya 1981, 113–15 [chap. 8, ḥadīth 13]).

Extreme they surely are. But what is their origin? The strange remark that God's "feet were in greenness" will give us a clue, for it will begin to make sense if we suppose it is based on Exod. 24:10—"they saw the God of Israel, and under his feet was something resembling a construction of sapphire stone, like the heaven itself for purity"—and on the midrashim expounding that passage (Halperin 1988, 217–20).

As for God in the shape of a youth, the Jewish antecedents of this idea are particularly clear. Midrashic texts describe how God appeared to the Israelites at the Red Sea in the form of the handsome young man of the Song of Songs. A hekhalot text found in the Cairo Genizah warns prospective travellers to the divine throne that they will see a "youth" who looks almost the same as God and that they must be careful not to worship him. This "youth" plays a major role elsewhere in the Hekhalot, which normally (e.g., 3 Enoch) identify him with Metatron (Halperin 1988, index 5, s.v. "youth").

I suggest that these "extremist" claims are among many Jewish elements Islamicized by early Shi'ites and incorporated into their version of Muhammad's *mi'rāj*. The orthodox Twelvers repudiated these *mi'rāj* traditions, as they did much of their Shi'ite heritage, as "extremism" (*ghuluww*) (Hodgson 1955). Yet the traditions survived. They continued to be transmitted, through channels I am not yet able to define. Majlisī took them up, in bowdlerized form, centuries afterward.

VI

The hypothesis I have advanced is in accord with the recent (and ongoing) researches of Steven M. Wasserstrom, who has argued that the early Shi'ites used Jewish concepts in the shaping of their doctrines, their communal self-definition, and their theory of authority. We need not, Wasserstrom points out, take literally the charges of Muslim heresiographers that Shi'ism was the invention of a converted Jew, 'Abdallāh b. Sabā (Friedlaender 1909–10; Hodgson 1960–); or that Shi'ites are the "Jews of Islam" (Wasserstrom 1985). (The Shi'ites themselves shared the latter perception [Rubin 1979, 53–55].) These claims may nonetheless represent a correct perception that early Shi'ites were prepared to learn from Judaism. Some of their thinkers, who perhaps were indeed of Jewish origin, had profound understanding of and sympathy with some of the teachings of the midrashim and the Hekhalot. Like the second- and third-century Christian intellectuals who undertook the "despoiling of the Egyptians"—the appropriation, for Christianity, of the intellectual treasures of Hellenism (Crouzel 1985, 210–11)—these thinkers set themselves to retrieve for Islam the nuggets of divine wisdom preserved in an outworn faith. They thus transformed certain features of Jewish ascension lore into subtle and effective confirmations of their belief that Muḥammad and 'Alī were preexistent luminaries, all but divine.

Contemplating the traditions of the Hekhalot, these early Shi'ites saw them as the work of kindred spirits. They acted accordingly.

Their perception, I would add, may well have been correct. It may perhaps serve us as a guide to understanding the mysterious individuals who created the Hekhalot.

NOTES

First delivered at the Southeastern Regional meeting of the American Academy of Religion (Atlanta, March 17, 1991); then, in revised and expanded form, at the University of Chicago conference "Other Realms: Death, Ecstasy and Otherworldly Journeys in Recent Scholarship" (May 16–17, 1991). I thank Professor Steven M. Wasserstrom for having carefully read both versions of the paper and for having provided me with many helpful comments and bibliographical suggestions. It is impossible to think back upon the Chicago conference without feeling overwhelming sorrow for Professor Ioan Culianu, one of the conference's organizers, a gentle scholar of great integrity, brutally murdered only a few days after the conference's end.

1. Gen. R. 78:1 (Theodor and Albeck 1965, 915–17); Lam. R. 3:23 (Buber 1963–64, 66b–67a); Ex. R. 15:6.

2. From Greek *ryakion,* "lava stream" (Levy 1969, 264–65).

3. Schaefer 1981, no. 54 (= 3 Enoch, chap. 36); 180–86, 530–36, 790–96, 810–16.

4. The distance of a five-hundred-year journey, which Majlisī uses in this passage to indicate the distances between the celestial "curtains or partitions," is a staple measurement in rabbinic cosmology, occasionally taken up in Muslim traditions. I give references in my *Faces of the Chariot* (Halperin 1988); see index 6, s.v. "Five hundred year journey."

5. It is possible to trace it back further, into the Talmud and even into the apocalypses, as belief in an angel whose name incorporates God's own (Scholem 1960, 43–55; 1961, 67–70; Segal 1977, 60–73).

6. I have found one other hekhalot derivative of the Talmud's Elisha story: Schaefer 1981, no. 597 (translated in Halperin, 1988, 410).

7. Schaefer 1981, nos. 178–80; parallels in nos. 527–30, 787–90, 807–10.

8. BT Ḥullin 91b; Gen. R. 68:12 (Theodor and Albeck 1965, 788). I know of two references in the Hekhalot to Jacob's celestial image. Schaefer 1981, no. 411, describes how "Jacob's face lights up before Adiriron Yahweh, God of Israel," when the worthy traveller enters the celestial realms. Schaefer 1981, no. 164, charges the celestial traveller—much like Muḥammad in Majlisī's *mi'rāj*—to "bear witness to [the Jewish people] on my behalf of what you have seen, what I do to the image of Jacob's face that is engraved on my throne of glory. When you say before

me, *Holy* [*holy, holy*], I bend over it, hug and kiss it, embrace it so that my hands are on my shoulders."

9.   Majlisī (1982) repeats this point in a different context (151): "The companions of the prophet were greatly amazed at all this, and said, It is strange that even wild beasts love and revere Aly. Mohammed replied, If you wonder at this, what would be your feelings were you to know in what estimation Aly is held in heaven! Verily, at Sidret-ul-Muntaha, I saw his image which God had placed there to gratify the burning desire of the angels to behold him, and the angels humbled themselves and bowed before the image more reverently than these wolves have done to Aly himself."

10.   In one debate, for example, the Jews claim that Moses "is more excellent than thou art, for God spoke four thousand words to him, whereas He has not spoken to you at all." Muḥammad replies to this that God "caused me to be borne to the seventh heaven on the wing of Jibraeel, and I passed Sidret-ul-muntaha, that station of the archangel, and came to the pillar of the empyrean, where I heard a voice saying, I am the Lord, besides whom there is no Lord . . . All this is certainly superior to the favors bestowed on Moosa" (Majlisī 1982, 102; similarly, 118, 131, 135).

11.   Written at some time between the accession of the Caliph Man-ṣūr (754 c.e.) and Ibn Isḥāq's death (767); survives in an epitome by Ibn Hishām (d. 833) (Guillaume 1955; Newby 1989).

12.   ʿṬabarī has God tell Muḥammad: "I have exalted your name, to the extent that no one can mention me without making mention of you" (Renaud 1987, 286; cf. 280). Renaud explains this as referring to Muḥammad's presence, along with God, in the Muslim profession of faith. It hardly seems to presuppose Majlisī's derivation of the name Muḥammad from the divine title *Mahmūd*.

13.   Majlisī's biography of Muḥammad is filled with expressions of hatred for Jews. Outside the *miʿrāj* section, I have found in it few traces of Jewish influence.

14.   Five centuries later, Suyūṭī (d. 1505) similarly represents Muḥam-mad as telling Ibn ʿAbbās that God "caused me to ascend to His heaven, and gave me one of His own names, for the Lord of the Throne is *mahmūd* (praised) and I am Muḥammad." Shortly after this, Suyūṭī incorporates a story, similar to one I have already cited from Majlisī, in which Muḥam-mad explains to the Jews how he is superior to Moses: "Glory be to Him who took His servant by night (xvii, 1), for He bore me up on Gabriel's wing till He brought me to the seventh heaven, and I passed beyond the Sidra tree of the Boundary at the Garden of Resort (Liii 14, 15), till I caught hold of a leg of the Throne, and from above the Throne came a voice: 'O Muhammad, I am Allah. Beside Me there is no other deity.'

Then with my heart I saw my Lord" (Jeffery 1962, 333–36). In several ḥadīths, quoted by Ibn Ḥanbal, Bukhārī, and Tirmidhī, it is Moses who lays hold of a leg of the throne; the detail is borrowed from the Jewish ascension traditions (Halperin 1988, 486–87).

15. Rāzī's *miʿrāj* contains an important parallel with the hekhalot traditions, which I have not seen in Majlisī. God says to Muḥammad: "I have exalted your name in such a manner that, whatever you learn concerning the laws of my faith, you will retain" (Piemontese 1987, 314–15). This is very suggestive of the *Sar Torah* theme in the Hekhalot: by reciting the proper incantations, the adept is able effortlessly to remember whatever Scripture and Mishnah he has learned (Halperin 1988, 376–83, 427–46). The regular collocation of Scripture with Mishnah, in *Sar Torah*, may help explain Rāzī's next sentence, which, to judge from Piemontese's translation, begins: "In place of the Torah, I have given you the *mathānī* . . . " (cf. Qurʾān, 15:87, 39:23). Rāzī tells a story stressing the superiority of Muḥammad's praises of God over those of the angels (Piemontese 1987, 310). This theme, to which I have earlier alluded, pervades the rabbinic *merkābāh* traditions (Halperin 1988, 137–41, 396–405).

16. Ghaitī (Jeffery 1962, 621–39) also mentions Ismāʿīl; his numbers are the same as Majlisī's, and he adds that Ismāʿīl is "Master of the lowest heaven, dwelling in the air, and never mounting up into that heaven nor coming down on to the earth save on the day of the Prophet's death" (627).

17. Majlisī (1982), whom these extremes evidently alarmed, has Muḥammad say to ʿAlī: "Verily, were it not that I fear a sect of my followers will say of you, what the Nasara affirm of Eesa, I would this day declare some things in your praise, so that you would pass no company that would not gather the dust on which you tread, for the blessing it confers" (285–86).

18. Compare also Revelation 3:21, 22:1–5.

19. *Ṣamad;* "solid" is a possible meaning (Newby 1973, 127–30). Ibn Bābūya's source attributes this latter statement to three Shiʿite intellectuals of the middle of the eighth century: Hishām b. Sālim (al-Jawāliqī), Ṣāḥib al-Ṭāq (= Muʾmin Ṭāq?), and (ʿAlī b. Ismāʿīl) al-Maythamī. Steven M. Wasserstrom points out to me that Shahrastānī (1076–1153) similarly credits Hishām with this belief (Vadet 1984, 304). Is the idea somehow linked to Ezek 1:27?

REFERENCE LIST

Alexander, P., trans. "3 (Hebrew Apocalypse of) Enoch." In James H. Charlesworth, *The Old Testament Pseudepigrapha*, vol. 1. Garden City, N.Y., 1983.

Asín, Miguel. *Islam and the Divine Comedy.* Translated and abridged by Harold Sunderland. London, 1926.

Asín Palacios, Miguel. *La Escatología Musulmana en la Divina Comedia.* 3rd ed. Madrid, 1961.

Braude, William G., trans. *Pesikta Rabbati: Discourses for Feasts, Fasts, and Special Sabbaths.* 2 vols. New Haven, 1968.

Brockelmann, Carl. *History of the Islamic Peoples.* Translated by Joel Carmichael and Moshe Pearlmann. New York, 1960.

Buber, Salomon, ed. *Midrasch Echa Rabbati: Sammlung agadischer Auslegungen der Klagelieder.* Tel Aviv, 1963–64. Originally published 1899.

Corbin, Henry. *Spiritual Body and Celestial Earth: From Mazdean Iran to Shi'ite Iran.* Translated from the French by Nancy Pearson. Princeton, 1977.

Crouzel, Henri. *Origène.* Paris, 1985.

El-Azma, Nazeer. "Some Notes on the Impact of the Story of the Mi'rāj on Sufi Literature." *Muslim World* 63 (1973), 93–104.

Fischel, W. J. "Persia." *Encyclopedia Judaica,* vol. 13, cols. 313–16. Jerusalem, 1971.

Friedlaender, Israel. "'Abdallah b. Saba, der Begruender der Šī'a, und sein juedischer Ursprung." *Zeitschrift fuer Assyriologie und verwandte Gebiete* 23 (1909), 296–327; 24 (1910), 1–46.

Friedmann, Meir, ed. *Pesikta Rabbati: Midrasch fuer den Fest-Cyclus und die ausgezeichneten Sabbathe.* Tel Aviv, 1963. Originally published 1880.

Guillaume, A. *The Life of Muhammad: A translation of Ibn Ishaq's Sirat Rasul Allah.* Lahore, 1955.

Halperin, David J. *The Faces of the Chariot: Early Jewish Responses to Ezekiel's Vision.* Texte und Studien zum antiken Judentum, vol. 16. Tübingen, 1988.

Hodgson, M[arshall] G. S. "'Abd Allāh b. Saba'." In *Encyclopedia of Islam,* 2nd ed., 1:51. Leiden, 1960–.

———. "How Did the Early Shî'a Become Sectarian?" *Journal of the American Oriental Society* 75 (1955), 1–13.

Huart, Cl. *Le Livre de la Création et de L'Histoire.* Vol. 4. Paris, 1899–1903.

Ibn Bābūya, Abū Ja'far Muḥammad b. 'Alī. *Al-Tawḥīd.* Beirut, 1981.

Ibn Bābūya, Abū Ja'far Muḥammad b. 'Alī. *Ma'ānī al-Akhbār.* Najaf, 1971.

Jeffery, Arthur. *A Reader on Islam: Passages from Standard Arabic Writings Illustrative of the Beliefs and Practices of Muslims.* The Hague, 1962.

Jellinek, Adolf, ed. *Bet ha-Midrasch: Sammlung Kleiner Midraschim und vermischter Abhandlungen aus der aeltern juedischen Literatur.* 3rd ed. Jerusalem, 1967. Originally published 1855–77.

Kappler, Claude, ed. *Apocalypses et Voyages dans l'Au-delà.* Paris, 1987. Steven M. Wasserstrom called my attention to this volume.

Levy, Johanan. "Remainders of Greek Phrases and Nouns in 'Hechaloth Rabbati.' " In *Studies in Jewish Hellenism.* Jerusalem, 1969. Originally appeared in *Tarbiz* 12 (1940–41), 163–167 (Hebrew).

al-Majlisī, ʿAllāma Muḥammad Bāqir. *The Life and Religion of Muhammad: Hiyat al-Qulub.* Vol. 2. Translated by James L. Merrick. San Antonio, 1982. Originally published 1850.

Momen, Moojan. *An Introduction to Shi'i Islam: The History and Doctrine of Twelver Shi'ism.* New Haven, 1985.

Moosa, Matti. *Extremist Shiites: The Ghulat Sects.* Syracuse, 1988.

Newby, Gordon D[arnell]. "Sūrat al-'Ikhlāṣ: A Reconsideration." In Harry A. Hoffner, ed., *Orient and Occident: Essays Presented to Cyrus H. Gordon on the Occasion of His Sixty-fifth Birthday.* Kevelaer/Neukirchen-Vluyn, 1973.

Newby, Gordon Darnell. *The Making of the Last Prophet: A Reconstruction of the Earliest Biography of Muhammad.* Columbia, S.C., 1989.

Nicholson, R. A. "An Early Arabic Version of the Miʿrāj of Abū Yazīd al-Bisṭāmī." *Islamica* 2 (1926), 402–15.

Piemontese, Angelo M. "Le Voyage de Mahomet au Paradis et en Enfer: Une Version Persane du Miʿrâj." In Kappler 1987, 293–320.

Renaud, Etienne. "Le Récit du Miʿrâj: Une Version Arabe de L'Ascension du Prophète, dans le Tafsîr de Tabarî." In Kappler 1987, 267–290.

Rubin, U. "Pre-existence and light: Aspects of the concept of Nūr Muḥammad." *Israel Oriental Studies* 5 (1975) 62–119.

———. "Prophets and Progenitors in the Early Shīʿa Tradition." *Jerusalem Studies in Arabic and Islam* 1 (1979) 41–65.

Schaefer, Peter. *Synopse zur Hekhalot-Literatur.* Texte und Studien zum Antiken Judentum, vol. 2. Tübingen, 1981.

Scholem, Gershom G. *Jewish Gnosticism, Merkabah Mysticism, and Talmudic Tradition.* New York, 1960.

———. *Major Trends in Jewish Mysticism.* 3rd ed. New York, 1961.

Segal, Alan. *Two Powers in Heaven: Early Rabbinic Reports about Christianity and Gnosticism.* Leiden, 1977.

Sells, Michael. "3 Enoch (Sefer Hekhalot) and the Mi'raj of Abu Yazid al-Bistami." Paper read before the American Academy of Religion, 1989.

Ṭabarsī, Faḍl b. Ḥasan. *Majmaʿ al-Bayān fī Tafsīr al-Qurʾān.* Vol. 5. Beirut, 1986.

Theodor, Julius, and Chanoch Albeck, eds. *Midrash Bereshit Rabbah: Critical Edition with Notes and Commentary.* 2nd ed. 3 vols. Jerusalem, 1965.

Vadet, Jean-Claude, trans. *Muhammad ben ʿAbd al-Karîm al-Shahrastâni: Kitâb al-Milal, Les Dissidences de l'Islam.* Paris, 1984.

Wasserstrom, Steven M. "Sefer Yetzira and Early Islam." Paper read before the American Academy of Religion, 1985.

Yann, Richard. *Le Shi'isme en Iran: Iman et revolution.* Paris, 1980.

CHAPTER 14

The Role of the Anima Mundi as Mediator between the Divine and Created Realms in the Twelfth Century

Bernard McGinn

Connecting the divine and the human realms—heaven and earth, the ideal and the imperfect—has never been an easy task. In addition to researching the accounts of descents of heavenly beings to earth and ascents of special humans to higher realms, a field to which Ioan Culianu made so many notable contributions, it may be worthwhile to take a look at another mode of mediating between the above and below that has enjoyed a long tradition in western speculation: the belief in the *anima mundi*, or World Soul, as an essential link between God and creation.

The story of the World Soul has a rich history. This chapter will concentrate on one period when speculation on the *anima mundi* was especially pronounced, the twelfth century. My purpose is not to uncover new materials (most of these texts are sufficiently well known), nor is it to provide an encyclopedic survey (though there is no full account at present). Rather, I intend to study these texts and the traditions they utilized in order to cast some light on the question of divine mediation and created autonomy. How did the World Soul help to bring the divine and created realms together? Why was it largely abandoned after a brief period of major interest in the early twelfth century?

In order to get some handle on these questions it will be necessary to start with Plato, though blaming it all on Plato would be a mistake. Plato's *Timaeus* was responsible for the classic formulation of the doctrine of the Cosmic or World Soul, the *anima mundi*, but belief in a single great animating principle of the universe, the integrating link between the intelligible and sensible realms, was central to much in Greek thought and flourished especially among those thinkers we label "Stoic" and "Neoplatonic."[1] The *Timaeus* is a complex symbiosis of "likely story" (*eikos mythos* [29b]) and "likely explanation" (*eikos logos* [53d]).[2] Though modern interpreters like Hans-Georg Gadamer have argued for a "demythologized" reading of the text, which would see it primarily as a combination of a teleological and a mathematical causal explanation of the universe based on the axiomatic acceptance of the reality of the Forms or Ideas,[3] in the Platonic tradition the dialogue's deliberately ambiguous mode of self-presentation left it open to a wide variety of readings. The account of the World Soul (primarily in 34a–40d), "acknowledged since ancient times to be the most mysterious and difficult section of the work,"[4] can be approached from many perspectives. Though it may well be that Plato's primary intent was to provide an explanation for the self-movement, or *autokinēsis*, of the All,[5] he also made it clear that the issue of mediation was central. Since "it is not possible that two things alone be joined without a third, for there must be an intermediary between them" (31c), it is necessary that Soul (*pyschē*), as a "third thing," be placed in the middle between indivisible being that remains always the same and the divisible being found in bodies (35a). From the perspective of the history of the Platonic tradition, the World Soul's role as the essential mediation between the ideal and the material realms is the foundation of its other functions as principle of universal motion, vitality, and harmony.

The World Soul may strike us today as a curious piece of baggage—a mythic fiction out of place in philosophy, physics, and even theology—yet there was a time when the *anima mundi* was integral to both scientific and religious speculation. During the first forty years of the twelfth century, in the cathedral schools of northern France, when philosophy, physics, theology, and poetry interacted in a way reminiscent of how the four primal elements were thought to have mingled in the formation of the universe, the *anima mundi* served as a crucial link in what we might call early attempts at a unified field theory that would show the inner harmony not only among the human sciences but also between human *scientia* in general and the divine *sapientia* of theology. What is more, through the identification of the *anima mundi* with the Holy Spirit, some thinkers experimented with a new way of understanding the Christian triune God's mediating activity. These speculations about the *anima mundi* provoked considerable discussion and eventual condemnation, and so it has been easy to dismiss them. Some have argued that their proponents were not original thinkers. In a noted revisionist essay, R. W. Southern said, "All their thoughts were old thoughts. They had the strength to make old thoughts live again, but they could not add to them."[6] In order to show why I think Southern is wrong, I shall briefly survey the development of thought on the World Soul up to the twelfth century.

Whatever doubts the Atomists and Epicureans had, the respectable schools of ancient philosophy all taught the existence of the World Soul. Besides the foundational text found in the *Timaeus*, which was available in the Middle Ages through the partial translation of Chalcidius, a number of other ancient expositions were also known to medieval authors. Stoic ideas of the World Soul, found in such texts as Cicero's *De natura deorum*, Seneca's *Naturales quaestiones*, and some famous lines in Anchises' speech in the sixth book of the *Aeneid*, saw the universal spirit both as general providence and in materialistic fashion as an "intus spiritus" which was really an "igneus vigor" found in all things.[7] Stoic thought on the World Soul is not a little ambiguous, since many of the key texts influential in the Middle Ages mingle notions of the Cosmic Logos with those of a more Platonic Cosmic Soul. Standard Middle Platonic thought on the World Soul as an intermediate principle was also available to medievals in the *De Platone et eius dogmate* of the second-century author Apuleius.[8]

In Neoplatonism the World Soul played a decisive role. In the thought of Plotinus the World Soul, or "Soul of the All," is presented in two broad ways. Frequently it is equated with the third hypostasis in the emanational descent (e.g., *Enneads* 2.3.17, 2.9.1–2, 5.1.2–10), but other texts bifurcate the third hypostasis into an upper Soul, which contemplates the Intellectual Principle, and the lower Soul, which actually gives life to the universe (e.g., *Enneads* 2.1.5, 2.3.9, 5.2.1).[9] The Latin followers of Plotinus sometimes tended to simplify this complexity, thus making it easier to identify the World Soul with the "third" in the divine realm.

Though Plotinus's own writings were not available to medieval

authors, many of the texts that corroborated and at times compli-
cated Plato's account of the World Soul were much influenced by
Neoplatonism. The most important of these for the twelfth-
century theorists were Chalcidius (fourth century), who not only
translated the *Timaeus* but also provided it with an extensive commentary,[10] and Macrobius, whose *Commentarium in Somnium
Scipionis* (c. 400) was an important medieval textbook.[11] The *Asclepius,* a philosophical-religious treatise ascribed to Mercurius or
Hermes Trismegistus, the greatest of pagan sages, also spoke of the
World Soul,[12] as did Martianus Capella's *De nuptiis Philologii et
Mercurii* and Boethius's famous cosmological poem found in book
3 of the *De consolatione philosophiae.*[13]

But what of the church fathers? Was the *anima mundi* to be
found among the champions of Christian orthodoxy? Abstracting
from Greek witnesses not known in the West,[14] we find that Latin
patristic evidence is slim with the exception of Augustine, whose
testimony is ambiguous.[15] The Bishop of Hippo considered the
issue of the World Soul a "magna atque abdita quaestio,"[16] one
that, like the problem of the origin of the human soul, he was never
quite able to decide. In his early philosophical treatises *De immor-
talitate animae* (387) and *De musica* (389), Augustine admitted the
existence of a soul that animated the "mundus animal,"[17] but
when he reviewed these texts in his *Retractationes* he was more
cautious, calling such statements rash. However, he notes,

> that this world is an animate being, as Plato and numerous other
> philosophers thought, I have not been able to investigate by solid
> reasoning, nor have I found that I accept this idea on the author-
> ity of the Sacred Scriptures. Hence something said by me, too, in
> the book *De immortalitate animae,* which can be interpreted in
> this way, I have noted was said rashly—not because I maintain
> that this is false, but because I do not understand that it is true
> that the world is an animate being.[18]

In this passage, as in earlier ones in *De civitate Dei* where he
reviews pagan teaching on the *anima mundi,* Augustine insists that
even if there is such a thing as a World Soul it is not to be wor-
shipped as a god.[19] But it is important to note that in the second of
the five commentaries Augustine wrote on the creation account in
Genesis, the *De Genesi ad litteram liber imperfectus* (393–94),
he admitted that Gen. 1:2 ("spiritus Dei superferebatur super

aquam") could signify a living soul that moves the universe and all that is in it. And since in his later commentary, the *De Genesi ad litteram* (401–15), he held that this verse indicated the part the Holy Spirit played in creation, a sanguine interpreter might be tempted to put the two interpretations together, though this would be far from Augustine's intent.[20]

The teachings of Plato, Macrobius, Boethius, and Martianus Capella led to some speculation on the *anima mundi* during the ninth century. John the Scot, good Platonist that he was, briefly discussed the evidence of Plato and Vergil in book 1 of his *Periphyseon*,[21] and in his commentary on Martianus Capella he identified the World Soul with the mysterious *entelechia*.[22] He was followed in this by his pupil Remigius of Auxerre.[23] We also find the World Soul in a contemporary St. Gall commentary on Boethius's *De consolatione*,[24] and Ratramnus of Corbie wrote a refutation of the view that Augustine had taught that the soul is at once one (i.e., universal) and many.[25] These few references, however, do not go beyond what was available in the tradition. Above all, none of these authors saw the World Soul as the Holy Spirit.

Around the year 1100 there was a remarkable outburst of interest in the *anima mundi,* one that took old ideas in new and surprising directions. The reasons for this outburst of interest were both scientific and theological. In the twelfth century, Plato was not only the *magnus gentium theologus*[26] but also *Plato physicus*, the master of cosmology. Use of the *Timaeus*, surprisingly sparse until the eleventh century, saw a dramatic increase between roughly 1050 and 1150.[27] This is shown not only by the surviving manuscripts of Calcidius's version[28] but also by the commentaries that indicate that the dialogue had an important role in the lecture halls of the cathedral schools that were revolutionizing higher education.[29] As R. W. Southern put it: "On the Creation he [Plato] had something to say which could be found nowhere else. On this subject, therefore, he was essential."[30]

This interest in the *Timaeus* was not to be a lasting one. "The *Timaeus* was mastered, only to be dropped," as Margaret Gibson said,[31] and much the same is true for scholastic use of the other "physical" texts of the Platonic tradition, especially Macrobius and Boethius's *De consolatione.* Southern spoke of the *Timaeus* as a kind of doorway into the world of natural science, a doorway that was soon left behind as newly translated texts in cosmology, astronomy, astrology, medicine, and psychology became available.[32] Still, doorways are necessary things, and this one also formed an unusual type of threshold upon which a number of different disciplines and interests met and underwent mutual enrichment.

Honorius Augustodunensis, a monastic author of the early twelfth century, summed up the scientific status of the first book of the Bible when he said, "Genesis, which speaks of the natures of things, belongs to physics (*physica*)."[33] This being the case, enterprising cosmologists of the era were invited to inquire into the coherence between Plato and Moses, that is, to show that the scientific account of the formation of the world found in Plato was fully compatible with the authoritative scriptural text on creation. In the *De civitate Dei* Augustine had already noted the agreement of Plato and Moses on divine goodness as the motive for creation.[34] Early twelfth-century thinkers, such as Abelard, William of Conches, and Thierry of Chartres, were to try to show even greater consonance.

Physica, however, was not the only motivation behind early twelfth-century speculation on the *anima mundi*. Equally important, though more difficult to detect because it was less explicitly formulated, was a deep new concern for how the created universe mediated the divine presence, especially the presence of the triune God. As Winthrop Wetherbee put it:

> That the visible universe is a coherent cosmos, informed by soul and modelled on an ideal exemplar, was fundamental, and to the extent that the world soul and the archetype were seen as manifestations of God, expressions of his wisdom and goodness, they could render his activity accessible to reason through the visible universe.[35]

Twelfth-century speculation on the World Soul, in other words, was at least partly dependent on a desire to find new ways of mediating between God and the world, of joining heaven and earth. For Christians this mediation raised important trinitarian questions, ones that especially concerned the role of the Holy Spirit.

The history of twelfth-century theology of the Holy Spirit remains to be written, but it can be argued that this era was a particularly vibrant one for pneumatology. Johannine and Pauline texts provided a scriptural foundation for Christian belief that the Spirit had a special role in mediating the divine presence in the inner life of each Christian. On the basis of these texts, William of Saint-Thierry created the first explicitly pneumatological, or "Spirit-centered" trinitarian mystical theology in Latin Christianity in the 1130s and early 1140s. Toward the end of the century Joachim of Fiore, in more daring fashion, advanced his trinitarian theology of history, which looked forward to a coming *status* of the Holy Spirit marked by the triumph of the *intelligentia spiritualis* of the scriptures. Though never as fully developed as these mystical and historical pneumatologies, the early twelfth-century identification of the Holy Spirit with the *anima mundi* can take its place as a distinctively cosmological way of discerning the presence and action of the Spirit in the very structure of reality.

The basic division among proponents of the *anima mundi* in the twelfth century is between those who were willing to identify it with the Holy Spirit and those who regarded it only as a created principle of vitality in the universe. The former view, representing a daring break with the Augustinian position, was eventually condemned at the Council of Sens in 1140 and largely abandoned. The latter position was gradually transformed into speculation on and poetic presentation of Natura, the World Soul's daughter or at least successor in later medieval thought. The simple division, however, masks some complex interactions and subtle developments.

Peter Abelard was among the first literary witnesses to the identification of the *anima mundi* with the Holy Spirit. In his earliest theological work, the *Theologia summi boni* (c. 1118–20), he insisted, like Anselm before him, that he had tried to meet his students' demands for "rational and philosophical expositions."[36] As a part of these expositions he defended the use of the terms *potentia, sapientia, bonitas* as proper names for the Persons of the Trinity and also expatiated on how the *anima mundi* of the philosophers is really the Holy Spirit.[37] The length of Abelard's treatment and his awareness of the problems connected with this view indicate that the identification was probably not invented by him but was rather a question already under discussion in the schools.[38] Despite the fact that the *Theologia summi boni* was condemned and burned at Soissons in 1121 (apparently not on the grounds of its thoughts about the *anima mundi*),[39] Abelard did not hesitate to include its teachings in his subsequent theological textbooks, notably the *Theologia Christiana,* whose three redactions date between 1122 and 1138, and the *Theologia scholarium* (also called *Introductio in Theologiam*), which saw some five redactions in the period between 1133 and 1140.[40] The treatment is fairly similar in all three works, but that of the *Theologia Christiana* is the most developed.

The first book of the *Theologia Christiana* is concerned with what Peter Lombard was later to call the "fides antiquarum," the extent to which the mysteries of faith, in this case the Trinity, were known to the Jews through the Old Testament (1.8–53) and to pagans through their sages (1.54–117).[41] Abelard, unlike most other proponents of the World Soul–Holy Spirit identification, was more interested in the economy of revelation than in cosmology and natural processes.[42] Though he held that the revelation given to the pagans was only partial, he insisted that the evidence of Plato, Mercurius, Macrobius, Vergil, and others showed a clear acceptance of the three Persons, the Father as the highest God, the Son as the *Mens* or *Nous* born from him, and the Holy Spirit as the *anima mundi* coming from both (1.68).[43] Naturally, he began with Plato:

> First, let us diligently consider what Plato says about this soul, from whom other philosophers have taken what they have about it. He distinguishes the World Soul as the third Person from God and *Nous,* and pursuing a longer and closer description, he gives a complete account of it both in itself and in its effects.[44]

Abelard's exegesis of the *Timaeus* text on the World Soul and other ancient *auctoritates* was designed to show their full conformity with Christian teaching. Benign interpretations of passages that might create difficulties abound: the philosophers said "made" (*factum*) when they really meant "begotten" (*genitum*) or "originated from" (*ex ipso esse*) (1.70, 113); the Soul consists of both undivided, unchanging substance, and divided substance because the Holy Spirit is simple in itself but multiple in its effects (1.74–77); the location of soul in the midst of the world (*Timaeus* 34b) signifies that God's grace is available to all (1.87); and so on. Abelard followed Macrobius in asserting that many of the texts of Plato and others on the *anima mundi* need to be read figurally *per involucrum* (1.89, 97, 103–7, 109)— "Otherwise Plato, the highest of philosophers, would be the greatest fool!"[45] The most important effect of Abelard's use of *involucrum* is to avoid problems about the relation of the World Soul to individual souls and to highlight his theological reading of the life conveyed by it: "Human souls give animal life to our bodies; the World Soul which, if I'm not mistaken, the philosophers understood as the Holy Spirit, gives spiritual life to our souls by the distribution of his gifts."[46]

In book 4 Abelard once more returned to the philosophers' evidence, making more precise the important distinction introduced in Book 1 between the Third Person of the Trinity as simple eternal love in itself and the Third Person as vivifying *anima,* that is, as given to creatures in a multiplicity of graces. "There is an eternal procession of the Spirit according to love (*affectus*), because he willed in this way from eternity; there is a temporal procession of the Soul according to what has been made (*effectus*)."[47] This distinction between *affectus* and *effectus* was to become central to the Abelardian school. In his contemporary *Expositio in Hexaemeron,* Abelard, like Augustine before him, interpreted the Spirit borne over the waters of Gen. 1:2 (or warming [*fovebat*] the waters, as another version has it) as the Holy Spirit.[48]

After the condemnation of his view at the Council of Sens in 1140 (more on this below), even Abelard retreated. In his late logical work, the *Dialectica,* he rejected his long-standing position, denying the identification of World Soul and Holy Spirit because this would make the Third Person less than the Father and Son, and claiming that any kind of World Soul is impossible because it would imply two souls in each person.[49] If Abelard surrendered, the same was not true of all his followers. The equating of the Holy Spirit and the World Soul was widespread in the texts belonging to the School of Abelard.[50] This is not surprising in compilations from before the condemnation, such as the *Sententiae Parisienses* (c. 1125),[51] *Sententiae Florianenses* (c. 1130),[52] *Sententiae Hermanni* (date uncertain),[53] and the *Commentarius Cantabrigiensis* (c. 1140).[54] In the *Sententiae Parisienses* and the *Sententiae Hermanni* the activity of the Holy Spirit extends to the whole domain of vivification and thus appears more cosmologically oriented than Abelard himself. The identification is also found in some texts after 1140. The *Ysagoge in Theologiam,* written sometime in the 1140s, a work that combines Abelardian themes with Victorine ones, cites Vergil, Solomon, and Plato as it claims that the Holy Spirit is the World Soul.[55] Robert of Melun, a student of Abelard writing in the 1150s, was more circumspect, noting that the claim made sense but was not to be taught or preached, because Church authority did not support it.[56]

The second major proponent of the doctrine of the World Soul in the early twelfth century was William of Conches, who, according to John of Salisbury, was a student of Bernard of Chartres.[57] The complexity of his views on the *anima mundi,* as well as disagreement about the canon and chronology of his writings, make his position harder to characterize.[58] Though he can be linked with Abelard in identifying the World Soul as the Holy Spirit, William did so in his own way. William was interested in theological questions, but he was not a theologian. John of Salisbury knew him as the "grammaticus de Conchis," and his writings are not theological textbooks or scriptural commentaries but philosophical *summae* and commentaries on school texts in the arts and sciences—Plato, Boethius, Macrobius, Martianus Capella (lost), Priscian, Vergil (lost), and Juvenal.

Peter Dronke has demonstrated the originality of William's understanding of the philosophical use of *fabula* (what we might call "mythic fiction") developed in his early *Glosa super Macrobium* (probably before 1120).[59] Here the Master dared to use not just the "likely story" of the philosopher but also ancient myths about the gods to demonstrate the *anima mundi:*

> Because philosophers claim that the World Soul is shared out among all physical beings, though it does not exercise the same activity in them all . . . , and because Bacchus is a name for the World Soul, that is why they invented a fable (*integumentum*) with hidden meaning about Bacchus.[60]

In this context the *anima mundi* functions only as a cosmological principle of vivification, similar to what the ancients had admitted; but a subsequent text speaks of the "anima mundi, que secundum quosdam est Spiritus Sanctus" and suggests that William accepted, if hesitatingly, the identification.[61] His position becomes clearer in another early work, the *Glosae super Consolationem Boethii,* which says:

> The World Soul is the natural energy [*vigor*] by which some things have the power only to be moved, others to grow, others to sense, others to judge. Ask what that energy is? It seems to be that the natural energy is the Holy Spirit, that is, the divine and beneficent concord from which all things possess being, movement, growth, sensation, life and judgment.[62]

An even more daring *fabula* is invoked as revealing the *anima mundi* in notes on Martianus Capella's *De nuptiis* found in a Florence manuscript. Dronke argues that they are not actually by William but do reflect his teaching.[63] Here Hymen, the god of sexual union whose hymn opens the work, signifies many things, not least the natural power of propagation, which, in a way not fully explained, is also seen as "the Holy Spirit, who infuses an ardent charity in all things. He is called the god of weddings, that is, he composes the holy conjunction of elements."[64] The same text goes on to identify Hymen's father, Bacchus, with the World Soul. Dronke suggests that here we have a kind of imperfect parallel to Abelard's distinction between two aspects of the Holy Spirit (i.e., *affectus, effectus*), but the distinction might also reflect the bifurcation of higher and lower World Soul to be found in authors like Macrobius.[65] A subsequent passage on *endelechia* as World Soul tries to turn the tables on objections to its identification with the Holy Spirit by saying that it would be heretical to think that any merely created spirit could have such powers.[66] (This might be an addition made after 1140.) It is clear, then, that both Abelard and William identified the Holy Spirit with the *anima mundi*, though each did so in his own way.[67]

Based on the rich treatment of these early texts, William's better known brief entry on the World Soul in his *Philosophia mundi* (c. 1125), described as "the first general survey of the physical universe in the twelfth century,"[68] merely summarizes his position by claiming that there are two possible meanings of the *anima mundi—spiritus sanctus* and *naturalis vigor*.[69] His enigmatic statement that the World Soul is not a soul in the sense that individual souls are refers his readers to his *Glosae super Platonem*, William's lengthiest discussion, which appears to date from the 1130s, though its final recension may come later. In the *Glosae* the issue of the analogous nature of the World Soul does not really seem to be taken up in the detailed exegesis of *Timaeus* 34b–39e (a *Tractatus de anima mundi* as the manuscripts call it). William's treatment here is also more cautious than his earlier ones. While he did discuss the cosmological role of the World Soul as the *naturalis vigor* of the universe in a predominantly Stoic fashion,[70] he spent more time on the mathematical and astronomical details of Plato's account, and he avoided a detailed pneumatological interpretation, beginning with an agnostic remark: "Some say this spirit is the Holy Spirit, but I neither affirm it or deny it."[71] Nevertheless he later, without comment, identified the *tercium genus animae* (*Timaeus* 35a) with the Holy Spirit.[72] Perhaps William sensed that the inquisitors were at the door, or he may have begun to realize the difficulties involved in his youthful views.[73] After the condemnation of Sens, the revision of the *Philosophia mundi* called the *Dragmaticon* (composed in the late 1140s) significantly passes over the World Soul in silence. In one place here Master William even felt compelled to assure his readers that "Christianus sum, non Academicus."[74]

The identification of the World Soul with the Holy Spirit was common in the schools in the decades between 1120 and 1140. For a time the World Soul seemed to be almost as omnipresent in academia as it was supposed to be in the cosmos. An interesting discussion is found in an author who shared many of the concerns of William of Conches—Thierry of Chartres, who may have been Bernard of Chartres' brother and who wound up as chancellor of the school at Chartres.[75] Thierry commented on rhetorical texts and composed a famous handbook of the liberal arts, the *Heptateuchon*, but he also displayed a more theological side, as his commentaries on Boethius's theological tractates and his treatise on creation, *De sex dierum operibus* of the 1130s show.[76] This last work has been seen as an example of Chartrian "naturalism" because of its attempt to "win for physical theory a relative independence from theology," as Raymond Klibansky claimed.[77] But, as R. W. Southern has suggested, "the great achievement of Thierry . . . was precisely the opposite one of combining the evidence of Revelation and the secular texts."[78] Thierry's work is marked by the confidence characteristic of Anselm and Abelard that faith and reason—in this case the reason of the physical philosophers—could be shown to be in perfect harmony. He might well have defended his concentration on the explanation of Genesis "secundum physicam et litteram"[79] by citing Augustine's distinction of the four aspects of the existence of all created things and assuring his readers that he was dealing with only the second and the third of these.[80] Thierry's use of an unusual mathematical proof for the Trinity found among some twelfth-century authors,[81] as well as his acceptance of both the theological and the cosmological interpretations of the *anima mundi*, make eminent sense within this context. He cites Mercurius on the cosmic *spiritus*[82] and then goes on to say,

Plato in the *Timaeus* calls the same spirit the World Soul.
Vergil speaks in this way about it:
> In the beginning, seas and lands, deep heaven,
> And the pale globe of the moon and Titan's stars
> Were nourished by a Spirit within (Aen. 6.724–26)

The Jews spoke about the Spirit as operative in this way—Moses
says, "The Lord's Spirit was borne over the waters" (Gen. 1:2);
David, "The heavens were established by the Lord's Word" (Ps.
32:6); Solomon says of this Spirit, "The whole earth is filled with
the Lord's Spirit" (Wis. 1:7). Christians call it the Holy Spirit.[83]

A number of other school texts from the first half of the twelfth
century stress the cosmological aspect of the Holy Spirit's activity as
the *anima mundi*. An anonymous commentary on the *Timaeus*
partially edited by Tullio Gregory is close to William of Conches in
its discussion of how Plato's *anima mundi* is both the Holy Spirit
and the "vigor naturalis rebus insitus."[84] The *Commentum* on the
first six books of the *Aeneid,* usually attributed to Bernardus Silvestris and thought to have been written c. 1125–30, never comes
right out and calls the *spiritus intus* of *Aeneid* 6.726 the Holy Spirit,
but it certainly implies it when it says, "It is called soul from its
office, because from the fact that the divine spirit which always
existed gave life to some things, it is therefore called soul. Hence
Plato and the other philosophers speak of it as created, that is,
because it vivifies created things and works in them."[85] This agrees
with texts found in a commentary on Martianus Capella that is
probably by the same author,[86] but it disagrees with what is found
in Bernard's authentic *Cosmographia*. Either Bernard abandoned
his early views, or this is another argument that the two commentaries are really not from his pen.[87] Bernard has, with rather more
justice than Thierry, been seen as experimenting with "naturalistic"
explanations of the *anima mundi;* but it is difficult to separate
natural science from theology in the undifferentiated world of early-
twelfth-century thought, as the identification of the Holy Spirit with
both the World Soul and the souls of the seven planets in the
astronomical treatise known as the *Tabulae Massilienses* shows.[88]

Interest in the *anima mundi* was by no means absent from the
theology of the cloister in the twelfth century, though identifying
World Soul and Holy Spirit was apparently rare. At the beginning
of the well-known Paris manuscript (Bibl. Nat. lat. 6734, f. 55) of
the compendium of John the Scot's *Periphyseon* known as the

Clavis physicae, put together by Honorius Augustodunensis, there is an unusual pictorial presentation of the *anima mundi* among a series of drawings that M.-T. d'Alverny called "l'une des plus parfaites expressions de l'activité imaginative des hommes du xiie siècle."[89] The regal female figure, surmounted by sun, moon, and stars, proclaims by inscription and banner that she is "anima mundi que est vegetabilis in arboribus, sensibilis in pecoribus, rationabilis in hominibus." Under her feet appears an inscription reflecting the tripartite Platonic division of the soul (*rationabilitas, concupiscibilitas, irascibilitas*). It is clear that we are dealing not with a pneumatological interpretation but with the World Soul as the immanent vivifying principle of the universe, a point further strengthened by the quadrangular frame with inscriptions of Aristotelian inspiration representing the combinations of the four elements. As d'Alverny remarks, this illustration is more dependent on Chalcidius and Macrobius than on the *Periphyseon,* and thus may well not be from Honorius himself.[90] The *Clavis* does, however, discuss the *anima mundi* in one important passage and elevates it to the "created and creating" level of the primordial causes.[91] Though this personified portrait of the World Soul is unusual, the tradition of triangular diagrams attempting with more or less success to convey the mathematical proportions of the *anima mundi* is found in a number of examples, including the Ghent manuscript of Lambert of St. Omer's *Liber Floridus* dating from about 1120.[92]

Later in the century there are some intriguing textual witnesses to the *anima mundi* from monastic circles. Perhaps the richest is that of Hildegard of Bingen in her *Liber divinorum operum* from the early 1160s. The first vision of this work concerns *caritas,* seen as a "summa et ignea vis" involving three basic aspects: that of soul insofar as it gleams forth in water; that of reason (*rationalitas*) as found in the sun, moon, and stars; and that of life as it breathes in every form of air and wind.[93] Hildegard's polyvalent World Soul may seem close to the vitalistic conception found in the *Clavis physicae* illustration and elsewhere, but in a somewhat confusing, if undeniably original fashion, she connects this immanent life with the divine Life itself.[94] Arnold of Bonneval, a Benedictine abbot and friend of St. Bernard, writing in the late 1150s, goes a step further, one more in line with the early-twelfth-century academics we have seen, in speaking of the *anima mundi* as the Holy

Spirit, if only in a fairly tentative way.[95] The Cistercian Isaac of Stella, deeply influenced by the tradition of Chartres, although he does not speak of the Holy Spirit as the World Soul, does talk of the universe as a "magnus animal," a position that implies one vital universal principle.[96] Thus it is clear that the identification of the World Soul and the Holy Spirit was not only widespread in schools but also not unknown in the cloisters. Nevertheless, the idea entailed major problems, theological, philosophical, and scientific. The weight of these were to lead to the condemnation of Sens in 1140.[97]

Augustine had warned against any attempt to see the World Soul as divine, and his objections doubtless lay behind the often tortured explanations used by those who accepted the identification with the Holy Spirit. Plato's classic account also caused problems. He had spoken of the *anima mundi* as "made" by the Demiurge (34c)—a position that, from a Christian perspective, seemed to entail a subordinationism that made the Holy Spirit less than the Father and the Son. Abelard and others countered this by claiming that Plato really meant "originated from" when he said "made." But this was no answer to a third and graver difficulty, namely, the pantheism that seemed to follow from making a divine person, the Holy Spirit, immanent within the cosmos as its vital principle, the Soul of the World.[98] Such an identification would also seem to imply the eternity of the universe and thus conflict with Christian belief in the temporal character of creation. The author of the anonymous *Timaeus* commentary edited by Tullio Gregory had an answer for this: "I confess that the Holy Spirit is what he is from eternity, but he is not the World Soul from eternity."[99] Many of the proponents of the identification of World Soul and Holy Spirit also tried to address the pantheism issue through some kind of distinction between the Holy Spirit taken in himself and the Holy Spirit's multiple, temporal, life-giving presence in the world. But these explanations do not appear to have carried much weight, especially against the Augustinian teaching that God's activity in creating and sustaining the universe is the work of all three persons of the Trinity acting as one transcendent cause. The particular mediation of the Holy Spirit was to be sought not on the cosmological level but within the action of grace in the interior of the soul.

These arguments, of course, did not affect the traditional inherited views of the *anima mundi,* those of a vitalistic rather than pneumatological nature. For example, the *Compendium philoso-phiae,* a text sometimes—but probably incorrectly—ascribed to William of Conches, outlines five views on the *anima mundi.*[100] The first rejects its existence, the second identifies it with the sun, and the third identifies it with the Holy Spirit. All three are judged wrong. The fourth view, the traditional one seeing it as the *natu-ralis vigor,* is allowed, but the author prefers the new fifth position, which, basing itself on Boethius and Calcidius, holds that "fatum vel series vel divina dispositio est anima mundi."[101] The *Compen-dium* shows dependence on Hugh of St. Victor's educational hand-book, the *Didascalicon,* written after 1125, in which the *en-telechia* is identified with the human soul (as some Carolingian commentators had done).[102] In his second *Homilia in Eccle-siasten,* Hugh recognized the Stoic source of the Vergilian "intus spiritus" (*Aen.* 6.726) that provides life to the universe, though he sought to qualify its corporeal character.[103] There were also twelfth-century commentaries on Plato's dialogue that insisted that the World Soul was some form of created spirit.[104]

The strong reaction against seeing the *anima mundi* as the Holy Spirit came not from the theologians of the schools but from those of the cloisters. It was part of a wider conflict between the schools and the cloisters upon which much has been written. From the perspective of the history of the doctrine of the Holy Spirit as the mediator between the divine and the human world, it can be described as a conflict between cosmological and mystical under-standings of the Spirit's mediation.

Abelard had been a controversial figure for years before Wil-liam of Saint-Thierry wrote the letter to Bernard of Clairvaux and Geoffrey of Chartres in 1139 that began his downfall.[105] In this epistle the fifth of the thirteen objectionable propositions was "Quod Spiritus Sanctus sit anima mundi." In the treatise that William sent along with the letter, it is clear that the monastic theologian was more concerned with other aspects of Abelard's Trinitarian errors than this one, though in chapter 5 William does take up the World Soul, accusing Abelard of advancing theological novelties, of contradicting Augustine, and of compromising divine transcendence.[106] Bernard's famous Letter 190, his *Tractatus de erroribus Petri Abaelardi* sent to Rome with a list of nineteen prop-ositions, also spends more time on other aspects of Abelard's views on the Trinity, dismissing the World Soul problem with the caustic remark, "The more Abelard sweats to make Plato a Christian, the more he shows himself a heathen."[107] Bernard's letter appears to have been written after the meeting of French bishops and ecclesiastics at Sens in 1140 that condemned the nineteen propositions.[108] The condemnation was upheld by Pope Innocent II,[109] and it spelled the end of most attempts to interpret the *anima mundi* as the Holy Spirit.

Although William of Conches was not formally censured, he too encountered serious opposition. At about the same time as Abelard was being attacked, a novice fleeing the world made the mistake of bringing along a copy of the *Philosophia mundi* to the Cistercian house of Signy, where the former Benedictine abbot of Saint-Thierry, William, was then residing as a simple monk. William soon sent Bernard another treatise, *De erroribus Guillelmi de Conchis,* which attacked the Master's teaching on the Trinity and on creation.[110] William the monk lambastes William the Master primarily on the basis of the Sabellian and Abelardian implications of his analysis of the divine proper names and relations, but he also makes it evident that he considers William's identifying the World Soul with the Holy Spirit as entailing an illegitimate economic view of the Trinity unacceptable to the true *ratio fidei.*[111] William concludes: "The scientist [*physicus*] and philosopher has been given up to an evil meaning [Rom. 1:28] by scientifically philosophizing about God."[112]

This is not the place for more discussion of the conflict between Bernard and Abelard, about which too much has been written, or the conflict between the two Williams, about which too little has been written.[113] William of Saint-Thierry was no theological obscurantist, as his profound pneumatological treatises on the Trinity show. It is obvious, however, that he was rigidly opposed to the easy confidence of some of his contemporaries that physics and philosophy had an important role in Trinitarian speculation. Both Abelard and William of Conches were eventually compelled to agree.

Was there any room left for speculation on the World Soul after the defeat of 1140? Apparently so, though not for long. A few followers of Abelard, as we have seen, continued to adhere to the identification, while other writers upheld the wisdom of the past, which saw the *anima mundi* as the *naturalis vigor* to be found in all things. But if the *vigor* were only *naturalis,* the philosopher-physicists of the twelfth century were bound to begin to ask hard questions. The flood of new scientific literature translated from Greek and Arabic made the pursuit of exact particular knowledge of nature and its processes a more attractive option than the presentation of what we might call the premature unified field theory represented by World-Soul speculation.[114] Philosophically, the traditional objection, so often discussed by Carolingian and twelfth-century authors,[115] that the admission of a World Soul implies two souls in each human still bore much weight. Might it not be easier to admit that there was indeed a general principle inherent in the whole creation, but that this would be better called *"natura"* than *"anima mundi"*? Before this solution became general, however, there were a few further creative attempts to deal with the *anima mundi.*

Bernardus Silvestris's striking cosmological poem the *Cosmographia* was dedicated to Thierry of Chartres and read in the presence of Pope Eugene III in 1147. It is a good illustration of one solution to the problem, that suggested by Winthrop Wetherbee when he says "poetic intuition is finally the only means of linking philosophy and theology, pagan *auctores* and Christian doctrine, *sapientia* and *eloquentia.*"[116] The many links between philosophy, theology and poetry that marked the twelfth century are too complex to be investigated here,[117] but in the case of Bernardus Silvestris, at least, we can well agree with Theodore Silverstein when he says "And what philosophy could not do, poetry might."[118]

The orthodoxy of the Christianity to be found in Bernard's *Cosmographia* has provoked considerable debate. Is the poem basically orthodox Christian cosmology in poetic disguise, or does it include naturalistic elements incompatible with faith?[119] The Christian Trinity makes no direct appearance in the work, but it can be argued that the *involucrum* created by Bernard both reveals and conceals it in artful ways. In the first book, or "Megacosmos," the feminine creative trinity of Noys, Natura, and Silva, who are theophanies of the hidden God, by their mutual efforts give form to all that lies hidden in the womb of *Yle.* The exact nature of the reality portrayed in these personifications is not easy to determine.[120] The World Soul, under the Ciceronian-Calcidian-Carolingian title of Endelechia, emanates from the semidivine Noys to give life to all things through its sacred marriage to Mundus:

> From the very source, then, of this our life and light, there issued
> forth by a sort of emanation the life, illumination, and soul of
> creation, Endelechia. She was like a sphere, of vast size yet of
> fixed dimensions, and such as one might not perceive visually,
> but only by intellect . . . Now by her birth this Endelechia was
> closely and intimately related to Noys. Lest so glorious a bride
> should protest that the universe spawned by mother Silva was an
> unworthy husband, Providence arranged the terms of a special
> compact, wherein material and heavenly nature might arrive at a
> consistent harmony by way of congruent proportions.[121]

Not since Vergil had the World Soul been portrayed with such
poetic power. It is clear that she is not divine, however, whatever
her mother's status is.[122]

Another unusual treatment of the *anima mundi* also designed
to protect divine transcendence and involving a distinction of trini-
ties is that found in the treatise known as the *De septem septennis*.
The seventh group of sevens discussed here contain the seven principles of creation. The first principle, *aeternitas* or *necessitas*, is
identified with the Christian Trinity and explained in the mathematical way found in Thierry: "From this highest and eternal Trinity descends a kind of trinity of perpetual things." The next three
principles are *possibilitas* or matter, *finalitas* or form, and *actu-
alitas* or "the universal movement of all things."[123] The author
goes on to say that "This motion is called Nature by Mercurius,
World Soul by Plato, fate by some, and a divine disposition by
theologians."[124] The final three principles are the *lex astrarum*,
mundus, and the *machina mundi*. The notion of descending trini-
ties was taken from one of Thierry's commentaries on Boethius's
De Trinitate, but there the identification with the World Soul is not
explicit.[125]

These exotic solutions found few if any followers. In the ex-
panding world of twelfth-century scientific views, a universal concept like the World Soul, with its theological and philosophical
difficulties, had less and less of a future. The easiest thing to do
with the *anima mundi* was to see it as just a metaphor for *natura*.
Calcidius had spoken of the works of the World Soul as *opera
naturae*,[126] and Hermann of Carinthia, a student of Thierry, in his
De essentiis of 1143 had already taken the hint when he wrote,
"We can call *natura* by the same name Plato used in speaking of
the *anima mundi*."[127]

Tullio Gregory has studied this gradual transformation of the World Soul into "Dame Kynde" in the latter part of the twelfth century,[128] and there is no need to repeat the story here. It is worth noting that speculation on the World Soul never totally died out in the Middle Ages, though it was never again at the cutting edge of the interaction of religion, science, and philosophy. In the thirteenth century, Bonaventure rather misleadingly claimed that Augustine had rejected the idea that the world was animated.[129] Thomas Aquinas, although he cautioned that the *anima mundi* should not be considered as God or as divine in any way,[130] at least in his early commentary on the *Sentences* seems to allow the *corpus caeleste* an angelic mover that could be analogously called a "soul."[131] Meister Eckhart, that pronounced Platonist, in two places in his Latin works speaks of God as the *anima mundi* as if the Council of Sens had never happened, though the concept does not play any essential role in his thought.[132]

Still, the idea of the World Soul, or at least something very much like it, seems almost impossible to kill in any final way. Renaissance Neoplatonists like Marsilio Ficino, Giovanni Pico della Mirandola, and Leone Ebreo, revived it in forms deeply influenced by its Platonic and Neoplatonic past. It has been given new life in sundry times and places in more recent centuries, and it cannot be said to be totally extinct in our age if we consider the implications of the thought of someone like Teilhard de Chardin, another thinker who sought to unite science and theology.

The early-twelfth-century scientist-theologians seemed outmoded even to their immediate successors, let alone to modern views. But perhaps something can be said in their favor. In M.-D. Chenu's fine phrase, "the twelfth century featured an essentially religious discovery of the universe through a discovery of Nature,"[133] and speculation on the *anima mundi* played a vital, if temporary, role in this process. Richard McKeon has also reminded us that "The twelfth century was a period in which poets and philosophers were engaged on the same themes, and the poetic expression of philosophy as well as the philosophical criticisms of poetry reflect the basic theological problem of the relation of faith and reason."[134] In these debates over the role of reason and faith, those who identified the World Soul with the Holy Spirit made special efforts to give equal attention both to the claims of the physical sciences and to those of the science of faith. In their attempts to bring together

faith and reason, as well as in their daring pneumatological interpretation of the *anima mundi*, Abelard, William, Thierry, and others, not unlike ancient voyagers to the heavenly spheres, sought to
be mediators who would join heaven and earth.

NOTES

This essay is a revised version of a talk originally given at "Science
and the Humanities," a symposium for the opening of the new Crerar
Science Library at the University of Chicago. I would like to thank Stephen Gersh and several anonymous readers for a number of helpful suggestions.

1. J. Moreau, *L'Âme du monde de Platon aux stoiciens* (Paris,
1939) is a standard account.

2. The excellent commentary of Francis M. Cornford, *Plato's
Cosmology*, first published in 1937, remains helpful for all questions
concerning the *Timaeus*. More recently, see the penetrating study of Hans-
Georg Gadamer, "Idea and Reality in Plato's *Timaeus*," in *Dialogue and
Dialectic: Eight Hermeneutical Studies on Plato* (New Haven, 1980) 156–
93. On the relation between *mythos* and *logos* in Plato's doctrine of the
soul, see David Tracy, "Argument, Dialogue and the Soul in Plato," in
Philip E. Devenish and George L. Goodwin, eds., *Witness and Existence:
Essays in Honor of Schubert M. Ogden* (Chicago, 1989) 91–106.

3. See Gadamer, "Idea and Reality," 190–93.

4. Ibid., 165.

5. Ibid., 166.

6. R. W. Southern, "Humanism and the School of Chartres," in
Medieval Humanism and Other Studies (New York, 1970) 83.

7. Cicero, *De natura deorum* 2.22–28; Seneca *Naturales quaestiones* 1, praef. 13; and Vergil, *Aeneid* 6.724–32. On Stoic influence in
the Middle Ages, see Gerard Verbeke, *The Presence of Stoicism in Medieval Thought* (Washington, D.C., 1983); and Michael Lapidge, "The
Stoic Inheritance," in Peter Dronke, ed., *A History of Twelfth-Century
Western Philosophy*, (Cambridge, 1988) 81–112.

8. Apuleius, *De Platone et eius dogmate* 1.9.199–200. On the
World Soul in Apuleius, see Stephen Gersh, *Middle Platonism and Neoplatonism: The Latin Tradition*, 2 vols. (Notre Dame, 1986) 1:250–52,
260–63, 308–9.

9. For Plotinus's teaching, see H. J. Blumenthal, "Soul, World
Soul and Individual Soul in Plotinus," *Le Néoplatonisme: Colloque In-
ternationale du Centre National de la Recherche Scientifique, Royaument
9–13 juin 1963* (Paris, 1971) 55–66.

10. *Timaeus a Calcidio translatus commentarioque instructus,* ed. J. H. Waszink, Corpus Platonicum Medii Aevi, Plato Latinus 4 (London/Leiden, 1962). In the commentary see especially caps. 26–39, 51–55, 99–118, etc. On the debate over the dating of Chalcidius, contrast John Dillon, *The Middle Platonists 80 B.C. to A.D. 220* (Ithaca, 1977) 401–8, which argues for an early-fourth-century date, with Waszink's introduction (pp. xii–xv), which prefers the late fourth century. See the discussion of Chalcidius on the World Soul in Gersh, *Middle Platonism and Neoplatonism,* 2:474–79.

11. *Macrobii Commentarii in Somnium Scipionis,* ed. J. Willis (Leipzig, 1963), esp. 1.6, 14, and 2.2. For a detailed discussion, see Gersh, *Middle Platonism and Neoplatonism* 2:538–43, 551–58, 562–70.

12. *Asclepius,* in A. D. Nock, ed., *Corpus Hermeticum,* vol. 2 (Paris, 1960), 14 (p. 313), 16 (p. 315), and 29 (p. 337).

13. Martianus Capella, *De Nuptiis Philologiae et Mercurii,* ed. A. Dick (Leipzig, 1925), esp. bks. 1.1–7, and 68; and Boethius, *De consolatione philosophiae,* ed. L. Bieler (Corpus Christianorum 94; Turnhoult, 1957) bk. 3, metrum 9 ("O qui perpetua").

14. E.g., Eusebius of Caesarea, *Praeparatio Evangelica* 11.20 (J. P. Migne, *Patrologia Graeca* [hereafter *PG*] 21:901); Ps.-Basil (Didymus the Blind), *Contra Eunomiam* 5 (*PG* 29:769–73); Theodoret, *Evangelium veritatis* (*PG* 83:852).

15. Salvian of Marseilles, *De gubernatione dei* (J.-P. Migne, *Patrologia Latina* [hereafter *PL*] 53:29) is an exception.

16. The quotation is from *De consensu evangelistarum* 1.23.35 (*PL* 34:1058). In following Augustine's views on the World Soul, I have been helped by Vernon Bourke, "St. Augustine and the Cosmic Soul," *Giornale di Metafisica* 9 (1954) 431–40.

17. *De immort. an.* 15.24–25 (*PL* 32:1033); *De mus.* 6.14.44. (*PL* 32:1186). Another early text in *De quan. an.* 32.69 (*PL* 32:1073) is more ambiguous.

18. *Retract.* 1.11.4 (*PL* 32:604; cp. also 1.5.3).

19. *De civ. Dei* 7.29, 10.2, 13.16–17 (*PL* 41:219, 279–80, 387–90; cp. *De vera rel.* 10.18).

20. *De Gen. ad lit. lib. imperf.* 4.17 (*PL* 34:226–27, a text not qualified in the *Retract.*); and *De Gen. ad lit.* 1.6–8.12–24 (*PL* 34:250–51). For another patristic exegesis of Gen. 1:2 that could be read as suggesting a World Soul, see Ambrose, *In Hexaemeron* (*PL* 14:150). There is also a sermon of Augustine that the Maurist edition holds inauthentic only on the grounds of its assertion that Gen. 1:2 teaches the existence of the World Soul; cp. Bourke, "St. Augustine and the Cosmic Soul," 437–38.

21. *Periphyseon* 1.31, in *Iohannis Scotti Eriugenae Periphyseon (De Divisione Naturae): Liber Primus*, ed. I. P. Sheldon-Williams (Dublin, 1968) 114–16. See also the remarks in *Periphyseon* 3.38, ed. I. P. Sheldon-Williams (Dublin, 1981) 290–92.

22. The term *entelechia* (actuality) originates with Aristotle's definition of the soul in *De anima* 2.1 (412a). In Cicero's *Tusculanae disputationes* 1.10.22 the word *endelechia* appears as a description of the World Soul, which may be either a confusion for *entelechia* or an early Aristotelian cosmological term. For the history of the relation and use of these terms (which rapidly became conflated in the tradition), see Jean Pépin, *Théologie cosmique et théologie chrétienne* (Paris, 1964) 206–16. Chalcidius discusses *entelechia* in his *Commentarium* caps. 222, 225, and 227, and it appears as a personification in Martianus Capella's *De nuptiis* 1.7 and 2.213. See Johannes Scotus Eriugena, *Annotationes in Marcianum*, ed. Cora E. Lutz (Cambridge, Mass., 1939) 10–11. On the Carolingian interpretations, see G. Mathon, "Jean Scot Érigène, Chalcidius et le problème de l'âme universelle," *L'homme et son destin d'après les penseurs du moyen âge* (Paris/Leuven, 1960) 361–75.

23. Remigius of Auxerre, *Commentum in Martianum Capellam*, bks. 1–2, ed. Cora E. Lutz (Leiden, 1962) 76, 207.

24. For a description see Peter Dronke, *Fabula: Explorations into the Uses of Myth in Medieval Platonism* (Leiden, 1974) 85–88, 157. For the background on early medieval use of Boethius, see Pierre Courcelle, "Étude critique sur les commentaires de la Consolation de Boèce (ixe–xve siècles)," *Archives d'histoire doctrinale et littéraire du moyen âge* 12(1939) 5–140 (later incorporated in his *La Consolation de philosophie dans la tradition littéraire: Antécédents et Postérité de Boece* [Paris, 1967]); and R. B. C. Huygens, "Mittelalterliche Kommentare zum *O qui perpetua*," *Sacris Eruditi* 6(1954) 373–427.

25. See Philippe Delhaye, *Une controverse sur l'âme universelle au IXe siècle* (Analecta Mediaevalia Namurcensia 1; Namur, 1950).

26. The phrase is from the Cistercian Isaac of Stella in his *Sermo 24* (*PL* 194:1769c). For a study, see B. McGinn, "Isaac of Stella on the Divine Nature," *Analecta Cisterciensia* 29(1973) 4–46.

27. M. Gibson, "The Study of the Timaeus in the Eleventh and Twelfth Centuries," *Pensamiento* 25(1969) 183–94. On twelfth-century Platonism the latest survey is by Tullio Gregory, "The Platonic Inheritance," in Dronke, *History of Twelfth-Century Western Philosophy* 54–80.

28. See the chart in R. W. Southern, *Platonism, Scholastic Method and the School of Chartres*, The Stenton Lecture, 1978 (Reading, 1979) 14.

29. See Gibson, "Study of the Timaeus," 188, which lists seven

commentaries. On the use of the *Timaeus* in the schools, see also Winthrop Wetherbee, *Platonism and Poetry: The Literary Influence of the School of Chartres* (Princeton, 1972) 28–36.

30.   Southern, *Platonism*, 9.

31.   Gibson, "Study of the Timaeus," 190.

32.   Southern, *Platonism*, 10, 13–15.

33.   Honorius Augustodunensis, *Selectorum Psalmorum expositio* (*PL* 172:270b).

34.   *De civ. Dei* 11.21 (*PL* 41:334–35), citing *Timaeus* 37c and 29d. For a twelfth-century notice, see Isaac of Stella, *Sermo* 24 (*PL* 194:1769d).

35.   Winthrop Wetherbee, "Philosophy, cosmology, and the Twelfth-Century Renaissance," in *A History of Twelfth-Century Western Philosophy* 25. Wetherbee cites a text from William of Conches in this connection that highlights the trinitarian aspect of the manifestation of nature.

36.   The *Theologia summi boni* was edited by H. Ostlender, *Peter Abaelard's Theologia 'Summi Boni,'* (Beiträge zur Geschichte der Philosophie und Theologie des Mittelalters 35.2–3; Münster, 1939). The comment about its intent is taken from Abelard's *Historia calamitatum*, ed. J. Monfrin (Paris, 1967) 83.

37.   *Theologia summi boni*, 13–20.

38.   For a survey of Early Scholastic texts on the *anima mundi* concentrating on Peter Abelard, see Ludwig Ott, "Die platonische Weltseele in der Theologie der Frühscholastik," in Kurt Flasch ed., *Parusia: Festgabe für Johannes Hirschberger*, (Frankfurt, 1965) 307–31. Peter Dronke in *Fabula*, 58–59, speculates that Bernard of Chartres, who was teaching at least as early as 1114, may have been the source—an attractive, but with our present knowledge unprovable, assertion.

39.   See D. E. Luscombe, *The School of Peter Abelard* (Cambridge, 1969) 104.

40.   We are fortunate now to have the excellent edition of the *Theologia Christiana* and the shorter versions of the *Theologia Scholarium* in *Petri Abaelardi Opera Theologica*, ed. E. Buytaert (Corpus Christianorum. Continuatio Mediaevalis 12; Turnhoult, 1969). The introduction gives a full discussion of the dating and relation of the three *Theologiae*. For a brief conspectus, see E. F. Little, "The Status of Current Research of Abelard," *Arts libéraux et philosophie au moyen âge* (Montreal/Paris, 1969) 1122.

41.   Book 2 goes on the defend the appeal to pagan letters, while Books 3 and 4 treat the Trinity from the dialectical point of view. Book 5 begins, but does not complete, an enlargement on the proper understanding of the Trinity.

42.   See Wetherbee, "Philosophy, cosmology," 37–38.

43. The source for this is Macrobius, *In Som. Scip.* 1.2, 14.

44. *Theologia Christiana* 1.69 (ed. Buytaert, 100).

45. Ibid., 1.106 (ed. Buytaert, 116). In the next paragraph, Abelard defends Macrobius's "mystical" interpretation (pp. 121–22). On Abelard's understanding of *involucrum*, see Dronke, *Fabula*, 55–67; and Wetherbee, *Platonism and Poetry*, 40–41.

46. Ibid., 1.108 (ed. Buytaert, 117).

47. Ibid., 4.147 (ed. Buytaert, 338).

48. *Expositio in Hexaemeron* (*PL* 178:735–36). In c. 753 of the same text, Abelard notes Augustine's hesitations about the World Soul. This text has a more cosmological flavor than is usual in the *Theologiae*, but see *Theologia Christiana* 4.143 (ed. Buytaert, 337).

49. *Dialectica* 5.1 (ed. de Rijk, 558–59). Abelard claims the error belongs to those "qui allegorie nimis adherentes" (558, line 26).

50. The basic discussion is in Luscombe, *The School of Peter Abelard*, though Luscombe's view (e.g., 123–26) that because Abelard was using allegory or *involucrum* he cannot, strictly speaking, be accused of identifying the World Soul and the Holy Spirit seems mistaken.

51. *Sententiae Parisienses*, Pars 1, in A. Landgraf, ed., *Écrits théologiques de l'école d'Abélard* (Leuven, 1934) 6, 16–18.

52. *Sententiae Florianenses*, cap. 17, ed. H. Ostlender in *Florilegium Patristicum*, fasc. 19 (Bonn, 1929) 7.

53. *Sententiae Hermanni*, cap. 18 (*PL* 178:1720d–1722a).

54. *Commentarius Cantabrigiensis in Epistolas Pauli e Schola P. Abaelardi*, ed. A. Landgraf, 4 pts. (Notre Dame, 1937–45), see the comment on Rom. 1:21–23.

55. *Ysagoge in Theologiam*, bk. 3, in Landgraf, *Écrits théologiques*, 257–58.

56. Robert of Melun in his *Sententiae* 1.296, as discussed in Luscombe, *The School of Peter Abelard*, 285. A similar view was expressed by Alexander Neckham in his *Speculum speculationum*, on which see Nicholas Häring, *Commentaries on Boethius by Thierry of Chartres and his School* (Toronto, 1971) 47, n. 95. John of Salisbury rejects the identification in *Metalogicon* 4.16.

57. John of Salisbury, *Metalogicon* 1.5, 24. On the controverted question of William's schooling, see Peter Dronke, "New Approaches to School of Chartres," *Anuario de estudios medievales* 6(1969) 121–23.

58. The fundamental work on William remains that of Tullio Gregory, *Anima mundi: La filosofia di Guglielmo di Conches e la scuola di Chartres* (Florence, 1955), which resumes some of this author's articles noted below. For the general background, the older work of J.-M. Parent, *La doctrine de la création dans l'École de Chartres* (Paris/Ottawa, 1938), retains much value. Among other studies of William on this issue, note

Peter Dronke, "L'amor che move il sole e l'altre stelle," *Studi medievali,* 3rd series, 6(1965) 410–13; Wetherbee, "Philosophy, cosmology"; Gregory, "The Platonic Inheritance"; as well Dorothy Elford, "William of Conches," in Dronke, *History of Twelfth-Century Western Philosophy* 308–27.

59. See Dronke, *Fabula,* chap. 1. See also Edouard Jeauneau, *"Lectio philosophorum": Recherches sur l'École de Chartres,* pt. 1 (Amsterdam, 1973).

60. The translation of Dronke in *Fabula,* 24, based upon the text he gives on p. 70. For a discussion, see 23–25, 104–06.

61. The text is from a Copenhagen manuscript cited in Dronke, *Fabula,* 174–76, commenting on Macrobius, *In Som. Scip.* 1.14.6. The hesitation seems to involve Macrobius's statement that the highest God creates the World Soul from himself ("de se creat"), on which the commentator notes "Si hoc dicatur de spiritu sancto, hereticum est quod ait 'creat.'" This might be a later gloss, reflecting the situation after 1140.

62. I translate here from the text cited in Southern, *Platonism,* 23, n. 27. William's *Gloss* on Boethius has been studied by Winthrop Wetherbee, *Platonism and Poetry,* 92–104. A similar passage is found in the "Sigtuna" glosses on the *Timaeus,* edited by T. Schmid, which some hold was an early product of William's pen; see "Ein Timaioskommentar in Sigtuna," *Classica et Mediaevalia* 10(1948) 239.

63. See Dronke, *Fabula,* chap. 3 (the textual evidence is presented in "Appendix B," 167–83).

64. I am using the translation of Dronke, *Fabula,* 103, from the text of Florence, Naz. Conv. Sopp. I.1.28, f. 50v..

65. The Plotinian teaching on the bifurcation of *psychē* was influential on Macrobius's presentation. See Gersh, *Middle Platonism and Neoplatonism* 2:551–70.

66. For the text, see Dronke, *Fabula,* 116–18, with a discussion on 110–13.

67. T. Gregory in *Anima mundi,* 145, and his article "L'*Anima Mundi* nella filosofia del XII secolo," *Giornale critico della filosofia italiana* 30 (1951) 503, is misleading in suggesting that Abelard is purely mystical and allegorical, while William is cosmological. There are, indeed, differences between the two, but they are complex interaction of various elements as recognized in Dronke, *Fabula,* 176.

68. Southern, *Platonism,* 17.

69. *Philosophia mundi,* 1.15, ed. Gregor Maurach (Pretoria, 1974) 15–16.

70. See Lapidge, "The Stoic inheritance," 110.

71. See *Guillaume de Conches: Glosae super Platonem,* ed. Edou-

ard Jeauneau (Paris, 1965) cap. 71 (p. 145). The treatise on the World Soul extends from cap. 71 to 102 (pp. 144–88).

72. Ibid., cap. 74 (pp. 148–50). But contrast this with the discussion in cap. 94 (p. 176), which says that the *anima mundi* is only "like" the Creator.

73. Elford, "William of Conches," 326–27, argues that William's "confidence in the consistency and dynamic order of the natural world" eventually made the identification of the Holy Spirit and the World Soul unnecessary.

74. *Dialogus de substantiis physicis,* ed. G. Grataroli (Strassburg, 1567) 306.

75. For the evidence on Thierry's life, see N. Härring, "Chartres and Paris Revisited," *Essays in Honour of Anton Charles Pegis* (Toronto, 1974) 279–94. For a recent survey, Peter Dronke, "Thierry of Chartres," in Dronke, *History of Twelfth-Century Western Philosophy,* 358–85.

76. The text was first edited by N. Häring, "The Creation and Creator of the World according to Thierry of Chartres and Clarenbaldus of Arras," *Archives d'histoire doctrinale et littéraire du moyen âge* 30(1955) 137–216, with a valuable commentary. A subsequent, improved text appeared in N. Häring, *Commentaries on Boethius by Thierry of Chartres,* 555–75. See the discussion in Southern, *Platonism,* 31–34.

77. R. Klibansky, "The School of Chartres," in Marshall Clagett, Gaines Post, and Robert Reynolds, eds., *Twelfth-Century Europe and the Foundations of Modern Society* (Madison, 1966) 8. See also, Dronke, "New Approaches," 133–39.

78. Southern, *Platonism,* 28, and also the remarks on 39–40. See also Häring, "The Creation and Creator," 154–57, 180.

79. *De sex dierum operibus,* cap. 1 (ed. Häring, 555).

80. Augustine, *De Gen. ad lit.* 6.10.17 (*PL* 32:346). This text is not cited by Thierry, but it was central to his student Clarenbald's exposition in his *Tractatulus,* cap. 23 (see Häring, "The Creation and Creator," 207).

81. *De sex dierum operibus,* caps. 30–47 (ed. Häring, 568–75). On this, see Edouard Jeauneau, "Mathématiques et Trinité chez Thierry de Chartres," in his *"Lectio Philosophorum,"* 93–99; and Southern, *Platonism,* 36–40.

82. *De sex dierum operibus,* cap. 26 (ed. Häring, 566), citing *Asclepius* 14 and 16 (ed. Nock, 313, 315).

83. *De sex dierum operibus,* cap. 27 (ed. Häring, 566–67).

84. Paris, Bibl. nat. MS. lat. 8624, ff. 17r.–24v., in Tullio Gregory, "Nuove note sul platonismo medievale: Dall'*anima mundi* all'idea di

natura," *Giornale critico della filosofia italiana* 36(1957) 37–44 (two other views are also mentioned).

85.   *The Commentary on the First Six Books of the* Aeneid *of Vergil Commonly Attributed to Bernardus Silvestris,* ed. Julian Ward Jones and Elizabeth Frances Jones (Lincoln, 1977) 121. Other mentions of the *anima mundi* in the text are less clear (cp. 41, 109, 119). See the review of this volume by Theodore Silverstein in *Speculum* 54(1979) 154–57.

86.   Unedited, but see the fragments given in Jones and Jones, *Commentary on the* Aeneid, 134–36; and those in Wetherbee, *Platonism and Poetry,* 267–72. Ibid, 123–24, presumes the author was Bernardus. Against the Bernardine authorship is Brian Stock, *Myth and Science in the Twelfth Century: A Study of Bernard Silvester* (Princeton, 1972) 33–40.

87.   The doubts about authorship are summarized in Jones, and Jones, *Commentary on the* Aeneid, ix–xi.

88.   See the discussion in Pierre Duhem, *Le systeme du monde* (Paris, 1915) vol. 3, 204–5. Cf. P. Courcelle, *Consolation de philosophie,* 314–15.

89.   M.-T. d'Alverny, "Le cosmos symbolique du XIIe siècle," *Archives d'histoire doctrinale et littéraire du moyen âge* 20(1953) 31 (d'Alverny gives a detailed analysis of the illustration on 69–81). For the text and illustrations, see *Honorius Augustodunensis: Clavis Physicae,* ed. Paolo Lucentini (Rome, 1974).

90.   D'Alverny, "Cosmos symbolique," 70, 73.

91.   *Clavis physicae* cap. 211 (ed. Lucentini, 167–68). In his *Hexaemeron* (PL 172:254d) Honorius interprets Gen. 1:2 as signifying the Holy Spirit's work of "vivificatio," in line with much patristic exegesis.

92.   *Lamberti S. Audomari Canonici Liber Floridus,* ed. Albert Derolez (Ghent, 1968), f. 222r. (p. 443 of the facsimile). Simpler examples can be found in William of Conches, *Glosae super Platonem* (ed. Jeauneau) 153–58.

93.   Hildegard of Bingen, *Liber divinorum operum* (PL 197:743–44).

94.   In the words of *Caritas-anima mundi* herself: Sed et officialis sum, quoniam omnia vitalia de me ardent; et aequalis vita in aeternitate sum, quae nec orta est, nec finietur, eademque vita se movens et operans Deus est, et tamen haec vita una in tribus viribus est (744a).

95.   Arnold of Bonneval, *Liber de cardinalibus operibus Christi* 12 (PL 189:1672–73).

96.   Isaac of Stella, *Epistola de anima* (PL 194:1882c).

97.   The philosophers' conceptions of the World Soul had already been rejected in the late eleventh century by Manegold of Lautenbach in

chapter 2 of his *Liber contra Wolfelmum,* edited by W. Hartmann in the *Monumenta Germaniae historica: Quellen zur Geistesgeschichte des Mittelalters* 8 (Weimar, 1972), 47–48.

98. For a brief overview of medieval struggles over materialistic pantheism, see Verbeke, *The Presence of Stoicism,* chap. 2.

99. Gregory, "Nuove note," 43.

100. Edited by Carmelo Ottaviano, "Un brano inedito della "Philosophia" di Guglielmo di Conches (1080–1145)," *Archivio di Storia della Filosofia* 1(1932) 133–45; 2(1933) 16–51. Gregory, *Anima mundi,* 28–40, denied the attribution to William; Southern, *Platonism,* 23–24, thinks it may be authentic.

101. Ottaviano ed., 36–37.

102. *Didascalicon* 1.1. Jerome Taylor in *The Didascalicon of Hugh of St. Victor* (New York, 1961) 22–28, 178–80, suggests that Hugh was criticizing Abelard and William.

103. Hugh of Saint Victor, *Homiliae in Ecclesiasten* 2 (*PL* 175:136), and the discussion in Lapidge, "The Stoic inheritance," 109–10. Hugh's willingness to admit an "occultam naturae vim," but avoidance of the term *anima mundi* presaged the dominant view of the second half of the twelfth century. See also *De tribus diebus* 18 (*PL* 176:828).

104. See the commentary from an Avranches manuscript edited by E. Jeauneau, "Gloses marginales sur le Timaeus," *Sacris erudiri* 17(1966) 87–89.

105. Ep. 326 in Bernard's corpus. For a critical edition, see J. Leclercq in the *Revue Bénédictine* 79(1969) 377–78.

106. *Disputatio adversus Petrum Abelardum* (*PL* 180:265–66). A second *Disputatio* against Abelard edited in *PL* 180:283–328, under William's name, but actually by Thomas of Morigny, briefly attacks the notion of the *anima mundi* as implying subordinationism (cc. 321c–322a).

107. Ep. 190.4.10 (J. Leclercq et al., *Sancti Bernardi Opera* 8, p. 26).

108. On the condemnation at Sens, see Luscombe, *The School of Peter Abelard,* chap. 4; and E. Little, "Bernard and Abelard at the Council of Sens," *Bernard of Clairvaux: Studies Presented to Dom Jean Leclercq* (Washington, D.C., 1973) 55–71.

109. Ep. 194 in Leclercq et al., *Sancti Bernardi Opera* 8, 46–48.

110. *PL* 180:333–340.

111. Ibid., cc. 334, 335b–c, 338.

112. Ibid., c. 339a.

113. There are brief remarks in Eugenio Garin, *Studi sul Platonismo medievale* (Florence, 1958) 62–68. For William of St. Thierry's scientific interests in medicine, which are surprisingly close to those of his

opponent, see B. McGinn, "Introduction," in *Three Treatises on Man: A Cistercian Anthropology* (Kalamazoo, 1977) 29–35.

114.   See the first two parts of Charles Homer Haskins, *Studies in the History of Mediaeval Science* (New York, 1967); and Elford, "William of Conches," 326–27.

115.   E.g., Arnold of Bonneval (*PL* 189:1673a–b); Anonymous Commentary in Gregory, "Nuove note," 42–43; *De mundi constitutione* (*PL* 90:902–3); William of Conches, *Philosophia mundi* 1.15.

116.   Wetherbee, *Platonism and Poetry,* 4 (see also 67).

117.   Along with Wetherbee's book, two older studies retain their value: Richard McKeon, "Poetry and Philosophy in the Twelfth Century: The Renaissance of Rhetoric," in R. S. Crane, ed., *Critics and Criticism, Ancient and Modern* (Chicago, 1952) 297–318; and Theodore Silverstein, "The Fabulous Cosmogony of Bernardus Silvestris," *Modern Philology* 46(1948–49) 92–116.

118.   Silverstein, "Fabulous Cosmogony of Bernardus Silvestris," 116.

119.   Etienne Gilson attacked older and cruder views of Bernardus's paganism and pantheism in his "La cosmogonie de Bernardus Silvestris," *Archives d'histoire doctrinale et littéraire du moyen âge* 3(1928) 5–24. Silverstein largely agreed with Gilson but doubted the tendency to dualism in Bernardus that Gilson had detected. Among other scholars who have discussed the issue, see Wetherbee, *Platonism and Poetry,* chap. 4; Brian Stock, *Myth and Science in the Twelfth Century,* which sees Bernard's position as a kind of "existential naturalism" (e.g., 280–83). Important discussions are also found in the introductions and notes to the edition *Bernardus Silvestris: Cosmographia* by Peter Dronke (Leiden, 1978); and the translation by Winthrop Wetherbee, *The Cosmographia of Bernardus Silvestris* (New York, 1973).

120.   Besides Silverstein, *Cosmographia of Bernardus Silvestris,* see Peter Dronke, "Bernard Silvestris, Natura and Personification," *Journal of the Warburg and Courtauld Institutes* 43(1980) 16–31.

121.   *Cosmographia,* Megacosmos 2.15 (ed. Dronke, 103). I have used the translation of Wetherbee, *Cosmographia,* 74. For a discussion of *Endelechia* as World Soul, see *Platonism and Poetry,* 164–66; Stock, *Myth and Science,* 122–25; and especially Silverstein, *Cosmographia of Bernardus Silvestris,* 114–16.

122.   In *Cosmographia of Bernardus Silvestris,* Silverstein shows how Bernard maintains the transcendence of his superessential God by carefully distinguishing between the *Verbum Dei* and its manifestation in *Noys* (110, 113).

123.   *PL* 199:961c–d.

124.   Ibid., c. 962a.

125.   Häring, *The Commentaries on Boethius,* 80–81. See Stephen Gersh, "Platonism-Neoplatonism-Aristotelianism: A Twelfth-Century Metaphysical System and its Sources," in Robert L. Benson and Giles Constable, eds., *Renaissance and Renewal in the Twelfth Century* (Cambridge, 1982) 518–19.

126.   Calcidius, *Commentarium,* cap. 177 (ed. Waszink, 206).

127.   Hermann of Carinthia, *De essentiis,* ed. Manuel Alonso (Comilles, 1946) 63. On Herman, see Charles Burnett, "Hermann of Carinthia," in Dronke, *History of Twelfth-Century Western Philosophy,* 386–404.

128.   Gregory, "Nuove note."

129.   *In 2 Sent.* d. 14, p. 1, a. 3, q. 2, resp.

130.   *Summa theologiae* 1a, q. 3, a. 8; *Summa contra gentiles* 1.27, 2.42, 3.120.

131.   *In 2 Sent.* d. 14, q. 1, a. 3, resp. et ad 3.

132.   *Expositio libri Genesis* n. 112, in *Meister Eckhart, Die deutschen and lateinischen Werke: Die lateinischen Werke* (Stuttgart, 1936–) 1:266; and *Expositio libri Sapientiae* n. 299 (2:632).

133.   M-D. Chenu, *Nature, Man and Society in the Twelfth Century* (Chicago, 1968) 48.

134.   McKeon, "Poetry and Philosophy," 314.

Early Modern

CHAPTER 15

Death and the Distribution of Sacral Power in Early Japanese Mythistory

Gary L. Ebersole

Endings test language, trying to the limit its capacity to reveal and
communicate primordial meanings. Whereas myths of creation and
origin reach toward the imaginative limits of primal chaos or
sublimity, images of demise measure language against the final,
outer reaches of experience and against the very end—both
termination and *telos*—of meaning itself.
                    —Lawrence E. Sullivan, *Ichanu's Drum*

The attempt to attain knowledge of the past is also a journey into
the world of the dead.
—Carlo Ginzburg, *Ecstasies*

In this essay I will look briefly at a few mythic narratives from
early Japan dealing with death, but from a different perspective
than has generally been adopted by scholars. I will not be interested in reconstructing the early Japanese views of death, the otherworld, and afterlife.[1] Nor will I privilege myths of the origins of
death, as many historians of religions have done,[2] for to do so is to
imply, as Sullivan does in this chapter's first epigraph, that the
primary function of myth is "to reveal and communicate primordial meanings."[3] Yet, to borrow Clifford Geertz's terms, myths
provide both models of the world or cosmos and models for living
in it. In this study, as we undertake a journey into the world of the
dead (i.e., of the early Japanese) à la Ginzburg, the focus will be on
myths of death as narrative models for living (or merely surviving)
in the phenomenal world.

Many definitions of "myth" (singular) have been based primarily on myths of origins. This essay seeks to call the wisdom of this procedure into question insofar as privileging such narratives functions implicitly to devalue those serving other functions. In their efforts to distinguish myth as a special and privileged form of discourse and imaginative creativity, historians of religions have often deflected attention from the more mundane uses of myths by historical agents.

Some myths from early Japan concerning encounters with sacral power and death are, I want to argue, best understood as cautionary tales. If they provide paradigmatic models, these are for living in the world; moreover, these are provided through negative examples of defeat or death. Such myths do not tell how the world and humans came to be the way they are but rather portray the world and the power relations that obtain within it. They portray the world as filled with competing loci of sacral power and, consequently, as inherently dangerous. Through representing paradigmatic narratives of this agonistic situation, they also provide practical guidance as to how to survive in this world.

Below we will look briefly at a few mythic narratives from the earliest extant Japanese mythological texts, the *Kojiki* (712) and the *Nihonshoki* (720). In these tales, in which deaths occur prematurely and unnecessarily, death is represented resulting from an individual's failure to recognize the actual and/or proper distribution of sacral power in various different loci or situations. Analyzing a few of these narratives of "mythistory" will enable me to shed light on early Japanese representations of death and of sacral power. Special attention will be paid to where sacral power is located in these texts, how it is distributed, what the texts suggest the proper spheres for the exercise of specific kinds of sacral power to be, and so on. I hope to show that the mythic texts from early Japan preserve traces of that period's real power struggles among historical agents holding different understandings of the distribution and locations of sacral power.

SACRAL POWER IN EARLY JAPANESE MYTH

We must begin with a glance at the way sacral power (frequently equated with the term *kami*) in early Japan has generally been represented by scholars. Many historians of religions have suggested that the early Japanese held the phenomenal world or nature *in toto* to be sacred (or at least potentially so). H. Byron

Earhart, for instance, cites the famous nativist scholar (*kokugaku-sha*) Motoori Norinaga (1730–1801) in support of this position:

> Generally speaking, [the word] "*kami*" denotes, in the first place, the deities of heaven and earth that appear in the ancient texts and also the spirits enshrined in the shrines; furthermore, among all kinds of beings—including not only human beings but also such objects as birds, beasts, trees, grass, seas, mountains, and so forth—any being whatsoever which possesses some eminent quality out of the ordinary, and is awe-inspiring, is called *kami*.

Earhart is led to conclude, "The identity of *kami* is so elastic that perhaps the best general term for understanding *kami* is the notion of the sacred."[4] Joseph M. Kitagawa's influential description of the religious world of meaning of the early Japanese is similar. According to Kitagawa, this religious world was a "monistic world of meaning" in which the people

> took it for granted that the natural world was the original world . . . they did not look for another order of meaning behind the phenomenal, natural world—at least until they came under the influence of Sino-Korean civilization and Buddhism. The one-dimensional meaning structure of the early Japanese is implicit in the term *kami*—the root *mi* plus the prefix *ka*. According to Tsuda [Sōkichi],
>
>> "*Mi* may be interpreted as a material thing or an embodied spirit possessing some kind of divine potency, or as a non-corporeal spirit, in either case believed to possess an intrinsic magic power, or established as an object of worship. Among corporeal objects of this nature may be numbered such physical elements as fire, water, wood and stone; certain animals; celestial bodies such as the sun and the moon; man-made objects such as swords and mirrors; agricultural products such as grain; and other objects of a similar nature. As for non-corporal spirits, these include any non-visible elements or attributes having the power to exert some form of strong or violent influence on Nature or to affect man's existence."
>
> Usually the term *kami* refers to all beings that are awesome and worthy of reverence, including both good and evil beings. It would be misleading to consider the religion of the ancient Japanese, which came to be known later as Shinto—the way of the *kami*—as nature worship. While it accepted the plurality of the *kami* as separate beings and objects, its basic affirmation was

the sacrality of the total world (cosmos) permeated as it was by the *kami* (sacred) nature.

The unitary world of meaning of the early Japanese is also evident in the ancient myths concerning a three-dimensional universe—the plain of high heaven (*Takama-no-hara*), the manifest world (*Utsu-shiyo*), and the nether world (*Yomotsu-kuni*). These three realms are portrayed as almost interchangeable, in that certain *kami* and heroes move back and forth freely among them."[5]

These and similar generalized descriptions of *kami* or sacral power are accurate as far as they go. All of the things mentioned—deities, persons, mountains, swords, grass, and so forth—are indeed referred to as *kami* somewhere in the extant myths from early Japan. However, these general descriptions tend to be misleading, insofar as they fail to indicate explicitly that *not all* persons, mirrors, mountains, birds, and so on were held to be sacred. Nor do they acknowledge that not all individuals shared the same evaluation of the sacrality of specific loci of power. Moreover, even those objects, geographical sites, and persons that were widely understood to be sites of sacral power were not all held to be equally powerful. In the myths of early Japan one finds sacral power to be widely distributed in the world, but that is not to say that it is ubiquitous or equally distributed. Nevertheless, most of the secondary literature suggests that the world of the early Japanese ("permeated with *kami*-nature") was universally appreciated as being sacred. Moreover, most presentations suggest that this religious world was largely pacific and free of conflict; that there was, in other words, a general and easy consensus concerning the sacrality of the world.

In the passage cited above, Kitagawa is surely correct in noting that in the myths from early Japan only "certain *kami* and heroes move back and forth freely among [the three cosmological realms]." Yet, like most commentators, he ignores the political dimensions inherent in the acknowledged fact that only "*certain*" beings have this ability or, perhaps, prerogative. That is, he does not comment on the significance of the fact that the myths represent this special status, not to mention many other claims of hierarchical (and even ontological) difference, as "natural." Yet, it is only by glossing over such distinctions, drawn in the texts themselves, that Kitagawa can make the broad generalization that "While [Shinto] accepted the plurality of the *kami* as separate beings and objects, its basic affir mation was the sacrality of the total world . . . permeated as it was by the *kami* (sacred) nature."

Similarly, in Tsuda's discussion of the particle *mi* in *kami,* cited above, he notes that this may be either a corporeal or noncorporeal site of potency or something "established as an object of worship." Here human agency in establishing certain objects, sites, and persons as the repositories of sacral power is clearly implied, yet this is subsequently not an object of serious inquiry. As a result, one is left with the false impression that while there were a multitude of *kami* and innumerable sacred sites and objects in Japan, these were finally all of a piece and uniform in their sacrality.

Such representations may in part be a legacy of the nativist scholars' ideological romanticization of the ancient period as a Golden Age of sorts.[6] Yet, to a remarkable degree many of the myths from early Japan are concerned with what I would call "the politics of sacral power." By this phrase I seek to indicate (and to focus our attention on) (1) the contestational process over which sites, objects, persons, and so forth are to be represented as repositories of sacral power and (2) the manner in which the relative sacrality or power of different loci, brought into contact, is contested in the texts. Rather than presenting a general and static "snapshot" of sacral power in early Japan, as most scholars have done, I will attempt to capture something of the dangerous agonistic contests waged among those who made competing claims of possessing sacral power as these are represented in selected mythic narratives. A glance at a few myths will demonstrate that sacral power or *kami*-nature was not held by the early Japanese to be evenly distributed, nor was there an easy consensus concerning the distribution of this power. Myths do not carry a single meaning, of course; they are multivalent. While fully recognizing this fact, I will make no attempt here to explore all of the possible meanings found in the myths treated. Instead, I will content myself with merely highlighting the narrative representations of the agonistic historical process of locating or "placing" sacral power—spatially, temporally, and hierarchically.

THE YAMATO-TAKERU TALE

One finds many myths from early Japan wherein various loci of sacral power are brought into contact with potentially violent results, sometimes even resulting in death. The tale of Yamato-

takeru, found in both the *Kojiki* and the *Nihonshoki,* is an especially rich source for investigating the competition among different claims of sacral power precisely because it is the story of the
ultimate failure of a person of great promise and power due to
his ignorance of the politics of sacral power. More specifically,
Yamato-takeru's death is represented as a result of his ignorance of
the real source of his power and the appropriate spheres (temporal
and spatial) where it might effectively be exercised. In this tale we
find acts and sacred objects out of place, ill-fated assumptions
concerning both the locus and agency of power, and finally a fatal
act of misrecognition.

In a famous "reading" of the Yamato-takeru tale, Ivan Morris
takes it to be the paradigmatic story of a romantic tragic hero who
epitomizes the Japanese cultural valorization of "the nobility of
failure."[7] While this is a suggestive interpretation, I prefer to think
of the Yamato-takeru narrative as a cautionary tale, a Machiavel-
lian lesson, if you will, on the politics of sacral power. For the sake
of brevity, here I will treat only the *Kojiki* version of the Yamato-
takeru tale (and only part of that) and not the sinified version in
the *Nihonshoki.*

As the *Kojiki* myth begins, this prince, a son of Emperor Keikō,
is known as "Ōusu-no-mikoto." The emperor hears of two beautiful young sisters in one of the provinces and desires to possess them
as wives. To this end, he sends his elder son, Ōusu-no-mikoto, to
bring the women to him. However, this prince marries them himself and sends back substitutes; moreover, he then refuses to appear at the morning and evening meals in the imperial palace, a
symbolic action indicating his rebellion against his father. The
younger son, Ousu, is consequently sent to bring his brother back
forcibly. Instead of doing this, however, he kills his older brother,
dismembers the body, and unceremoniously discards it.

Emperor Keikō is frightened by this demonstration of Ousu's
violent nature, so he decides to send Ousu out of the capital again.
This time he is dispatched to the western provinces with orders to
subdue two rebellious brothers, the Kumaso-takeru, "the Brave of
Kumaso." Before setting out on this mission, Prince Ousu visits his
aunt, Yamato-hime, the sacred priestess of the Ise Shrine, and receives three items from her—an upper garment, a skirt, and a
sword (later known as the "Kusanagi-sword" and one of the imperial regalia). Prince Ousu uses the first two magical items to dis-

guise himself as a beautiful young woman and thus is able to have himself invited into the Kumaso-takeru's heavily fortified headquarters, where he is seated between them at a banquet.

At this point the prince seems poised to realize yet another stunning triumph. When the Kumaso-takeru are intoxicated, Ousu uses the sword from the Ise Shrine to slay them. Before expiring, however, one of the Kumaso-takeru asks the prince his name and Ousu replies:

> "I am the son of Emperor O-Tarashi-hiko-oshiro-wake, who dwells in the palace of Hishiro and rules Oyashimaguni; and my name is Yamato-oguna-no-miko. Hearing that you Kumaso-takeru were unsubmissive and disrespectful, he dispatched me to kill you."
>
> Then Kumaso-takeru said: "Indeed this must be true. For in the west there are no brave, mighty men besides us. But in the land of O-Yamato there is a man exceeding the two of us in bravery! Because of this I will present you with a name. May you be known from now on as Yamato-takeru-no-miko [the Brave of Yamato]!"
>
> . . . From that time, he was called Yamato-takeru-no-mikoto to praise his name. Then as he returned, he subdued and pacified all of the mountain *kami,* river *kami,* and *kami* of the sea-straits.[8]

Let me interject a few brief comments here on essential details of the myth up to this point. It should be noted that Ousu is able to deceive and then defeat the Kumaso-takeru, as well as various *kami* of mountains, rivers, and straits through the agency of the items obtained from the Ise priestess. However, if we may anticipate subsequent episodes of the myth, there is a crucial detail that most commentators have missed: the Kumaso-takeru achieve a posthumous victory of sorts by praising Ousu and "planting" a false synecdochic relationship in his mind by having him assume the name Yamato-takeru. That is, *given the informing logic (i.e., the operative politics of sacral power) of this myth,* with the assumption of the name "Yamato-takeru," Ousu's downfall is already determined. When Ousu is seduced by an appeal to his ego into assuming this new name, with its implied synecdochic relation among the land, his person, and his power, he is in a sense already doomed because, as we have seen, his real power is represented as coming from the objects obtained from the Ise Priestess. While he possesses the power to do away with a disobedient and recalcitrant prince by himself, this power or ability is not necessarily sufficient or appropriate in other situations and in relation to other loci of sacral power.

The succeeding episodes of the myth support this reading. Yamato-takeru's sacral power is represented as coming from a specific place, the Ise Shrine (i.e., the imperial family's clan shrine), yet it is portable and transferable. This power is invested by Yamato-hime, the Ise priestess, in specific objects—an upper garment, a skirt, and a sword—which Ousu carries with him. Blinded by hubris, however, Yamato-takeru ceases to recognize these as the source of his power; instead, he mistakenly assumes that this power is instantiated in his person. This leads him to believe himself invincible and no longer subject to the restrictions and limitations that bind others. Again, his subsequent actions recounted in the myth confirm this interpretation. Among other things, he brazenly breaks a taboo by having sexual intercourse with one Miyazu-hime during her menstrual period. This act represents a blatant disregard for propriety; it is an act that is out of place, since it is performed at an inappropriate time.

As if this were not bad enough, the situation is then exacerbated by another failure on the part of Yamato-takeru to recognize the source of his power. As he does off on his next adventure to subdue the *kami* of Mount Ibuki, Yamato-takeru leaves the sacred Kusanagi sword behind with Miyazu-hime. We pick up the myth as he arrives at the foot of Mount Ibuki.

> At this time [Yamato-takeru] said: "I will take the *kami* of this mountain with my bare hands." [Thus saying], he went up the mountain. Then on the mountain he met a white boar the size of a cow. Thereupon he spoke out [*kotoage shite*] and said: "This is the *kami*'s messenger, which is here transformed into a white boar. I will not kill it now, but will kill it when I come back." [Thus saying], he went up. At this time, [the *kami*] caused a violent hail storm and dazed Yamato-takeru-no-mikoto.[9]

Yamato-takeru is fatally wounded by the hail. In vain he struggles to return home but dies on the way. For our purposes here, we need not follow this myth to its conclusion, with the deceased Yamato-takeru turning into a white bird and flying off over the sea, pursued by his grieving wife and children. Instead, let us concentrate on *the immediate cause of Yamato-takeru's death*, which consists of two instants of misrecognition: (1) he fails to recognize the *kami* of the mountain and (2) he fails to recognize the source and locus of his own power, as well as its proper spatiotemporal sphere of efficacy. Just as was the case with his tryst with Miyazu-hime, he mistakenly assumes that he can exercise his power at any time because he carries it within himself ("I will take the *kami* [deity] of this mountain with my bare hands"). That is, he assumes a synecdochic relationship between himself as agent and his power or agency. In assuming the name Yamato-takeru he also comes to believe that he embodies the sacral power of the land of Yamato.

In this myth, then, sacral power is found in various places—in the Ise Shrine, in the objects carried from Ise, in the *kami* of the mountain, and so forth—which are brought into a contestational relationship. Significantly, the tale makes it clear that power and efficacy is *not* invested in the person of this imperial prince; any power he wields is borrowed, as it were, from elsewhere. Needless to say, this situation mirrors the actual sociopolitical status of an imperial prince in Japan, whose power and prestige came almost exclusively from his spatial and social proximity to the emperor.[10] Let us not forget that, as the historical chronicles of early Japan inform us, princes who ignored this "fact" often found themselves facing summary execution or exile.

One final detail merits our attention. In this mythistory, Yamato-takeru suffers a fatal pummeling in a hailstorm wrought by the *kami* of the mountain. Here, perhaps, we may glimpse a mythic representation of the conflict in early Japan between two different forms of religiosity—one found in older local mountain cults, the other in the newly emerging religio-political ideology-*cum*-genealogy of the descent of the imperial family from Amaterasu-ōmikami, the sun goddess. This myth, in other words, may be seen as portraying an uneasy, even antagonistic, relationship between two different understandings of where greater sacral power is located—in the mountains or in the persons of the imperial family members. Support for this position may be found in other narratives from this period that concern the encounter of a mountain *kami* and an emperor. One such encounter, preserved in two different versions, must suffice here. We will begin with the *Kojiki* account.

> On [one] occasion, when the Emperor [Yūryaku] was ascending Mount Katsuragi, all of his many attendants were dressed in dyed blue garments to which red cords were attached. At the time people who were exactly like the emperor's entourage were

climbing the mountain from the opposite side. Both the appearance of their garments and the people themselves were so much alike as to be indistinguishable.

Then the emperor, seeing this, inquired saying: "There is no other king in this land of Yamato. Who is this who comes in this manner?" The style of the reply was also the same as the emperor's own words. At this time, the emperor was greatly enraged and fixed his arrow. His many attendants also all fixed their arrows. Then the other people also fixed their arrows.

Hereupon the emperor again inquired, saying: "In that case, say your names. We will all say our names and then shoot our arrows." This time, the reply was: "Since I have been asked first, I will say my name first: bad fortune with one word [*magakoto hito-koto*], good fortune with one word [*yogoto mo hito-koto*], the word-deciding deity Hito-koto-nushi-no-ōkami am I!" At this, the emperor was afraid and said: "I am struck with awe, O my great deity! I did not know that you had a corporeal form [*utsushi omi aramu to wa*]." Thus saying, beginning with his own great sword and bow and arrows, he had his many attendants take off the garments they were wearing and reverentially presented them. Then this Hito-koto-nushi-no-ōkami, clapping his hands, accepted these offerings. Thus, on the emperor's return, from the mountain top to the entrance of Mount Hatsuse, this *ōkami* escorted him back.[11]

The *Nihonshoki* account of this encounter is significantly different. It reads:

4th year, Spring, 2nd month. The Emperor went a-hunting with bow and arrows on Mount Katsuragi. Of a sudden a tall man appeared, who came and stood over the vermilion valley. In face and demeanor [*kao-sugata*] he resembled the Emperor. The Emperor knew that he was a *kami*, and therefore proceeded to inquire of him, saying:—"Of what place art thou Lord [*izu ko no kimi zo*]?" The tall man answered and said:—"I am a *kami* in visible human form [*arahitogami*]." Do thou first tell thy princely name, and then in turn I will inform thee of mine." The Emperor answered and said:—"We are Waka-take no Mikoto." The tall man next gave his name, saying:—"Thy servant is Hito-koto-nushi-no-kami." He finally joined him in the diversion of the chase. They pursued a deer, and each declined in favour of the other to let an arrow fly at him. They galloped on, bit to bit, using to one another reverent and respectful language, as if in the company of *hijiri*. Herewith the sun went down, and the hunt came to an end. The *kami* attended on the Emperor and escorted him as far as the Water of Kume. At this time the people all said:—"An Emperor of great virtue!"[12]

These two passages purport to recount the same event, yet, as I have suggested, they differ in significant ways. What is at issue in these different narrative representations of the encounter of an emperor and a *kami* on Mount Katsuragi is, I want to argue, at the heart of the politics of sacral power in early Japan. While it is impossible to identify the individual narrators in both cases, it is nevertheless clear that historical agents differed in their evaluation of the relative distribution of sacral power. In these two versions we encounter an interesting rhetorical difference revolving around the issues of recognition and rank as well as those of similarity or identity and difference. In the *Kojiki* version, Hito-koto-nushi is referred to as an *ōkami*, a "Great *kami*," while he is styled only "*kami*" in the *Nihonshoki*. Moreover, in the *Kojiki* version, the emperor initially does not recognize the deity as a *kami*, but rather is nonplussed because this being is his mirror image. (One thinks here immediately of the most famous instance in Japanese mythology of the misrecognition of a mirror image—that of Amaterasu when she has hidden herself in a cave, plunging the cosmos into darkness, until she hears raucous laughter outside, peeks out, and mistakes her own reflection in a mirror for another *kami* who she is told has replaced her.) In the *Kojiki* the person the emperor meets both looks and acts exactly like himself, and even their entourages are identical. When the *kami* discloses his identity, though, the emperor humbly makes an offering to him of his weapons and the garments of his attendants. If these two beings are identical in appearance, actions, and even in terms of external trappings, they are nevertheless somehow still hierarchically marked in terms of their power and sacrality, with the mountain *kami* emerging as preeminent.

In the *Nihonshoki* version, on the other hand, the emperor immediately recognizes the being he encounters, a giant who still resembles him in facial feature if not size, as a *kami*, but the *kami* also recognizes him as the emperor. Significantly, the mountain *kami* uses a polite and humble form of address in speaking to the emperor, while Yūryaku treats this *kami* courteously and as an equal. The text clearly implies, though, that this was magnanimous on the emperor's part since his rank and status were more exalted.

According to this account, it was the emperor's magnanimous attitude and courteous actions that earned him recognition as a "virtuous emperor."

At issue in these two accounts is the relative rank and sacrality of this *kami* and the emperor. Japanese scholars have long pointed to the declining fortunes in ancient Japan of the Katsuragi clan, as it came under the hegemonic control of the imperial clan, as the historical "fact" lying behind this narrative of mythistory. Such an historical reality may have been there, of course, yet euhemerist explanations such as this are finally inadequate—not to say banal—in understanding myths. Of more import and interest is the way in which these texts rhetorically represent a historical and structural tension in early Japan between two competing paradigms of the locus of sacral power, which we glimpsed in the Yamato-takeru tale.

The *Kojiki* version privileges locative sacrality and the magical power of words (*kotodama*) over the claim of ontological or instantiated sacrality in the person of the emperor. That is, in the *Kojiki* it is of determinative importance that the incident takes place on Mount Katsuragi, the domain of Hito-koto-nushi-no-ōkami. He is specifically referred to as "the Great *kami* of Katsuragi, Hito-koto-nushi." Emperor Yūryaku, while possessing *kami*-nature himself, like all sovereigns according to the religio-political ideology of direct descent from Amaterasu, nevertheless must recognize the superior status and sacral power of Hito-koto-nushi on *Mount Katsuragi*. Hito-koto-nushi's power clearly comes from the place. There is a twofold synecdochic relationship drawn: first, between the place and the *kami* and, second, between the *kami* as agent and the agency whereby his power is exercised (i.e., the ability to determine anyone's fortune for good or ill with one word is identical to the name of this *kami*—Hito-koto-nushi). In the *Nihonshoki* account, however, one finds a somewhat clumsy rhetorical attempt to counter the inherent narrative power of this synecdochic relationship—clumsy because no clear countervailing relationship of identity is drawn.

A powerful and rhetorically effective counterpoint to the claims concerning sacral power represented by the *Kojiki* account of the encounter of Emperor Yūryaku with Hito-koto-nushi on Mount Katsuragi was mounted, however, in the late seventh century in the mythistory spun by oral reciters associated with and employed by

the imperial family. If the *Kojiki* narratives of mythistory emphasized a paradigm of locative sacrality, the oral performative ritual
poetry of, say, Hitomaro suggested that the person of the sovereign
(or in other cases an imperial prince) is so sacred that his or her
mere presence can qualitatively transform any place into a sacred
site.

For a single example of a rhetorical representation of this paradigm of the sacral power instantiated in the person of the sovereign
overwhelming all other competing loci, let us turn to *Man'yōshū*
1.38–39. There Hitomaro proclaims that when Empress Jitō travels to the detached palace in Yoshino, the local inhabitants, including the *kami* of the land itself, all pay homage to her and serve her.
Hitomaro represents the local *kami* as recognizing and bowing to
the superior sacrality of the empress. As a *chōka* or public performative oral verse, *MYS* 1.38–39 was no doubt recited before a
large crowd gathered for a ritual occasion.

yasumishishi	Our Lord
wago ōkimi	who rules in peace,
kamu nagara	a very *kami*,
kamusabisesu to	manifests her divine will
Yoshino-gawa	and raises towering halls
tagitsu kōchi ni	above the Yoshino riverland
takadono o	where waters surge,
takashirimashite	and climbs to the top
noboritachi	to view the land.
kunimi o seseba	On the mountains
tatanazuku	folding upward around her
aokaki yama	like a sheer hedge of green,
yamatsumi no	the mountain *kami* present their offerings.
matsuru mi-tsuki to	They bring her blossoms in springtime
harube wa	to decorate her hair
hana kazashimochi	and, when autumn comes,
aki tateba	they garland her with yellow leaves.
momichi kazaseri	And the *kami* of the river
yukisou	that runs alongside the mountains
kawa no kami mo	make offerings
ōmi-ke ni	for her imperial feast.
tsukaematsuru to	They send cormorant forth
kamitsu se ni	over the upper shoals,
ukawa o tachi	they cast dipper nets
shimotsu se ni	across the lower shoals,

sade sashiwatasu	mountain and river
yamagawa mo	draw together to serve her—
yorite tsukauru	the reign of a *kami* indeed!
kami no mi-yo kamo	

yamagawa mo	A very *kami*
yorite matsureru	whom mountain and river
kamu nagara	draw together to serve,
tagitsu kafuchi no	she sets her boat to sail
funade suru kamo	over pools where waters surge.[13]

The primary aim of this verse is to proclaim the divine *kami*-nature of the empress. "As a *kami*" (*kamunagara*) the empress "acts out of her *kami*-nature" or "manifests her *kami*-nature" (*kamusabisesu to*) in climbing the Yoshino hill and performing a land-viewing ritual (*kuni-mi*), which is represented as bringing blessings, fertility, and prosperity to the country. According to Hitomaro, time and space both revolve around the person of the empress. In his rhetorical representation of the politics of sacral power, the *kami* of the mountains and the river recognize the superior power of the empress and, thus, worship her. The seasonal cycle also participates in this recognition of the priority of the claims of ontological or instantiated sacrality over locative sacrality by garlanding the empress in spring and autumn. This fact, Hitomaro proclaims, proves that the present reign of Empress Jitō is truly that of an august *kami* (*kami no miyo kamo*).

In an important sense one can say that the symbolic power of the land-viewing ritual was based on the conflation of what Kenneth Burke would have called scene-act, scene-agent, and scene-agency ratios.[14] That is, place, person, act, and agency are all immediately related and asserted to be appropriately so related. Sacral power was already invested in the mountains and riverland (the scene) in the *kami*, but here the claim is pressed that it is the presence of the divine sovereign (the agent) on the summit, performing the ritual viewing of the land and pronouncing words of praise or *yogoto* (the act and agency), which alone is efficacious in promoting fertility and prosperity.[15]

The rhetorical claims proffered above are based on the *presence* of the sovereign or imperial prince as a living *kami*, yet the inverse case can equally occasion powerful rhetorical representations. That is, if the presence of the sovereign qualitatively transforms a site, so does the *absence of the sovereign, especially that occasioned by death.* The *banka* (funeral laments) from early Japan are based upon this symbolic equation. In *Man'yôshû* 1.29–31, for instance, Hitomaro speaks of the Omi area, which, "though a barbarous place" (*hina ni wa aredo*), was immediately transformed into a sacred place when Emperor Tenji (r. 662–71) built his palace there at Otsu.[16] At the time Hitomaro visited the site, however, this capital had been abandoned for many years, the buildings were crumbling, and the grounds were overgrown with grass and weeds. Yet, by recalling the former grandeur of the place resulting from the sovereign's presence, Hitomaro rhetorically heightens the sense of physical and emotional devastation wrought in the wake of his absence. In *MYS* 1.29–31, even the local *kami*, to whom these verses were addressed, are represented as still longing for the emperor:

Omi no araretaru miya o suguru toki, Kakinomoto Asomi no Hitomaro no tsukuru uta	Poem by Kakinomoto Hitomaro on passing the ruined capital at Omi

tamatasuki	Since the reign
Unebi no yama no	of the Master of the Sun
Kashiwara no	at Kashiwara
hijiri no miyo yu	by Unebi Mountain
aremashishi	of the jeweled sleeve cords,
kami no kotogoto	all *kami* who have been born
tsuga no ki no	have ruled the realm under heaven,
iya tsugitsugi ni	each following each
ame no shita	like generations of the spruce,
shirashimeshishi o	in Yamato
sora ni mitsu	that spreads to the sky.
Yamato o okite	What was in his mind
aoniyoshi	that he would leave it
Nara yama o koe	and cross beyond the hills of Nara
ikasama ni	beautiful in blue earth?
omōshimeseka	Though a barbarous place
amazakaru	at the far reach of the heavens,
hina ni wa aredo	here in the land of Omi
iwabashiru	where the waters race on stone,
Omi no kuni no	at the Otsu Palace
Sasanami no	in Sasanami
Otsu no miya ni	by the rippling waves,

ame no shita	the Emperor,
shirashimeshikemu	the divine Prince,
Sumeroki no	ruled the realm under heaven.
kami no mikoto no	Though we hear
ōmiya wa	this was the great palace,
koko to kikedomo	though they tell us
ōtono wa	here were the mighty halls,
koko to iedomo	now it is rank
harugusa no	with spring grasses.
shigeku oitaru	Mist rises
kasumi tachi	and the spring sun is dimmed.
haruhi no kireru	Gazing on the ruins of the great
momoshiki no	palace,
ōmiyadokoro	its ramparts thick with wood and
mireba kanashimo	stone,
	I am filled with sorrow.

hanka	Envoys
Sasanami no	Cape Kara in Shiga
Shiga no Karasaki	at Sasanami
sakiku aredo	you are as before, but
ōmiyabito no	you wait for the courtiers'
fune machikanetsu	boats in vain.

Sasanami no	Waters in the deep bends
Shiga no ōwada	of Shiga's lake at Sasanami
yodomu tomo	you are calm, yet
mukashi no hito ni	you can never meet again
mata mo awameyamo	those people from the past.[17]

This verse is built upon the mythico-symbolic complex of imperial divine descent from the sun goddess. The emperor had transformed a desolate site into a mighty capital by his presence, but with his death (here euphemistically referred to as "crossing the hills of Nara") the capital had been abandoned. The forlorn state of the site, however, is rhetorically used by Hitomaro as "proof" of the sacral power of the person of the emperor.

In this brief excursus we have seen how the mythic narrative of the death of Yamato-takeru may be usefully revisioned by focusing on the politics of sacral power in early Japan. We have also found the same informing symbolic logic in that myth, other narratives of mythistory, and even in other literary genres from early Japan. I hope to have demonstrated something of what is to be gained by refocusing on the politics of sacral power in these various narrative and rhetorical representations, not the least of which is the restoration of historical human agents, with different and competing desires and valuations of the world, in our own discussions and representations of myth. Let us end where we began, with the line from Carlo Ginzburg: "The attempt to attain knowledge of the past is also a journey into the world of the dead."[18] In our "journeys" as historians of religions, we need to acknowledge the various individuals, factions, and communities among the dead rather than continuing to consign them in our narrative reports to a homogenous population as "the Japanese," "the Yanoama," and so forth and, thus, to anonymity.

NOTES

1. I have treated these topics in an earlier study. See *Ritual Poetry and the Politics of Death in Early Japan* (Princeton, 1989).

2. Mircea Eliade and Lawrence E. Sullivan come to mind here. Cp. Eliade, "Mythologies of Death: An Introduction" in *Occultism, Witchcraft, and Cultural Fashions: Essays in Comparative Religions* (Chicago, 1976) 32–46; and Lawrence E. Sullivan, *Icanchu's Drum: An Orientation to Meaning in South American Religions* (New York, 1988) especially 468–80, 660–72.

3. Sullivan, *Ichanu's Drum*, 469.

4. H. Byron Earhart, *Japanese Religion: Unity and Diversity*, 3rd ed. (Belmont, Calif., 1982) 8. The Norinaga quotation is from Shigeru Matsumoto, *Motoori Norinaga, 1730–1801* (Cambridge, Mass., 1970) 84. While using the term *the sacred* as a rough equivalent of *kami* may have the advantage of suggesting the diffuseness of the latter, I am uncomfortable with this since *kami* is a noun, while *the sacred* is an adjective masquerading as a noun.

5. Joseph M. Kitagawa, *On Understanding Japanese Religion* (Princeton, 1987) 44. The internal quotation is from Tsuda Sōkichi, "The Idea of Kami in Ancient Japanese Classics," *T'oung Pao* 52 (1966) 294.

6. A famous modern example of the persistence of the nativist representation of this cultural age is the introduction to the Nippon Gakujutsu Shinkōkai translation of the *Man'yōshū* (New York, 1965). There one finds, for instance, highly suspect statements such as the following:

> Genuineness of thought and feeling pervades all the Manyō poems, with scarcely any trace of vanity or frivolity. The prevailing atmosphere is happy, bright and peaceful. Frontier-guards departing for distant shores pledge their loyalty to the Throne and frankly record their personal

loves and the sorrows of separation, but never a murmur of grudge or resentment. A sanguinary and martial spirit is conspicuous by its absence . . . [one finds instead] a charming revelation of the close intimacy and friendliness that characterized the relationship between sovereign and subject in ancient Japan. (xiv)

For the ideologically informed representation of the religion of early Japan, see ibid., xxxviii–xlvii.

7.   Ivan Morris, *The Nobility of Failure: Tragic Heroes in the History of Japan* (New York, 1975).

8.   Donald Philippi, trans., *Kojiki* (Tokyo, 1968) 235. For the original, see *Nihon koten bungaku taikei* (Tokyo: Iwanamishoten, hereafter *NKBT*), 1:208–11.

9.   Philippi, *Kojiki,* 246, slightly adapted. See also *NKBT* 1:218–19.

10.   For a fuller analysis of this point, see Ebersole, *Ritual Poetry and the Politics of Death,* 45–49.

11.   Philippi, *Kojiki,* 360–61, slightly adapted. See *NKBT* 1:316–17.

12.   W. G. Aston, trans., *Nihongi* (Rutland, Vt., 1972) 1:341–42, slightly adapted. See *NKBT* 67:466–67.

13.   Ian Hideo Levy, trans., *The Ten Thousand Leaves* (Princeton, 1984) 57–58, slightly adapted. For the original, see *NKBT* 4:30–31.

14.   See Kenneth Burke, *A Grammar of Motives.* (Berkeley, 1969). Originally published by Prentice-Hall in 1945.

15.   This claim of exclusive prerogative, which reserves to the sovereign or her or his representatives the right and ability to perform this ritual, was apparently challenged by other historical agents who climbed various hills to perform similar rites. These ritual performances should be understood as explicit challenges to the throne. They also represent a common expression of the politics of sacral power, for by occupying specially delineated sites marked out for ritual purposes one could symbolically assume the role others would reserve to themselves. See, Ebersole, *Ritual Poetry and the Politics of Death,* 23–30.

16.   For a translation of this verse, see Ian Hideo Levy, trans., *The Ten Thousand Leaves* (Princeton, 1981) 53–55. The original may be found in *NKBT* 4:26–27. For a fuller "reading" of this verse from a history of religions perspective focusing on the ritual performative aspects of the verse, see Ebersole, *Ritual Poetry and the Politics of Death,* 65–72. There I also explain why Levy's translation of the two poetic envoys must be amended to capture the fact that the verses were directed to the *kami* of the place.

17.   *NKBT* 4:26–27; Levy, *The Ten Thousand Leaves,* 53–55,

adapted. The translations of the envoys are my own. For a fuller treatment of these verses, see Ebersole, *Ritual Poetry and the Politics of Death*, 65–72.

18. Carlo Ginzburg, *Ecstasies: Deciphering the Witches' Sabbath* (New York, 1991) 24.

CHAPTER 16

To Hell and Back: Death, Near-Death, and Other Worldly Journeys in Early Medieval China

Robert Ford Campany

"To Hell and Back"—in choosing this phrase as my title, I'd intended a simple play on words. As used in American English, the phrase builds metaphorically on the extreme distance and otherness of hell to describe a journey to some place in this world that, like hell, is not only far away but typically difficult to reach and often distinctly unpleasant once one has arrived. Here, of course, the wordplay was going to consist of taking the metaphor literally in a talk about stories of actual journeys to hell and back again. But when I told my dear teacher Tony Yu about my title, he said I should see Audie Murphy's movie of the same title. And, as usual, his advice was excellent.

In *To Hell and Back* (made in 1955), Murphy—who was the most decorated American soldier in World War II—plays himself. Unexpectedly, there were two things about the movie that struck me as directly relevant to my own discussion. First, Murphy is a noncommissioned soldier, an *ordinary* guy (no West Point specialist) who happens to excel at gutsy ground combat, and the film stresses his ordinariness throughout. He could be anybody. Second, there is not only the reality and immediacy of the film—a real war hero playing himself—but also its tonality of *everydayness* even in the face of death, a tonality often expressed through grim humor. This quality is clearest in the scene, late in the European war, of a tank and infantry battle in eastern France in which Murphy, acting alone, holds off whole platoons of the advancing enemy by remaining in an exposed forward position and calling in pinpoint artillery fire over a radio transmitter. At the moment when the German troops are almost on top of Murphy, the artillery officer on the other end of the line asks frantically, "How close are they?" Murphy says coolly, "Hold the phone and I'll let you talk to 'em."

In China from the third to the seventh centuries of the common era, the Other World of death, the afterlife, and the realm of spirits and gods was being massively modified by the assimilation of Buddhist doctrine and practice. The influx of Buddhism spurred a grand series of adjustments in and new mappings of the otherworldly terrain. The translation of Buddhist scriptures into Chinese revealed an entire cosmology. It laid bare not only the doctrines of karma and rebirth but also definite mechanisms by which death and rebirth were regulated, including ritual vehicles for the participation of the living in these processes. And, to specialists, it imparted techniques of meditation and visualization by which the other worlds of Buddha-realms and pure lands could be constructed even in the midst of this world by the power of mind. Meanwhile, partly in reaction to Buddhism's impact, China's own indigenous higher religion—Taoism—began to map its own otherworldly terrain. Here the mapping was done not by translation but by revelation (itself actually a kind of translation): female and male deities residing in levels of the heavens so exalted that they had never before been known began descending and speaking to a few select individuals, whose writings on what they saw and heard formed the nucleus of a scriptural canon to rival that of the foreign religion. These revelations, which claimed to encompass and supercede Buddhist teachings, taught a new vision of the ranks of heavens, the true shape and nature of the earth, and the complex sinuosities of the subterranean realm. They, too, described definite mechanisms by which death and afterlife were regulated, as well as ritual vehicles for the involvement of the living. They, too, imparted a variety of techniques—visualization, respiration, alchemical preparations, diet—by which divine Perfected beings could be summoned from other worlds to the midst of this world, and through which the adept could hope to travel in spirit to the highest heavens and to the farthest reaches of the earth, even to the distant isles and mountains where transcendents dwelt and rare herbs of immortality grew. In both cases, then, other worlds that were by nature fantastic and glorious—of a beauty and a radiance indescribable in human language—were made accessible to those few adepts with the leisure and resources needed to master the specified techniques.

But alongside these specialized religious techniques and texts, other genres of texts charted the newly revealed worlds in more public forms. Among these were large numbers of tales, typically written by and about laypersons of the lower and middle strata of the official class or ordinary monks and nuns, describing journeys to and from the realms of the dead, of the gods, and of the celestial buddhas. These tales focus on the Audie Murphys of the religious world, ordinary men and women who—usually, not by their own design, but by fate or accident—journey to, or receive a visit from, the spirit-world and then describe what they have experienced.[1] And in these tales, the other world that the ordinary protagonist discovers and describes is often surprising, not for its fantastic otherworldliness, but precisely for its similitude to this familiar world of ours. Hence the inflection of my subtitle: "Death, Near-Death, Afterlife, and *Other Worldly Journeys* in Early Medieval China."

In what follows, I want, first, to illustrate these two themes—the ordinariness of the protagonist-traveler and the worldliness of the other world he or she discloses—by discussing just a few of the many examples of two selected story-types from this large corpus of narratives: the death-summons and the return from death. (A closely related story-type that I do not treat here is that of the ghost appearance.[2]) Then in each case I want to compare these story-types to closely related motifs in canonical or more mainstream Buddhist and/or Taoist texts in order to show exactly how the tales differ in emphasis from the other texts. This comparison will illustrate a more general point that bears some pondering: how common plots and action-structures can be used in a culture to make substantially different points about the other world and thus do different religious work. Finally, I will conclude by reflecting on why, in their cultural and religious context, the authors of these tales shaped them in the ways they did.

THE DEATH-SUMMONS

The essential background on the medieval Chinese concept of the personal metaphysics or physiology of death is this: as in most other cultures I know, death was taken to be a disintegration of elements the conjunction of which constitutes life. There was, on the one hand, the body, which upon death became the object of mourners' ritual attentions. On the other hand, there were not one but multiple souls, grouped into two basic types: the *po* or earth-soul or *yin*-soul, which upon death, whatever else it was thought to do, descended into the earth, usually to linger in the vicinity of the tomb; and the *hun* or cloud-soul or *yang*-soul, whose proper destiny was to ascend upwards into the atmosphere or journey outward into the cosmos, though in this period, largely due to Buddhist influence, it was coming to be thought of as first detoured through an array of underground "earth-prisons" for judgment and purgation. Metaphysically speaking, these three basic elements of the person were not distinct kinds of substance (à la "matter vs. spirit") but were all one substance—*qi* or vital energy—found in various *degrees* of subtlety or turbidity.

Now, reflecting the bureaucratic cast of Chinese afterlife imagery in this and earlier (as well as later) periods, death is usually pictured in the tales I will speak of as an official summons to the cloud-soul to assume a government post in the other world, delivered by low-level message bearers or lictors and an escort party.[3] Here are two of the more straightforward examples:

> During the Jin [Dynasty], when Wang Wendu was subduing the Guangling area, he suddenly saw two escort officers carrying a summons-placard written in swan-head script coming forward to summon him. Greatly perturbed, Wang asked the escorts: "What office am I to hold?" The escorts replied: "You are summoned to serve as North-Subduing General, Commandant of Xu and Yan Provinces." Wang said, "I've already held this office. Why am I being summoned again?" The spirits [*gui*] said: "That was only in the human realm. What you are now to serve in is a celestial office [*tianshang guan*]." At this Wang was very frightened. He then saw that a whole crowd of dark-clad men and black-jacketed lictors had come to welcome him to his post. Shortly afterwards, Wang died.[4]

> Liu Qingsong of Guangling got up one morning and saw a man clad in court attire handing him a tablet which said: "Summoned to serve as Governor of Lu Commandery." When this exchange was done, the man departed and was seen no more. The next day he came again and said, "You should now report to your post."

Qingsong knew he must die, so he instructed his wife and children in domestic matters, then took a bath. That evening a carriage and horses appeared, with an escort party to the left and right. Qingsong suddenly expired. Then his family members all saw him mount the carriage and set off toward the south. After about a hundred paces he gradually ascended [into the air], then vanished.[5]

These stories are typical in that the protagonists do not welcome their summons, despite the fact that it means they will occupy an office in the other world and thus avoid consignment to the nameless masses of the dead not of the official classes. These two protagonists do not think of avoiding or challenging the summons: they apparently take it to be as inevitable as death itself. In other tales, however, complications arise—and they are just the sort of complications one would expect in a narrative tradition that imagined death as a summons to official duty.

During the Han, Zhou Shi of Xiapei [in Shandong] was once traveling to Donghai. On the way he met a lictor who was carrying a scroll-book and who asked for a ride. When they had gone a little over ten *li*, the lictor told Shi: "I have something to do. I am leaving my book here on your boat. Be sure not to open it." After he'd gone, Shi snuck a peek at the book. It was a list of various dead people; and the last entry was his own name. Soon the lictor returned to find Shi still looking at the book. The lictor said angrily, "I told you not to look, yet you did anyway!" Shi knocked his head on the floor till blood ran. After a long time, the lictor said, "I am grateful for your carrying me such a long way. But I cannot expunge your name from this book. Go back home today and do not emerge from your house for three years, and you will escape. And tell no one that you have seen my book."
    Shi then returned home and did not go out. After over two years had passed, his family began to think him very odd. Then a neighbor died, and Shi's father grew angry and insisted that he pay his condolences. Shi had no choice; he was compelled to go out the door, and as soon as he did he saw the lictor, who said: "I told you not to come out for three years. Now that you have come out, what else is there to be done? Because of my attempts to avoid seeing you, I have suffered whipping and beating. Now that I have seen you, there is no other choice. Three days from now, at noon, I will come to take you." Shi returned home in

tears and told his family the whole story. His father did not believe him, but his mother stayed by his side day and night. At noon on the third day, [the lictor] indeed showed up to take him, and so he died.[6]

In the traditional Chinese moral economy, to receive a favor is to incur an irrevocable obligation of repayment; so here, though it costs him dearly, the otherworldly lictor repays the protagonist's favor by offering a set of conditions by which to avoid his destined end. Once the conditions are violated, however—the lictor's obligation to Zhou Shi having been satisfied—he must perform his duty as an otherworldly functionary and "take in" the unfortunate man. There are other stories in which the protagonist manages to talk his way out of the summons by "nominating" others to take his place or by citing precisely the same factors living Chinese used to excuse themselves from official duty in *this* world —unworthiness, illness, or an aged parent in need of care.[7]

What I mean by the "worldliness" of the other world and the ordinariness of the protagonists in these tales comes into sharper focus when we compare how the same motif of the death-summons is treated in canonical religious literature from the same period. Take, for example, the famous case of Shangqing Taoist scriptures, revealed to the visionary Yang Xi over the period 364–70 and passed to his associates in the governing class, Xu Mi (303–73) and his youngest son Xu Hui (341–c. 370). One of these scriptures contains the following account of a dream of Yang Xi's in which the young Xu Hui was summoned. The writer is Xu Hui.

> In the third year of the Xingning reign-period [365], on the 27th of the fourth month, Master Yang dreamt he saw a man dressed in a vermilion robe and basket cap, holding two tablets in his hands. Projecting from his robe were two other tablets. He summoned Xu Yufu [i.e., Xu Hui] to appear. On all the tablets were written characters in green, which said, "Summoned to serve as chamberlain." A moment later I [i.e., Xu himself] appeared. Yang pointed to me and said, "This is young Master Xu." I myself said, "I am supposed to have thirteen more years. If you summon me now, I will not yet have acquired an understanding of the proper forms of procedure [as required by the post]." The other answered, "If such is the case, you may submit a protest,"

and I composed one, stating that I had not yet come to understand the procedural norms, but that I was just then diligently working at it and required an additional thirteen years. He then bowed to me and departed.[8]

Strikingly absent here is the tonality of everydayness we saw in the tales. First, Xu Hui's reasons for seeking an extension of his stay in this world are different: he dares not mention such worldly concerns as family obligations, illness, or even some vague form of unworthiness; his sole reason for petitioning for reprieve from the summons is that he might continue to study the esoteric "procedures" being progressively revealed to Yang Xi in the scriptures. Second, the context of the account differs utterly from that of the tales: at the time of this dream Xu Hui had recently taken up ascetic retreat on the sacred hills of Mao Shan in order to devote himself full time to visualization and perhaps alchemical practices; the divine visitor is an emissary from the same Shangqing heavens that were in communication with Yang Xi. In other words, the death-summons in this case—although not in the tales—comes to a religious adept in the context of a total program of religious life, itself understood as a preparation in this world for one's more exalted role in the divine hierarchy of the unseen world. The chief similarity to the tales is that here, too, the death-summons constitutes an untimely interruption: like his counterparts in the tales, Xu Hui is depicted as far from overjoyed at his summons (yet— note again—for different reasons), despite the high rank he is promised;[9] and he seems to have only temporarily delayed its execution, as he died five years later instead of the requested thirteen: "He burnt incense," runs the account of his death, "and did obeisance on the stone altar at the entrance to the north cavern [of Mao Shan]. Then he prostrated himself and did not arise. When, the following morning, they discovered his body, it was as if he were still alive."[10] The writer then adds the telling comment: "From this it is clear that he was deliberately seeking 'concealed transformation,' cutting off early the dust of the world." This marks a final and important difference from the way the death-summons is handled in the tales: although they may be ambivalent about leaving so soon, ultimately this world—for Taoists of this period at least—is mere "dust" and impurity, a training ground due for obliteration in the imminent apocalypse, not a place in which any adept would want to linger. Hence the ritual suicide by consumption of deadly but divinizing alchemical potions for which some adepts were known—and which may have been the reason Xu Hui himself appeared "as if still alive" the morning after his death.[11] By sharp contrast, in the culture of the tales it is life in this world that is precious. One is rarely in a hurry to leave it for an other world that in any event seems not very different from this world, except for the single and most unfortunate fact that one is dead.

THE RETURN FROM DEATH

If death is imagined as a summons, it is a summons to undertake a journey: the cloud-soul of the newly dead must travel to a distant place to take up its post or to join the ranks of the dead at one of several standard, cosmic destinations. But there are many stories of ordinary people who succeed in returning from death to reinhabit their bodies and, often after a brief recovery period, tell the living of their experiences in the other world.[12] Here is an example from the tale literature:

> In the first year of the *jingping* reign-period [423], a certain man in Qu'e died of illness. He saw his father up in heaven, and his father said to him: "According to your tally records you ought to have lived eight more years; but instead you've had the unexpected misfortune to die and enter the realm for the punishment of sins. I've tried to get you placed, but there are no vacancies in the offices now. There was a vacancy only with the Duke of Thunder [one of several types of rain deities], so I'm filing a request to fill this post." So he dispatched the request to the higher authorities, and the son was able to fill this position. He was then sent up to Eastern Liao [in Manchuria]. He rode on the Dew Carriage while the Ox scattered water in all directions. He wasn't even halfway [back?] when he received new orders to go to Western Liao. When he was finished there he returned, saw his father, and desperately pleaded to go back [to life], saying he did not like his job. So his father sent him back, and he was able to revive.[13]

This story plays in an unusual way on the motif of the "mistaken summons," in which the dead protagonist returns to life because his or her death-summons was delivered too early by otherworldly officials; for here, although the protagonist has died eight years ahead of his destined time, he remains in the unseen world.[14] More typical of return-from-death tales is the role (as seen here) of a dead relative or friend in negotiating on the protagonist's behalf— negotiations that sometimes become amusingly complex. In this case, the reason for the protagonist's return to life is that his new otherworldly job is not to his liking. In other tales, people return for a host of similarly "worldly" reasons: because they were mistakenly summoned instead of someone else with the same name or physical appearance; because they prove inept at the post they are given; because they recommend a better candidate for the job; because they know someone on the inside of the bureaucracy who is able to get them shipped back to life; because they persuade spirit-officials to let them return to take care of orphaned children or widowed spouses in this world; or because they successfully slip bribes to difficult doormen.[15]

During these same centuries, Buddhist authors—both monks and laymen—were writing and collecting tales similar in form but with some significant differences in content. Here is one example.[16]

Li Qing, a native of Yuqian [Village] in Wuxing,[17] served under [Duke] Huan Wen as Commander in Chief, Adjutant Supervisor of Garrisons, and Protector-General. While in office he contracted an illness, whereupon he returned home and died. After some time had passed he revived. He said that at first he received orders from men carrying pennants[18] and saying that "the Duke" wanted to see him. Qing thought it must be [Duke Huan] Wen summoning him, so he got up, fastened his belt, and set out. Upon going out the door he saw a bamboo sedan chair and was told to get in it. Two men carried it along as quickly as if they were galloping horses.

They arrived at a vermilion door, where [Qing] saw [his old acquaintance] Ruan Jing,[19] who at that time had been dead for thirty years. Ruan asked Qing, "When did you arrive? Do you have any news of my family?" Qing said, "Your family is extraordinarily wicked." Ruan wept profusely at this, then asked: "Do you know how my own sons and grandsons are doing?" "They're all fine," Qing answered. Ruan said, "I'll see to it that you are released. Can you take care of my family?" Qing replied, "If you can do as you say, I couldn't possibly repay your kindness." Ruan then said, "The official in charge of this office, the

monk Sengda, has been very kind to me. I will plead with him."
He then went inside [the bureau] for a long time.

Someone then was sent out to announce: "The four-storied
temple outside the gate was erected by this office. Sengda ordinarily enters this temple at dawn to worship. You should go there
to make your request of him." So Qing went to that temple,
where he saw a monk who said to him: "Seven lifetimes ago you
were my disciple. Having received blessings now over seven lifetimes, you have become lost among the pleasures of the world
and have forgotten your original [good] karma. Because you've
turned your back on good and embraced evil, you deserve severe
punishment; but [from] today you can [still] repent and mend
your ways. Tomorrow a monk will appear in order to help you."

Qing got back in his sedan chair and passed a bitterly cold
night. The next morning the monk Sengda indeed appeared at
the temple, and Qing prostrated himself before him. Sengda told
him, "You should reform your heart toward good, taking refuge
in the Buddha, the Dharma, and the Sangha. If you accept the
Triple Refuge, you can avoid a violent death. Take heed of this:
otherwise, you'll undergo suffering!" Qing at once accepted [the
Refuge]. Then he saw the monk Sengda had mentioned the day
before, and [Sengda] knelt before this monk and made the following request: "This man was my disciple in a former life.[20] He
forgot the truth and disobeyed the Dharma. For this he was
about to undergo punishment. But, aided by his previous karma,
he has now taken the Refuge, and so I ask that he be extended
mercy and forgiveness." The other monk replied: "Because he
was formerly a person of merit, he may be spared."

With that he was returned to the same vermilion door as
before, from which a messenger shortly emerged and said: "Officer Li, you may now depart." Then Ruan also came out, gave
Qing a green bamboo staff, and told him to close his eyes and
mount it. Qing did as he was told, and suddenly found himself
back at his house. In the house people were wailing. It was so full
of neighbors and relatives that he couldn't get inside. Just then
someone returned with the coffin they'd bought, and the family
and guests went out to look at it, leaving only the corpse [inside]
on the floor. Qing went in and approached his corpse. When he
smelled its stench, he was reluctant to return to it. But then the
people outside started crowding back in again, and before he
knew it he had reentered the corpse, and thus he revived.

So [as promised] he took care of Ruan's family, dividing up
their residences. Thereupon he devoted his heart to the Three

Treasures, remained faithful to the Buddha's teachings, and became a virtuous [lay] disciple.[21]

As glimpsed in this and many similar tales, the Buddhist afterlife is, in one sense, no less "worldly" than its counterpart in tales not obviously Buddhist in orientation: here too there is a spiritual bureaucracy, and here too it is possible to negotiate a return to life based on prior relationships and the exchange of favors. But there are also differences that show how Buddhist authors bent this motif to their own ends. Most obvious is the moral valorization, which is even more strongly emphasized in other stories' graphic depictions of the torments inflicted on sinners. More subtle is the mention of Li Qing being disgusted at the stench of his own corpse—a theme frequent in canonical Buddhist literature and related to actual meditation practices used to realize the impermanence of the self. Furthermore, the Buddhist return-from-death tales, as in this case, almost always note the effect on the protagonist (as well as on others who hear) of his or her experience in the other world: both the experience and its secondary narration profoundly transform human beings by impressing upon them the reality and gravity of Buddhist teachings concerning karmic retribution. While the non-Buddhist return-from-death tales are equally concerned to map the unfamiliar terrain of the new afterlife introduced during this period, they rarely seem intended to admonish the reader to adopt any specific practices or beliefs other than a healthy conviction that the soul survives death and may be judged according to its merits and faults. Thus they rarely conclude as the Buddhist stories almost always do by noting the protagonist's transformation.

A final difference between Buddhist and non-Buddhist return-from-death tales is that it was not unusual for the latter to be turned to polemical use. Here is a conveniently brief example.

> Li Tong of Pucheng died, then after three days returned [to life]. He said he had seen the monk Fazu expounding the *Suramgama sūtra* for King Yama. He had also seen the Taoist Wang Fou: he was chained down and begging for forgiveness from Fazu, but Fazu refused to let him go because he had betrayed the Sage [i.e., the Buddha] and only came to regret it after his death.[22]

The Taoist Wang Fou mentioned in this tale was the author of *Scripture on the Conversion of the Barbarians* (*Huahu jing*), an infamous anti-Buddhist tract that, as best as can be judged from surviving fragments, maintained that the Buddha was merely an avatar of the Taoist sage Laozi and that the "religion" he founded was nothing more than a cosmic plot to render the purportedly noxious Indian race extinct by mandating clerical celibacy.[23]

Once more I would like to emphasize the special character of these tales, both Buddhist and non-Buddhist, by comparing them to literature produced closer to the Buddhist and Taoist mainstreams. First, so far as I am aware, this motif of return-from-death is virtually nonexistent in scriptural texts of either tradition: the motif itself, in other words, and not just the way it is dealt with in the tales, seems to be noncanonical. Second, when we do find journeys to hell and back in scriptures of this period, the journey is (to my knowledge) almost always made by a deity, religious adept, or shamanic visionary, not—as in the tales—by any ordinary monk and certainly not by laypersons.[24] The classic exemplar is the Buddhist figure of Mulian (the Chinese version of the Indian Maudgalyāyana), a shamanic monk who spiritually travels to hell to rescue his mother's soul from torment. Even in noncanonical, quite "popular" narratives of Mulian's exploits, such as the "transformation texts" found at Dunhuang, his meditative powers and spiritual vision are heavily emphasized, as is his arduous training. Mulian, though he may be a spiritual hero, is not presented as a figure capable of being emulated by ordinary readers and hearers of his story; his experiences are not seen as typical.[25] Third, there are (nonnarrative) canonical texts in both traditions that seek to describe the afterlife world with a thoroughness and a programmatic specificity largely absent from tale literature. And these cosmological texts portray the spirit-world—both the hells and the heavens—as a *fantastic* terrain, where the joys of the blessed far outshine this world in splendor and where likewise the pains of the karmically unfortunate are exaggerated in the extreme.[26] Once again, in sharp contrast to these various textual traditions, the return-from-death tales without exception concern quite ordinary men and women; and the unseen world they disclose is often surprising, not for its indescribable wonders, but for its familiarity. Some tales even go so far as to record the protagonist's explicit statement that what he or she saw while dead was "no different from this world."[27]

CONCLUSION

Surveying the cultural and religious context of the tales I've discussed, two features stand out. First, the early medieval period was a time in which many among the official class in China were sceptical of the soul's survival after death and the reality of the spirit-world. Their scepticism had a long and distinguished pedigree in the agnosticism of the Confucian tradition in which they had all, to varying degrees, been schooled and in the critical rationalism of the great first-century thinker and essayist Wang Chong and others like him. Second, there had been recent and profound changes in the shape and character of the other world, including a massive bureaucratization of what had earlier been a more mythological set of images—perhaps a religious response to the profound changes in Chinese culture inaugurated by the bureaucratic and administrative mentality of the Han empire—and, even more recently, the coming of Buddhism, which fit quite well with the bureaucratic trend while also adding moral valorization, karmic etiology, and procedural complexity to the indigenous afterlife images.

Responding, first, to the scepticism of their age, these authors crafted arguments in narrative form. The tales are clearly intended to impress, persuade, convert, and convince their readers that, as one author put it, "the spirit world is no lie." These authors, quite unlike the authors of texts who wrote from within the religious establishments (whether for an elite or a popular audience), sought not so much to construct a schematic order or procedural system for the other world as simply to move their readers to take it seriously as a reality. The Buddhist and non-Buddhist tales are no different in this respect; they differ only in the particular shape of the other world they portray and, more precisely, in the claims that world makes on how one lives in this world.

Responding, secondly, to the recent changes in the afterlife, these authors sought above all to domesticate it. "Domestication" as a religious act can take many forms: I have in mind here not so much the mapping and ordering, "locative" sort of domestication —though the tales to a small extent can be seen as doing this as well—as the sort of domestication that makes the other world a "home" with a recognizably human face, a human space in which there is room for maneuver and negotiation, a regime comfortable for its fallibility, friendly in its benign corruption.

The narrative features I've highlighted—the ordinariness of the protagonists, the worldliness of the other world they report—were an apt vehicle for this persuasive and domesticative enterprise.

The ordinary protagonists in these tales are passive; things happen to them; they do not and need not undertake the active regimens of the specialist in order to make contact with the other world. Further, the social roles they are depicted as occupying are precisely the sorts of roles occupied by those who read the tales. Since, like Audie Murphy, these otherworld travelers could be anybody, their reports took on more rather than less credibility, and the experiences they report are immediately relevant because they are of the same sort that readers may expect for themselves.

Those experiences of the other world, moreover, were more rather than less credible to readers precisely because of their "worldliness." In their concreteness and immediacy of detail, and especially in the all-too-human quality with which they invest the other world, the accounts created a series of analogies and linkages to familiar aspects of life. They then, as it were, invited the reader to project or extend them outward beyond the boundary separating life from death, so that, though the boundary was left intact (if rendered slightly more permeable), the world on its other side was rendered an increasingly habitable space, well suited to the cultural expectations of the middling literati for whom it was thereby so carefully prepared.[28]

The authors of these tales, then, acted as psychopomps, leading their readers' imaginative souls on a tour conducted in the mode not of meditative visualization but of realistic narration.

NOTES

This Chapter was written expressly for oral delivery to a non-Sinological audience at the 1991 conference held at the Divinity School of the University of Chicago and organized by Ioan Culianu. Having considered revising it into a more recognizably and numbingly academic format by adding further evidence, documentation, and elaboration, I decided to leave it in its original form except for a few very minor changes, fully aware of its shortcomings as a "research article" of the sort that is supposed to impress specialists, deans, and tenure committees. Ioan invited me to join the conference rather late after Professor Anthony Yu had to withdraw. It was a daunting assignment, but something in Ioan's gentle humanity persuaded me that I could and should give it a try. I will always cherish his memory and resent whoever it was that denied him a full life and us a valuable colleague. I am grateful to Professor Yu for his oral comments delivered at the conference, and hope that he will pardon me for retaining the opening gambit on Audie Murphy's movie (which, as the reader will discern, does have a relationship to what I say here) even though he did not seem to find it amusing.

1.   They are *ordinary* in the sense that they are rather common-place monks or laypersons—and, often, not even particularly pious laypersons—not powerful religious specialists, shamans, highly accom-plished adepts, or wonder-workers. Few, however, are of the peasant class; most are of the lower grades of the official class.

2.   The best overview of the premodern Chinese ghost tale is An-thony C. Yu, "'Rest, Rest, Perturbed Spirit!' Ghosts in Traditional Chi-nese Fiction," *Harvard Journal of Asiatic Studies* 47:2 (1987) 397–434. For the period under discussion here, see also my "Ghosts Matter: The Culture of Ghosts in Six Dynasties *Zhiguai*," *Chinese Literature: Essays, Articles, Reviews* 13(1991) 15–34. For a study of the entire genre of texts of which the ones cited here constitute a very small proportion of exam-ples, see my *Strange Writing: Anomaly Accounts in Early Medieval China*, forthcoming from SUNY Press.

3.   Contrast other Chinese images such as that of the poetic funeral lament in the *Zhaohun* (Summons of the soul), where it is the living who summon the soul of the dead *back to the body*: see the translation in David Hawkes, *The Songs of the South* (Harmondsworth, 1985) 219–31.

4.   Item 158 in the tale collection *Youming lu*, in Lu Xun, ed., *Gu xiaoshuo gouchen, Lu Xun sanshinian ji* (n.p., 1941) 284. This work is hereafter cited as *LX*. Compare the versions in the seventh-century Bud-dhist encyclopedia *Fayuan zhulin, juan* 56 (712, register b, vol. 53 in the Taishō shinshū daizōkyō edition [Tokyo, 1924–34], hereafter cited as *FYZL*), and in the tenth-century court-sponsored encyclopedia *Taiping yulan, juan* 606.

5.   *Youming lu* item 217 (*LX* 301); cp. the text in the tenth-century compendium *Taiping guangji, juan* 321, item 5. This work is hereafter cited as *TPGJ*.

6.   Item 8 of *juan* 5 of the twenty-*juan* version of *Soushen ji* by Gan Bao, hereafter cited as *SSJ*; I have used an edition published in Taibei by Shijie shuju in 1982. Cp. the version in *FYZL* 46 (639a).

7.   See, e.g., *SSJ juan* 5, item 7, amusing in its elaborate negotia-tions between the protagonist Wang You and his would-be divine patron and summoner, Zhao Gongming. Wang begs off because of his aged mother. Compare *Yiyuan juan* 5, item 23, in which the skilled carpenter Shi Xiuzhi dodges his summons to the court of the divine Governor of

Taishan to make chairs by suggesting that one Liu Zheng be appointed instead. Liu indeed dies soon thereafter, while Shi survives. I have used the edition of the *Yiyuan* (attributed to Liu Jingshu) published in *Shuoku* (Taibei, 1963) 1:66–87.

8.   *Zhengao* (fascs. 637–40 in the *Zhengtong daozang* [Shanghai, 1925–27]) *juan* 17, p. 5b, line 10-p. and p. 6a line 6; translation following Michel Strickmann, "On the Alchemy of T'ao Hung-ching," in Holmes Welch and Anna Seidel, eds., *Facets of Taoism: Essays in Chinese Religion* (New Haven, 1979) 129, with his Wade-Giles romanizations converted to Pinyin for the sake of uniformity.

9.   The promise is also extended more poetically by the Perfected One Clear Numinosity at *Zhengao* 2.13a.6–10.

10.   *Zhengao* 20.10a.10–10b.2, thus far following Strickmann's translation; the following comment of Tao Hongjing is translated by me.

11.   Strickmann, "On the Alchemy," 159–62, discusses further the cases of Zhou Ziliang and of Tao Hongjing himself; the scene of Zhou's suicide is one of the most graphic, touching, and realistic in all Taoist literature. Note that both Zhou Ziliang and Tao Hongjing had visions or dreams of death-summons from spirits, recounted in the *Zhoushi mingtong ji* (*Daozang* fasc. 152) and discussed by Strickmann. Note that although Zhou's summons, like Xu's, was untimely—in this case it was forty-six years early—the transcendent who informed him of it asked, "But why should you continue to linger on among men, sowing sins?" (*Mingtong ji* 1.11a.5, following Strickmann, "On the Alchemy," 161).

12.   I have treated this story type in "Return-from-Death Narratives in Early Medieval China," *Journal of Chinese Religions* 18(1900) 91–125, giving a bibliography on the topic and translating some sixteen stories as examples.

13.   *Youming lu* item 241 (*LX* 308); Lu Xun cites as his source for this item *TPGJ juan* 373, but I am unable to locate it there or (so far) elsewhere.

14.   Compare the statement by a dead man who returns to urge his nephew to more faithful observance of lay Buddhist precepts: "I was not supposed to die when I did, but I was needed in the gods path of rebirth (*shendao*, i.e. *devagati*) to help count up the [sins and merits on] spirits' registers" (in *Mingxiang ji* item 101 [*LX* 516–17]).

15.   For further examples and discussion, see Campany, "Return-from-Death Narratives," 114–20.

16.   I am preparing a separate article on Buddhist return-from-death and related tales in this period. For other published translations, see, *infra alia*, the story of Zhao Wenruo in Donald Gjertson, *Miraculous Retribution: A Study and Translation of T'ang Lin's "Ming-pau chi,"* (Berkeley Buddhist Studies Series 8; Berkeley, 1989) 32–33; the story of

Yuan Zhizong in Campany, "Return-from-Death Narratives," 119–20; and the story of Zhao Tai in Karl S. Y. Kao, ed., *Classical Chinese Tales of the Supernatural and the Fantastic* (Bloomington, 1985) 166–71.

17.   The *FYZL* version places him in the Song period, but the *TPGJ* version gives no date. *LX* says the date should probably be Jin, not Song. I omit any mention of the period, which is in any case irrelevant to the plot.

18.   This is an unusual feature of messengers or lictors in these tales, and it is probably a signal of the Buddhist nature of the afterlife— pennants, banners, streamers, and pained curtains being commonly mentioned in Buddhist tales of this period but only rarely mentioned in other tales.

19.   As is usual in these tales, the text from here on refers to Ruan Jing by his given name, Jing. But because of its similarity to Qing, the protagonist's name, I will use his surname, Ruan, in the remainder of my translation to prevent confusion on the part of the reader.

20.   The surviving versions of the text differ here. This reading makes the most sense to me, though Lu Xun, for reasons unexplained, thought otherwise.

21.   *Mingxiang ji* item 29 (*LX* 472–73); cf. *FYZL juan* 95 (988c–989a) and *TPGJ juan* 379, item 2. There are minor discrepancies in wording among these versions but none that affect the basic sense of the story.

22.   *Youming lu* item 264 (*LX* 320).

23.   See Erik Zürcher, *The Buddhist Conquest of China* (Leiden, 1972) chap. 6.

24.   Not, that is, unless guided by a spirit, in the relatively rare motif of "tour of hell"—e.g., *Mingxiang ji* item 101 (cited above), much less prominent in China than it was in roughly contemporary Western traditions as shown by Martha Himmelfarb, *Tours of Hell: An Apocalyptic Form in Jewish and Christian Literature* (Philadelphia, 1983).

25.   See esp. Victor H. Mair, *Tun-huang Popular Narratives* (Cambridge, 1983) 87–121, for a complete translation of the transformation text (*bianwen*); and, for the best discussion of Mulian as "shaman," see Stephen F. Teiser, *The Ghost Festival in Medieval China* (Princeton, 1988) chap. 5. Paradigmatic Taoist travelers to hell, if there are any—figures parallel, that is, to Mulian—probably arose later; I am so far unaware of any such theme in Six Dynasties Taoist literature.

26.   In the case of Taoism, I have in mind early cosmographic "marvels" texts such as the *Shizhou ji* (Record of the Ten Continents), recently translated by Thomas E. Smith in "Record of the Ten Continents (Translation)," *Taoist Resources* 2.2 (1990) 87–119; others of a similar nature include *Dongming ji* and the *Shenyi jing*. These, in turn, all look back to

the *Shanhai jing* as their precursor. There are also Tao Hongjing's famous, if somewhat futile, attempts to systematize the jumble of what the Shang-qing revelations had to say about the organization and layout of the unseen world: see esp. *Zhengao, juan* 15–16, for the regions and organization of the realm of the dead, and, for the entire system schematized, his (*Dongxuan lingbao*) Zhenling weiye tu (*Daozang* fasc. 152), for a summary of whose structure see Michel Strickmann, "The Mao Shan Revelations: Taoism and the Aristocracy," *T'oung Pau* 63 (1977) 9, n. 13. More vivid than these formal schemes, however, are of course the actual descent accounts contained in the revelations to Yang Xi, with their dazzling descriptions of the various male and female transcendents and perfected ones whom Yang had the good fortune to meet. On early Chinese Buddhist underworld cosmographies, see Teiser, *The Ghost Festival*, chap. 6.

27.   For two examples—there are many more—see Campany, "Return-from-Death Narratives," 124, n. 73.

28.   A number of comparisons might be made with the roles (specifically) of *narrative* in constructions of other-worldly images discussed in such works as Carol Zaleski, *Otherworld Journeys: Accounts of Near-Death Experience in Medieval and Modern Times* (New York, 1987), and Jacques Le Goff, *The Birth of Purgatory*, trans. Arthur Goldhammer (Chicago, 1984).

CHAPTER 17

Sir Henry Vane: Mystical Piety in the Puritan Revolution

W. Clark Gilpin

In the summer of 1652, Sir Henry Vane the Younger was nearing the fortieth year of his life and the height of his political career. Perhaps no individual except Oliver Cromwell himself had done more to secure parliamentary victory in the civil wars with Charles I, to guide the fortunes of the Long Parliament, or to chart the foreign policy of the Commonwealth. From his youthful misadventures as governor of Massachusetts Bay in the 1630s, when he took the side of Anne Hutchinson and the antinomians against John Winthrop and the leading ministers, to his political apprenticeship with John Pym in the opening days of the Long Parliament, to the administrative skill he displayed as treasurer of the navy, Vane had developed the political acumen and the single-minded, occasionally even ruthless, pursuit of his objectives that made him one of the principal architects of the Puritan Commonwealth. Meanwhile, beginning with his successful negotiation of the Solemn League and Covenant between Parliament and the Scots in 1643, Vane had also earned a reputation as a leading and persistent advocate of religious toleration. His friend John Milton celebrated these achievements in July of 1652 with a sonnet, "To Sir Henry Vane the Younger:"

> Vane, young in years, but in sage counsel old,
> Than whom a better Senator ne'er held
> The helm of Rome . . . /To know
> Both spiritual power and civil, what each means,
> What severs each, thou hast learnt, which few have done.

The bounds of either sword to thee we owe.
Therefore on thy firm hand religion leans
In peace, and reck'ns thee her eldest son.[1]

Within a year, however, Cromwell had expelled the Long Parliament, and Vane had retired to his estates at Belleau, Lincolnshire, skeptical about what he regarded as the arbitrary power
of the Protectorate. There he began to publish his religious views,
both in such tracts as *The Retired Mans Meditations* (1655) and in
private prophesying sessions. His contemporaries were baffled.
Obscure allegories and mystical theology of "peculiar darkness"
seemed to have replaced the incisive oratory and diplomatic phrasing that for a full decade had made Vane "Parliament's draftsman"
for documents of political moment.[2] Pragmatic political judgment
was apparently submerged in millenarian enthusiasm, and Vane's
opinions came to be connected in the popular mind with sectarian
fanaticism, the abortive plots of the Fifth Monarchy Men, even
messianic pretensions. Hence, his later efforts to return to the political arena were greeted both with mistrust of his motives and
with fear of his acknowledged abilities. Cromwell imprisoned him
briefly in 1656 for publishing *A Healing Question,* a "seditious"
critique of the Protector's dependence on military force. And, following the restoration of the Stuarts, Vane was again imprisoned
and then executed in 1662, primarily, as Bishop Burnet recalled,
because of "the great opinion that was had of his parts and capacity to embroil matters again."[3]

But although his contemporaries—not to mention later
historians—generally combined respect for his political wiles with
the suspicion that his theological writings were, in the phrase of
David Hume, "absolutely unintelligible," Vane himself believed
that it was precisely the intersections between his religion and
political leadership that charted the course of his life.[4] Hence, any
effort to understand this leading figure within seventeenth-century
Puritanism must address the question of whether Henry Vane's
theological and political views represent, in some sense, a coherent
system. In raising this question, it is important to recognize that
Vane was a *lay* theologian who appropriated theological language
for his own purposes and in his own way. Although his thought
had a rough symmetry and what might be called an "experiential
logic," Vane was not systematically consistent or fully aware of the

theological implications of particular positions he espoused. By *system* I do not, therefore, intend to suggest that Vane's beliefs composed a logical system or a systematic theology. They perhaps bore greater resemblance to a gravitational system in which various opinions were held in more or less regular orbits by a central mass that was itself noticeably influenced by the tug of the encircling bodies. In the present essay, I shall argue that the center of this system was a mystical religious experience by which, as Vane himself described it, "faith is wrought in the soul, giving Christ an actual inhabitation and abode there, as . . . the causer and begetter of the soul into actual membership with himself, in his heavenly and spiritual human perfection."[5]

The *first* step in pursuing the coherence of Vane's thought is thus to associate him with the type of Puritan piety that Jerald C. Brauer, James F. Maclear, and Philip F. Gura have denominated "spirit mysticism" or "radical spiritism."[6] As a distinctive form of mystical spirituality, "Spiritism placed its major stress," these scholars have asserted, "not on a transitory union experience, but on the life lastingly transfigured by the possession of the Spirit."[7] This diverse movement of piety on the "radical wing" of Puritanism had its historical outcroppings in New England's antinomian controversy, among the spiritual preachers of the New Model Army, and in the rise of Quakerism.

Geoffrey F. Nuttall, in *The Holy Spirit in Puritan Faith and Experience,* argued that "the Puritan movement, in its various phases, has evinced itself to be a movement towards immediacy in relation to God," and he therefore concluded that the spiritist tradition of "radical Puritan devotion" represented a key to the development of Puritanism as a whole.[8] Without placing spiritism in the central role that Nuttall suggested, I would nonetheless assert that it was a highly significant strand in the complex fabric of Puritan piety and that Henry Vane was a particularly prominent representative of this strand. Some understanding of his religiosity, therefore, usefully complements research on "mainstream" Puritan piety, especially the excellent work of Charles E. Hambrick-Stowe.[9] And, in the tradition of William James, I would further suggest that examination of Henry Vane's piety will perhaps disclose certain general traits of Puritan piety, made "prominent and easy to notice in those religious experiences which are most one-sided, exaggerated, and intense."[10]

Second, by describing spirit mysticism as one strand in a larger fabric of piety, I wish to emphasize both that Vane's intellectual tools for reflection were appropriated from the larger Puritan tradition of experimental divinity and also that mystical experience gave the tradition a particular twist. Indeed, in Vane's piety we see Puritanism's meditative imagination in the full exercise of its freedom. The world, society, and his own duty were drawn into thematic unity by what William Haller has called "the characteristic Puritan version of the age-old epic of man's spiritual striving . . . the drama of sin and grace, of the war between Christ and Satan, experienced immediately in the soul."[11] But the drama was rewritten throughout in order to place at its center immediate, mystical union with Christ. Vane's spirit mysticism dramatized the death and rebirth of religion in order to express a comprehensive religious vision of the political order (and disorder) of the age, the nature of the church, and his own salvation.

As the quotation from Haller suggests, the tools for reflection and expression that Vane appropriated from Puritan experimental divinity were not, fundamentally, particular doctrines or specific ideas. Consider a contrasting example: Michael McGiffert has interpreted the piety of the Puritan minister Thomas Shepard by arguing that "Puritans looked for security from and within a system of ideas that was fairly clear, consistent, and stable—intended, like all such systems, to explain and organize experience." And, among the doctrines of this "theological system," McGiffert then proceeded to list original sin, total depravity, and limited atonement.[12] Henry Vane, like Thomas Shepard, turned to the inherited theological tradition for the means to explain and organize experience. But the ordering form Vane found there, I shall propose, was not a doctrinal system but rather an interlocking set of biblically derived metaphors.[13]

For two generations these ruling metaphors—the wilderness pilgrimage, the house of God, the mystical marriage, the divine covenant—had cast upon a cosmic screen the formative social experience of Puritanism as a fellowship of those "called out" from superficial and degenerate religion into disciplined commitment to the cause of God. For Vane, these metaphors established an arena of discourse within which, as lay theologian, he had considerable latitude to cast his own interpretations in the contexts of prophesying sessions, family exercises, and private meditation. Their intellectual potency resided largely in their capacity to thematize around a single image the various spheres of human existence: personal life, the institutions of society, and the fundamental order of nature and history. The house of God, to take one of these metaphors as an example, represented at one level the personal, mystical union in which believers "follow God's invitation of them into the secret chambers of his presence, and do dwell in his house, (a building not made with hands, in the person and spirit of Christ)."[14] It was, as well, a godly and contrite England, into which "it may please God to come . . . for his temple and the place of his habitation and rest, wherein he shall abide forever."[15] And, it was Christ the eternal Word of creation, whose person was "that eternal house of the Father, wherein are many mansions," who established "the platform and exemplary patern" of the cosmos and who set all things and all peoples in their proper array.[16]

These same metaphors also suggested to Vane thematic unities within Scripture and opened avenues for that personal appropriation of the Bible that had been a perennial objective of the experimental divinity. In one of the classics of Puritan devotion, *The Practice of Pietie*, Lewis Bayly had advised the reader of Scripture to "apply these things to thine owne heart, and reade not these Chapters as matters of Historicall discourse; but as if they were so many Letters or Epistles sent downe from God out of heaven unto thee."[17] Henry Vane's religious meditations liberated this appeal for personal appropriation from its context in ministerial traditions of exegesis and made the Bible a vast allegory of the soul's union with Christ. The metaphors of Puritan piety became the medium by which he correlated the Bible with personal and public experience; and the stories of Cain and Abel, of Abraham's wanderings, or of Paul's afflictions were "interiorized" as steps in the spiritual journey of self and society toward the eschatological Bridegroom. The fact that these metaphors had sufficient flexibility to make such correlations possible Vane took for evidence of Christ's

> indwelling presence in the heart, comparing itself in the mind and understanding of the Saint, with the testimony which is given of it self in the Outward Word: and by discerning the perfect Analogie and Harmony that springs up between both, answering one another as face answers face, the believer receives such certainty and satisfaction in the mind of God made known,

as warrants him in the delivery and declaration thereof unto others.[18]

In this harmonization, the written word of the Bible worked in "subserviency unto the living Word" indwelling in the faithful, and this "living unwritten Word of God," vivified the written words "and is made use of as the key to open them."[19]

A *third* preliminary point is that the form and coherence of Vane's faith was influenced by the social prominence of his family and his own changing political position during the era of the Puritan Revolution. His father, Sir Henry Vane the Elder, had advanced himself in the court of Charles I as a member of the Privy Council and, eventually, secretary of state. During the 1630s, the elder Vane acquired substantial estates and, moving without political mishap to the parliamentary side, he left at his death in 1655 a significant inheritance to the younger Sir Henry. Coupled with this aristocratic background, Vane's own prominence in affairs of state led him to ponder the import of mystical religion for responsible action on the public scene. In particular, Vane's theological meditations underwent development as he sought to bring them to bear upon three major political issues of the age: the relation of religious liberty to reformation, the character of the magistrate's responsibility for religion, and the relation of Christian faith to the moral ordering of society.

In what follows, I shall argue that Vane articulated the mystical indwelling of Christ as an experience of spiritual death and rebirth. This interpretation became the axis on which he turned other biblically derived metaphors, such as the wilderness pilgrimage or the heavenly marriage, in order to explain salvation history and present social duty. Mystical death of the self imaginatively shaped his religious universe and, maintained by private devotional disciplines, was the organizing center of his religious persona. It was, at once, the source for his rhetoric of self-denying public service and for his opponents' exasperation with his religious arrogance.

MYSTICAL PIETY AND THE PERSONAL PILGRIMAGE

The substance of Vane's theological ruminations first came to public attention in *The Retired Mans Meditations* (1655), a rambling treatise of more than four hundred pages written during his retreat from public life after Cromwell's expulsion of the Long Parliament. In this tract, Vane located the mystical experience within the larger pattern of conversion and sanctification that ordered the personal pilgrimage of faith. By their mystical union with the indwelling Christ, Vane wrote, Christians "enter with Christ within the veyl, and are admitted into the sight and enjoyment of God in the very brightness of his glory . . . partaking after this manner of the divine nature itself, wherein they see God face to face . . . conversing with him, as friend speaks with friend."[20] He did not, however, identify this transformative vision of God with conversion (his own conversion had occurred when he was a student of fourteen or fifteen).[21] He presented it instead as a subsequent and separate event. After Christians had been brought by conversion "out of the corrupt, degenerate state of nature" into "the earthly Canaan . . . not in the letter only, but in the spirit," Vane believed that some individuals would receive "another Call, or second voice to the soul, causing it to sojourn as a stranger, even in the land of promise: and to look upon this earthly Jerusalem, as no abiding City: but that, out of which it must also pass into a heavenly Country, the Jerusalem that is above."[22]

This "second voice to the soul" was heard by the saints only after an initiatory "trial" of spiritual death, when Christ departed and the soul was abandoned to desolation "in a dry and barren wildernesse." Having previously experienced the converting ministry of Christ through Scripture, preaching, and sacraments, the soul had to be brought into "Conformity with Christ in his death"; and this time of trial mystically recapitulated Christ's own suffering, crucifixion, and entombment. All natural powers and mental faculties had "death passe upon them," so that they had no "possibility of acting in rebellion, resistance or contradiction to the Law of the heavenly nature and mind, set up by faith." Not until this "death" of Christ was "perfected in them" would souls be raised in Christ to new and perfect knowledge. "According to the steps and degrees of this death" of the self, Vane concluded, "doth the approach and increase of this higher life let it self in upon them."[23] Through mystical death and rebirth the first faith of the saint was extinguished and the self emptied of its motive power to be reconstituted by the Christ, who now indwelled, inhabited, or took up abode in the soul, lifting it to immediate vision of God and becoming the active moral principle of the saint's life in the world. Just as, in the resurrection of the body, that which had been corruptible rose incorruptible, so now mystical death and rebirth annihilated "mutable" faith and raised up faith "immutable."

Vane elaborated the significance of mystical death and rebirth by a parallel interpretation of the heavenly marriage, which depicted the experience as the transition from a first marriage to a second, and higher, one. Christ, "after he hath become a Bridegroom and married Husband unto true beleevers, in and by his first appearance" in conversion, would "wholly dissolve that marriage-band betweene them" and separate himself from the saint. But this privation would end when Christ returned "with everlasting mercies to embrace them, and be married unto them in the light and life of his second appearance, not only supplying to them again that wherein he was withdrawn from them, but adding over and above, a fuller and more abundant communication of life and glory; which, untill this death or withdrawing of his be perfected in them, they are not capable subjects perfectly to receive and inherit."[24] The heavenly marriage had now, in Vane's opinion, been changed from a "mutable" covenant—"capable of Divorce"—into the immutable covenant that was a foretaste of the beatific vision.[25]

The previous, mutable covenant granted knowledge of the divine will in mediated form: through the external creation, the Bible, the ministry and sacraments of the visible church. In ascending beyond these "fleshly" media to direct converse with God, the mystical saint achieved not only an insight into the eternal world but also a spiritual discernment that penetrated the motives of human action. It had long been the conviction of the Puritans that, in the words of John Preston, "there is a sagacitie given to the Saints, a certaine new qualitie, that others want [lack], by which they are able to finde out the steppes of Gods way."[26] But this had typically been construed as an ability to test the spirit of one's own motives against the standard of Scripture. For Vane and the camp of radical spiritism, it became as well a capacity to discern the spirit by which others were motivated. His follower and first biographer, George Sikes, summarized the radical spiritist view in a reference to Vane himself.

Whoever is partaker of the divine nature or spirit of Christ . . .

lives undeniably in a spirit and discerning, superior to what is to be found in any first-creation nature whatsoever, humane or angelical. He that lives in this spirit, knows not onely this or that man by personal converse, but humane nature, mankind, what it amounts to, how 'twill act, where it will be next. He comprehends it, knowes the most curious and otherwise imperceptible motions of every wheele in it . . . Many believed in Christ; but he knew what kind of Faith they had, a temporary one, that onely that cast out the devil, and made them men again, wash'd their humane nature, not baptized them into the divine. He would not therefore trust them, for he knew all men.[27]

Hence, although Vane's religious rhetoric invariably emphasized the death and abasement of the self and of self-interest, this transformation of the self by the indwelling Christ had the effect of elevating Vane to the pinnacle of a spiritual hierarchy.

In *The Retired Mans Meditations,* Vane described the pilgrimage toward mystical union as one that traversed a threefold hierarchy of the natural, the legal, and, finally, the evangelical covenants. In this, and in his polemical propensity to identify much that passed for Puritanism with the legal covenant of works, Vane's exposition stood in continuity with the Hutchinsonian side of the antinomian controversy in New England some twenty years earlier. However, during the imprisonment that would culminate in his execution in 1662, Vane refined this threefold covenantal structure by distinguishing between two levels of the evangelical covenant. This portrayal of the Christian life, which had the significant purpose of acknowledging the authenticity of faith that did not include mystical experience, was most clearly set forth in two posthumously published theological tracts: *Two Treatises* (1662) and *A Pilgrimage into the Land of Promise* (1664). In both works, Vane distinguished between those saints of the immutable covenant who had received "the Holy Ghost, in the single portion of it" and those who had received the "double portion" of the Spirit.

Among these Children of the Resurrection . . . the immortal life, wherewith they are quickned by Christ, as he is the giver of the Holy Ghost is of two sorts, as to the degree and measure of the glory thereof. First, Such, wherein Men and Angels are equal: And the Second, Such, wherein some Men are made in such manner Christ's Equals, the Lamb's or Bridegroom's Wife that lies in his bosom, that they are the Angel's superiours.[28]

By this means, Vane distinguished between persons whom he re-garded as fully "evangelical" Christians and those (like himself) who by mystical death and rebirth had ascended yet another rung in the hierarchy of saintship. In the language of scriptural typol-ogy, these two groups of saints were the "two flocks" ultimately destined "to be gathered into one sheepfold"; they were both "Abrahams seed . . . that in all changes of time remain the pure invisible church."[29] But they experienced the "immutable" faith of the saints in two differing degrees or "measures."

MYSTICAL PIETY AND THE DISPENSATIONS OF HISTORY

While on the one hand biblically based metaphors were interi-orized as the spiritual narration of the soul's transformation, on the other hand these transformed saints acted on the "outward" stage of providential history. Their presence testified not only to the internal coming of Christ but also to his eschatological return in judgment and the approaching kingdom of the saints. The pil-grimage of the individual soul had, in other words, its counterpart in the great human pilgrimage of redemption. The natural, legal, and evangelical covenants of the soul; the first and second appear-ances of Christ; the wilderness of time in Christ's death or absence—all of these had their parallels in the dispensations of history stretching from Adam to the millennium.

In its broad themes, Vane's theological narrative of the great pilgrimage shared most of the commonplaces of the Puritan vision of history, but again, these were reworked in order to make mysti-cal death and resurrection the key to history's culmination. As Henry Vane recounted the matter, humanity had passed first through the covenant of nature, within which natural reason, the "candle of the Lord," constituted "that light that enlightens every one that comes into the world." by this inner light the individual could discern the divine law not only in external creation but also in "the work or impression of the law in their owne hearts."[30] But the natural conscience was easily misled by its limited capacity for rational discernment and by its propensity, as fallen nature, to pursue self-interest rather than divine truth. Hence, this first cove-nant was superseded by the law of Scripture, a dispensation in which the written word acted as a "Schoolmaster," making explicit the original natural law and pointing toward the coming of "the true Spiritual light." This second historical dispensation, the "ministry of the law," had taken two forms, one recorded in the Old Testament and the other in the New; its adherents were "Israel according to the flesh, whether under the Law or under the Gospel." But neither form of this second covenant provided more than temporary rest on the "pilgrimage to the land of promise," and like the personal spiritual pilgrimage the whole history of redemption was passing through the death of one dispensation toward the new life of another. The epoch of "Christs own personal ministry in the flesh" was in a "dying and declining state," but "the yet more glorious day of Christs second appearance and dispensation in Spirit, is at hand."[31]

In the transition to the new age, there existed among the members of the visible church as "a select number of hidden and beloved ones, kept through the power of faith unto salvation, without whom the rest would be a Sodom, and Gomorrah."[32] The final age of "Christs personal appearance in the Spirit" was being prefigured in the appearance of these spiritual saints who were the precursors of Christ's millennial advent. Wonders loomed on the horizon and, in Vane's reading of the times, the spiritual saints—especially those with the "double portion" of the Spirit—were the two witnesses foretold in the eleventh chapter of Revelation whose preaching, persecution, death, and resurrection would inaugurate the reign of Christ. His own imprisonments, on behalf of what he regarded as the truth of Christ, did little to dampen his hopes that he was numbered among the persecuted prophets. Angelic emissaries populated the heavens, the true witnesses of faith were stepping forth to speak with spiritual tongues, and the mystical Christ had become Jacob's ladder, whereby the saints traversed the invisible realms "in the state of souls seperate from the body." As late as 1662, Vane still anticipated the full disclosure of a spiritual or "angelicall ministry" in which those "called into this ministry, shal be found speaking with the tongues, not of men only, but of angels." The consequences, "both for cleernes and certainty of the matter preached, and the power of that spirit in which it is ministered, shal be beyond all that hath yet bin seen or experienced in the church."[33] These miracles would culminate in the earthly kingdom, when Christ shall give and derive to his body (the general assembly of the first-borne, whose names are written in heaven) authority to be the only Potentates, Lords of Lords . . . next and immediately under Christ their head; and this, as well as in reference to the regulating and well-ordering the service of God in the societies of Saints and all his true worshippers; as in reference to the governing and well-ordering the natural and outward converse of men in their humane societies, during the reigne of Christ upon earth the thousand years.[34]

This reading of history displayed Vane's ambivalence toward the church and its population of "fleshly" and "legal" Christians. On the one hand, the visible church was the nursery and schoolmaster for authentic Christianity and it had its own, albeit limited, measure of truth. But on the other hand, this "worldly Church" had long displayed "the fury of the Serpent" in its persecution of both the spiritual saints and those "natural men" who stood outside its pale of influence. Its day had passed. Vane very rarely, therefore, made the appeal for restoration of the church's primitive, apostolic order in the manner so characteristic of standard Puritan rhetoric (but note the exception in Vane's comment on family worship below). The Spirit was leading the Puritan movement not backward to an original purity but forward to the new age.

Although as a young dissenter Vane may have had some scruples regarding the outward forms of worship,[35] throughout most of his life he shared the opinion of such other spirit mystics as William Dell and John Saltmarsh that the historic sacraments were mere types that prefigured and were being superseded by the immediate presence of Christ in spirit. He did not oppose the use of baptism or the Lord's supper but simply regarded them as the withered husks of an order now passing.[36] Providential history as a whole, like the spiritual journey of the individual, must endure the death of its first faith in order to culminate in direct, unmediated knowledge of God. Meanwhile, the mystical saints "soujourne in tents, in the outward land of Canaan, the streets of the visible church, and various self-chosen ways of visible worship" and focus the eyes of faith instead upon the "land of promise in spirit, whilst it is yet at a great distance and very far off."[37] In this transitional age, Vane exercised his own piety primarily in regular household devotions and, in an exhortation to his family on the day before his execution, compared himself to Abraham and the patriarch's practice of "Family-worship":

> There were, in his time, no formed Churches or Societies of a larger kind . . . embodying themselves and walking in communion together. That which he was capable to do, he did. He catechized and instructed his Relations, spreading abroad amongst them the savour of the riches of that Grace, which (through mercy) he was partaker of. This was the state of the true Church, then, as to its outward form. If the larger visible Societies, and collective Bodies, or Churches of Saints be now interrupted, this Family-way of Religion and Worship may be kept up, and so things return to their primitive way again, as in the dayes of Abraham.[38]

MYSTICAL PIETY AND THE SOCIAL COVENANT

Vane's covenantal theory not only set forth a sequential theology of history but also provided a theological explanation for the composition of the contemporary social order, its political turmoil and contending religious parties. Still more important, it was the basis of his proposals for social concord and a viable political settlement. His ruminations on the theme of covenant had shifted, so to speak, from its eternal and temporal dimensions to its spatial ones. He now inquired how responsibility to divine covenant could be made the basis for a stable political order that was not only "godly" but also open enough to comprehend religious diversity.

In *The Retired Mans Meditations,* Vane argued that the "threefold kingdom of Christ" in the contemporary world was composed of all who lived righteously under one of the three covenants: natural, legal, or evangelical. Although he believed that the first two covenants were "mutable" and that persons of natural or legal conscience fell short of the eternal glory of salvation reserved for "the spiritual seed," nevertheless in this life, they lived acceptably before God, who perhaps intended that some of them would yet receive the "greater light and mercy" of salvation. In short, God "will punctually perform what lies on his part, in giving to the righteous man, the righteous mans reward; according to the tenor of the promises, covenant, and light they live under."[39] Through exercise of the "natural good conscience . . . there is no man that comes into the world, wherever he be born or educated, but is in a capacity of being respected by God, as a natural and righteous man."[40] To this extent, Vane esteemed the Quakers, with their doctrine of the inner light, as persons living righteously according to the covenant of nature, even though this righteousness was quite inferior to that enacted by grace "in unity and similitude of spirit" with Christ.[41]

Within this covenantal framework, Vane asserted both that the natural law was the proper foundation for human government and also that each covenant should be respected for the legitimate "measure of light" it cast upon human conduct. Characteristically, he did not insist that a good magistrate must be Christian but instead declared that "the more illuminated the Magistrates conscience and judgment is, as to *natural justice and right*, by the knowledge of God and communications of light from Christ, under any of the three dispensations before mentioned; the better qualified is he to execute his office."[42]

When Vane applied these theories to the political scene, he concluded that "the good old cause" for which the Puritans had contended included two principal elements: guarantee of the people's "natural rights in civil things" and "true freedom in matters of conscience."[43] These themes were most fully explored in two political tracts of the 1650s: *Zeal Examined* (1652) and *A Healing Question* (1656). The first, although published anonymously, may be identified as Vane's work by circumstantial, stylistic, and substantive evidence. It called for "liberty of conscience in matters of religion" and particularly for the toleration of Roman Catholics. When it drew reaction, it was upheld in *The Examiner Defended* (1652) by Roger Williams, who was living at the time in Vane's London residence.[44] *A Healing Question* was published in response to Cromwell's declaration of a public fast, in which the protector proposed that divine guidance be sought in the religious and political settlement of the nation. Vane answered that the party of "honest men" had become divided when self-interest took precedent over concern for the common good, and he proposed settling the government by calling a "convention of faithful honest, and discerning men, chosen for that purpose by the free consent of the whole body of adherents" to the cause of natural rights and religious liberty. This convention would fashion "the particulars that by way of fundamental constitutions shall be laid and inviolably observed as the conditions upon which the whole body so represented doth consent to cast itself into a civil and politic incorporation."[45]

Although space does not permit a general treatment of Vane's political thought, three issues mentioned at the beginning of this essay serve to illustrate the connections between his mystical piety and his views on politics and society: the relation of religious liberty to reformation, the character of the magistrate's responsibility for religion, and the relation of Christian faith to the moral ordering of society.

First, Vane shared the conviction of Roger Williams and John Milton that truth "ever thrives best in fair and open debates."[46] The cause of the faithful was most endangered, he believed, when "through confidence in our present Attainments, we are barred from receiving any new Discoveries of Truth," and he appealed to the experience of the nation for evidence that "our late troubles" came from "the growth of that persecuting Principle that would endeavor by outward Force to impose one way of Worship upon all Men."[47] Precisely because too much concern with the outward ordinances of the church fostered intolerance, he hoped his readers would "follow the Lord in any steps wherein he pleases to appear, and not to expect all thy nourishment from such Ordinances as may be wither'd to thee, when thou mayest receive the bread and water of eternall life through any other channel in a more immediate and experimentall way."[48] An age when the Spirit was disclosing things "beyond all that hath yet bin seen or experienced" and was disclosing them not through social institutions but through immediate illumination of individual saints was, Vane believed, a poor time to place the coercive power of the state on the side of the past.

Second, as this comment suggests, Vane believed the primary task of the magistrate in the advancement of religion was to stand aside and "let light come forth upon equall terms with the darkness."[49] Although in the early 1640s he had favored establishing a board of clerical commissioners to oversee religion, he joined Roger Williams, most of the Baptists, and his younger brother, Charles, in opposing such a scheme when it was proposed by the Independent divines in 1652. All religious views should have an open hearing unless they intended to establish themselves by "oppression and bloudy practices" and thereby violated the natural rights of conscience. In that case, the magistrate had rightful authority to intervene and insure that "the great Whore" of religious persecution was "rewarded double in the same Cup of Bloud which she hath filled to the Saints."[50]

Third, Henry Vane's spiritist interpretation of covenantal theology combined with his desire for a comprehensive and stable political settlement to produce a distinctive form of millenarianism. He believed that "the honest party" in the realm included not only the saints but persons from among all three of the divine covenants and that government should be such as would "best answer the public welfare and safety of the whole." Such a government depended upon the fundamental right of "honest men" to place "meet persons in the place of supreme judicature and authority among them, whereby they may have the use and benefit of the choicest light and wisdom of the nation that they are capable to call forth, for the rule and government under which they will live."[51]

This appeal to fundamental right was not, however, a move toward democratic political theory but only an assertion that the natural covenant was the foundation of the political order, a foundation that could not be arbitrarily violated by those in power. By the covenant of common good, the people entrusted themselves to persons endowed with "the choicest light and wisdom of the nation" in order that the whole might be preserved. In his view, it was the mystical saints who had the clearest discernment of this common good, who precisely by mystical death of the self had transcended "that great Idol, Self-Interest," and who would ultimately emerge in the approaching millennium as the leaders of the honest party. These were "heavenly men, qualified with a discerning peculiar to the spiritual seed" who would exact justice on those who "presume to offend against the principles of natural good and right, held forth in and by the righteousness of the first Covenant [of nature]."[52] Reflected light from these immutable saints would shed a glow of earthly felicity throughout the "threefold kingdom of Christ," and "the nations . . . shall walk in her light, all the world over, and be happy and glorious also, but changeable."[53]

What emerged, then, in Vane's theological meditations on society was *an aristocracy of the mystical saints,* tolerant of those possessed of lesser measures of discernment, willing to share political power with them in a transitional epoch but ultimately destined to govern by the prerogatives of superior spiritual endowment. His combination of mystical piety with concern for comprehensive political order distinguished his views from those held by others on the radical wing of the Puritan Revolution. The Fifth Monarchy Men, for example, had begun in the early 1650s advocating rule by the saints alone. But Vane, although intrigued by their millenarian speculations, remained skeptical of this position, opposed the Nominated Parliament partly for that reason, and eventually attracted one of the Fifth Monarchy leaders, John Rogers, to his position while the two were imprisoned together in 1656.[54] Despite this difference from the Fifth Monarchy Men, Vane did anticipate an earthly kingdom. His mystical piety thereby differed in emphasis from that of other radical spiritists such as William Erbery and John Saltmarsh, who stressed that the "spiritual reign" of Christ would be "a kingdom inward and spiritual" and who sharply criticized hopes for a literal rule of the saints.[55] Finally, Vane's theory of the social covenant differed from the more democratic position of Levellers such as John Lilburne, who generally held Vane in disdain. Vane employed his spiritist convictions not to advocate a "radically egalitarian view of society"[56] but instead to insist that prior to all outward forms of government—whether in church or state—there existed an affective loyalty to "the cause," which was the measure of virtue in public life and the foundation upon which just institutional forms must be built. This common loyalty was the actual substance of government, and where it existed, he declared himself willing to work within any particular political system, including the traditional one of king, lords, and commons.[57]

These debates among radical Puritans about the millennium and democracy were expressions of the more general Puritan hope for establishment of the godly commonwealth. Hence, Henry Vane's deployment of these ideas in an effort to influence the shape of the commonwealth exhibited in extreme form the tensions within Puritan political theory as a whole. These tensions arose and ultimately brought the Puritan political experiment to ruin, I believe, because the Puritans derived political authority and social harmony from personal, affective, or experiential appropriation of the authoritative law of God. But this reliance on the godly disposition of the heart for the building of political institutions seemed unable to account for the diversity of religiously based political views that in fact emerged. Vane attempted to account for this diversity and to incorporate it into a political settlement through his notion of the three interlocking covenants, in which citizens could live diverse but legitimately "righteous" public lives. But, because he shared the Puritan drive for personal holiness and *true* godliness, he sought also to elaborate a spiritual aristocracy who, through mystical death and rebirth, deserved (and would receive) ultimate political authority in the approaching political millennium. This mystical basis for his political theory ultimately failed to undergird his efforts for religious tolerance and comprehension.

NOTES

1. John Milton, "To Sir Henry Vane the Younger," in Merritt Y. Hughes, ed., *John Milton: Complete Poems and Major Prose* (New York, 1957) 161.

2. Vane was defended against charges of theological obscurity by his friend and biographer, George Sikes, in *The Life and Death of Sir Henry Vane* (London, 1662) 7. His skill as a drafter of political documents has been emphasized by Violet A. Rowe, *Sir Henry Vane the Younger: A Study in Political and Administrative History* (London, 1970) 250.

3. Gilbert Burnet, *Bishop Burnet's History of His Own Time*, ed. Thomas Burnet, vol. 1 (London, 1753) 228.

4. At the turn of the century, historians perceived Vane as an early apostle of democratic, constitutional government: James K. Hosmer, *The Life of Young Sir Henry Vane* (Boston, 1889); William W. Ireland, *The Life of Sir Henry Vane the Younger* (New York, 1906); John Willcock, *Life of Sir Henry Vane the Younger, Statesman and Mystic (1613–1662)* (London, 1913). In a twist on this tradition, George Calvin Rogers argued that Vane's thought contained an unresolved tension between a millenarian vision of the rule of the saints and a rhetoric of republican government grounded in the agreement of the people: "Sir Henry Vane, Jr.: Spirit Mystic and Fanatic Democrat" (Ph.D. dissertation, University of Chicago, 1953). More recent scholarship has concentrated on the political aspect of Vane's life: Rowe, *Henry Vane*; and Margaret A. Judson, *The Political Thought of Sir Henry Vane the Younger* (Philadelphia, 1969). For one illustration of Vane's own sense of the interconnection of piety and public life, see the letter written to his wife just prior to his execution, reprinted in Ireland, *Henry Vane*, 454–62.

5. Henry Vane, *The Retired Mans Meditations* (London, 1655) 223.

6. Jerald C. Brauer, "Puritan Mysticism and the Development of

Liberalism," *Church History* 19(1954) 99–108; James Fulton Maclear, "The Making of the Lay Tradition," *Journal of Religion* 33(1953) 113–36; Philip F. Gura, *A Glimpse of Sion's Glory: Puritan Radicalism in New England, 1620–1660* (Middletown, Conn., 1984) 49–92.

7. Maclear, "Lay Tradition," 127.

8. Geoffrey F. Nuttall, *The Holy Spirit in Puritan Faith and Experience* (Oxford, 1946) 134, 136, 137.

9. Charles E. Hambrick-Stowe, *The Practice of Piety: Puritan Devotional Disciplines in Seventeenth-Century New England* (Chapel Hill, 1982).

10. William James, *The Varieties of Religious Experience: A Study in Human Nature* (New York, 1902) 45.

11. William Haller, *The Rise of Puritanism* (New York, 1938) 18, 34.

12. Michael McGiffert, ed., *God's Plot: The Paradoxes of Puritan Piety: Being the Autobiography and Journal of Thomas Shepard* (Amherst, 1972) 10–11.

13. Cf. Nigel Smith, *Perfection Proclaimed: Language and Literature in English Radical Religion, 1640–1660* (Oxford, 1989) 229–30.

14. Henry Vane, *A Pilgrimage into the Land of Promise, by the Light of the Vision of Jacobs Ladder and Faith* (London, 1664) 69.

15. Henry Vane, *A Healing Question: Old South Leaflets*, vol. 1, no. 6 (Boston, n.d.).

16. Vane, *Pilgrimage*, 3.

17. Lewis Bayly, *The Practise of Pietie*, 12th ed. (London, 1620) 245–46.

18. Vane, *Retired Mans Meditations*, 18.

19. Ibid., 19.

20. Ibid., 138.

21. Sikes, *Henry Vane*, 7–8; *The Tryal of Sir Henry Vane, Kt., at the Kings Bench* (London, 1662) 88.

22. Vane, *Retired Mans Meditations*, 228.

23. Ibid., 289–91, 296–97, 301, 305.

24. Ibid., 289–92, 305.

25. Ibid., 331.

26. John Preston, *The New Covenant; or, The Saints Portion*, 3rd ed. (London, 1629) 192.

27. Sikes, *Henry Vane*, 95; Vane, *Retired Mans Meditations*, 128, 137–38.

28. Henry Vane, *Two Treatises* (London, 1662) 18.

29. Vane, *Pilgrimage*, 103–4, 106.

30. Vane, *Retired Mans Meditations*, 126–29, 145; Vane, *Pilgrimage*, 5–6.

31. Vane, *Retired Mans Meditations,* 128, 133, 195–96, 208; Vane, *Two Treatises,* 20–38; Vane, *Pilgrimage,* 5–9, 10, 21–22.

32. Vane, *Pilgrimage,* 68–69; Vane, *Two Treatises,* 44–45.

33. Vane, *Two Treatises,* 57–58, 72–73; Vane, *Pilgrimage,* 2–5, 85–89, 90–91.

34. Vane, *Retired Mans Meditations,* 409.

35. "Letter from Sir Henry Vane, the Younger, to His Father," *Proceedings of the Massachusetts Historical Society* 12 (1871–73) 246.

36. Sikes, *Henry Vane,* 48; [Henry Vane], *Zeal Examined* (London, 1652) 38–42.

37. Vane, *Pilgrimage,* 68–69.

38. Sikes, *Henry Vane,* 156.

39. Vane, *Retired Mans Meditations,* 126–29, 179–80, 209.

40. Ibid., 183.

41. Ibid., 184–85.

42. Ibid., 388 (emphasis added).

43. Vane, *Healing Question,* 1–6.

44. Cf. James E. Ernst, *Roger Williams: New England Firebrand* (New York, 1932) 318–19.

45. Vane, *Healing Question,* 1–2, 14.

46. Vane, *Zeal Examined,* 20.

47. Ibid., 4, 24.

48. Ibid., 41.

49. Ibid., 23.

50. Ibid., 412; Vane, *Retired Mans Meditations,* 388.

51. Vane, *Healing Question,* 1–3.

52. Vane, *Retired Mans Meditations,* 410–11.

53. Ibid., 412; Vane, *Pilgrimage,* 106, 110.

54. B. S. Capp, *The Fifth Monarchy Men: A Study in Seventeenth-Century English Millenarianism* (London, 1972) 121, 125, 139.

55. William Erbery, *A Call to the Churches* (London, 1653) 35–40; John Saltmarsh, *Sparkles of Glory* (London, 1647) 21–25.

56. Cf. Gura, *Sion's Glory,* 77–78.

57. Hosmer, *Henry Vane,* 327.

Contemporary

CHAPTER 18

Death and Near-Death Today

Carol Zaleski

DEATH DENIAL AND DEATH TABOO

The pervasiveness of denial of death in modern western societies has become axiomatic, thanks to broadly influential writings on this subject by Sigmund Freud, Geoffrey Gorer, Ernest Becker, and others. Yet whatever we consider axiomatic deserves a second look; and a second look reveals a dogmatic assumption underlying at least the Freudian strain in this literature: that the only rational way to face death is with an attitude of heroic acceptance of human finitude. From this viewpoint, intimations of immortality are but stratagems to evade the reality of death. Such a premise, whatever merits it may have as a moral tonic, can inhibit our appreciation for cultures and traditions that prefer to see death as a doorway to other realms.

To help us place the idea of "denial of death" in perspective, I will begin by reviewing three landmark works from earlier in our century, works that have in common the belief that it is morally incumbent on humankind to learn how to face death squarely.

In his 1915 essay "Thoughts for the Times on War and Death," Freud made what has become the classic statement on death denial:

> The second factor to which I attribute our present sense of estrangement in this once lovely and congenial world is the disturbance that has taken place in our attitude towards death . . .
>
> This attitude was far from straightforward. We were of course prepared to maintain that death was the necessary outcome of life, that everyone owes a debt to Nature and must

383

expect to pay the reckoning—in short, that death was natural, undeniable, and unavoidable. In reality, however, we were accustomed to behave as if it were otherwise. We displayed an unmistakable tendency to "shelve" death, to eliminate it from life. We tried to hush it up . . . Our own death is indeed unimaginable, and whenever we make the attempt to imagine it we can perceive that we really survive as spectators. Hence the psychoanalytic school could venture on the assertion that at bottom no one believes in his own death, or to put the same thing in another way, in the unconscious every one of us is convinced of his own immortality.[1]

Freud proceeds to unveil with masterful irony the paradoxes and subterfuges in our attitude towards death. While our own death may be unimaginable, he points out, the death of a stranger is entirely acceptable. In wartime, when stranger becomes enemy, we can even rejoice in his death. Such defensive strategies break down, however, when we face the death of a friend or relative. Part "me" and part "other," the friend who dies evokes ambivalent feelings of grief mixed with secret pleasure. The guilt this arouses reinforces our need to deny the reality of death:

By the body of his slain enemy primitive man would have triumphed, without racking his brains about the enigma of life and death. Not the intellectual enigma, and not every death, but the conflict of feeling at the death of loved, yet withal alien and hated persons was what disengaged the spirit of inquiry in man. Of this conflict of feeling psychology was the direct offspring. Man could no longer keep death at a distance, for he had tasted of it in his grief for the dead; but still he did not consent entirely to acknowledge it, for he could not conceive of himself as dead. So he devised a compromise; he conceded the fact of death, even his own death, but he denied it the significance of annihilation . . . During his contemplation of his loved one's corpse he invented ghosts, and it was his sense of guilt at the satisfaction mingled with his sorrow that turned these new-born spirits into evil, dreaded demons. The changes wrought by death suggested to him the disjunction of the individuality into a body and soul—first of all into several souls . . . The enduring remembrance of the dead became the basis for assuming other modes of existence.[2]

The evolutionist assumptions in Freud's essay have rendered it obsolete as an exercise in ethnography; nonetheless, the basic thesis and its moral overtones continue to influence us, perhaps more than we realize. Fated as we are to experience such conflicting attitudes, our hope lies, according to Freud, in cultivating as much impartial self-knowledge as we can muster, animated by a sense of duty. Concluding with the maxim: "if you would endure life, be prepared for death," Freud's essay reads like an Epicurean meditation on achieving philosophical composure in the face of death.

The sociological treatment of death denial has its roots in Geoffrey Gorer's famous essay on "The Pornography of Death," published in England in 1955.[3] Gorer was the first to suggest that death had replaced sex as our society's great "unmentionable," inverting the values of our Victorian ancestors, for whom death was a familiar, domestic reality. Gorer's essay profoundly influenced a generation of thanatologists, social theorists, and intellectual historians, including Philippe Ariès, of the *Annales* school, whose massive works tracing the changing face of death in Western culture conclude with a vision of death as "forbidden," "invisible," and "savage" in the modern world.[4]

Freud's "Thoughts for the Times" and Gorer's "The Pornography of Death" were followed in 1973 by Ernest Becker's *The Denial of Death*, a literate, at times rhapsodic, work indebted to Otto Rank and Kierkegaard, which argues that human culture is built upon dread of death, this dread being simultaneously the wellspring of our creativity and of our disabling neuroses.[5] These three works, highlights in a series of moral critiques of death denial in modern culture, have borne fruit in the death awareness movement (popularly associated in this country with Elisabeth Kübler-Ross) and in the efforts of consumer advocacy and reform movements to expose what they consider to be irrational or exploitative contemporary funeral practices.

Since the early 1970s, it would seem that the taboo concerning death has been lifted. We are now talking about death incessantly and with remarkable confidence. Popular literature on death and dying from Kübler-Ross and her followers, makes the prospect of death more bearable by mapping five stages of approach (denial, anger, bargaining, depression, acceptance).[6] Historical and ethnographic scholarship on death, though less evangelizing, has its own ways of controlling the subject, usually by emphasizing the cultural construction of death and mourning practices. What are these but attempts, shored up by scientific discourse, naturalistically to remove the sting of death?

To speak in the idiom of developmental psychology, it is tempting to think that North American middle-class society has been going through a prolonged adolescence, marked by identity crises, narcissism, and denial of death. Our current preoccupation with death, then, would not necessarily be a sign that this adolescence is ending. For adolescents, in addition to denying death (as evidenced by their risk-taking behavior and their frequently attested belief that their own death will be quick and painless) also think of death frequently, as a way of testing their emerging self-image.

If death anxiety cannot be cured by staring death down, or by talking death to death, then we may be left with the disconcertingly simple thought that our only recourse is wisdom, a quality that each person must cultivate according to the terms one's culture provides. Unflinching acceptance of human finitude is one option, but not the only one. By itself, it seems inadequate, for the mere uncensoring of death, like the uncensoring of sex, does not automatically lead to a more mature and responsible understanding.

Life cycle theorists—principally Erik Erikson and Robert Jay Lifton—while acknowledging the pervasiveness of pathological forms of death anxiety and denial, suggest that something more than merely exposing the "facts" about death is needed if human beings are to make sense of themselves in the face of death. For Erikson, the developmental process leads beyond establishment of psychosocial identity in the direction of generativity (that is, caring for the next generation), wisdom (which he defines as "informed and detached concern with life itself in the face of death itself"[7]) and integrity ("the acceptance of one's own and only life cycle and of the people who have become significant to it as something that had to be and that, by necessity, permitted of no substitutions"[8]). Accepting death is not enough; vital links must be created between "one's own and only life cycle" and the life cycle of a wider cosmos.

Robert Jay Lifton has investigated this question of vital links. He finds that when individuals or societies are prevented from cultivating images of death that hold out the promise of continued life or transcendence, their moral energy is soon sapped, and "psychic numbing" sets in. Lifton speaks of five modes of symbolic immortality: through one's children, through religious identification with a power beyond death, through one's creative works, through identification with the cycles of nature, and through "experiential transcendence" or ecstasy.[9]

Symbolic immortalities may not guarantee an unbroken temporal succession of personal existence after death; but they do provide some sense of continuity in the face of death. In such symbols, we may find shelter from the three kinds of death anxiety of which Paul Tillich spoke in his 1952 Terry lectures at Yale University (published as *The Courage to Be*): the anxiety of annihilation, of meaninglessness, and of despair.[10] They protect us from annihilation by relating us to society and cosmos, they protect us from meaninglessness by giving us a part to play in a communal narrative, and they protect us from despair by providing modalities of judgment and reconciliation.

IMMORTALITY AND ITS SYMBOLIC SURROGATES

Without attempting to catalogue the manifold ways that the world's cultures have provided for coming to terms with death, we can readily see what is promising in Lifton's scheme. The common achievement of the symbolic immortalities is to offer the individual a wider cosmos within which to dwell, nourished by a rich network of social, natural, and spiritual connections. They overcome isolation and are therefore both reasonable and adaptive, rather than illusory and regressive.

This is also the moral and political lesson Philippe Ariès wishes us to take home from his massive studies of death and society. In *The Hour of Our Death* as well as in his earlier work on childhood, he mourns the loss of community and the estrangement of individual consciousness, placing the blame at the door of secularism, nationalism, and liberal democratic ideologies.[11]

We can appreciate Ariès's insight about the perils of individualism, without necessarily adopting his inherent conservatism (even royalism). Indeed, recent interpreters of death in the West, seeing a crisis in human relations brought on by extreme individualism, have begun to move away from the Freudian call for heroic realism and to proclaim in its place an ethic of commitment and interconnectedness.[12] The consensus seems to be that individuality, as constructed in this society, has become too great a burden for any single person to bear alone.

Yet even to speak of the perils of individualism or of the need for the individual to find a wider cosmos in which to dwell is to use a distinctively modern idiom. Recent ethnographic and philosophical studies inspired by Marcel Mauss's 1938 lecture on the category of the person ("Une Catégorie de l"Esprit Humain: La Notion de Personne, Celle de 'Moi' ") show what a shifting category "person" can be.[13] The individualism of the modern West is only one way to parse the totality of human existence, and it can lead to fundamental errors in our scholarship; we tend to err in two opposing directions: either by importing alien categories of individuality and selfhood into our study of different societies or by assuming that notions of individuality are absent in those societies.

Attempts to account for the historical roots of modern individualism are legion. Some see Greco-Roman precursors, such as the evolution of *psychē* from its Homeric to its Socratic and Platonic conception as identified with reason and the ethical will; some credit the breakup of the *polis* and the increasingly individualistic understanding of the philosophic life, as found in the schools of the Stoics, Epicureans, Cynics. Others, such as Louis Dumont, hold that the most powerful force for individualism has been the Christian tradition: "Sociologically speaking, the emancipation of the individual through a personal transcendence, and the union of outworldly individuals in a community that treads on earth but has its heart in heaven, may constitute a passable formula for Christianity."[14]

Among more recent philosophical sources of modern individualism it is customary to cite, along with Descartes, the legacy of Kant, who influenced not only his successors but also his opponents to think of authentic selfhood as synonymous with freedom, accountability, moral autonomy, and inalienable rights. In the hands of democratic political and social theorists, who naturalized Kant's transcendental and unknowable self, this conception became a charter for individualism.[15]

Still, we have not arrived at the atomistic individual, until we take into account the impact of industrialism. Only in modern industrial societies does individualism become such an isolating force. Only now do we feel acutely that to exist as an individual is to be in peril, standing out exposed on the plain of being, an easy target for death.

In a world of atomistic individuals, the symbolic surrogates for immortality may fail to console. As Woody Allen puts it, "I don't want to achieve immortality through my works; I want to achieve immortality by not dying."

Suppose, however, that advances in medical technology were to make it possible to grant Woody Allen his wish. The thought of such a prospect has an unsettling effect; it raises hopes to an anxious pitch, while simultaneously intensifying the isolation of the individual who faces death.

Yet medical immortalism continues to receive serious attention from some of our more adventurous philosophers and religious thinkers. Robert Ellwood, in *The History and Future of Faith*, writes:

> As astounding as it may seem to those who have not been close to research in the field, it appears that managing the biochemical processes that bring about aging and death is feasible, and that sometime in the twenty-first century "immortality pills" or the equivalent, making life spans of many hundreds or even thousands of years the norm, may be available at the corner drugstore. At the end of *that* life span brain transplants to new, perhaps humanoid, organisms might prolong life unimaginably.[16]

It puts a strange spin on the millennialist hope to hear that we have been born just a few moments too soon to be present when the cure for death will be handed out. By proposing such a seemingly outlandish future and thus provoking, perhaps, an irrational "sour grapes" response, Ellwood does us a favor. For thinking through the problems with this scenario can bring clarity to one's views about death, identity, and eternal life.

The first problem, as Ellwood points out, is that this "immortality pill," far from bringing eternal life, gives humanity at best a bittersweet consolation prize for the loss of eternity. The Epic of Gilgamesh tells the same story. Pill or plant, such a cure is more likely to increase death anxiety than to overcome it. As death becomes rarer, it may be all the more fearsome; unprecedented longevity would merely extend our days of exposure to death and persuade us that we have all that much more to lose. Under such conditions, one can imagine developing an exaggerated fear of accidents.

Second, we are just as likely as Gilgamesh to lose the life-restoring plant from sheer forgetfulness or perversity. (As in the sleep test, which reveals that human nature, in its present condition, is not fit for eternal life).

Third, the prospect of life extension through brain transplants raises once again the knotty problem of mind/brain identity. Conceptions of an afterlife also raise this problem; no prescription for immortality worth its salt has ever promised to leave my habitual, cherished sense of "me" intact.

Supposing, however, that we do not lose the prize, and the immortality pill appears on schedule in, say, 2040. We might face devastating consequences from its use, as Ellwood points out: extreme over-population and consequent environmental collapse, leading both to war and to natural disasters. Ellwood suggests colonizing other worlds as a possible solution; and it is fascinating to note that here, once again, the thought of "other worlds" provides imaginative solace for the unbearable prospects we face in this world.[17]

We can only conclude that medical immortalism in its present form fails to provide a vital sense of continuity in the face of death.

NEAR-DEATH STUDIES

Another place we might look for a sense of continuity in the face of death is the recent proliferation of accounts of visionary and ecstatic near-death experience. Again the question will arise, whether our fascination with near-death testimony constitutes a new and especially virulent form of narcissistic death denial or whether it offers a valid way to come to terms with death. I would like to suggest that near-death testimony, though it indeed reflects the individualistic bias of our culture, nonetheless deserves to be taken seriously by scholars and religious thinkers.

Near-death experience first received widespread attention in 1975 with the publication of *Life After Life* by Raymond Moody.[18] A former philosophy professor turned psychiatrist, Moody began collecting stories of near-death experience while still in medical school. On the basis of 150 reports, Moody constructed a master narrative describing the "typical" near-death experience, which quickly became the standard source for portrayal of death and its aftermath in films and other popular media.[19]

Moody's book (an instant bestseller) inspired several ambitious clinical studies. The subject continues to receive attention, not only in the media, but also in journals of psychology and medicine and in the publications of professional societies for near-death studies in the United States, the United Kingdom, France, Norway, Holland, and Australia.[20]

In a 1981 survey by the Gallup organization, 15 percent of its U.S. sample reported having had a close brush with death; of that number, 34 percent claimed that the episode triggered ecstatic or visionary states of consciousness.[21] The frequency of this phenomenon is attested by other sources as well, but recent studies reveal greater variation in the content of near-death experience than the Moody narrative suggests.

The following features recur throughout contemporary accounts:

1. Separation from the body, sometimes accompanied by a "spectator" perspective, watching the scene of crisis from a distant or elevated vantage point.

2. Journey motifs, such as drifting through darkness, outer space, a "void," or a tunnel.

3. Encounter with deceased relatives or friends, or with a godlike or angelic presence (Moody's "being of light").

4. Review of one's past deeds in the form of a panoramic visual replay of memories (the life review). In cases of sudden encounter with life-threatening danger, this life review often takes precedence over other features.

5. Immersion in light and love. Many confess that this experience is indescribable. Cognitive and affective characteristics are fused. The keynote is a profound sense of security and protection, accompanied by a sense of receiving special messages or hidden truths. For some, this takes the form of an instantaneous, timeless, and comprehensive vision of the totality of existence.

6. Return to life, either involuntarily or by choice, to complete unfinished business on earth.

7. Transforming aftereffects, such as loss of fear of death, newfound zest for everyday life, and renewed dedication to the values of empathetic love, lifelong learning, and service to others. For some, these positive effects are accompanied by difficulties in adjusting to normal life.

The first reports on near-death experience in the media presented this testimony as exciting new evidence for an afterlife. In an effort to stem the tide of sensationalism, experts came forward from several quarters eager to attribute near-death experience to the mind-altering effects of drugs and anesthetics or to conditions which are part of the normal physiology of dying, such as oxygen deprivation, sensory isolation, elevated endorphin levels, and seizure activity in the brain. Near-death testimony was added to the list of targets for debunking attacks (along with metal-bending and trance channeling) by members of the Committee for Scientific Investigation of Claims of the Paranormal, a group of crusading skeptics.[22]

What both critics and researchers failed to notice was the striking evidence for the cultural shaping of near-death experience. They were unaware that what we call "near-death experience" today is nothing new. As this conference demonstrates, stories of people who return from death, bringing back eyewitness testimony about the other world, can be found in nearly every religious tradition; and although they have many similar features, such reports invariably portray this experience in ways that conform to cultural expectations. Had the critics realized this, they no doubt would have added it to their arsenal of arguments against the veridicality of near-experience.[23]

What are we to make of this testimony? None of the responsible researchers would claim that it is proof of an afterlife. This should not prevent us from taking it seriously, however, if only out of respect for the right of individuals to believe in their own experience. My own approach has been to acknowledge the physiological, psychological, and cultural conditions that shape visionary experience, yet at the same time to defend near-death testimony against its critics by shifting the focus from historical fact to narrative truth.

I have interpreted the near-death vision as a special kind of conversion experience, one in which the religious imagination transfigures the perceived world as a corollary to subjective transformation. As a conversion experience, a near-death episode can be evaluated in Jamesian fashion, with regard to its "fruits for life."

More speculatively, I suggest that near-death visions disclose the other world as an "imaginal" realm (to use Henri Corbin's term) in which the inner world is projected onto the stage of the imagination. The fruits of a near-death vision are found in its orienting power; and to those in our culture who are touched by hearing near-death testimony, it may legitimately offer, not a scientific endorsement of belief in the hereafter, but rather a narrative and imaginative pledge of continuity in the face of death.

IN MY BODY OR OUT OF MY BODY?

Now that we have had an overview of near-death testimony, I would like to focus on a particular question that has engaged me lately.[24] The question is: what can we learn from near-death testimony about the imaginative roots of our sense of self? What does it reveal to us about our understanding of personal identity?

One reason for current fascination with near-death testimony is that it speaks to an intense and widespread preoccupation in our society with problems of personal identity. This preoccupation is evident in the popularity of films that deal with body-swapping (*Big, All of Me,* etc.), in the proliferation of psychologies and therapies concerned with identity formation, and in the ongoing debate among professional philosophers concerning possible criteria for personal identity.[25]

Two aspects of near-death testimony are particularly revealing: the sense of separation from the body; and the retrieval, or creation, of memories during the life review.

In "Prophetic Voices," a public television documentary consisting of interviews with survivors of near-death experience, we hear vivid expressions of the sense of separation from the body.[26] A kindergarten teacher, Vita Ventra, tells us that she "zoomed" upwards, lost all sense of pain, and immediately realized that "I was out of body; I was no longer Vita; I had no gender; I was shapeless, odorless, and colorless." Another young woman describes looking down at her body with an attitude of serene detachment. "I wasn't in a body; I may have had a head or center; the rest of me was very loose. I wasn't my body. I was my mind, I say I was my spirit." The language sounds every bit as dualistic as Plato or Descartes. Yet it is an imaginative and dramatic dualism, closer in spirit to the multiple soul traditions of many cultures than to philosophical dualism. Often this dualism is accompanied by what I call "somatomorphism," in which the separated "I" takes on the forms and characteristics of a body. The principles of dualism and somatomorphism—which in the strictest philosophical terms might seem incompatible—appear as twin laws governing the imaginative construction of the self in the face of death. If we turn, now, to the life review, the narrative character of this construction will become more evident.

THE LIFE REVIEW

Although not an inevitable feature of near-death reports, the life review episode occurs in a wide variety of cases and holds special interest for our consideration of the relationship between death and personal identity. I would like to suggest that the life review functions in our culture as a visionary, imagistic therapy for identity confusion.

Even before the term *near-death experience* was coined, the idea that a drowning man sees his life pass before him had been planted in the popular imagination (where it quickly acquired the status of proverbial wisdom) by its treatment in several widely read nineteenth-century English and American memoirs and medical essays. Thomas De Quincey writes in his *Confessions of an English Opium-Eater*:

> I was once told by a near relative of mine that, having in her childhood fallen into a river, and being on the very verge of death but for the assistance which reached her at the last critical moment, she saw in a moment her whole life, clothed in its forgotten incidents, arrayed before her as in a mirror, not successively, but simultaneously; and she had a faculty developed as suddenly for comprehending the whole and every part.[27]

In the late nineteenth century, medical writers like Dr. William Munk, historian for the Royal College of Physicians in London, made a small industry out of collecting anecdotes like this in order to show that death need not be painful. In his book on *Euthanasia or Medical Treatment in the Aid of Easy Dying* (1887), Munk relates the experience of the famous British naval officer, Admiral Beaufort, when he fell off a ship into Portsmouth harbor as a young boy. As soon as Beaufort stopped struggling, a feeling of contentment swept over him, his mind calm but at the same time alert and invigorated, and he found himself reviewing his life in reverse chronological order:

> the whole period of my existence seemed to be placed before me in a kind of panoramic review, and each act of it seemed to be

accompanied by a consciousness of right or wrong, or by some reflection on its cause or its consequences; indeed, many trifling events which had been long forgotten, then crowded into my imagination, and with the character of recent familiarity.[28]

In 1892, the Swiss geologist and Alpinist Albert Heim published an article on thirty mountain climbers, himself among them, who had survived nearly fatal falls. For most of the survivors Heim interviewed, the experience of rushing headlong toward death was neither frightening nor painful; rather, they remembered feeling calm, detached from any sense of real danger, lucid, and even joyful. In many cases, this beatific experience was accompanied by a panoramic recall of memories. Heim's own account is typical:

> I saw my whole past life take place in many images, as though on a stage at some distance from me. I saw myself as the chief character in the performance. Everything was transfigured as though by a heavenly light and everything was beautiful without grief, without anxiety, and without pain.
>
> . . . I acted out my life, as though I were an actor on a stage upon which I looked down from practically the highest gallery in the theatre. Both hero and onlooker, I was as though doubled.[29]

Careful studies published by psychiatrist Russell Noyes, Jr., and clinical psychologist Roy Kletti have confirmed that visual replay of memories is indeed a widespread phenomenon, especially among accident victims suddenly faced with life-threatening danger.[30] A teen-aged motorcyclist involved in a head-on collision with a stalled car recalls seeing his life flash before his eyes "like lantern slides in quick succession."[31] A drowning victim remembers a kaleidoscopic vision of the events of his life: "they were going very fast like one of those strobe lights that you see today, like a real fast flip of slides, instant takes."[32] In these and countless other cases, certain features stand out as particularly tantalizing to interpret: the sense of self as spectator, the attitude of serene detachment, the comprehensiveness and simultaneity of the visual replay of memories, and the implication that the life review constitutes a final summation and judgment of one's character and history.

The sense of self as a spectator reminds us of Freud's dictum that "our own death is indeed unimaginable, and whenever we make the attempt to imagine it we can perceive that we really survive as spectators."[33] Accordingly, psychological interpreters of near-death experience have seen it either as a regressive reaction to the unacceptable prospect of death or, more charitably, as a healthy coping strategy designed both to maximize the chances for survival and to pave the way, if necessary, for graceful acceptance of death.

Noyes and Kletti explain the spectator viewpoint and the attitude of serene detachment as manifestations of "depersonalization," a syndrome that ordinarily would be treated as pathological but may be considered adaptive when it is triggered by situations of extreme danger.

Neurological explanations have been suggested as well. Involuntary panoramic visual recall of memories sometimes accompanies the "aura" preceding epileptic seizures and can be triggered by electrical stimulation of the temporal cortex. This has led some neuropsychologists to propose limbic lobe agitation (which can result from reduction in the brain's oxygen supply) as the neural basis for the life review.

Although the psychological and neurological explanations teach us a great deal about the conditions that give rise to the life review, they leave the work of interpretation unfinished. As Noyes and Kletti acknowledge, these experiences may have more than merely transient adaptive value: "the vastly alerted mind may be set to work upon final tasks . . . the individual nearing death may accept the reality before him and, from a transcendent perspective, capture a glimpse of his life in harmony with the universe."[34]

In *Otherworld Journeys,* I suggested that the contemporary experience of witnessing one's past deeds in the form of a movie or slide show may be an updated version of an ancient way of symbolizing postmortem judgment: the encounter with one's deeds (or thoughts, words, and deeds) in an externalized form. In the history of the world's religious traditions, this motif has appeared in guises as various as the mirror of karma, the book of deeds, the personification of virtues and vices, and the weighing of deeds. The one common thread that links all of these manifold expressions is the idea that at death or on a final day of judgment, each person sees himself and his works unmasked.

In contemporary accounts of near-death experience, the life review is primarily a consoling and therapeutic experience; but vestiges of its judicial function remain. The twenty-four year old survivor of a nearly fatal automobile accident recalls:

It was as if I were trying to decide whether or not I would like to be dead. I seemed to be weighing the "goods" and "bads" in life. I remembered bad stuff and felt kind of happy that I was dying. Then my mind would shift to something good: parents, girl-friends, successes, stuff like that.

. . . The good thoughts seemed to last longer than the bad ones. It seemed as though I was weighing life, thinking about what had happened and deciding whether or not it was worth continuing to live.[35]

When judgment appears as an explicit feature of contemporary accounts of the life review, the emphasis is on self-evaluation, learning, and growth rather than on judicial assessment and pun-ishment. The following example is typical for its reassuring treat-ment of these themes:

And into this great peace that I had become there came the life of Phyllis parading past my view . . . The reliving included not only the deeds committed by Phyllis since her birth in 1937 in Twin Falls, Idaho, but also a reliving of every thought ever thought and every word ever spoken PLUS the effect of every thought, word and deed upon everyone and anyone who had ever come within her sphere of influence whether she actually knew them or not PLUS the effect of her every thought, word and deed upon the weather, the soil, plants and animals, the water, everything else . . . I never before realized that we were responsible and accountable for EVERY SINGLE THING WE DID. That was overwhelming!

It was me judging me, not some heavenly St. Peter. And my judgment was critical and stern. I was not satisfied with many, many things Phyllis had done, said or thought. There was a feeling of sadness and failure, yet a growing feeling of joy when the realization came that Phyllis had always done SOME-THING . . . She tried. Much of what she did was constructive and positive. She learned and grew in her learning. This was satisfying. Phyllis was okay.[36]

In contemporary accounts, the life review sometimes takes place in connection with interrogation by a divine presence (Moody's "being of light"). Unlike traditional renditions of this theme (such as Islamic accounts of interrogation in the grave), however, this ques-tioning is as gentle and nonjudgmental as a session of Rogerian therapy. There are no real sins, only regrettable mistakes, which always turn out to be opportunities for learning and growth.

Contemporary near-death testimony thus proves to be as much a product of cultural expectations as the more traditional symbolic ways of envisioning and experiencing death. Comparative study compels us to acknowledge this cultural shaping and prevents us from treating contemporary accounts as more direct or privileged descriptions of the experience of death.

Nothing requires us, however, to declare the life review experience illusory. Although it is socially and culturally conditioned, and although it may be triggered by neural and psychological mechanisms, the life review is nonetheless a symbolic encounter in which real work—the imaginative construction of identity—gets done.

MEMORY AND IDENTITY: A MODEST CONSTRUCTIVIST PROPOSAL

If we accept the existentialist premise that the self has no nature, only history, then the life review may consummate that history, completing a process that normally accompanies aging. Parallels to the life review can be found not only in accounts of the afterlife but also in neuropsychological literature investigating the phenomenon of "elderly reminiscence."[37] As one ages and approaches death, vivid memories of youth may begin to surface unbidden, making the present fade by comparison.

Rather than seeing elderly reminiscence as a sign of deterioration, many psychologists interpret it as a constructive effort to achieve integration before death. For those who face death suddenly or prematurely, and are thus deprived of this experience of gradually collecting and reviewing images of the past, the life review perhaps serves as an accelerated way to accomplish one of life's essential tasks. Similarly, psychologists have noticed parallels between the life review and the vivid visual replay of memories that sometimes accompanies bereavement.[38]

Retrieval of memories, whether on the analyst's couch, or through casual reminiscence, is well known to be an unreliable source of historical information.[39] Yet, as I will suggest below, "narrative truths" may emerge from the collaboration between analyst and analysand, near-death survivor and interviewer, or visionary and culture.

Lawrence Sullivan has observed that public practices in response to death provide the occasion for separate histories to collide and fuse.[40] A close brush with death may, similarly, bring on the collision and fusion of the individual's separate histories.

Hence, many eschatological traditions describe more than one moment of death, more than one decisive ritual for disposing of the dead, and more than one final reckoning after death. Scholars have often been puzzled by this redundancy. Why, after all, would a deathbed judgment not be sufficient to set the final seal on an individual's character and destiny? Perhaps it is that while one act of narrative composition reaches completion at the moment of death, other story lines (represented in some traditions by multiple souls) come to fruition at a moment of greater communal significance: the day of judgment, the moment of rebirth, or the occasion of reburial when the individual rejoins the ancestors.[41]

The parallels among the life review, psychoanalytic retrieval of memories, autobiographical composition, and eschatological traditions with redundant burials and judgments help us to understand how the life review functions as a means of imaginative construction of the self in the face of death. Anticipation of death makes one acutely aware that personal identity is not a given—hence the impulse to gather together the discrete moments that make up a life and see them in memory as a simultaneous whole.

The life review neither depends upon nor necessarily supports belief in a substantial self that survives death. As Derek Parfit argues in *Reasons and Persons,* personal identity, as understood according to the usual philosophical criteria, "is not what matters"; a sense of vital continuity and integrity in the face of death can be achieved without it.[42]

If death is the end of life, then the life review is the gathering together of a self in order to make a true holocaust—a complete burnt offering of oneself.

The life review could also be seen as a work of translation, converting an individual lifetime from a temporal project, as existence under construction, into a complete structure or finished statement. From a theistic perspective, one might say that the consummation of a life is the completion of a thought in the mind of God or that the life review gathers one's past experiences into a comprehensive and simultaneous thought, which distantly echoes or approximates the comprehensive and simultaneous wholeness of divine thought.

Memory, then, is the key not only to identity but also to a sense of wholeness. This is what Augustine finds, when he reflects on the power of memory that enabled him to make his *confessio,* or sacrificial offering of his past. Like Hume, Augustine points out that we experience ourselves as fragmented; "I am divided between time gone by and time to come, and its course is a mystery to me."[43] Like everything else that is subject to time, we seem to be "coming out of what does not yet exist, passing through what has no duration, and moving into what no longer exists."[44] Such continuity as we do experience is a gift of memory, both private and communal. Significantly, it is through what Augustine calls the "higher memory" that he believes we can recover our true identity, in relation to the triune God. A constructivist understanding of memory and identity stops short of such a confession—but does not forbid it.

The salvific potential of memory (even when that memory brings with it conviction of sin) is conveyed by Tolstoy's harrowing vision of the life review in *The Death of Ivan Ilyich*:

> One after another images of his past came to mind. His recollections always began with what was closest in time and shifted back to what was most remote, to his childhood, and lingered there . . .
>
> And together with this train of recollections, another flashed through his mind—recollections of how his illness had progressed and become more acute. Here, too, the farther back in time he went, the more life he found. There had been more goodness in his life earlier and more of life itself . . . There was only one bright spot back at the beginning of life; after that things grew blacker and blacker, moved faster and faster. "In inverse ratio to the square of the distance from death," thought Ivan Ilyich.[45]

It is the life review, triggered by the immediacy of death, that makes it possible for Ivan Ilyich to realize that his life was "not the real thing" and to redeem his last moments by grieving and dying authentically.

Similarly, in T. S. Eliot's "Little Gidding," the last of the "gifts reserved for age to set a crown upon your lifetime's effort" is "the rending pain of re-enactment of all that you have done, and been." Yet in the bitter fruit of remembrance of past sins lies the seed of redemption: "this is the use of memory: for liberation."

In traditions that envision many lifetimes, the review of deeds is no less significant: it not only sums up and assesses the acts of a single life in a vast series but also represents a hope that transcends the series, leaving behind the calculus of merit and demerit, punishment and reward. That hope is to make one's life a perfect offering, in which attachment has been wholly immolated by transcendent knowledge, ascetic practice, or devotion, and in which actions therefore bear none of the bitter fruit of further bondage to samsara. Similarly, the recollection of past lives is presented as a significant meditative attainment even in Buddhist literature, where this experience of remembering serves as a harbinger of liberation rather than a proof of personal continuity.

What we learn about the imaginative construction of the self from the life review and its analogues in spiritual life thus appears to be compatible with widely differing ways of understanding personal identity. Yet we still need to find out more about the presence, absence, or variations of the life review in different cultures. We need to ask, cross-culturally, what sorts of things are remembered? What counts as a life history?[46]

According to Mircea Eliade, although the life review is found in many religions and folk traditions, it is preeminently an artifact of historical consciousness; for archaic religious consciousness, in contrast, personal identity is achieved by an *anamnesis* that abolishes time. Echoing the classical motif of the senectitude of the world, Eliade goes so far as to suggest that our culture's obsession with history may be a collective life review in the face of impending death: "Our Western civilisation, before it foundered, would be for the last time remembering all its past, from protohistory until the total wars. The historiographical consciousness of Europe—which some have regarded as its highest title to lasting fame—would in fact be the supreme moment which precedes and announces death."[47]

Eliade's observations are suggestive; but we must consider the possibility that he has exaggerated and idealized the contrast between archaic and modern consciousness. Not all the evidence is in yet; for now, we must be content to say that given the culturally specific character of life review experiences, we would not be warranted in using the life review to support (or to refute) a doctrine of the self as a substantial unity.

We are on safer ground if we treat the life review as a culturally shaped activity of imaginative unification of the self; as such, our study of the life review relativizes all doctrines of the self by pointing to their imagistic nature. Yet by preferring a constructivist to an essentialist model here, we are not obliged to deny the existence of an immortal soul. Modesty prevents us from taking a God's-eye view; our proper task is to acknowledge the empirical reality of fragmentation, marvel at the powers of imaginative construction of meaning, and fall silent before the ultimate mysteries of consciousness that may pass beyond this. We can thus take advantage of current scholarly explorations of the constructed character of bodily and mental awareness, without ending in skepticism.

As a thought experiment, we might apply this constructivist approach to Descartes. Is it possible that when Descartes says, "I think, therefore I exist," he is engaged in an imaginative construction of his sense of self? When he withdraws into his thoughts in the search for certainty, and envisions himself a spectator who looks down upon his body, is this not a speculative analogue to near-death experience? But Descartes will not allow us to pursue this analogy very far, for he attempts to cut himself off from his imaginative roots by declaring, "examining attentively that which I was, I saw that I could conceive that I had no body, and that there was no world nor place where I might be; but yet that I could not for all that conceive that I was not."[48]

Descartes attempts to be dualistic without being somatomorphic, without noticing, to use Mark Johnson's phrase, "the body in the mind."[49] What near-death testimony suggests, however, is that the imaginative power that makes the self a spectator also (and perhaps inevitably) creates for the self another world to live in and bestows form and figure on its thoughts.

To move beyond the current impasse in understanding questions of personal identity, we must recognize that our sense of self has its roots in an imaginative realm, where such contraries as dualism and somatomorphism, multiple souls and redundant judgments, coexist. What I am trying to suggest is that the imaginative character of our experience is not something we need to regret; exploring this realm further opens up new ways of appreciating the possibilities for authentic personal existence and continuity in the face of death.

Antony Flew, well known for his critiques of Cartesian assumptions about death and identity, once remarked that "the news of the immortality of my soul would be of no more concern to me than the news that my appendix would be preserved eternally in a bottle."[50] For Flew, it is an either-or situation; either I can unequivocally identify myself with a soul-substance, which departs at death, or I am not rationally entitled to think of myself as immortal. I must choose, so to speak, between Descartes and decomposition.

Yet there may be another alternative, if we consider the religious imagination and the stories it tells us about ourselves. If there is indeed a power great enough to resist mortal decomposition, that power might be found at work in the religious imagination, ever weaving fresh compositions out of our fragmentary, time-bound histories. Once we recognize the religious imagination as the power that composes and renews our life, then we no longer need to base our prospects for immortality on the invulnerability of an invisible internal organ.

NOTES

1. Sigmund Freud, "Thoughts for the Times on War and Death" (1915) in *Collected Papers*, vol. 4, authorized translation under the supervision of Joan Rivière (London and New York, 1959) 304–05.

2. Ibid., 310.

3. Geoffrey Gorer, "The Pornography of Death," in *Death, Grief and Mourning* (New York, 1965) 192–99. Reprinted from the British journal *Encounter*, October 1955.

4. See Philippe Ariès, *The Hour of Our Death*, trans. Helen Weaver (New York, 1981; reprint, New York, 1982); *Western Attitudes toward Death from the Middle Ages to the Present*, trans. Patricia M. Ranum (Baltimore, 1974); *Images of Man and Death*, trans. Janet Lloyd (Cambridge, Mass., 1985).

5. Ernest Becker, *The Denial of Death* (New York, 1973).

6. Elisabeth Kübler-Ross first presented her five-stage model to a wide public in *On Death and Dying* (New York, 1969).

7. Erik H. Erikson, *The Life Cycle Completed: A Review* (New York and London, 1982) 61.

8. Erik H. Erikson, *Identity and the Life Cycle* (New York, 1959; reprint, New York, 1980) 104.

9. Robert J. Lifton, "On Death and Continuity," in *The Life of the Self* (New York, 1976) 32–33.

10. Paul Tillich, *The Courage to Be* (New Haven, 1952).

11. Philippe Ariès, *The Hour of Our Death: Centuries of Childhood*, trans. Robert Baldick (New York, 1962).

12. See, for example: Ralph C. Johnston, Jr., *Confronting Death: Psychoreligious Responses* (Ann Arbor, Mich., 1988). Robert J. Kasten-

baum, *Death, Society, and Human Experience,* 4th ed. (New York, 1991). Robert Jay Lifton, *The Broken Connection* (New York, 1979). Robert Jay Lifton and Eric Olson, *Living and Dying* (New York, 1974). Alfred G. Killilea, *The Politics of Being Mortal* (Lexington, Ky., 1988).

13.   In Michael Carrithers, Steven Collins, Steven Lukes, eds., *The Category of the Person: Anthropology, Philosophy, History* (Cambridge, 1985).

14.   Louis Dumont, "A Modified View of Our Origins: The Christian Beginnings of Modern Individualism," in *Carrithers, Collins, and Lukes,* The Category of the Person, 99.

15.   Discussed by Steven Collins, in "Categories, Concepts or Predicaments? Remarks on Mauss's Use of Philosophical Terminology," in Carrithers, Collins, and Lukes, *The Category of the Person,* 46–82.

16.   Robert Ellwood, *The History and Future of Faith* (New York, 1988) 145.

17.   Ibid., 146.

18.   Raymond A. Moody, Jr., *Life after Life: The Investigation of a Phenomenon—Survival of Bodily Death* (Atlanta, 1975; reprint, New York, 1976).

19.   Moody's master narrative, in *Life after Life,* 21–23:

> A man is dying and, as he reaches the point of greatest physical distress, he hears himself pronounced dead by his doctor. He begins to hear an uncomfortable noise, a loud ringing or buzzing, and at the same time feels himself moving very rapidly through a long dark tunnel. After this, he suddenly finds himself outside of his own physical body, but still in the immediate physical environment, and he sees his own body from a distance, as though he is a spectator. He watches the resuscitation attempt from this unusual vantage point and is in a state of emotional upheaval.
>
> After a while, he collects himself and becomes more accustomed to his odd condition. He notices that he still has a "body," but one of a very different nature and with very different powers from the physical body he has left behind. soon other things begin to happen. Others come to meet and to help him. He glimpses the spirits of relatives and friends who have already died, and a loving, warm spirit of a kind he has never encountered before—a being of light—appears before him. This being asks him a question, nonverbally, to make him evaluate his life and helps him along by showing him a panoramic, instantaneous playback of the major events of his life. At some point he finds himself approaching some sort of barrier or border, apparently representing the limit between earthly life and the next life. Yet, he finds that he must go back to the earth, that the time for his death has not yet come. At this point he resists, for by now he is taken up with his experiences in the afterlife and does not want to return. He is overwhelmed by intense feelings of joy, love, and peace. Despite his attitude, though, he somehow reunites with his physical body and lives.

Later he tries to tell others, but he has trouble doing so. In the first place, he can find no human words adequate to describe these unearthly episodes. He also finds that others scoff, so he stops telling other people. Still, the experience affects his life profoundly, especially his views about death and its relationship to life.

20. See Moody, *Life after Life* and *The Light Beyond* (New York, 1988). Bruce Greyson and Charles Flynn, eds., *The Near-Death Experience* (Springfield, Ill., 1984). Kenneth Ring, *Life at Death: A Scientific Investigation of the Near-Death Experience* (New York, 1980) and *Heading Toward Omega: In Search of the Meaning of the Near-Death Experience* (New York, 1984). Michael B. Sabom, *Recollections of Death: A Medical Investigation* (New York, 1982). George Gallup, Jr., and William Proctor, *Adventures in Immortality: A Look beyond the Threshold of Death* (New York, 1982). Craig Lundahl, ed., *A Collection of Near-Death Research Readings* (Chicago, 1982). Robert Kastenbaum, ed., *Between Life and Death* (New York, 1979). Melvin Morse, *Closer to the Light* (New York, 1990). Articles on near-death experience have appeared in *The Journal of Nervous and Mental Disease*, *Lancet*, *Omega*, *The American Journal of Psychiatry*, and the *Journal of Near-Death Studies*, edited by Bruce Greyson and published by Human Sciences Press. *The Journal of Near-Death Studies* is affiliated with the International Association for Near-Death Studies.

21. Discussed in Gallup and Proctor, *Adventures in Immortality*.

22. For a discussion of efforts to explain near-death experience, see Carol Zaleski, *Otherworld Journeys: Accounts of Near-Death Experience in Medieval and Modern Times*, rev. ed. (New York, 1989) chap. 9, "Ecstatics and Statistics," and chap. 10, "Explanations and Counterexplanations."

23. For examples, see I. P. Couliano, *Out of this World: Otherworldly Journeys from Gilgamesh to Albert Einstein* (Boston, 1991); Zaleski, *Otherworld Journeys*, chap. 1; also Lawrence E. Sullivan, *Icanchu's Drum: An Orientation to Meaning in South American Religions* (New York, 1988) 524–48; and the articles in Lawrence E. Sullivan, ed., *Death, Afterlife, and the Soul*, selections from *The Encyclopedia of Religion* (New York, 1989).

24. Portions of what follows were presented previously at the Conference on Science and Religion, Columbia University, Arden House, January 19–21, 1990.

25. Don Browning has observed a shift in the kinds of personality disorders for which patients currently seek therapy. "There seems to have been a massive move away from the classical neurotic personality who has had an unsuccessfully resolved Oedipal problem that expresses itself in obsessive-compulsive, hysterical, or phobic difficulties of various kinds. Both Erikson and Kohut recognize this trend and with their respective

concepts of identity confusion and narcissism are trying to name the new sociocultural trends in human personality difficulties" (*Religious Thought and the Modern Psychologies* [Philadelphia, 1987] 208).

On the debate concerning criteria for personal identity, see Harold Noonan, *Personal Identity* (London: Routledge, 1989); Derek Parfit, *Reasons and Persons* (New York, 1984); Bernard Williams, *Problems of the Self*; Antony Flew, *The Logic of Mortality* (Oxford, 1987); S. Shoemaker and R. Swinburne, *Personal Identity* (Oxford, 1984); Anthony Kenny, *The Metaphysics of Mind* (Oxford, New York, 1990); Amélie Oksenberg Rorty, *The Identities of Persons* (Berkeley, 1976).

26.   "Prophetic Voices" public television documentary in which Kenneth Ring interviews four near-death experiencers. Produced for WGBY-TV, Springfield, Mass., by Andrew J. Silver, 1981.

27.   Thomas de Quincey, *Confessions of an English Opium-Eater*, quoted by Russell Noyes, Jr., "Dying and Mystical Consciousness," *Journal of Thanatology* (January/February 1971) 30.

28.   Quoted by Noyes, "Dying and Mystical Consciousness," 29.

29.   Albert Heim, "Notizen über den Tod durch Absturz," *Jahrbuch des schweizer alpen Club* 27(1892) 327–37. Translated by Russell Noyes, Jr., and Roy Kletti in "The Experience of Dying from Falls," *Omega* 2(1972) 45–52.

30.   In addition to the articles cited above, see the following articles jointly authored by Russell Noyes, Jr., and Roy Kletti: "Depersonalization in Response to Life-Threatening Danger," *Comprehensive Psychiatry* 18(July/August 1977) 375–84; "Depersonalization in the Face of Life-Threatening Danger: A Description," *Psychiatry* 39(1976) 19–27; "Depersonalization in the Face of Life-Threatening Danger: An Interpretation," *Omega* 7(1976) 103–14; "The Experience of Dying from Falls," in Richard A. Kalish, ed., *Death, Dying, Transcending* (Farmingdale, N.Y., 1980) 129–36; "Panoramic Memory: A Response to the Threat of Death," *Omega* 8(1977) 181–94.

31.   Noyes and Kletti, "Panoramic Memory," 184.

32.   Ibid.

33.   Sigmund Freud, "Thoughts for the Times on War and Death," 304–5.

34.   Noyes and Kletti, "Depersonalization: An Interpretation," 113.

35.   Noyes and Kletti, "Panoramic Memory," 186–87.

36.   P. M. H. Atwater, *I Died Three Times in 1977* (Dayton, Va., 1980) 22. See also her fuller account in *Coming Back to Life* (New York, 1988).

37.   Robert N. Butler, "The Life Review: An Integration of Reminiscence in the Aged," *Psychiatry* 26(1963) 65–76. See also Robert N.

Butler and M. I. Lewis, *Aging and Mental Health: Positive Psychological Approaches* (St. Louis, 1973).

38.   Colin M. Parkes, *Bereavement: Studies of Grief in Adult Life* (New York, 1972).

39.   See Donald Spence, *Narrative Truth and Historical Truth: Meaning and Interpretation in Psychoanalysis* (New York, 1982). Steven Kepnes, "Telling and Retelling: The Use of Narrative in Psychoanalysis and Religion," in Steven Kepnes and David Tracy, eds., *The Challenge of Psychology to Faith* (New York, 1982). E. Kris, "The Recovery of Childhood Memories in Psychoanalysis," *The Psychoanalytic Study of the Child* 11(1956) 54–88.

40.   Lawrence E. Sullivan, public lecture on "The Spectacle of Death" at Smith College, April 11, 1991.

41.   Cp. Lawrence E. Sullivan, *Icanchu's Drum*: "Elements of the personality unravel after death and components of the body and psyche are redistributed to their various postmortem abodes" 669. On multiple deaths, see 670.

42.   Parfit, *Reasons and Persons*, 245–306.

43.   Saint Augustine, *Confessions*, trans. R. S. Pine-Coffin (Harmondsworth, 1961) 11:29, 279.

44.   Ibid., 11:21, 269.

45.   Leo Tolstoy, *The Death of Ivan Ilyich*, trans. Lynn Solotaroff (New York, 1981) 122–23.

46.   For critical perspectives on autobiography, see Avrom Fleishman, *Figures of Autobiography: The Language of Self-Writing in Victorian and Modern England* (Berkeley, 1983) 1–108, 471–79; James Olney, *Metaphors of Self: The Meaning of Autobiography* (Princeton, 1972); James Olney, ed., *Autobiography: Essays Theoretical and Critical* (Princeton, 1980); Roy Pascal, *Design and Truth in Autobiography* (Cambridge, Mass., 1960); Jeff Todd Titon, "The Life Story," *Journal of American Folklore* 90(1980) 280; Karl Joachim Weintraub, *The Value of the Individual: Self and Circumstance in Autobiography* (Chicago, 1978).

47.   Mircea Eliade, *Myths, Dreams, and Mysteries*, trans. Philip Mairet (New York, 1960) 234–35.

48.   René Descartes, *Discourse on the Method* 1, in *The Philosophical Works*, trans. E. S. Haldane and G. R. T. Ross (Cambridge, 1934) 101; quoted and discussed by Antony Flew in *The Logic of Mortality*, 93.

49.   Mark Johnson, *The Body in the Mind: The Bodily Basis of Meaning, Imagination, and Reason* (Chicago, 1987).

50.   Antony Flew, "Death," in Antony Flew and Alasdair Macintyre, eds., *New Essays in Philosophical Theology*, (London, 1950) 270.

CONTRIBUTORS

Tzvi Abusch, Brandeis University

Robert F. Campany, Indiana University

Adela Y. Collins, The University of Chicago

John J. Collins, The University of Chicago

Nathaniel Deutch, Hunter College

Arthur J. Droge, The University of Chicago

Gary L. Ebersole, The University of Chicago

Michael Fishbane, The University of Chicago

W. Clark Gilpin, The University of Chicago

David Halperin, The University of North Carolina

Martha Himmelfarb, Princeton, University

Moshe Idel, The Hebrew University of Jerusalem

Bernard McGinn, The University of Chicago

Alan F. Segal, Barnard College, Columbia University

Jonathan Z. Smith, The University of Chicago

Guy G. Stroumsa, The Hebrew University of Jerusalem

BIBLICAL REFERENCES
INDEX

Gn 1, 71
1:2, 292–3, 297, 301
3, 227
26, 99–100
5:18–24, 103
15, 70
28:12, 275
49:22, 220–1

Exodus, 97, 100
1:26, 100
7:1, 51
20:21, 52
23, 112
24:3, 99
    20, 99
    21, 99, 107, 110, 112,
      273
24, 99
24:1, 220
    9–10, 45
25:19, 69
33, 111
33:18–23, 100
34, 111
34:29–35, 111

Leviticus
6:18, 187
7:1, 187
7:37, 187

Numbers
16:22, 198

Deuteronomy
5:31, 103
6:4–6, 189
6:4, 223

6:5, 113
10:14, 62
11:22, 183
30:12, 45
33:5, 52

I Kings
8:27, 62
18:42, 98

Isaiah
6:1, 21
6:6–9, 22
22:14, 199

Ezekiel, 100
1, 98, 140
1:26, 97, 100
1:28, 110
9:4, 228

Psalms, 100
25, 199
25:1, 201
32:6, 301
44:23, 184, 201
82:1, 101
89:36–7, 49
104:2, 259
109:22, 185
110, 52
110:1, 49
145:15, 221
147:40, 107

Proverbs
30:4, 45

411

Job
38:7, 99, 102

Lamentations
3:23, 272

Daniel, 100, 130
2:22, 259
7, 49–50, 66, 99, 174–6
  10, 272
  13, 99
9:18, 227
12, 96, 97
12:1–3, 96
  3, 99, 103, 104

Nehemiah
9:6, 62

Matthew
19:28, 50
25:31, 50
27:52, 144

Luke
22:30, 50 (n. 31)

Acts, 108

Romans
5:3, 114
6:4, 110
7:24, 114
8:10, 114
  13, 114
  17, 110, 114
  18, 110
  29, 110, 114
9:23, 110
10:9–12, 112
12:2, 113

1Corinthians
2:8, 110
12:3, 112
15:43, 113
  49, 110
16:22, 112

2Corinthians, 97, 108, 129
1:16, 114
2:3–9, 66
3:16–4:6, 110–1
4:4, 109
  15–7, 110
8:2, 114
10–13, 66
12, 61, 109
12:1–9, 108
  1, 67
  2–10, 67

Galatians
1, 108
1:16, 113
14:19, 113

Ephesians
1:17, 110
  18, 110
3:16, 110
4:10, 68
6:9, 68

Philippians
1:29, 114
2:6, 109, 112
  9, 112
  11, 112
3:10, 113
3:20–1, 113–4
3:21, 110
4:19, 110

Colossians
1:5, 68
1:15, 109
1:27, 110
3:1, 50
      4, 110

1Thessalonians
1:16, 114
2:14, 114
3:3, 114

2Thessalonians
1:4, 114

1Timothy
1:11, 110

Hebrews
1:3, 50, 110
4:14, 58

James
2:1, 109–10

Revelation, 79
3:21, 50
20:4, 50

NONBIBLICAL AUTHORS
AND WORKS

Abelard, 144, 294–7, 299, 304–5
    Diaelctica, 297
    Theologia Christiana, 296
    Theologia Scholarium, 296
    Theologia summi boni, 296
Abudarham, 188
Abulafia, Abraham, 211, 251–2, 255–6
Abulafia, Todros ben Joseph Ha-Levi, 256
Acts of Perpetua and Felicitas, 155–7
Adapa, 15, 17
Akiba, 127, 191–2, 254, 269
Alexander Polyhistor, 51
Albodini, Judah, 211
Angelet, Joseph
    Livnat ha-Sappir, 221–2
Apocalypse of Abraham, 61, 70–2, 77, 100–1, 124, 131
Apocalypse of Moses, 68
Apocalypse of Peter, 144–5
Apocalypse of Zephaniah, 101, 132
Apuleius
    De Platone et eius dogmate, 291
    Metamorphoses, 142
Aquinas, Thomas, 308
Aristophanes
    The Frogs, 144
Arnold of Bonneval, 302
Asclepius, 292
Augustine, 146–7, 300, 303–4
    De civitate Dei, 292, 294
    De Genesi ad litteram liber imperfectus, 292–3
    De immortalitate animae, 292
    De musica, 292
    Retractationes, 292
Avot de Rabbi Nathan, 186
Avraham ben Natan Hayarh i of Lunel
    Sefer ha-Manhig, 188
Azikri, Eliezer
    Milei de Shemaya, 210, 222
    Sefer Ḥaredim, 191, 194

Azulai, Hayyim Yoseph David
    Midbar Qadmut, 253

Bahiya ben Asher
    Commentary on the Pentateuch, 198, 253
Baraies, 128–30
Bamidbar Rabba, 52
2 Baruch, 71, 106
3 Baruch, 61, 71, 77–80, 130
Basilides, 85–6
Bayly, Louis
    The Practice of Pietie, 365
Bernard of Clairvaux, 302, 304–5
    Tractatus de erroribus Petri Abaelardi, 304
Boethius
    De Consolatione philosphiae, 292–3, 304
Bonaventure, 308
Būkha⁻ri, 281
    Ṣaḥiḥ, 276

Calvin, 144
Canticle of Michael, 43, 44
Capella, Martianus, 300
    De nuptiis Philologii et Mercurii, 292–3, 299
Celsus, 82–3, 86
Chalcidius, 291–2, 302, 307
Chong, Wang, 355
Cicero, 291
    De natura deorum, 291
Clement of Alexandria, 166
    Stromateis, 164
Community Rule, 53
Compendium Philosophiae, 304
Cordovero, Moses
    Èlimah Rabbati, 219
    Sefer Gerushin, 210–11
Cyprian
    On the Lapsed, 160

Damascius
    Life of Isadore, 143
Damascus Document, 54
Dante, 147
Dā'ūd Qaysarī, 277
Descent of Inanna/Ishtar, 15–7
Diogenes Laertius
    Lives of Eminent Philosophers,
    140–1
Diwan Abathur, 172
Dov Ber, 202–3
    Quntres ha-Hipta'alut, 202
Sha'ar ha-Teshuvah veha-Tefillah, 202

Ebreo, Leone, 308
Eleazar ben R. Yehuda, 188
Elimelekh of Lizensk
    Tzeṭl Qoṭon, 203–4
1 Enoch, 52–3, 141
    Book of the Watchers, 45–8, 62,
    72, 129
    Similitudes of Enoch, 50, 61,
    66–7, 97, 103–4
    Book of the Heavenly
    Luminaries, 73
    Epistle of Enoch, 50
2 Enoch, 61, 72–4, 77, 79, 101, 105,
    130
3 Enoch, 49, 101, 107, 141, 273
Epiphanius
    Against Heresies, 84, 86
Enuma Elish, 64, 71
Erasmus, 144
Erberry, William
    A Call to the Churches, 377
Etana, 15
Eudoxos, 69
Eusebius
    Church History, 163, 165
    Martyrs of Palestine, 163
    Vita Constantini, 143
Ezekiel the Tragedian
    Exagogue, 50–2, 141
    Moses, 101
4 Ezra, 71, 130, 132

Ficino, Marsilio, 308
First Thoughts in Three Forms, The,
    85

Gikatilla, Joseph, 251, 255
Gilgamesh, xi, 3–5, 8–12, 15
    Death of Gilgamesh, 4
    Gilgamesh and the Land of the
    Living, 3, 7
    Gilgamesh, Enkidu and the
    Netherworld, 3
Ghaitī, Najm al-Din al-, 270
Ginza Raba, 171–3, 175
Greek Magical Papyri, 125–6, 143–4
Gregory, Tullio, 303, 308

Hahn, Yosef Yuzpa (Noyrlingen)
    Yosef 'Ometz, 192–6
Hai Gaon, xi, xii, 97–8
Ha-levi, Abraham ben Eliezer
    (Berukhim), 216, 218–19, 233
Hekhalot texts, 124–8, 140, 269–83
    Hekhalot Rabbati, 127
    Hekhalot Zutarti, 127–8
Herodotus, 140
Hildegard of Bingen
    Liber divinorum operum, 302
Hodayot, 44, 53–5
Homer
    Odyssey, 142
Honorius Augustodunensis, 294,
    302
Hugh of St. Victor
    Didascalicon, 304
    Homilia in Ecclesiasten, 304
Hume, David, 362

Ibn Adret, Shelomo ben Abraham,
    256
Ibn Bābuya, 277, 281
Ibn Ishaq, 278, 281
    Life of the Prophet, 276
Ibn Latif, Isaac, 251, 255
Ibn Tabul, 231

Irenaeus
    Against Heresies, 82–7
Isaac ben Samuel of Acre, 255
Isaac ha-Kohen, 259
Isaiah Horowitz of Prague
    Shnei Luḥot haBerit, 196–7
Isaac of Stella, 303

Jacob ben Asher
    Arba'ah Turim, 191
Joachim of Fiore, 295
Joel Sirkis, 191
John Chrysostom
    Homilies on 1Cor. 4.7, 159–60
John the Scot
    Peripyseon, 293, 301–2
Joseph Moses of Zbarov
    Berit Abram, 259
Joseph of Hamadan, 255
Julian the Theurgist
    Chaldaean Oracles, 82, 126
Justin Martyr
    Second Apology, 161

Karo, Yosef
    Maggid Mesharim, 210, 228
    Shuilḥan Arukh, 189
Kojiki, 324, 331–5
Kruschev, Nikita, ix

Lambert of St. Omer
    Liber Floridus, 302
Leon, R. Moshe de, 251, 255
    Sefer ha-Rimmon, 189–91, 199
Levi apocryphon, 47,7
Life of Adam and Eve, 61, 68–70, 101
Life of Joseph, 84–5
Lombard, Peter, 296
Lucian, 157
    Death of Peregrinus, 157
    Menippus, or the Descent into Hades, 142
Luria, Isaac, 200–2, 212–7, 219

Luzzatto, Moshe Hayyim
    Derekh haShem, 191–2

Maimonides, 255–6
    Guide to the Perplexed, 204
    Mishneh Torah, 221
Ma'asheh Merkavah, 127
Ma'ayan Ḥokhmah, 272–3
Macrobius, 292–3, 296, 302
    Commentarium in Somnium Scipionis, 292
Majlisi, Muḥammad Baqir b. Taqi al-, 269–83
    Biḥar al-Anwar, 269–73
    Haya t al- Qulu b (The Life and Religion of Muhammad), 270
Man'yoshū, 335–7
Maqdisi, 278
    Book of Creation and History, 2776
Martyrdom of Carpus, Papylus and Agathonikes, 158–9
Martyrdom of Euplus, 163
Martyrdom of Marianus and James, 162–3
Martyrdom of Pionius, 162
Maqiû, 17–30, 65
Martyrdom and Ascension of Isaiah, 50, 61, 74–8, 101, 106, 129, 131–2, 195
Meir of Rothenberg, 191
Meister Eckhart, 308
Menah em Azariah of Fano
    Kanfe Yonah, 230–1
Melchizedek Scroll, 101
Mercurius, 292, 296, 307
Milton, John
    To Sir Henry Vane the Younger, 361–2, 375
Mingxiang ji, 351–3
Mishnah
    Ḥagigah, 109
    Berakhot, 183–4
Mithras Liturgy, 59, 83, 86, 124–5, 127
Moses ben Shimeon of Burges, 258

Nachmanides, 256
Nag Hammadi texts
    Apocalypse of Paul, 86
    First Apocalypse of James, 86
Nathan Neta Hanover
    Yevein Metzula, 193
Nihonshoki, 324, 332–5

Origen, 82–3
    Commentary of John, 102
    Contra Celsum, 83–4
    Philocalia, 102
Orphic Literature, 141–2

Paul, 46, 66–8, 95, 97, 101–3, 105–15
Pausanius
    Description of Greece, 142–3
Pesiqta Rabbati, 272–3
Philo, xii, 100
    Life of Moses, 51–2, 103
    Sacrifices of Cain and Abel, 103
    Questions and Answers on
        Exodus, 103
Pico Della Mirandola, Giovanni, 308
Pistis Sophia, 85
Plato, xii, 69, 82–3, 157, 203, 307
    Parmenides, 100
    Phaedo, 166
    Timaeus, 289–94, 296, 299,
        301, 303–4
Plotinus, 146–7
    Enneads, 291
Plutarch, 60
    On the Face of the Moon, 79
Poimandres, 81
Preston, John
    The New Covenant, 368
Psalm of Thomas, 144
Psalms of Solomon, 67
Ptolemy, 83, 87

Ratramnus of Corbie, 293
Remigius of Auxerre, 294
Reality of the Rulers, The, 84

Revelation of Joshua ben Levi, 145
Rashi, 263
Rāzī, Abu 'l-Futuḥ al-, 278
Robert of Melun, 297–8

Saltmarsh, John, 372, 377
    Sparkles of Glory, 377
Scripture on the Conversion of the
    Barbarians, 353
Seneca
    Naturales questiones, 291
Sha'are Ṣedeq, 218
Sifrei Deuteronomy, 184, 189–90
Sikes, George
    Henry Vane, 368–9, 373
Silvestris, Bernard
    Cosmographia, 301, 306–7
Simeon bar Yoḥ ai, 213
Simeon ben Menasia, 184–5, 188
Solomon Shlomeil of Dresnitz,
    213–14
Songs of the Sabbath Sacrifice, 126
Soushen ji, 347–8
Šūrpu, 65

Ṭabari, 276
Tabarsi, 280–1
Talmud (Babylonian)
    Berakhot, 191
    Ḥagigah, 49, 272, 274
    Menaḥot, 186, 194, 197
    Megillah, 187, 197
Tanḥuma, 52
Tertullian, 161
Testament of Abraham, 101–2
Testament of the Twelve Patriarchs
    Testament of Dan, 101
    T. Levi, 46, 48–9, 52–3, 62–6,
        72–3, 76, 79–81, 86, 130, 141
Thierry of Chartres, 294, 300–1,
    306–7
    De sex dierum operibus, 300
    Heptateuchon, 300
Tibetan Book of the Dead, xii
Tiqqunel Zohar, 255
Tosefta, 184

Valentinus, 87
Vane, Sir Henry, 361–78
  The Examiner Defended, 374
  A Healing Question, 362, 374
  Pilgrimage into the Land of
    Promise, 369
  The Retired Man's Meditations,
    362, 365–7, 372–3
  Two Treatises, 369
  Zeal Examined, 374
Vidas, Elijah de
  Reshit Hokhmah, 218, 222, 229
Virgil, 147
  Aeneid, 142, 291, 293, 301, 304,
    307
Vision of the Netherworld, xi, 15
Visions of Ezekiel, The, 272
Vital, Ḥayyim, 211–219, 222–233
  'Es Ḥayyim, 213, 226–7
  Sefer ha-Ḥezyonot, 210, 214
  Sha'ar ha-Haqdamot, 216–7
  Sha'ar ha-Kawwanot, 222–5
  Sha'ar ha-Yiḥudim, 212, 217
  Sha'ar Ruaḥ ha-Qodesh, 211–
    12, 215–17, 233
  Sha'are Qedushah, 211, 231–4

War Scroll, 43–4, 54
William of Conches, 294, 298–301,
  304–5
  Dogmaticon, 300
  Glosa super Macrobium, 298
  Glosae super Consolationem
    Boethii, 298
  Glosae super Platonem, 299
  Philosophia mundi, 299
William of Saint-Thierry, 295, 304–5
Wisdom of Ben Sira, 301

Yamato-takeru tale, 328–339
Yehuda Leib ha-Cohen of Anipola,
  263
Yohanan ben Zakkai, 186
Yonah, Moses, 230
Youming lu, 346–7, 350, 353

Zedekiah ben Abraham ha-Rofe
  Shibbolei Ha-Leqet, 188
Zhenjao, 348–9
Zohar, 96, 194–5, 198–9, 209–10,
  213, 221, 223, 228–31, 252, 255

MODERN AUTHORS INDEX

Abusch, T., 33, 34, 35, 388, 39
Andersen, F. I., 90, 91, 117
Anz, W., 59, 60, 87
Ariès, P., 385, 387, 403
Attridge, H., 90

Bacher, W., 250, 264
Baillet, M., 43, 44, 56
Becker, E., 383, 385, 403
Benin, S. D., 258, 266
Berger, P., xv
Betz, H. D., 121, 133, 143, 152, 153
Black, M., 58, 88, 116, 118
Bottéro, J., 35
Bousset, W., xvi, 57, 59, 60, 67, 87, 90, 92, 93
Brandt, W., 171, 178
Brauer, J. C., 363, 378
Burkert, W., 34, 143, 150, 151, 152

Charles, R. H., 88, 89, 90, 91
Charlesworth, J. H., 57, 116, 117, 118
Chenu, M.-D., 308
Cogan, M., 33
Collins, A. Y., 91, 136
Collins, J. J., 56, 57, 58, 90, 116, 119, 175, 179
Colpe, C., 148, 149
Cross, F., 173, 174, 175, 179
Culianu, I., xiii, xiv, xv, xvi, 60, 87, 91, 92, 93, 95, 120, 139, 154, 178, 283, 356, 405

Dahood, M., 57
de Jonge, M., 56, 89
De Quincey, T., 394, 406
de Ste. Croix, G. E. M., 161, 167, 168, 169
Dieterich, D., 144, 145
Dronke, P., 298, 309, 311, 313, 314
Dunn, J. D. G., 122

Earhart, H. B., 325, 339
Ebersole, G., 340, 341
Eliade, M., xv, 149, 339, 401, 109
Ellwood, R., 389
Eph'al, I., 33
Erikson, E., 386, 403, 405

Fine, L., 235, 236, 239
Fishbane, M., 33, 204, 205, 206, 207, 240, 246, 266
Flew, A., 402, 403, 406, 407
Fossum, D., 115, 116, 117, 120
Fox, R. L., 143, 152, 167, 168
Frend, S., 383, 384, 385, 403, 406

Gaylord, H. E., 91
Geertz, C., 323
Geller, M. J., 24
Gibson, M., 293, 311, 312
Ginzburg, C., 31, 38, 323, 339, 341
Gorer, G., 383, 385, 403
Gruenwald, I., 34, 56, 116, 120, 146, 152, 153, 265, 267

Halperin, D., 115, 126, 133, 134, 135, 150, 153, 240, 283
Hambrick-Stowe, C. E., 363, 379
Häring, N., 315
Hartman, L., 115
Hartog, F., 149, 150
Heim, A., 395
Hengel, M., 121
Himmelfarb, M., xvi, 48, 57, 120, 133, 134, 135, 136, 137, 145, 153, 359
Hurtado, L., 117

Idel, M., xi, xvi, 56, 115, 116, 126, 134, 136, 215, 234, 235, 236, 238, 241, 243, 264, 265, 266, 267, 268

Jacobsen, H., 58, 117, 150
Jacobsen, T., 24, 25, 33, 35
James, W., 363, 379
Jeremias, G., 58
Johnson, M. D., 90

Kirschner, H., xv
Kitagawa, J., 325, 326, 339
Kletti, R., 395, 396, 406
Klibansky, R., 300
Knibb, M. A., 58, 90, 117, 118, 136
Kobelski, P. J., 116
Kraus, H. J., 57
Kübler-Ross, E., 385, 403
Kuhn, H.-W., 58
Kuyt, A., 149, 153, 154
Kvanvig, H., xv, 33

Lambert, W. G., 64, 88, 90
Layton, 92, 93
Lévi, I., 145, 150, 153
Levy, I., 340
Lewis, I. M., 39
Lewy, H., 125, 134, 153
Lidzbarski, M., 178, 179
Lifton, R. J., 386, 403, 404
Lu, Xun, 357, 358, 359
Lunt, H. G., 70

Markus, R., 143, 152
Mauss, M., 387
McGiffert, M., 364, 379
McGinn, B., 311
McKeon, R., 308
Meeks, W., 51, 58
Meier, G., 33, 89
Meyer, M. W., 124
Milik, J. K., 88, 118
Moody, R. A., xv, 390, 404, 405
Morris, I., 328, 340
Mosca, P., 57
Munk, W., 394
Musurillo, H., 167

Newman, C., 116

Newsom, C., 126, 134
Neusner, J., 33, 58, 117
Nickelsburg, G. W. E., 56, 58, 116, 118, 136
Niditch, S., 56
Nilsson, 143, 151
Noyes, R., 395, 396, 406
Nuttall, G. F., 363, 379

Parfit, D., 399, 406, 407
Philippi, D., 340

Quispel, G., 116, 117, 120

Reiner, E., 34, 89
Rochberg-Halton, F., 65, 87, 89, 93
Rowland, C., 116, 120, 137
Rowland, R., 38
Rudolph, K., 172, 176, 178, 179

Sandler, P., 250, 264
Schaefer, P., 283
Schäfer, P., 126, 134, 135, 136, 145, 149, 153, 154
Schechter, S., 209, 234, 243
Schiffmann, L., 56, 241
Scholem, G., 96, 115, 120, 126, 134, 145, 148, 149, 154, 206, 209, 214, 234, 235, 236, 237, 238, 242, 245, 246, 250, 264, 265, 266, 267, 283
Schuller, E., 119
Segal, A., 57, 116, 117, 120, 122, 129, 136, 148
Sells, M., 276
Sikes, G., 378, 379, 380
Smith, G., 12
Smith, J. Z., 117
Smith, M., 44, 45, 54, 55, 56, 57, 115, 118, 123, 125, 126, 129, 133, 134, 136, 150
Southern, R. W., 291, 293, 300, 309, 311, 312, 314, 315
Sparks, H. F. D., 90, 91, 136
Stone, M. E., 118, 132

Strickmann, M., 358, 360
Stroumsa, G. G., 154
Sullivan, L. E., 323, 339, 398, 405, 407

Tabor, J. D., 57, 119
Talmage, F., 250, 264
Thompson, R. C., 65, 89
Tigay, J., 13
Tillich, P., 387
Tov, E., 33

Ulansey, D., 81, 92

van der Heide, 250
van der Horst, P. W., 58, 117, 119, 141, 150

VanderKam, J. C., 56
Vermes, G., 58
von Rad, G., 61, 87, 88

Wasserstrom, S. M., 990
Wells, L. S. A., 90
Werblowsky, R. J. Z., 214, 232, 235, 236, 237, 239, 247
Whittaker, M., 90
Wolfson, E. R., 205, 207, 234, 241, 242, 244, 245, 246, 247, 265

Yu, A., 356, 357

Zaleski, C., xv, xvi, 95, 360, 405